WITHDRAWN

BR   Rohrer, S. Scott, 1957-
515.5   Wandering souls
.R64   751091000176137
2010

NORTH ARKANSAS COLLEGE LIBRARY
1515 Pioneer Drive
Harrison, AR   72601

DEMCO

D0849440

Wandering Souls

The University of
North Carolina Press
Chapel Hill

S. SCOTT ROHRER

Wandering Souls

Protestant
Migrations
in America,
1630–1865

BR
515.5
.R64
2010

© 2010 The University of North Carolina Press
All rights reserved
Set in Dante
by Graphic Composition, Inc.
Manufactured in the United States of America

The paper in this book meets the guidelines for permanence
and durability of the Committee on Production Guidelines
for Book Longevity of the Council on Library Resources.

The University of North Carolina Press has been a member
of the Green Press Initiative since 2003.

Library of Congress Cataloging-in-Publication Data

Rohrer, S. Scott, 1957–
Wandering souls : Protestant migrations in America, 1630–1865 /
S. Scott Rohrer.
    p. cm.
Includes bibliographical references and index.

ISBN 978-0-8078-3372-8 (cloth : alk. paper)

1. United States—Church history. 2. Protestants—United States—
History. 3. Migration, Internal—United States—History. I. Title.
BR515.5.R64 2010
304.8'730882804—dc22

                                        2009033896

14 13 12 11 10   5 4 3 2 1

To the memory of my parents

George Smith Rohrer (1922–90)

Carol King Rohrer (1926–2006)

Hear my prayer, O Lord . . .
For I am a stranger with thee, and
a sojourner: as all my fathers were.
O spare me a little, that I may
recover my strength: before I go
hence, and be no more seen.
BOOK OF COMMON PRAYER

Wilderness is a temporary
condition through which we are
passing to the Promised Land.
COTTON MATHER

Contents

Tables, Maps, and Illustrations

PART ONE

Migration in America

Introduction

An Overview of Protestant Migrations, 1630–1865

A hitchhiker, a farmer. Consider these two tales from across the centuries: after the breakup of his marriage, an unemployed college teacher embarks on a restless journey in the 1970s. He pauses to pick up a hitchhiker near Potlatch, Idaho. The hitchhiker greets his benefactor with a question: "Do you want a free Bible course? . . . Jesus is coming." The professor shudders, wondering what he has gotten himself into. The hitchhiker is a born-again Christian and a member of the Seventh-Day Adventist Church who found Jesus after nearly dying in a car wreck during a mountain snowstorm. Having survived his brush with death, the man feels compelled to take to the road as a missionary and spread the Good Word. "Jesus hitchhikes in me. That's the work," he explains to the driver, William Least Heat-Moon. To back up his assertion, the hitchhiker cites Luke 14:23: "Then the master said to the servant, 'Go out into the highways and hedges, and compel *them* to come in, that my house may be filled.'" Heat-Moon finds the man a most curious companion. He can only conclude about this missionary-hitchhiker, "He seemed one of those men who wander all their lives. In him was something restless and unsatisfied and ancient. He was going everywhere, anywhere, nowhere. He belonged to no place and was at home anyplace."[1]

In the 1820s, a Puritan farmer unhappy with life in Concord, Massachusetts, sells the ancestral homeland, loads his belongings into a wagon, and heads to western New York with his family in search of fresh land and a religious new birth. This migration, so quotidian in its motives, was part of a far larger one out of New England and Pennsylvania that transformed New York's frontier into the "Burned-over District," a place that became famed by the 1820s for its revivalism and fiery religious spirit. "What New England was fifty years ago, the western section of New York . . . has in many respects already become," the *Orleans Advocate* observed in 1827. The migrants were a surprisingly diverse lot—the Congregationalists from old Puritan villages such as Concord were joined by Methodists, Baptists, Shakers, Quakers, and others. But this motley collection of religious believers shared two fundamental things: an attachment to emotional religion, and a predilection to migrate. For one historian of the district, the migrants' "moral intensity . . . was their most striking attribute." Emotional religion, he explained, was "a congenital characteristic, present at birth and developed throughout the youth of the section."[2]

Protestantism's contributions to Americans' wanderlust between 1630 and 1865 is a fascinating but little understood aspect of U.S. history. Modern treatments of migration, from Hollywood Westerns to scholarly books on the frontier, often ignore religion's role in mobility, citing instead the importance of land. The image of settlers headed west in Conestoga wagons for the chance to farm is deeply ingrained in the American psyche. During his cross-country jaunt, William Least Heat-Moon came across a North Carolinian who offered a novel theory on how Jimmy Carter, an obscure southern politician, had managed to win the White House in 1976: "He showed us he came from the land. To an American, land is solidity, goodness, and hope. American history is about land." One of the newest accounts of American expansion largely agrees: "The lure of all that land with its robust yields ensured a constant inflow of settlers, and the more who came, the more who followed," writes historian Richard Kluger. "After these irrepressible Americans consecrated their land as a nation . . . their territorial cravings only grew." A recent book on Andrew Jackson and the American "empire" put it even more baldly: "Land was the principal attraction for western settlement. . . . Land speculation dominated the thoughts of every man who journeyed west seeking a better life."[3]

Many contemporaries offered strikingly similar assessments. In an essay published in 1782, French-born J. Hector St. John de Crèvecoeur stressed land's importance to American democratic culture, especially when compared with Europe. "Here are no aristocratical families, no courts, no kings, no bishops, no ecclesiastical dominion, no invisible power giving to a few a very visible one," Crèvecoeur exclaimed. "Some few towns excepted, we are all tillers of the earth, from Nova Scotia to West Florida. We are a people of cultivators, scattered over an immense territory communicating with each other by means of good roads and navigable rivers."[4]

Such views of land's hold on migration have found their way into treatments of American Christianity by both modern historians and contemporary Protestant leaders. In general studies on religion in early America, historians recount how churches scrambled to keep up with their peripatetic parishioners, who scattered to the four winds in search of land and better economic opportunity. Eastern-based churches, which struggled with a shortage of ministers, lacked the resources to serve the needs of a growing population in the burgeoning West. The conclusion about the relationship of migration to religion was obvious and twofold: migration existed independently of religion, and Americans' mobility weakened Protestantism by drawing members away from their home churches to the frontier. Many leading Protestant lights from the Puritans onward thus believed that the wilderness posed a grave threat to the Protestant mission. "The great fear," as one historian described these worries, "was that the people of the West, being far removed from the civilizing and Christianizing influence of the settled communities of the East, would revert to 'barbarism' and subvert the moral order of society." Such beliefs rested on a Hobbesian view of human nature: place people in a state of nature, and violence and disorder would result. Religious authorities consequently worried about the wilderness and its potentially harmful effects on good Christians. New England Puritans were especially nervous about their brethren migrating to the frontier, fearing that these sojourners could degenerate into savagery. New Englanders saw the frontier as a dark, foreboding place that needed to be tamed and Christianized. Crèvecoeur agreed that America's open spaces could unmoor Protestants from their churches. In Europe, he explained, the continent's small spaces allowed religion to become a daily presence in people's lives. Europeans went to church regularly because they had churches nearby. "Zeal in Europe is confined; [but] here it evaporates in the great distance it has to travel," he wrote. "There it is a grain of powder inclosed, here it burns away in the open air, and consumes without effect."[5]

The real situation was far more complex and interesting. Migration and Protestantism shared a symbiotic relationship, with religion contributing to migration and migration contributing to religion. In fact, mobility did not weaken American Protestantism—it strengthened it. America's "open air," to borrow Crèvecoeur's evocative phrase, allowed two separate but related traditions—evangelism and a dissenting culture—to flourish. Both contributed to internal migration in protean ways that this book will fully explore.

Protestant dissenters from across Europe were drawn to America's shores—to the open spaces of the New World. Among the earliest arrivals were the Puritans. They embarked on a "Great Migration" in the 1630s that carried twenty-one thousand people across the Atlantic Ocean to the Puritan-founded Massachusetts Bay Colony, where settlers began the construction of a godly commonwealth, free from the supposed corruptions of the Church of England. A bewildering array of Anabaptists, Pietists, Evangelicals, and others from the Netherlands, France, Germany, and elsewhere followed. These pilgrims, many of them quite radical in their religious beliefs, settled mainly in Pennsylvania but also in New York, New Jersey, the Carolinas, and elsewhere.

Then they began to move about within America.

Puritans dissatisfied with the Massachusetts Bay Colony started heading "west," where they founded Connecticut and Rhode Island. Baptists facing Puritan harassment abandoned Boston for the more congenial clime of the South. Mennonites departed Pennsylvania for frontier Virginia, while Moravians went to backcountry North Carolina. Scotch-Irish Presbyterians scattered to every frontier they could find. The list goes on and on: Quakers, Lutherans, Dunkers, Shakers, Methodists—all migrated to points north, south, and west, clutching rudimentary maps along with their well-thumbed Bibles.

Because these exoduses were so common and so widespread, the challenge becomes not detecting religious migrations in America but making sense of their numbers and diversity. What lay behind all this mobility? What did the migrations have in common? What kinds of patterns did they form? What role did the American setting play in migration? Why were these migrations important? Although scholars of the various sects and denominations have studied individual migrations, no one has taken a comprehensive look at internal Protestant migrations in America. By exploring Protestant migrations from the 1630s, when Puritans arrived in New England, to the 1850s and 1860s, when two utopian groups (the Mormons and the Inspirationists) were making their way westward to Utah and Iowa, respectively, this book fills a gaping hole in the literature.

One way to make sense of the movements of religious groups is to focus on geography. Protestant migrations in early America radiated outward from three centers. One center was in northern New England. As early as 1631, Puritan dissenters began migrating for a variety of reasons. "Heading westward," though, meant undertaking migrations as short as thirty miles; longer ones involved sojourns of only a hundred miles. These were short-distance migrations that carried unhappy Puritans to the Connecticut Valley and to what became Rhode Island, Vermont, and New Hampshire. A second center formed later in Pennsylvania—specifically, in the Delaware Valley. William Penn's colony, founded in 1681, offered migrants the heady combination of religious freedom and abundant, fertile land. Radicals from across Europe eagerly embraced Penn's offer but did not linger in their new homes. From Pennsylvania, thousands of Protestant dissenters began moving south in the

1730s—first to Maryland and Virginia, then on to the Carolinas and Georgia. This migration to the southern backcountry was massive, and it did not stop until the American Revolution. Thus, a third center developed in the mid–eighteenth century. The South became home to the two fastest-growing evangelical sects, the Methodists and the Baptists, as well as to German-speaking Lutherans and to smaller groups such as the Moravians and Quakers. These groups, especially the Evangelicals, were every bit as restless as their dissenting colleagues from New England. From the Carolinas and Virginia, they began migrating in the revolutionary period and later to the Midwest and the West.

Religious migrations, as a result, consisted of three basic thrusts: westward from New England, southward from Pennsylvania, and northwestward from Virginia, the Carolinas, and Georgia. Such a geographical model, however, only hints at the complexity of what was going on. It oversimplifies the movements of Protestants (migrations continued out of New England in later periods, for example) and does not tell us why these Protestant pilgrims moved, only where and when.

Standard migration theories do not offer much help, either. One longtime favorite is the "push-pull" theory. Conditions in migrants' home regions or countries—depression, loss of jobs, lack of land—"pushed" them to move elsewhere. Setbacks in a home place worked in conjunction with the attractions of the migrants' destinations. In other words, the new home locale "pulled" the migrant with the lure of cheap land, plentiful jobs, political freedom, or some combination of them. This theory does contain relevance for certain religious migrations—for example, it helps to explain the movements of the Pietistic migrants discussed in chapter 4. Conditions in these Pietists' home congregations "pushed" them out of Maine, Pennsylvania, and Maryland, while cheap land in an appealing religious enclave "pulled" them to North Carolina. But this model fails to capture the complexity of Protestant migrations in all their variety, and it cannot explain how religious values fueled mobility.[6]

More recent theories have their own shortcomings. Some talk about "betterment" migrations, where people moved to improve themselves; "generational" migrations, where age determined who moved and when (the young tended to be more mobile than the middle-aged); or "chain" migrations, where people moved in family groups. The strength of these newer models lies in their ability to explain the social and economic underpinnings of mobility. They delve deeply into family life and the household economy to determine why someone would migrate. Much of what these studies have found is commonsensical: young people entering adulthood moved to find jobs; their aging parents, who were usually well established on farms or in crafts, tended to stay put. Such familial situations fit into both the betterment and the generational models: age and the desire to get ahead determine who goes or stays. Those older people with settled work situations are more rooted. Conversely, when the economy sours, the newly unemployed are more likely to try their luck elsewhere. The "wandering poor" were a common sight in sixteenth- and seventeenth-century England. These downtrodden souls took to the road in an effort to find work and food to survive. The chain-migration theory, meanwhile, is grounded deeply in social history. In rural Europe and America, dense kinship networks linked neighborhoods and villages. Studies based on the chain-migration theory untangle these relationships, concluding that many people moved in kinship groups. Often, younger sons migrated first and acted as a vanguard. They scouted out suitable places to settle, purchased land, built cabins, and put in crops. Their kin then followed.[7]

None of these models, however, adequately explains religion's role in migration or makes sense of the patterns that religious migrations formed. Again, this is not to say that conventional migration theories do not hold insights into the movements of the devout. They do. People of deep faith, after all, were still people: they needed to eat, to work, to find suitable shelter. As a result, they shared some of the same motivations as "secular" migrants. When the economy worsened, pilgrims felt the pain just as much as their less devout neighbors. Religious migrants also wanted land and good jobs, and for many of these migrants, kinship could and did help to shape their movements. Yet as the case studies in this book make clear, religious migrations differed fundamentally from secular movements: Protestant values motivated these migrants in profound ways.

Wandering Souls is organized around a different kind of model that peels back the layers of a religious migration to uncover its essential core. These migrations, for all their variety, shared a great deal. Utopians as well as sectarians needed land to fulfill their religious objectives, while Protestant groups of all stripes could face hostility or skepticism from nonbelievers. And religious fervor was common to nearly every Protestant migrant. Any pilgrim—Puritan, Presbyterian, Mennonite, Mormon—had formed a strong identity as a member of a Protestant group. In fact, Protestant migrations had so much in common that it is helpful to think of them as a prepared dish: they often shared a few essential ingredients, including religious fervor, land, family, internal conflicts, and a number of common seasonings. Yet each migration had its own flavor that owed its distinctiveness to the mix of ingredients used—in some migrations, family was more important; in others, internal conflict played a dominant role.

To make sense of the similarities and differences involved, this model sorts Protestant migrations into two basic patterns or types. It then isolates the key ingredients within each pattern and explains how they made a particular migration distinctive. Put another way, the migration model approaches Protestant migrations from different angles, highlighting the most important variables or themes that distinguished the various movements.[8]

The first and more common migration type involved religiously minded people moving to find some kind of spiritual and economic fulfillment. Pilgrims—usually individuals or families—migrated on their own initiative for complex, interlocking reasons. That is, religious, social, and economic factors intertwined to produce the migration of a religiously motivated individual, family, or congregation. Individual chapters focus on one key variable (or ingredient): the "new birth"; ethnicity and national identity; land and family; and a reformist drive. In this first type of migration, the main ingredient combined with a deeply felt faith and the various economic and social factors to induce a person or group to migrate within America. No one variable solely determined a migration; rather, a particular variable loomed larger in a particular migration than did a secondary variable such as land or family. Examples of individualistic migrations resulting from these four main ingredients abounded: a person struggling to achieve and maintain a new birth moves to join a congregation founded by like-minded Protestants; an immigrant presses on to the frontier to live among congregation members belonging to the national church of his homeland; a mother and father head to the southern backcountry to join a religious community where they can farm and raise their children among fellow believers; the reborn migrates repeatedly, seeking to spread the good news about Jesus and to spark religious reform. Such mobility was usually not church-led or -directed; it typically involved migrations undertaken by families or individuals, although exceptions occurred, as chapter 1 shows. Unlike in the second migration type, persecution or "utopian" motives did not drive these migrations; instead, the desire to find some kind of religious happiness did.

The second migration type involved classic religious migrations led by a church, congregation, or minister. A Protestant group moved en masse for one of three main reasons: to escape persecution by outsiders, to establish a religious utopia, or to mitigate internal conflict within a group. These migrations, while often quite complex, involved purer religious motivations than did the first migration type. That is, religious reasons loomed larger for these sojourners. Such migrations also were far better organized: church or congregational leaders typically decided who moved, when, and how. Members migrated at the behest of a Protestant leader or group and traveled in carefully selected companies organized by the church. Not surprisingly, these migrations often involved Protestant utopian groups—visionaries seeking to achieve some kind of Christian perfection. Thus the Mormons, in an effort to build a safe and lasting New Jerusalem in the Utah territory, formed "Pioneer Companies" and began traversing the Great Plains in 1846 after years of violence, ridicule, and harassment in the East and the Midwest. Classic religious migrations, however, could also involve Baptists or other Protestants not normally considered utopian. Instead, these migrations fall into the "classic" taxonomy because people moved as a unit and largely for religious reasons. A congregation or church wanted to practice its faith in peace on its own terms, and migration became the means to achieve that goal. By moving as a bloc, these groups attempted to leave behind their religious troubles.

Wandering Souls is divided into three sections, corresponding to the model's two migration types. Part 1, "Migration in America," sets the stage for all that follows. The first chapter offers a prototypical migration that explores the nuances of Protestant mobility and provides a baseline for comparison throughout the book. The decision by a Puritan group known as Thomas Hooker's Company to move to the Connecticut Valley from Massachusetts Bay in 1635 and 1636 was an especially complex Protestant migration, encompassing traits that fell into both migration types. The migrants moved as a congregational unit led by their minister, but a fascinating brew of religious, economic, and social motives underlay their decision to leave their Puritan home colony only a few years after their arrival from England.

Part 2, "The Protestant Sojourner," includes chapters 2–5 and examines the various impulses involved in the first migration type. That is, this section looks at the religious, cultural, and economic factors that propelled individual Protestants to move about in early America. The opening chapter explores one ingredient that made believers restless: sinners' desire to become reborn. Chapter 2 thus moves the story from seventeenth-century Puritan New England to eighteenth-century Anglican Virginia. It contrasts the restless wanderings of one renegade Anglican seeking to achieve a new birth to the relatively anchored existence of religiously indifferent Virginians living in the stable parish world of the state church. This chapter compares the two groups in an effort to demonstrate what an individual religious migration was and was not. Chapter 3 tells the tale of Scotch-Irish Presbyterians who flocked to the various frontiers in mid-eighteenth-century America. It highlights the intersection of religion, nationalism, and ethnicity in some immigrant groups' migratory patterns. Chapter 4 looks at another cultural phenomenon that contributed to mobility: the nexus of land, family, and religion. The chapter looks at Pietistical Moravians, a group of pilgrims known for their religious fervor. On the eve of the American Revolution, these Moravians moved from Pennsylvania to backcountry North Carolina, where they constructed family-based congregations centered on God and farming. Chapter 5 concludes the examination of the first migration type by looking at the role that the reformist and missionary impulse played in the movements of people to the frontier just after the American Revolution. The chapter focuses on the fastest-growing evangelical group, the Methodists, and it takes the reader to the Ohio Country shortly after the 1794 Battle of Fallen Timbers, when settlement of this midwestern frontier began in earnest.

Part 3, "Journeys of the Pure," explores the second migration type: classic religious migrations where Protestants moved as cohesive groups to achieve an important religious end. The case studies focus on the three main variables that contributed to migrations of this type: the role of the dissenting tradition; the role of utopian aspirations; and the role of persecution. Chapter 6 examines two dissenting congregations—one Baptist, one Puritan—to explain how internal conflict contributed to mobility. Chapter 7 tells the story of the Inspirationists, a German and Swiss group led by their prophet to Iowa in the mid-1850s after God told him to leave upstate New York and move west. The Inspirationists' deeper goal was to be left alone so that they could worship the Lord relatively free of outside "worldly" distractions. In antebellum America, utopian groups were becoming more numerous, as was persecution. The concluding chapter examines persecution's role in migration through the dramatic story of the Mormons, whose founder and prophet was assassinated in an Illinois jail in 1844. Repeated persecution motivated some sixteen thousand Mormons to migrate to a safer haven in the West between 1846 and 1852, the largest internal religious migration in U.S. history.

Two key themes emerge in these case studies. One is the restlessness of Protestant seekers. The desire to achieve salvation—to become reborn—was a true fault line in Protestantism. In a profound way, the desire to achieve a new birth transcended the differences of region, ethnicity, denomination, and era. The hitchhiker in 1970s Idaho, so "restless and unsatisfied," would have been easily recognizable to a seeker in the 1670s. Protestants who feared for their souls were literally restive and on the move. Their search for spiritual fulfillment and reinforcement often sent them scurrying to find Christian fellowship or to crusade for some kind of reform. Migration became an explicit means to build Christian community and to achieve spiritual renewal. Many Protestant migrants saw themselves as modern-day Israelites who needed to suffer in the wilderness before reaching the Promised Land. These Protestant migrants, as a result, shared an ethos, a belief that they were engaged in something larger and more important than themselves. Quite simply, they believed in the Lord and in what they were doing.

The second theme that emerges in the case studies is less universal but equally important: the role that the American environment and its dissenting culture played in internal religious migrations. J. Hector St. John De Crèvecoeur argued not only that America's open spaces undermined the religious life of the developing nation but also that America's fierce sectarianism harmed religious enthusiasm and that the presence of so many denominations and sects lessened religious identity and made people indifferent to religion.[9]

Crèvecoeur could not have been more wrong. Intense competition among and within the various Protestant groups led to a great battle for souls, and this spirited competition caused more people to join churches. The New World setting thus spurred religious migrations in two important ways. First, it encouraged a dissenting tradition. Lacking an established church and fostering a tradition of religious freedom that became codified in state and federal constitutions after the revolution, America attracted a multitude of religious sects and denominations. Ecumenicalism was a weak, lonely sibling of the dissenting tradition during this period, with far fewer adherents. Instead, Baptists, Methodists, Presbyterians, and others argued passionately over the rightness of their beliefs. The arguments represented more than heated competition among rival sects and denominations; they also constituted an intramural contest within groups. Individual congregations argued about doctrine, feuded over who should lead, and battled over where meetinghouses should be built. The angry losers in these disputes often left the area.

They had plenty of choices about where to go. And hence the second way that the American scene encouraged migration: land was plentiful and cheap. Unhappy with the home congregation, these dissenters could start their New Zions in other colonies or states, often on newly opened frontiers. The presence of so much land enabled people of faith to spread out, and land encouraged mobility by making it far easier for dissenters to move on. The combination of land and a dissenting tradition meant that America, especially during the revolutionary era, spawned a vigorous marketplace of religion that was liberal, individualistic, and aggressive. In such an atmosphere, laymen were encouraged to lead and to mold Protestantism in their own image, often by challenging church leaders and pursuing an individualistic version of emotional religion. The result, in the memorable words of historian Patricia Bonomi, was "one of high volatility. All is in motion as congregations gather, dispute, divide, and reconstitute themselves."[10]

In such protean ways did migration and a Protestant culture feed off of each other: the former strengthened the latter, and the latter contributed to the former. Migration enabled Protestantism to spread across the continent and its followers to recommit to the Lord, while religious values helped prod people to move. To fully explain this phenomenon, *Wandering Souls* focuses exclusively on Protestant groups. Protestantism was dominant in early America: the Jewish population was minuscule, and Catholics remained a small (albeit growing) minority until the Civil War era. Protestantism fostered a robust evangelical culture that resulted in two Great Awakenings, and it provided the prism through which ordinary people viewed their world. Gordon S. Wood, a preeminent historian of the revolutionary period, is struck by Protestantism's importance to Americans of that era. "Despite the growth of Enlightenment [values] among elites in the eighteenth-century America," he observes, "Protestantism in one form or another still remained the principal means by which most common people ordered and explained the world and made it meaningful. . . . For most ordinary people religion met personal and social needs not comprehended by rational philosophy or Whig ideology." For Bonomi, "The idiom of religion penetrated all discourse, underlay all thought, marked all observances, gave meaning to every public and private crisis."[11]

Deciding which Protestant groups to study and which to omit meant making some painful choices. Groups were not necessarily chosen based on their size or importance to American religious history. Instead, they were selected based on how well they could illuminate a larger theme within the book's religious migration model. For example, German-speaking Lutherans migrated within America for family and religious reasons, but the numerically smaller Moravians were selected to portray this theme based on their stronger records and smaller community. The Moravian enclave of Wachovia, North Carolina, with its carefully drawn borders, presents a controlled laboratory in which to better explain how religion, land, and family influenced migration.

The case studies were also chosen to provide a degree of chronological and geographical balance. *Wandering Souls*, in other words, strives to advance a story chronologically and geographically, beginning in New England in 1630, moving to the South in the eighteenth century, and ending in the West in the 1850s and early 1860s. Each chapter delves deep into the inner life of a Protestant group in an effort to answer one core question: what was it about Protestantism and America's dissenting culture that made Protestants so restless? The answers are compelling.

The First Frontier

Thomas Hooker and the New England Puritans

On the simplest level, a migrant of the nineteenth century would have understood. To the west lay land. As the Puritan settlers arrived on Massachusetts's shores during the Great Migration of the 1630s, the Connecticut Valley stood tantalizingly off in the distance, only a hundred miles from the coast. The valley was large, fertile, and beautiful. Thickly forested with aspen, elm, and other trees, it was home to an assortment of animals prized by fur trappers, including beavers, moose, and otters. But of greater importance to Puritan divines interested in cultivating the Lord's garden was the valley's potential as farmland. The meadows and alluvial terraces along the Connecticut River contained the finest soil in New England.

Thomas Hooker well understood the valley's potential and pitfalls. A revered Puritan minister and intellectual, Hooker spent his life thinking about God and the state of men's souls. Born in 1586 in Marfield, England, a hamlet in Leicestershire, he graduated from Emmanuel College in Cambridge and earned a prominent place in the Puritan movement because of his great intellect, devotion to the cause, and vigorous pen. He had come to the Massachusetts Bay Colony in late 1633 after a short exile in the Netherlands. Like others of the founding generation, he arrived with great hopes. New England represented a fresh start after years of struggle and persecution in England. In this new land, Puritan reformers envisioned creating a model commonwealth of piety that would shame their brethren across the sea into reforming the corrupt Church of England.[1]

Yet within three short years of his arrival in Massachusetts, Hooker and his "company" had departed for the frontier against the initial wishes of the colony's leaders, including Governor John Winthrop. That Hooker led a migration of some 160 people from Massachusetts Bay to found a frontier village that became Hartford, Connecticut, was one of the great ironies of early New

England history. Hooker, who denounced as dangerous the ideas of Roger Williams and Anne Hutchinson, was in many ways a defender of the Puritan orthodoxy. More interestingly, he was a theologian who believed that separation from society was a sin. He, like other Puritan ministers, preached repeatedly that God's people must put the church first and land and riches second. The central mission of Hooker's life was bringing people to Jesus Christ.

At its core, the migration of Hooker and his people represents a mystery. *Why did he do it?* Why did he abandon the Massachusetts Bay Colony so early in its history? What lure did the frontier hold for a religious group determined to create a godly commonwealth and reform Protestantism? Would the combination of rich, bountiful land, Indian "savagery," and an "empty" wilderness prove fatal and lead the saintly astray from God's ways? In another mystery, Hooker, a prolific writer, never fully explained his reasons, though he hinted at them. And his answer, such as it was, makes one thing clear: the 1636 migration was as rich and furrowed in its complexity as the land Hooker's Company was coming to farm.

A Harvest of Troubles

Hooker arrived in Boston on September 4, 1633. He was accompanied by his family; by his assistant, Samuel Stone; and by numerous other members of his former congregation in Essex County, England. After spending eight weeks aboard the *Griffin*, a three-hundred-ton ship that sailed from England's Downs in early July, the émigrés did not dally in Boston but pressed on to their new home at Cambridge, then called Newtown, a village that had been readying for Hooker's arrival for a year.[2] By European standards, Newtown was not much to look at. It was a colonial town in a colonial outpost of a small island nation. Visitors, however, were impressed with the place despite the fact that Newtown was only a few years old and was not yet home to Harvard University. Situated on the banks of the Charles River, Newtown "is one of the neatest and best compacted Townes in New England," William Wood wrote in 1634, "having many faire structures, with many handsome contrived streets." Inhabitants had taken care in constructing the town. At the first town meeting held in the newly completed meetinghouse in 1632, participants decreed that all houses had to be roofed with "slate or board, and not with thatch." They also decided "that no person whatever [shall set] up any house in the bounds of this town [without] leave from the major part."[3] Echoing Wood's assessment, Edward Johnson proclaimed Newtown a "comely" place with "well ordered streets." In September 1633, Hooker and his party found themselves in a bustling river town that at one time had hoped to become the colony's capital and a rival of Boston. In Johnson's view, the town not only was pretty but also was home to inhabitants who were "in a thriving condition in outward things also, both Corne and Cattell, Neate and Sheepe, of which they have a good flocke, which the Lord hath caused to thrive much in these latter days than formerly."[4]

The arrival of Hooker and the rest of his company in 1633 and 1634 added to this picture of prosperity. Their presence boosted the town's population by more than a hundred, and as early as 1635, homes had been built on fifty of the sixty-four house lots. Beneath the seeming prosperity, however, lay serious tensions resulting from several causes. One obvious problem was that the émigrés from Essex did not choose to live in Newtown. The vanguard of Hooker's Company had come to Massachusetts Bay in 1632 and settled in Mount Wollaston, a town forming south of Boston. But these members' selection of Mount Wollaston as their home landed them in the middle of one of the first political feuds in the colony's young history.[5]

In 1630, Deputy Governor Thomas Dudley had led an effort to found Newtown. In a still-dangerous wilderness society competing for inhabitants, Dudley reasoned that the erection of a secure, fortified town would draw settlers. His more ambitious hope was that the town would grow enough to become the capital of Massachusetts Bay. At the end of 1630, the General Court agreed that a site a mile from Watertown—Dudley's town—would become the colony's central fortified town. The magistrates also agreed to settle there the following spring, and Dudley became confident that Newtown would indeed become the colonial capital. He went ahead and built his house on the site. Governor Winthrop started to construct a residence there, too, but then had a change of heart. He concluded that Boston, located on the sea, offered more advantages as a commercial and political capital. He had workers remove the framing of his house and transport it to Boston. The other magistrates followed Winthrop's lead, and none built homes in Newtown. Boston thus became the capital of Massachusetts Bay.[6]

Dudley was distressed about this turn of events and unhappy with Winthrop's leadership on other fronts, and he sniped at the governor over the next two years. Winthrop saw one simple way to partially mollify the unhappy deputy governor: encouraging newcomers—specifically, the early arrivals in Hooker's Company—to settle in Newtown. Accordingly, in August 1632, the General Court ordered the first settlers from Hooker's English congregation to relocate to Newtown, and the court agreed to procure a minister for Newtown, a significant concession at a time when the competition among

In May 1636, Thomas Hooker (center) led the main group of migrants through the wilderness to the Connecticut Valley; members of his company were linked by kinship, nationality, and Puritanism. (Bettmann / CORBIS)

congregations for pastors was fierce. That minister, of course, was "the revered and faithful" Thomas Hooker.[7]

Hooker learned quickly upon his arrival that he was not joining a contented congregation happily building a new Eden in the New World. He was joining a congregation that had been forced to move within the first year of its landing to a town it had not chosen. Winthrop was interested primarily in mollifying Dudley and strengthening Newtown so that it would survive as a community. The happiness of Hooker's Company came third. Ironically, Winthrop succeeded all too well in his effort to help Newtown grow. As new arrivals established homes, inhabitants soon began to complain that the town was too crowded and that they had no place to expand. Newtown was hemmed in by the Charles River and by Watertown and Boston. Where commentators praised Newtown's compactness, the Essex contingent complained of a lack of room. Forced to leave Mount Wollaston, Hooker's Company found itself on a spit of land that it said from the outset was inadequate for farming. Newtown's boundaries were exceedingly narrow: the town was nearly eight times as long as it was broad, and farmers' meadows were on the opposite side of the Charles. One settler, John Pratt, was so unhappy with the place that he sent a letter to friends in England complaining that "the state of the country . . . was nothing but rocks, and sands, and salt marshes." Residents concluded that their economic future was bleak unless they acquired more land.[8]

The General Court initially was sympathetic to residents' wishes to move as long as they did not leave Massachusetts Bay. In 1634, the court granted the settlers permission to find a site within the colony. In late May of that year, a party of town residents explored the Merrimack River in an effort "to find a fit place to transplant themselves," Winthrop recalled. Yet despite the large number of potential sites within Massachusetts, the settlers were not satisfied with any of their options. In July, town residents' ultimate goals became clearer: they sent six men to explore the Connecticut River, outside the boundaries of Massachusetts Bay, and the party returned with enthusiastic reports about the valley's great potential.[9]

In September, Hooker and the residents asked the General Court for permission to relocate there. In arguing their case, Newtown's representatives stressed the practical. According to Winthrop's account of the debate that took place "over divers days" in early September 1634, "the principal reasons for their removeall were their want of accommodation for their Cattle," which prevented the inhabitants from making an adequate living and from being "able to maintain their ministers." The lack of space had another

NORTH ARKANSAS COLLEGE LIBRARY
1515 Pioneer Drive
Harrison, AR 72601

practical effect, the petitioners said: it would hurt Newtown's prospects of expanding, meaning that residents there could not "receive any more of their friends to help them." Hooker added that the Puritan commonwealth had made a "fundamental error" in placing the towns "so near each to other." The Newtown petitioners also tried to explain why they found Connecticut so enticing, and they again stressed the practical: the valley's "fruitfullnesse & Comodiousnesse." If that was not reason enough, they helpfully pointed out to the magistrates that good Puritans needed to claim this rich prize in Connecticut before the Dutch or other English did. Their final justification for migrating was possibly the most annoying to opponents of expansion. They simply wanted to move. In Winthrop's words, they had a "strong bent of their spirits to remove thither."[10]

Practical reasons all, with land as the dominant theme. But was it all about land? Winthrop indicated in one journal entry that it was. These English farmers, he wrote, complained "of straitness for want of land, especially meadow."[11] The General Court's assistants, however, grasped the religious implications of the petitioners' efforts to leave Massachusetts Bay. If Newtown's unhappiness was truly just about land and meadows, they pointed out, its residents could be "accommodated at home by some enlargement which other towns offered." Or the residents could "remove to Merimack, or any other place within our patent."[12]

Foes of expansion honed in on the real issue involved in Hooker's request to leave Massachusetts Bay: the long-standing danger separatism posed to Puritan society. They expressed this fear quite lyrically: "The removing of a candlestick is a great judgment, which is to be avoided."[13] At heart, then, the debate was not really about land but rather about whether to go or to stay. And ironically, all sides—including Hooker—agreed that separatism was a bad thing. For opponents, the settlers' departure from Newtown would weaken Massachusetts Bay and its mission in the New World. For supporters, the migration would extend rather than harm the Puritan domain. The two sides came to opposite conclusions but shared a common vision of Puritanism that derived from the very nature of this religious reform movement and the Great Migration of the early 1630s.

Puritanism and the Great Migration

Puritanism sought primarily to save rather than to abandon the Church of England. The movement traced its origins to the early years of Queen Elizabeth's reign, in the 1560s, when a group of reformers dissatisfied with the English church pressed for change. For these reformers, the Church of England, established by Henry VIII in a fit of pique with Rome so that he could marry Anne Boleyn, had not gone far enough to banish the relics of detested Catholicism. Thomas Hooker put the problem succinctly: King Henry had "cut off the head of Popery, but left the body of it yet within his realm!" Catholicism itself was gone, but many of its rituals remained. In the years following Henry's death in 1547, the English church lurched toward a more Protestant structure, adopting clerical marriages, a Protestant Book of Common Prayer, and communion tables in the naves, among other things. The nascent Protestant church was strong enough that it survived the attempts of Henry's daughter, Queen Mary, to restore Catholicism to the realm. Mary's death and Elizabeth's 1558 accession to the throne saved Protestantism in England.[14]

But what kind of Protestantism was it to be? For the emerging Puritan movement, the answer was the wrong kind of Protestantism. Elizabeth, these reformers feared, was committed to a halfway reformation that would preserve much of the Catholic structure from Henry's time. They criticized everything from the ornate dress of the clergy to the laity's signing with the cross. The Puritan movement was aptly named. It sought purity in the church. In practice, this reform drive meant that the movement wanted to simplify church ritual, return power to congregations, and keep the theological underpinnings of the church anchored firmly in Calvinism (which said that God preordained who would be saved and who would be damned) rather than Arminianism (which said that people could achieve salvation through their own will). Led by an energetic clergy, the Puritans by the 1620s had a large following, primarily among the middle class and based in Greater East Anglia, London, and southwest England.

The Great Migration, which began in 1630 and ended in 1642, was rooted in the belief that the reformation had stalled and that the only hope of salvaging it was by transporting Puritanism across the ocean to the American wilderness. The policies of King Charles I in the late 1620s had contributed to contemporaries' fears that the Puritan cause was in trouble. From the reformers' perspective, Charles was hostile to Protestantism both within England and on the Continent. The Stuart monarch failed to support the Calvinist Dutch and Germany's Protestant states against the Catholics. Just as ominous was the king's support of the High Church party. Charles installed William Laud as bishop of London, and the hated Laud aggressively sought to curtail the Puritan movement, increase the king's power, and establish Arminianism throughout the realm. For Laud and the king, the church was an extension of the state. England could have but one national church; in their eyes, Puritan efforts to create a community of saints undermined the national church and the king's authority. They thus saw the Puritans as a cancer spreading from within, threatening the church's health by converting both the clergy and the laity to its reform movement.[15]

Prominent Puritan ministers found themselves hauled before Laud's High Commission to answer charges that they were nonconformists threatening the stability of the church. Laud's strategy was brutally simple. He would imprison or kill the most effective and influential Puritan ministers. In the spring of 1629, Laud's commission began its work in earnest. Hooker was one prominent target. He had been building an impressive ministry at St. Mary's Church in Chelmsford, Essex, during the 1620s. Hooker never directly attacked the church leadership, but he criticized the "enemies to God's faithful ministers" as well as the persecutors of the "Ministers of Grace." The High Commission suspended Hooker from his lectureship and ordered him to post a bond guaranteeing his reappearance before the board if summoned. The Puritan minister was not cowed, however, and he continued "his former practices," in the words of one unsympathetic rector, by working with young ministers and by preaching in lay members' houses. Hooker's defiance alarmed his opponents and warmed his supporters, with both sides petitioning Laud to argue the case for and against his removal. In July 1630, the High Commission ordered Hooker to appear; he declined, well understanding that a stiffer punishment awaited him. After conferring with his friends, Hooker decided to go into exile in the Netherlands.[16]

Hooker's experience was duplicated across England. With increasing harassment of the Puritan ministry and its followers, with the High Church party in ascendancy, and with the king dissolving Parliament to keep members from helping their Puritan allies, many Puritans reluctantly decided that they would have to leave. This decision came after a great deal of soul-searching and was replete with ironies. A small group of Puritans had previously rejected the national church as hopeless and argued that separatism was the only alternative. These Puritan radicals saw the world through narrow lenses: society consisted of true believers and the hopelessly corrupt, and the former could do little to save the latter. Separatists thus withdrew to Holland or to Plymouth Plantation in America, where they could construct the kind of godly community they wanted. Most Puritans, however, rejected this version of separatism as wrongheaded because it would cut them off from English society and defeat the purpose of the reform effort—reclaiming England for true Protestantism. By 1630, the situation had changed, and Puritan leaders and followers alike faced the simple but cruel dilemma of whether to leave or to stay. Indeed, one biographer of John Winthrop considered separation the "central problem of Puritanism": "It was the question of what responsibility a righteous man owes to society. If society follows a course that he considers morally wrong, should he withdraw and keep his principles intact, or should he stay?"[17]

Hooker wrestled with this dilemma as well, concluding in 1631 that he had to get out of England. If he stayed, he would face Laud's wrath. A colleague of Hooker's, John Cotton, agreed and defended his and Hooker's decision to flee. According to Cotton, he and Hooker initially felt inclined to remain and battle Laud's forces. Yet to stay in England and fight the High Church party carried huge risks. Cotton compared their plight to that of Peter, whom God had advised "to suffer and [be] led along to prison and to death." Christianity had a long history of martyrdom, and Cotton and Hooker considered going that route, but, Cotton said, his parishioners "dissuaded me from that course, as thinking it better for themselves and for me and for the church of God to withdraw myself from the present storm and to minister in this country to such of their town as they had sent before thither." An exiled minister, in short, could accomplish far more good than could a dead or imprisoned one.[18]

Puritan leaders who denounced separation came up with another important rationale for leaving England. Drawing on a millennial view of history, they believed that England had a mission to redeem Christendom and to restore Europe's earlier religious unity by bringing all Christians to reformed Protestantism. Thus, they likened their withdrawal to the New World to an errand into the wilderness. By leaving England, the Puritans would have the opportunity to create a model community. By the sheer force of its example and the power of its prayer, this community would convert England and by extension the world. Winthrop famously called this model community a "City upon a Hill," a place where "the eies of all people are upon Us." Puritan Edward Johnson used nearly identical language. In his *Wonder-Working Providence*, he described New England as "lights upon a Hill more obvious than the highest mountain in the World." Puritans could accomplish more as God's agents in the forests of America than in England, where they faced imprisonment and harassment. Hooker eventually came to agree with this reasoning. In England, he warned darkly in a farewell sermon, "God is going, his glory is departing, England hath seene her best dayes, and now evill dayes are befalling us: God is packing up his Gospell, because no body will buy his wares." Departure offered Puritans a chance to reverse this unfolding disaster.[19]

With calamity on the way, individual Puritans in the 1630s had several choices. They could stay in England and hope for the best. They could seek refuge in the Netherlands, where a small Puritan community was forming among the Dutch Calvinists. Or they could take their chances in America with Winthrop and the Massachusetts Bay Company. Puritanism was never a monolithic movement, and various members chose among the three options depending on individual conscience and circumstance.

Some twenty-one thousand Puritans chose America, following the lead of John Winthrop, a wealthy Puritan landowner from Suffolk who was elected governor in October 1629, while still in England. Winthrop organized the first wave of the Great Migration, procuring ships, provisions, and passengers. In March 1630, he boarded the *Arbella* and set off for America, carrying the Massachusetts charter with him. One thousand men, women, and children accompanied him or followed shortly thereafter.[20]

In 1631, Hooker opted for the Netherlands for both practical and philosophical reasons. Having defied Laud, he needed to get out of England quickly. As his modern biographer has put it, Hooker "found it much easier and quicker to arrange for transportation to Holland than to New England, especially in the winter months, for the transatlantic ships left later in the spring." Hooker, unlike Winthrop, was not quite ready to give up on England. He still retained a sliver of hope that the Puritan movement could regain the initiative over Laud and his party.[21]

Hooker's hopes were soon dashed when he found himself embroiled in the middle of a raging debate among English Puritans in Amsterdam over congregationalism and separatism. The English church's pastor, John Paget, favored a presbyterian system that placed power not in the hands of the congregation but with ruling synods of church elders. He accused Puritan congregationalists of being "separatists"—radicals who sought to separate from society to create the purest form of church possible, a church that would consist only of the elect. When Hooker left England, members of the Amsterdam church wanted the congregation to hire Hooker as an assistant, and they talked Paget into inviting Hooker to give a trial sermon. The decision about hiring Hooker became a contest of wills between those who insisted that the congregation had the right to hire pastors and Paget, who countered that the right lay with church leaders. In the midst of this controversy, Paget demanded that Hooker explain his views on separatism and congregationalism. Forced to answer, Hooker conceded that "to separate from the faithful assemblies and Churches in England as no true Churches is an error in judgement, and a sin in practice."[22]

But unlike Paget, Hooker believed that separatists deserved mercy because they were guilty only of an error in judgment. At first glance, Hooker's position reeked of hypocrisy because he had separated from the Church of England and fled the country. Hooker's views on separation, however, were complex. He denied being a separatist; he insisted that he supported something called nonseparatist congregationalism. Nonseparatists wanted not to destroy the Church of England but to save it by creating true churches within the larger church's congregations. Nonseparating congregationalists condemned the English church for its papist errors and took on the task of reforming the church from within. By withdrawing temporarily, Hooker and his allies hoped to better effect the reforms they believed were needed. And for Hooker, the ultimate way to save the church was by leading a thorough reformation in the hearts of church members by bringing them to Jesus Christ. Reform, in short, began with individuals. This very evangelical notion had its counterpart in Germany among a group of religious reformers known as Pietists, who established small conventicles of believers within the larger church in an effort to spark a second Protestant reformation.[23]

Amid all the arguing and maneuvering, Hooker left Amsterdam and accepted an assistant's post in the Dutch town of Delft. But he found no peace there either. Once again, Hooker landed in the middle of an intense debate over congregationalism and church control and again tried to explain his position, publishing several tracts. But Hooker realized that his position in the Netherlands had become nearly as tenuous as it had been in England. He began to look elsewhere for refuge.[24]

While Hooker was struggling to make his Netherlands exile work, his followers had to decide where to go. Most opted for a new start in Massachusetts Bay, devising complex rationales for crossing the Atlantic that mirrored their later decision to move within New England. Their thinking was dominated by religious factors, including the twin desires to escape a corrupt England and achieve purity in their congregations and in themselves, but economic and social forces loomed large as well. Despite their lofty mission to redeem humanity, the Puritans were never utopians who ignored the exigencies of daily life.[25]

Promotional literature stressed not only the spiritual advantages of crossing the Atlantic but also the material blessings that awaited religious pioneers who came to America. Assessing New England's prospects in the early 1630s, William Wood described a wondrous scene to those Puritan farmers used to scratching out a marginal existence on small, unproductive plots in England. In Massachusetts, he noted, there were "divers places neare the plantations, great Meadowes, wherein grow neither shrub not Tree, lying low, in which Plaines growes as much grasse, as may be throwne out with a Sithe, thicke and long, as high as a man's middle; some as high as the shoulders." The land was rich, the wildlife was varied and abundant, and the natural resources were nearly endless. The chance to own more land and to increase one's material blessings in the New World thus helped to entice many wavering pilgrims to cross the Atlantic.[26]

In the Puritan mind, the material and the religious blended almost seamlessly. English Puritans wanted a "competency"—a degree of economic independence for their households. By providing adequately for their families, heads of households could ensure that their members lived good and orderly lives. Such lives, in turn, underpinned the pursuit of the spiritual. Moving to America thus offered migrants the opportunity simultaneously to take care of their families' worldly and spiritual needs. Thomas Dudley captured the complexity of motives in a March 1630 letter in which he explained exactly what kind of person would thrive in the Puritan commonwealth then taking shape: "If any godly men, out of religious ends, will come over here to help us in the good work we are about, I think they cannot dispose of themselves nor of their estates more to God's glory and the furtherance of their own reckoning." Worshiping God and prospering materially—such were the seemingly paradoxical goals of a majority of the migrants.[27]

Hooker's followers, who numbered about 160 souls, shared these complex motives. They came from Greater East Anglia, a region consisting of five counties in eastern England that supplied several thousand people to the Great Migration. East Anglia was an industrial and commercial powerhouse in the fifteenth and sixteenth centuries, taking advantage of its proximity to London, the sea, and numerous rivers to develop strong trade links with the Continent. The region also had a rich agricultural tradition. Essex County, the home of Hooker and his company, produced cereals, meats, and various dairy products for the London market. The region as a whole was a leading cloth producer. Braintree and Chelmsford, home to many members of Hooker's group, were market towns northeast of London. The turmoil surrounding Laud's religious crackdown overlapped with an economic depression in East Anglia that lasted from 1620 to 1640. The region was overpopulated, the cloth industry was in decline, and unemployment was rising. Nature contributed to Anglia's agony: heavy rains in the early 1620s harmed harvests, and a plague hit in the mid-1620s. Malnutrition became a serious problem, leading to a smallpox outbreak in some areas. Winthrop, who lived in northern Anglia, lamented, "This lande grows wearye of her Inhabitantes, so as man which is the most pretious of all Creatures, is neer more vile and base, then the earthe they treade upon, and of lesse prise among us than an horse or a sheepe." For Puritans already worried about England's religious future, these problems provided further evidence of God's displeasure and additional incentives to migrate.[28]

As the research of historian Roger Thompson has shown, Puritan migrants abandoned East Anglia for New England in three main waves—1630, 1634–35, and 1637–38. Most emigrants were married, according to Thompson: 443 men and 427 women, versus only 262 unmarried men and 83 unmarried women. Relatively few gentlemen left England: 52 percent of the emigrants were middle-class artisans and farmers. This profile was representative of the overall Puritan migration to New England: migrants generally were from the middle class, traveled in family groups, and were older. Such demographics contrast starkly with those of seventeenth-century migrations to the Caribbean, the Chesapeake, and elsewhere in the New World, in which most migrants were young, male, and single. These men often lacked the resources to pay for their passage and thus came to the New World as indentured servants, pledging seven years or so of labor in exchange for their passage. Religious motives were largely absent among the members of these groups, who came almost solely for the chance to improve their material lives.[29]

In 1633, two developments pointed Hooker to America. Most of his former parishioners had migrated to New England, and his exile in the Netherlands had gone badly. Hooker, as a result, had fewer options than had been open to him in 1631. As his biographer has noted, "The last remaining haven in the English-speaking world for the practice of the power of godliness and heart religion seemed to be the new settlements in New England."[30] Hooker's decision to come to America thus became relatively easy. In spring 1633, he secretly reentered England to secure passage to New England. In July, he, Cotton, and Hooker's new assistant, Samuel Stone, boarded the *Griffin* for yet another exile. After the ocean crossing, Hooker was reunited with his old parishioners in Newtown, where he at last was free of the quarrels of the church in England and Holland. In America, he believed, he would have the freedom to construct a godly society.[31]

But the creation of this new society did not go as planned. Like an unwanted visitor appearing at the door, the issue of separation and whether to go or to stay quickly reappeared in Hooker's life, and he found himself standing before the General Court in 1634 attempting to explain why his unhappy congregation wanted to migrate west to the Connecticut Valley. This theologian opposed separation in principle and understood that a Puritan could not turn his back on society; nevertheless, Hooker supported his followers' efforts to migrate to the frontier. In one sense, the migrants' decision to cite land as their main reason for moving constituted an effort to skirt the whole issue of separatism. They were, in effect, telling the General Court that they were not leaving the Puritan commonwealth but merely extending it. Foes of expansion, however, would have none of that reasoning. They viewed the proposed migration to Connecticut as old-fashioned separatism. The departure of Newtown's residents from Massachusetts Bay, they maintained, would weaken the whole fabric of society: "In point of Conscience they ought not to depart from us being knit to us in one body, & bound by oath to seek the well-far of this commonwealth." Opponents also argued that because Hooker was a leading Puritan, his removal would "not only draw many from us, but also divert other friends that would come to us." Thus, the migration of Hooker and his followers would harm the colony's prospects and undercut the reform mission that Puritans had undertaken by leaving England.[32]

On an even deeper level, the opponents of expansion believed that the Newtown settlers' removal would violate the covenant that formed the basis of society in Massachusetts Bay. In the words of Puritan William Bradshaw, the covenant represented a "free mutuall consent of Believers Joyning and covenanting to live as Members of a holy Society togeather in all religious and vertuous duties as Christ and his Apostles did institute and practise in the Gospell." Underpinning Puritan covenant theory was the belief that all members had to sacrifice their individual interests for the collective good, that the health and safety of the commonwealth depended on the interdependence of its various parts. Hooker, ironically, agreed that any person who entered a community "must . . . willingly binde and ingage himself to each member of that society to promote the good of the whole." Bound by a covenant, Hooker believed, a church could form a far "stronger tye." Winthrop put it more forcefully to his fellow passengers as the *Arbella* made its way across the Atlantic in 1630: "We are entered into Covenant with [the Lord] for this worke. . . . For this end, wee must be knitt together . . . as one man." For many of the magistrates, this responsibility formed the crux of the problem with the Newtown congregation's request to move to the Connecticut frontier. By leaving, Hooker and his people not only would be violating the solemn agreement that they had agreed to when they settled in Massachusetts Bay but also would be harming the entire society.[33]

If Newtown's residents had wanted to remain in Massachusetts Bay, none of these issues would have been a problem. The settlers would still have been part of the commonwealth and would not have been breaking any covenants. But Hooker's Company wanted to leave Massachusetts Bay. Worse, they wanted to go west, to the frontier. The magistrates' reaction to Newtown's request was intimately tied to the Puritan conception of the wilderness. The frontier, they believed, was populated by wolves and "savage" Indians and was something to be feared by all civilized Puritans. Bradford called the American wilderness "hidious and desolate," while others labeled it "howling" and "vast." Religion and European notions of civilization mingled in the Puritan mind to produce such views. Puritans believed, as did other Englishmen in the New World, that the wilderness was untamed and uncultivated. They saw the supposedly virgin forests of America as diametrically opposed to English gardens, which human labor cultivated and improved. Thomas Shepard Jr. defined a wilderness as a place of darkness, desolation, and evil that threatened to reduce man to a "lost" condition. In a telling phrase, Hooker likened sin to a wilderness "overgrown with weeds." By moving to the frontier, Hooker's people could degenerate into savagery. Classical humoral physiology, which argued that human beings were creatures of the climate that they inhabited, supported such assertions. "This notion," in the words of one modern historian, "led to the obvious conclusion that a people could not leave their native environment, as in the process of colonization, and retain indefinitely their native identity."[34]

Clashing with the numerous pressures against expansion was Puritans' sense that they had a religious duty to tame the wilderness. The frontier might have been a savage place, but the Puritans had a mission to conquer it and turn it into the Lord's garden on both a physical and spiritual level. The Puritans viewed themselves as the elect people, the moral descendants of the Jews. They derived this belief from Genesis, where God instructed Abraham's children to "increase and multiply and replenish the earth and subdue it." On a literal level, this admonition meant going out and clearing the land so that English-style villages could be built. On a spiritual level, it meant, in Hooker's words, overcoming great trials in a "vast and roaring Wilderness" before "they could possess that good Land." After arriving in Connecticut, Hooker explicitly reminded his congregation that they were children of Israel who needed to survive the hardships of frontier living. The wilderness experience thus mirrored the preparation for conversion. A member of the elect had to undergo a difficult period of vocation before achieving justification. Redemption came only after great trials.[35]

The conflicting pressures regarding expansion buffeted the General Court as it debated whether to grant Newtown's request to move to the Connecticut Valley. Fifteen of the court's twenty-five deputies supported the move. As the elected representatives of the towns, the deputies very likely saw it as in their best interests to permit the migration. An affirmative vote would set a precedent that would allow towns to expand. Eight of the eleven assistants (at-large court members), including John Winthrop, voted against the proposed migration. Two individual votes show just how muddled the situation had become: Dudley, who had recently replaced Winthrop as governor, backed Newtown's request even though the residents' departure would severely weaken his town in the short run. Deputy Governor Roger Ludlow voted against the petition even though he moved to Connecticut a year later and helped found Windsor. Most assistants concluded that expansion was not in the colony's best interests. Even though eighteen court members supported the removal and seventeen members opposed it, the assistants insisted that the measure was defeated because the colony's charter stipulated that six assistants had to support a bill for it to pass. The deputies protested this veto, Winthrop said, "and upon this grew a great difference" between the two sides, and neither would yield. Not knowing how to resolve the standoff, "the whole Court agreed to keep a day of humiliation to seek the Lord" and asked Hooker to preach a conciliatory sermon. He refused, citing "his unfitness for that occasion." Instead, Cotton took on the unpleasant task of trying to reconcile the two sides. In the end, the court shelved the matter and offered Newtown a compromise: the town could have thirty acres from neighboring Watertown, along with a chunk of land along "Muddy River" that belonged to Boston. Winthrop optimistically believed that Newtown would be satisfied with this offer of land.[36]

He could not have been more wrong. Newtown residents were already using the thirty acres, and such a small allotment hardly met their need for more meadow. The Boston land was on the opposite side of the river from Newtown and was accessible only by boat, an inconvenience in good weather and wholly impractical in bad. The compromise, in short, did nothing to assuage the residents' unhappiness. Newtown soon gained important allies, however. Inhabitants of Watertown, a "plantation for Husbandmen Principally," and Roxbury also began complaining that they did not have enough land. Faced with rising demands for inland expansion, the General Court allowed residents of those two towns to move on two conditions—that their new settlement not "prejudice another plantation" and that "they continued under this government." They and residents of Dorchester ignored both stipulations. In the summer of 1635, a small party of residents left Watertown and Dorchester for the Connecticut Valley, with the Dorchester group trespassing on land belonging to Plymouth Colony. The assistants' efforts to stop inland expansion had failed, and the General Court now had no practical way of keeping Hooker and his congregation from leaving the colony.[37]

In the summer of 1635, Newtown's residents resumed their plans to relocate to Connecticut. A vanguard of about sixty men, women, and children began

New England, 1636: Hooker's Company headed west to Springfield from Newtown, then pivoted south by following the eastern bank of the Connecticut River to the Connecticut Valley, where its members founded Hartford.

selling their homes in Newtown, and in mid-October they moved to Connecticut, settling just north of a small Dutch fort. In May 1636, Hooker and the remainder of the congregation followed.

The migrants took an approximately 110-mile overland route west to the valley, largely following Indian trails. Puritan explorers, including several in Hooker's party as well as John Oldham, an Indian trader, had navigated the route several times. Hooker estimated optimistically that the trip would take five days. The émigrés' journey began on the north bank of the Charles River and proceeded west through Watertown. The party consisted of about one hundred people and a large train of baggage and livestock, including 160 cattle. The route, which in time became known as the Bay Path or the Connecticut Path, carried them north of Cochituate Pond and past the towns

TABLE 1.1. Wealth of Hartford Settlers, Seventeenth Century, by Estate Inventories

VALUE OF ESTATE (IN POUNDS)	% OF TOTAL	AVERAGE WEALTH (IN POUNDS)
< 100 (n = 20)	21	48
101–600 (n = 72)	59	292
601+ (n = 24)	20	1,370
Total (n = 116)		445

Source: Wills.

of Weston, Wayland, and Framingham. The migrants continued on to the site of modern-day Springfield in what is now western Massachusetts before pivoting south for the final descent into the lower Connecticut Valley, where they traveled along the east side of the Connecticut River. The approximately two-week journey went fairly smoothly, although Hooker's wife had to be carried in a horse litter. By the end of 1636, only eleven families remained in Newtown. Winthrop reported this turn of events quite matter-of-factly in his journal: "Mr. Hooker, pastor of the church of Newtown, and the most of his congregation went to Connecticut."[38]

The migrants were a fairly homogeneous group. Eleven of the twelve men in the 1635 vanguard were married, as were twenty-seven of the thirty men in the 1636 group. In all, 81 percent of the men who came to the new settlement before 1640 were married. These men overwhelmingly were in their twenties and thirties, and most were members of the middle class. This demographic profile mirrored that of the Puritan transatlantic migration earlier in the decade, which had been led not by single men in their early twenties but by married men in their thirties and early forties. Despite its middle-class orientation, the Newtown migration was distinguished by the large number of members of the gentry who participated. Fifty percent of the men in the 1635 migration and 40 percent of the men in the 1636 migration belonged to the gentry.[39]

Hooker was the undisputed spiritual leader, but he was accompanied by some impressive talent from the political and economic realms. One notable was John Haynes of Essex County, England, described by a letter writer as "a very godly man of Mr. Hooker's charge." Haynes, who had come to Massachusetts with Hooker aboard the *Griffin*, was one of the wealthiest men in Newtown, leaving behind an estate of fifteen hundred pounds at his death in 1654. According to his son, Hezekiah, John helped finance the "first planting" at a considerable cost to the family fortune in England. Haynes served briefly as governor of Massachusetts Bay before his departure from Newtown, and he became Connecticut's first governor in April 1639. Also notable was George Wyllys, a merchant and trader who had far-flung interests that extended to several sugar plantations in Antigua. This wealthy squire did not travel to the frontier in 1636 but instead dispatched his steward, William Gibbons, and twenty men to do the grubby work of clearing a home site, building a house, and launching a farm. Wyllys and his family moved to Hartford in 1638. He was promptly elected a magistrate to Connecticut's General Court, and he served as governor in 1642, three years before his death.[40]

Far more typical of the migrants was John Pratt, a farmer with a wife and two sons who had come to Massachusetts from Wood Ditton in Cambridgeshire during the Great Migration. In late 1635, he found himself hauled before the Massachusetts Court of Assistants for saying "divers things" that Winthrop believed "were untrue and of ill report." The magistrates, extremely sensitive about the colony's reputation, summoned him to explain the complaints he had expressed in his letter to England. A contrite Pratt appeared before the court on November 3 and tried to clarify his meaning. In a subsequent letter, he backed off much of what he had said. Unhappy as he was, Pratt remained a good Puritan who would not defy the magistrates. The founders of Hartford thus shared the bond of home, hearth, and Puritanism. Nearly all hailed from Greater East Anglia; most were from Essex County; and many knew Hooker in Chelmsford. Those who did not got to know him well in Newtown. These tight-knit members of Hooker's Company were linked by kinship, nationality, and religion.[41]

An "Old" Society in a New Land

The mystery of why Hooker and his followers moved to the Connecticut frontier only deepened after 1636. Along the Connecticut River, Hooker's people now had the freedom to implement their vision of what a godly society should be, much in the same way as the Pilgrims in neighboring Plymouth as well as countless religious visionaries before and since.

Hooker's Company settled on a site that the Indians called Suckiaug ("black earth"). The Connecticut River's 410 miles (100 more than the Hudson River to the south) teemed with shad and salmon. The river was so imposing that it earned a variety of nicknames among those visitors and early Americans who laid eyes on it. Impressed by its sheer size, the Indians called it Kwinitekwa ("Long River"). The Dutch were more prosaic, referring to the river simply as Versche ("Fresh Water River"). One later American writer noted that travelers could not adequately describe its "uncommon and universal beauty."

Hooker's people were equally impressed. They referred to it repeatedly as the Great River. A second, less imposing river, the Little River, bisected the site as well.[42]

Hartford's founders had several options as they surveyed the meadows and forests bordering the Connecticut River. They could opt for large single-family farms of several hundred acres, as migrants to frontiers in Maine, upstate New York, and the West did. Or they could keep the Puritan village common to Massachusetts Bay. A third option was a middle ground between the dispersed American-style settlement and the Puritan village: the original inhabitants could construct a village but permit farmers to own large consolidated holdings beyond the village green. Hooker's Company chose to retain the familiar landscape of Newtown and England, a decision that was both surprising (given the settlers' repeated complaints about the lack of room in Massachusetts Bay) and not so surprising (given their English Puritan heritage).

Hooker and his followers thus built an English village on the frontier. The wide, swift-moving Connecticut River helped determine where the migrants constructed their homes and how they moved about. Residents erected no houses directly along the river's banks. Instead, the Little Meadow served as a buffer between the village and the Connecticut, which frequently flooded during the spring. A sizable number of migrants settled on the opposite side of the Little River, with Hartford dividing into a north side (where Hooker lived and the meetinghouse was located) and a south side that contained an ox pasture.[43]

Communal values loomed large in the shaping of Hartford, and these values mixed with business ones. As in Newtown, the two-story meetinghouse became the focal point of village life. The migrants' homes huddled around this central square and radiated to the north and south. For the town founders and church elders, the benefits of such a system were obvious and multifold. A village proper would keep the town unified and enable everyone to attend worship services. In addition, it would permit town and church leaders more easily to monitor the behavior of the saintly and not-so-saintly. If all the settlement's inhabitants lived off on their own in the "howling" wilderness, they could and would stray from the Lord's ways. Individualism, not congregationalism, would triumph in such a place.[44]

The town meeting kept tight control of land distribution and set aside meadows and pasture for everyone's use. The meeting decreed in 1639 that "noe new divesion of land shall be made by the Inhabetants of either side of the River without the knowledge and Consent of the whole" and barred inhabitants from felling "Anny Tymber tree in anny Common ground." More-

TABLE 1.2. Original Inhabitants' Landholdings in Hartford

	AVERAGE NUMBER OF PARCELS	AVERAGE ACRES PER PARCEL	AVERAGE TOTAL HOLDINGS PER PERSON
Small landowners			
(< 51 acres) (n = 70)	7	2.8	20
Medium landowners			
(51–199 acres) (n = 48)	13.6	6.6	90
Large landowners			
(200+ acres) (n = 16)	17	32	546
Total (n = 134)	10.3	10.4	107

Source: *Original Distribution of the Lands in Hartford among the Settlers, 1639* (Hartford, Conn., 1912)

over, it opted for small, scattered individual holdings beyond the village green. The town meeting wanted holdings to be kept "just and equal," because all residents were the Lord's people. However, those migrants who helped finance the move and the purchase of the site received more land than did less well-off members of Jesus' flock. The founders thus deftly mixed the communal and the material in laying out Hartford. Original proprietors—those migrants who had contributed financially to the move to Connecticut—received two-acre house lots and additional holdings; poorer inhabitants received small lots of one acre or less at the "Townes Courtesie."[45]

Despite the repeated pleas in Massachusetts Bay for more land and despite the availability of land in the Connecticut Valley, first-generation proprietors owned an average of only 107 acres spread out over ten parcels. Even the wealthiest members of the community—John Haynes, George Wyllys, and their ilk—owned an average of only 546 acres, and that amount was divided among seventeen parcels. The poorest proprietors averaged seven holdings that totaled 20 acres. More tellingly, Edward Stebbin possessed 180 acres spread over thirty parcels, an average of 6 acres per plot. Richard Lord owned forty-two parcels scattered across Hartford that totaled only 251 acres—again, an average of 6 acres. John Maynard owned 56 acres: his main lot contained his house and the standard 2 acres, on which were located his "tenement," barn, stable, outhouses, garden, and orchard. He had one rod in the Little Meadow, one acre on the east side of the Great River, and four acres in the "little ox pasture." His largest holding from the original 1639 division consisted of 10 acres in the cow pasture.[46]

Hartford's landholdings were spectacularly small when compared with the holdings of the gentry and middle class elsewhere in British North America in the late seventeenth and early eighteenth centuries. Along the northern and southern frontiers throughout the colonial period, wealthy Americans built up huge landholding empires of 10,000 or more acres. Even settlers of middling means bought 200-acre farms in North Carolina and other parts of the southern backcountry.[47] John Pratt, by contrast, who so loudly proclaimed that he wanted more and better land, acquired twenty-one tracts in Hartford totaling only 116 acres, although he had the resources to buy far more. At his death, he left an estate of more than five hundred pounds, an amount that placed him and his family in the upper ranks of the middle class.[48]

In the end, the migrants' landholdings in Connecticut differed little from their holdings in Newtown: inhabitants in both places owned small, scattered fields.[49] The similarities with Newtown did not stop at the cow pasture but also involved the congregation itself. In both form and spirit, Hartford's First Church closely resembled the congregation that members had left behind in May 1636. Hartford's congregational founders began by solemnly agreeing to a covenant, where they likely pledged to "freely give ourselves to ye Lord to walke in communion with him . . . and to yeeld obediance to all his Command and to submit to his government." Hartford's Articles of Faith proclaimed the virtues of the congregational way: "We believe that any number of Christians, duly organized, constitute a church of Christ, the special ordinances of which are Baptism and the Lord's Supper."[50] The 1638 constitution of Connecticut, which then consisted of Hartford, Windsor, and Wethersfield, advised towns within the colony to form an "orderly and decent Government established according to God." For their part, the first magistrates pledged to "enter into Combination and Confederation togather, to maytayne and presearve the liberty and purity of the gospells of our Lord Jesus." In the interests of maintaining a godly community, Hartford's town meeting in the early years sought both to keep out undesirables (the poor and strangers with "evill maners or opinions") and to regulate behavior.[51]

Despite Hooker's removal to the frontier in a new colony, he remained active in Massachusetts Bay's ecclesiastical affairs. Hooker may have "abandoned" the neighboring commonwealth, but he also was a devout Puritan who could be found defending religious orthodoxy and the unity of the saints. One important instance occurred in 1637, when Hooker returned to Boston to serve as co-moderator at a synod called to resolve the crisis spawned by Anne Hutchinson and her antinomian followers. At the synod, Hooker helped craft the compromise that for a time preserved the New England Way.[52]

Hartford's founders, in short, were not radicals who sought to build a religious utopia in the woods. The congregational way remained the center of their intellectual universe, and this fact meant that the Newtown migrants replicated what they knew in Massachusetts—the tight-knit congregational village, with members living within walking distance of the meetinghouse. Such "conservatism" again raises the central question of why they moved. The migrants could have just as easily stayed in Newtown and saved themselves the bother, danger, and expense of relocating to the frontier. And the dangers involved in this move were very real. Hooker's Company had turned its back on all it had built in Newtown. Most members were starting over for the third time in four years. The tiny village was isolated from Boston and was far inland, meaning that its economic prospects were far from certain. The migrants' isolation from Massachusetts Bay also meant that their physical safety was not assured. In 1636, the dominant military power in southern New England was not the English or the Dutch but the Native Americans. The Indians, especially the Pequots, made Puritan leaders in Boston and elsewhere exceedingly nervous about the safety of the isolated Connecticut settlements. A 1634 Pequot attack that led to the deaths of John Stone, the captain of a trading bark on the Connecticut River, and his crew heightened Puritan fears that the Indians wanted to drive the weak and scattered English from the valley. Hooker and his people arrived in Connecticut in the middle of a last-ditch diplomatic effort to resolve the crisis between the Puritans and the Pequots. The effort failed, and the two sides fought a two-year war that began in 1636, intensified in 1637, and ended in the rout of the Pequot people. Thus, almost upon their arrival, Hooker and his followers found themselves involved in a deadly war with the Pequot Indians, although the fighting took place to the south and Hartford itself was never attacked. As the largest town along the upper Connecticut, Hartford had to supply the most men and contribute the most money among its sister settlements.[53]

No one clear incident or reason explains why Hooker and his followers abandoned Massachusetts Bay. Rather, the migration resulted from a number of independent motivations that worked together. The broad forces at work in 1636 were foreshadowed in the migrants' decision to leave England and cross the Atlantic for Massachusetts Bay in 1632 and 1633. Religion and land, in other words, mingled in complex ways to spur internal migrations in Puritan New England, just as they had in the transatlantic migration.

Despite their small holdings in Hartford, land *was* important to the migrants. Pratt and others were not being insincere when they complained about Newtown and the lack of land. The settlers truly prized the valley's rich soil and bountiful meadows. They wanted to leave behind the rocky soil of coastal Massachusetts. As farmers in a new Eden, Hartford's founders wanted to grow wheat, oats, barley, and vegetables—to engage in mixed farming, in other words—while raising livestock. They greatly valued cattle and looked almost rapturously at the meadows along the Great River. Indeed, one Massachusetts writer commented in 1633 that young bulls were "wonderful dear here. There is none to be gotten but at a great price. A cow is worth here twenty-five pounds; a calf . . . ten pounds, and none to be gotten." Land, moreover, carried a spiritual component. Owning more land enabled Hooker's people to better pursue a competency. In the Connecticut Valley, they would have more freedom to achieve their material and spiritual goals. For all of these reasons, land was important to Hartford's founders, including Hooker, who profited quite nicely from the move to Connecticut. The man of God eventually owned one of Hartford's largest holdings, at 375 acres, and at his death in 1647, he left an estate of more than eleven hundred pounds. Such wealth placed him in the town's upper tier.[54]

Land was not a complete answer, however, as the Massachusetts Bay assistants pointed out in 1634; it was just one reason Hooker's Company left Newtown. Ironically, given the relative orthodoxy of Hooker and his followers, religious goals also influenced the migration to Connecticut and the direction that Hartford took. Hooker obviously had strong ideas about how a congregation should be run, and he laid out his vision in the *Survey of the Summe of Church-Discipline*, a book-length tract that captured the ambiguity of this Connecticut migration. Hooker both supported Puritan orthodoxy and passionately argued for a brand of Puritanism that put more moderate church leaders on edge. Historians of Puritanism have long speculated that he was unhappy with the direction that the Bay Colony was taking and that his relationship with Cotton had taken a turn for the worse.[55] Contemporaries as well sensed a rivalry between the two men, prompting William Hubbard to write that "two such eminent stars, such as were Mr. Cotton and Mr. Hooker, . . . could not well continue in one and the same orb." The suspicions were widespread enough that Winthrop felt compelled in 1635 to deny that any rivalry existed: "Mr. Hooker is like to go [to Connecticut] next year, [but] not for any difference between Mr. Cotton and him . . . for they do hold a most sweet and brotherly communion together." Eminent historian Perry Miller, writing in the 1950s, first discounted reports of a rivalry between the two ministers but later changed his mind, becoming "fully persuaded that the purely personal rivalry between Hooker and Cotton was much more of a factor in this removal than I had naively supposed."[56]

No hard evidence indicates that Hooker's rivalry with Cotton was heated enough to cause Hooker to leave Massachusetts Bay. Moreover, their most serious differences arose *after* the 1636 migration. Yet the two ministers clearly were not of one mind on church polity, and these differences likely factored into Hooker's decision to migrate west. Their most important disagreement involved requirements for church membership. As Calvinists, Puritans believed that God preordained who was saved and that the conversion process involved five intricate steps. The first step was *election*, in which an all-powerful God decided who would be saved or damned. The second stage involved *vocation*, where an individual came to understand his sinful nature and was offered the opportunity to turn to God and salvation. The third stage was *justification*, in which a person was "reborn" and his or her soul was redeemed. After achieving justification, the person entered *sanctification*, where he or she became a member of the elect. The final stage was *glorification*, which theoretically saw the removal of any doubt that the person was saved.[57]

In practice, determining whether someone had undergone justification and entered glorification was quite difficult and engendered considerable debate among Puritan theologians. Cotton and Hooker shared some common ground in this debate, but they also had significant differences: the former held people to a higher standard in meeting the test of glorification than did the latter. Cotton wanted applicants to demonstrate "infallible" signs that they had been saved and were now visible saints. Hooker agreed that Puritan congregations needed to rigorously screen new church members to ensure that applicants were truly of the elect. Hooker unhesitatingly believed that "Visible Saints only are fit Matter . . . to make up a visible Church of Christ." And he opposed extending baptism to children whose parents were not full members. But Hooker criticized the practices of the Massachusetts Bay Colony and Cotton as overly restrictive. He also criticized the Pilgrims and other separatists for their excessive emphasis on purity and piety among the faithful. He believed that it was nearly impossible for a mere human to fully divine what was inside someone's heart, making it inevitable that some of the nonelect would mistakenly become full congregation members. "The Church," he wrote, "consists of some who are faithfull and sincere hearted: some counterfet and halfe hearted. Some really good, some really bad." So, Hooker concluded, "only those who appear so bad and vile should not be accepted." Others who appeared to be sincere should be allowed in. By starting anew in the wilds of Connecticut, Hooker had greater freedom to pursue his ministry and his evangelical vision for a "true" church. He would have more leeway to conduct congregational affairs because he would literally be farther from the prying eyes of Boston's meddling magistrates. Thus, the new birth and the debate over church membership were important underlying causes of the migration.[58]

Lessons from Puritan New England

Hartford's story is interesting not just because of the personalities involved and the particulars of its migration but also because its themes and patterns resonate elsewhere in New England and America. There, in the wilderness, miles from the growing seaport of Boston, the Protestant migration model was distilled to its purist form. Protean economic, social, and religious factors drove the mobility of Hooker's Company. Such a mix of motives was not unusual in New England. Puritan migrations elsewhere followed similar patterns.[59]

One historian has labeled the settlement process in early New England "a reshuffling," as people sought a place that satisfied their spiritual and economic needs. Most migrants from England arrived in Massachusetts in the summer and spent a few weeks in port, where they tried to educate themselves about the best places to settle. Fewer than one in six heads of households opted to stay in the port cities, and the majority of those who did so were craftsmen who concluded that such a town was the best place to set up shop. The rest of the migrants "would spend their first year or two moving about the region, and most would finally choose for their permanent home a newly founded community where they might still obtain farms near the town center."[60]

Puritans therefore were quite mobile. In Hartford, 45 percent of the original inhabitants moved at least twice in New England; 41 percent moved three times; and 14 percent moved four or more times. Their most popular destinations were Hadley, Farmington, Saybrook, Norwalk, and Wethersfield. In early Connecticut, according to historian Jackson Turner Main, a quarter of the migrants pushed on to other places, including north into Massachusetts. Another historian found that 80 percent of migrants who left London in 1635 moved at least once in New England, and most moved twice. In all, migration from Connecticut's three river towns led to the founding of Fairfield, Farmington, Haddam, Killingworth, Middletown, Norwalk, Stratford, and Woodbury.[61]

The dynamics between religion and land evolved somewhat over the seventeenth century. Hartford witnessed the change through the problem of "outlivers"—inhabitants who lived a distance from the meetinghouse or across the river from the main village or "plantation." Outlivers wanted the

TABLE 1.3. Mobility among First Generation, Hartford

NUMBER OF MOVES	NUMBER OF SETTLERS (N = 145)	%
2	65	45
3	60	41
4	20	14

Source: J. Hammond Trumbull, ed., *The Memorial History of Hartford, Connecticut, 1633–1884* (Boston, 1886), vol. 1.

freedom to worship in their own meetinghouses, but this desire for separate houses of worship was tied closely to their desire for consolidated holdings farther from the town center. After 1640, as the population grew, New England villages became more spread out. This growth undermined the religious and social unity envisioned by the founding generation and led to dissent within congregations. The original plan in Hartford and elsewhere in New England was that all residents would be within walking distance of the meetinghouse. Such a goal forced farmers to own many tracts at a considerable distance from the home lot. Small, scattered holdings meant that farmers spent a considerable part of their day traveling to and from their fields. Thus, a spatial design meant to promote harmony instead ultimately produced division. Farmers simply got tired of walking to their far-flung fields. Town leaders resisted the consolidation of holdings because such a change would mean that homeowners would be living farther from the meetinghouse. The lurking danger here was individualism: people off on their own in the wilderness would be living for themselves, not for the Lord.[62]

And over time, the land pressures that had been present in Newtown in 1633 returned, though they worked differently in Hartford in the late seventeenth century. In Newtown, the first generation of settlers did not have enough space, so they moved to the frontier. By contrast, the land pressures of the mid- and late seventeenth century were more generational. Fathers ran out of room for their sons, forcing the second and third generations to migrate. Connecticut's population grew 58 percent between 1670 and 1700 and 280 percent between 1700 and 1730. Most of this growth occurred east of the Connecticut River because of the flood of migrants from southeastern Massachusetts. In Hartford, sons moved frequently to nearby Wethersfield and Windsor as early as the 1640s to acquire farms. Thomas Lord, for example, had seven children who scattered to Wethersfield, Stonington, and Saybrook. Lord had arrived in Hartford in 1636 and owned a one-acre house lot on the Little River. His nine parcels totaled only 58 acres, and his four sons looked elsewhere for land. Thomas Jr., the eldest, acquired landholdings in Hartford and Wethersfield and died with an estate of more than two hundred pounds.[63]

Inheritance practices of the mid–seventeenth century also encouraged sons to migrate.[64] In only a few instances did Hartford's fathers divide their lands equally among their sons and daughters. Instead, like their "secular" counterparts, they followed the English practice of bequeathing the bulk of the land to a favored son, usually the firstborn, and then awarding varying distributions of land, goods, and money to the rest of their children. Merchant William Whiting was no typical settler—at his death, he left behind an estate of nearly three thousand pounds—but his treatment of his seven children was quite typical. His namesake and oldest son was to inherit his father's house and land when he reached age twenty-one. His father also left him a hundred pounds "more than I give to either my sonne John or Samuel." And John and Samuel each received a hundred pounds more than their two sisters.[65] Unlike German-speaking settlers, who often shared and shared alike, the English played favorites. Primogeniture was the dominant practice in England during the early modern period because of the scarcity of land there. Maintaining the viability of the family estate mandated that it not be subdivided. Although the practice of passing on land to eldest sons did not survive intact in the New World, the idea that fathers should favor one or two sons did. English fathers generally believed that devolving most of the family land to one member would best protect the family estate. Daughters rarely received land; instead, fathers left them livestock, household goods, and other personal property. Uneven treatment meant that sons wanting to marry and acquire farms often had to look outside of Hartford. Newly married women moved along with their husbands.[66]

Some seventeenth-century mobility trends were obvious and commonsensical. The earliest migrants settled New England's best areas—the coast and the major river valleys. Internal migration first ran westward from Massachusetts Bay to the Connecticut Valley and then to Long Island, New Jersey, and western New York, simultaneously shifting northward to what became New Hampshire and Maine as those lands opened. Historian John Frederick Martin has shown the importance of the profit motive in the founding of many Puritan towns. Founders established business corporations and awarded town lands to investors who had helped finance the purchases. As settled areas filled up, later generations were forced to move. In the most general terms, the young were the most restless. And the experience of individual towns showed that mobility trends could be quite complex. In Windsor, Connecticut, founded in 1637, a year after Hooker arrived at what became Hartford, the most mobile members of that river town were not the second generation but the first. In Guilford, however, family demographics told a different story. The larger the family, the more likely that children had to migrate. When there was only one heir, that child tended to stay.[67]

These economic and social pressures could send religious migrations off in new directions, with religion always present as an undercurrent. In Windsor, the most stable residents tended to be original members of the church or those who quickly became active in congregational life. Those church members who did move had stayed in Windsor far longer (twenty years) than non-church-members who left (thirteen years). Social factors loomed large as well. According to historian Linda Auwers Bissell, single people without family ties in Windsor were twice as likely to migrate. Second-generation sons tended to stay put. Poor economic conditions and religious turmoil often dictated the timing of migrations, as did the opening of new towns.[68]

Despite the great diversity, seventeenth-century migrations in New England shared one basic characteristic. Good Puritans had to decide whether to go or to stay. Most went.

The Protestant Sojourner

Migration and the New Birth

Devereux Jarratt and the Anglicans of Virginia

Devereux Jarratt was, at heart, an optimist. In 1752, he had the opportunity to escape the drudgery of farm work to open a school in the frontier county of Albemarle, Virginia. But Jarratt was also a realist with a wry sense of humor who well understood what he was getting himself into. Becoming a teacher meant migrating to the backcountry from New Kent County in Tidewater Virginia with virtually no money and with only the clothes on his back. He did not even own a horse. The lure of a new life, however, proved irresistible to the nineteen-year-old Jarratt. "I readily embraced the proposal [to open the school], and soon packed up my *all*," he recalled years later. He would be traveling light. "My whole dress and apparel consisted in a pair of coarse breeches, one or two oznaburgs shirts, a pair of shoes and stockings, an old felt hat, a bear skin coat." To lend a little dignity to his appearance, the aspiring schoolteacher acquired "an old wig" from a slave, commenting wryly that in this status-conscious society, "people were not obliged, you know, to ask how I came by it." If they did ask, "I suppose I was wise enough not to tell them."[1]

Jarratt then borrowed his brother's horse and saddle and said his good-byes. It would be a lonely ride. The young schoolteacher was not a member of a "company," as Thomas Hooker, a Puritan minister, and his charges had been when they migrated from Newtown, Massachusetts, to the Connecticut frontier in 1636. Jarratt did not travel with a congregation—he was an Anglican, and an indifferent one at that. And no idealistic vision of a New Jerusalem awaited him in the hills of Albemarle County. Jarratt, unlike Hooker, was not a new arrival to America; he was a Virginian, born in 1733 in New Kent and raised by parents of modest means. "I was the youngest child of *Robert Jarratt* and *Sarah* his wife," he recalled in the autobiography that he wrote in the 1790s. "My grand-father was an Englishman, born, I believe, in the city of *London*, in Devereux county." Jarratt's father was a carpenter of some local renown, a "mild, inoffensive man, and much respected among his neighbors." Devereux and his brothers and sisters "always had plenty of plain food and raiment, wholesome and good," but he grew up with no great expectations of material success or social grandeur. "My parents neither sought nor expected any titles, honors, or great things, either for themselves or children. Their highest ambition was to teach their children to read, write and understand the fundamental rules of arithmetic. . . . They wished us all to be brought up in some honest calling, that we might earn our bread, by the sweat of our brow, as they did."[2]

Jarratt was raised in Tidewater Virginia, Hooker in the English hamlet of Marfield. Both men became servants of God. But they were born in different centuries in different lands on different continents. One was a colonial, the other a native-born Englishman. Jarratt learned about the unfairness of life at an earlier age than did Hooker. "When I was between six and seven years of age," Jarratt recounted, "I had the misfortune to lose my father, by a very sudden stroke." The consequences were immediate. Devereux's oldest brother, Robert, inherited all the family land, although Devereux was to get twenty-five pounds—a sum he considered princely—when he turned twenty-one years old.

Different as he was from Hooker, Jarratt shared a few traits with his predecessor. Both men were the products of middle-class families. Both showed academic prowess at an early age. According to Hooker's biographer, "By the age of eight or so [he] had learned to read English prose with facility and to handle pen and ink confidently, if not particularly handsomely. These were the usual requirements for admission to a grammar school." For Jarratt, a different kind of skill stood out. "The retentiveness of my memory was very extraordinary," he wrote. "Before I knew the letters of the alphabet, I could repeat a whole chapter in the Bible, at a few times hearing it read."[3]

And like Hooker, Jarratt began attending school at about age eight. He was modest about his accomplishments during his five years of formal schooling. "I learned to read in the Bible, (though but indifferently) and to write a sorry scrawl, and acquired some knowledge of Arithmetic." More misfortune befell Jarratt when he was twelve or thirteen: his mother died, and "no further care was bestowed on my education." He went to live with his oldest brother, who "allowed me in all the indulgences a depraved nature, and an evil heart could desire. I mean, he was at no pains to correct my morals, or restrain me from any of the vices of the times."[4]

Religion was not then much a part of Jarratt's life. "I followed the way of my own heart, and walked in the sight of mine own eyes, not considering, as every one ought, *that for all these things God would bring me into judgment.*" Jarratt's waywardness was hardly unusual in Chesapeake Virginia. His fellow Virginians likewise enjoyed their horse racing and cards. Living with his brother, Devereux worked as a farm laborer, performing "ploughing, harrowing, and other plantation work." He did not mind the first two tasks, but found the third very "irksome." At about age seventeen, he was finally "allowed to quit the plow, and to betake myself to the business of a carpenter, with my second brother *Joseph.*" This new occupation also failed to satisfy Jarratt, and he yearned for the classroom: "I was not contented with the small degree of learning I had acquired, and wished for more knowledge, especially in figures. My friends and acquaintance, I dare say, thought me a topping scholar—but I knew better." Jarratt studied on his own during his two-hour midday breaks, "and being now of an age for better discovering the nature of things, I made a greater progress in the real knowledge and use of figures, in one month, than I had done in years, while at school."[5]

He must have made considerable progress, because the "fame of my learning sounded far. One *Jacob Moon,* living in Albemarle county, about one hundred miles from New Kent, had also learned how learned I was." Moon, a native of New Kent, likely learned of Jarratt's promise through acquaintances or friends, and when Jarratt was nineteen, Moon "sent me word, that he should be glad to employ me as a schoolmaster." Jarratt eagerly agreed.[6]

His migration was about to begin.

Young Jarratt did not need the permission of any General Court to move. Nor was he breaking any covenant by leaving. Separation posed no deep philosophical dilemmas for society or the Anglican Church. Indeed, Jarratt did not move for overt religious reasons. His migration to Albemarle in 1752, however, represented the beginning of a long spiritual journey that ended with his "rebirth" and his ordination as an Anglican minister.

Jarratt's wanderings reveal much about Tidewater Virginia and the role—or, more accurately, the lack of the role—of the state church in mobility and society. The Chesapeake of the seventeenth and eighteenth centuries was a region of paradoxes. English immigrants established a tobacco culture in the seventeenth century, but religion and the church remained important to them, albeit in a different form than in New England and at a different level of intensity. These Virginians lived in a dispersed plantation society that lacked strong communal bonds, yet the Anglican parish became central to community. Nevertheless, religious fervor did not run as deep in Virginia as it did in Puritan New England.[7]

Jarratt's story points to these paradoxes and more. Although he grew up indifferent to religion, he eventually became so religious that he devoted his life to the church as a pastor. As minister of Bath Parish in Dinwiddie County, Jarratt became an outspoken member of the church's small evangelical wing as well as a critic of the church itself. He thus embodied Virginians' complex and difficult relationship with church and with God. His story, moreover, points to something deeper and even more fundamental about Anglicanism and the nature of religious migrations in Protestant America. It points to the role that the new birth and dissent played in the mobility of devout believers. Jarratt, after all, was not just restless; he was restless spiritually for reasons that even he did not fully understand at age nineteen or twenty.

The Wanderings of Devereux Jarratt

For the orphaned young man from New Kent, the frontier represented a chance to escape a life he did not particularly like. He would not grow tobacco out west; he would cultivate the minds of young boys in the field of education. Albemarle was as good a place as any to pursue such dreams. Located some eighty-five miles west of Richmond, this frontier county, which was formed in late 1744, was nestled between the Blue Ridge Mountains to the west and the Fluvanna River to the east. Its main town was Charlottesville. One of the county's early leaders was Thomas Jefferson's father, Peter, who helped organize Albemarle, became a justice of the peace, and served on the court of chancery. Arriving in the county after a two- or three-day ride astride his borrowed horse, Jarratt made himself at home at the residence of Moon, who was the overseer for Colonel Richard Cocke of Surry County. Jarratt soon encountered disappointment. "I quickly discovered the number of pupils would be far short of what I had been made to expect," he recalled. "The prospect was gloomy and forbidding." Jarratt's school struggled financially, and so did he.[8]

During his year with Cocke's overseer, Jarratt began his spiritual awakening, but not because of anything that Moon did. The family, according to Jarratt, was "just as ignorant of religion, as I was, and as careless about it." Albemarle remained a sparsely populated frontier when Jarratt arrived in 1752, and "there was no minister of any persuasion, or any public worship, within many miles. The Sabbath day was usually spent in *sporting*: and whether *this* was right or wrong, I believe, no one questioned." Amid this barren religious scene, something unexpected happened: a visitor left a copy of eight sermons preached in Glasgow by famous evangelist George Whitefield. These sermons piqued

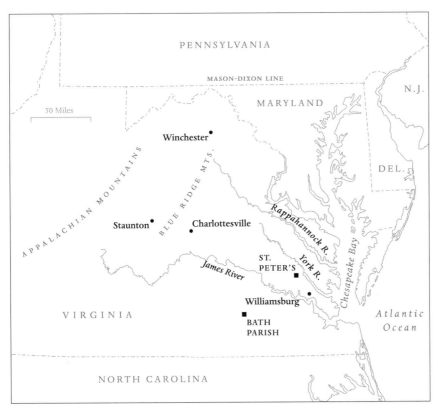

Virginia, 1750s: Devereux Jarratt traveled widely throughout the colony. He worshiped at St. Peter's as a child and got his first teaching job near Charlottesville. He became minister at Bath Parish.

Jarratt's curiosity but accomplished little else. He may have been a teacher, but Jarratt considered himself "a poor reader" who "understood little" of the sermons. Still, this fortuitous event introduced him to some strange concepts such as *"New-light"* and got him to thinking. Jarratt began to realize the wrongness of the dissolute lifestyle he, his family, the Moons, and Virginians in general pursued. Jarratt experienced no quick conversion to God's ways. Instead, he remained confused about the state of his soul and what he was supposed to do to save it. Further depressing his spirits was his bad health: he became "violently attacked [at Moon's] with a *quotidian* ague." He remained ill and completely miserable for some nine months: "In the paroxisms I frequently wept, at the thought of my being in a land of strangers, at a great distance from the place of my nativity, and my nearest relations," he recalled. "But of *God*, and my estrangement and distance from *him*, of the salvation of my soul and a future state, I had little or no concern. Such a degree of blindness and insensibility had fallen upon me."[9]

Jarratt had done little to prepare for this migration; he departed on a whim after receiving Moon's offer. Not surprisingly, given the lack of planning, the scheme did not work out well. His school was struggling, his health was poor, his pockets remained empty, and he was desperately homesick. Jarratt could have returned to New Kent, but instead, he did something quintessentially American: he moved again, opening a school at the home of Abraham Childers in Albemarle. "Here I wished to pitch my tent for the whole year," he optimistically declared, "as I found the manners of that family very much to the taste of my depraved mind." Jarratt may have felt the first stirrings of religious awakening while at the Moons, but he was not yet ready to put behind his life of debauchery. Instead, he joyfully partook of the *"merriment* [and] *buffoonery"* the Childerses offered. His new school brought in even less income than the previous enterprise, and "with great reluctance," Jarratt moved a third time, clinging to the hope that he could make a go of running a school in the Virginia backcountry.[10]

Two things changed this time. He went to live with a wealthier family headed by "a gentleman, whose name was *Cannon*. He was a man of great possessions, in lands, slaves, &c &c." And contrary to stereotypes that Evangelicals came almost exclusively from poorer backgrounds, Cannon's wife was quite religious. Jarratt tried to control his nerves as he entered the Cannons' residence one Sunday afternoon: the carpenter's son from a modest New Kent home was "very shy of *gentlefolk.*" Something else bothered him as well. "There was another very fearful circumstance, which added to my perplexity: for I had been told, that the lady of the house was a *New-light*, and of sentiments so rigid and severe, that all levities of every kind must be banished from her presence, and every species of ungodliness must expect a sharp reproof from her." Jarratt was unsure about how to act around this devout lady. He wanted to make a good impression and to avoid receiving her "reproof." He decided he needed to "induce the pious matron to think I was not destitute of religion. This put me upon a *project* entirely new to me, I mean, *to act the hypocrite.* I had no intention of being religious, but wished to appear so, in order to gain her good opinion."[11]

When Jarratt arrived, he found her reading a religious book and soon learned that she liked to study the sermons of John Flavel, a seventeenth-century Presbyterian divine. The plantation mistress asked Jarratt to join her for the readings. He accepted the invitation, since it was "agreeable to my purpose of playing the hypocrite." But Jarratt understood little of what he heard:

"Flavel's sermons are too experimental and evangelical, for one, so ignorant of divine things, as I was, to comprehend." He continued the charade for six or eight weeks, meeting with the lady of the house for religious readings that produced in him only "fatigue and drowsiness."[12]

Despite his boredom, he eventually began to understand the sermons. One especially stood out. "It pleased God, on a certain night, while she was reading, as usual, to draw out my attention, and fix it on the subject, in a manner unknown to me before." Its text was Luke 24:45, "Then opened he their understanding." It was a defining moment for him. "I must have known before this, that I was a sinner . . . but nothing ever came home to my heart, so as to make a lasting impression, till now. The impression followed me to bed—arose with me in the morning, and haunted me from place to place, till I resolved to forsake my sins, and try to save my soul."[13]

Jarratt, as Thomas Hooker could have told him, was experiencing vocation, the frightening realization that he was a sinner who needed to open his heart to Jesus Christ. Jarratt called his pain a "distress," a wonderfully understated way of saying "that I was a stranger to God and true religion, and was not prepared for death and judgment." Mrs. Cannon was overjoyed at the transformation occurring in her irreligious schoolmaster. She was so happy that she insisted he remain with the family for the whole year. Jarratt agreed, but his progress remained halting, and his path from vocation to justification was strewn with difficulties. As Jarratt lamented, "The best resolutions I made, were too weak to bear the shock of temptation," and he constantly slipped back into his old destructive behavior and then had to restart the process. The depressing cycle again left Jarratt miserable. Half saved, half sinner, "I had religion enough to make me frequently uneasy—but never to make me happy. Sinning and repenting—repenting and sinning was the round, in which I went for many months."[14]

Jarratt was stuck in another kind of cycle as well. He kept moving in the hope that he could establish a thriving school that would enable him to make a comfortable living and achieve some respectability. With a troubled mind, Jarratt left the Cannons to return to Moon's after Moon assured the schoolmaster that he would have an enrollment of twelve or thirteen students. Religion intruded each time Jarratt moved. The first move introduced him to the sermons of Whitefield, the Great Awakener. The second move put him in extended contact with a New Light devotee who got him to understand the evangelical way. The third move now did something equally important. It shook up the smug views that Jarratt was developing about the nature of sin and the role of the new birth.

Moon's family was vastly amused by the transformation in their formerly fun-loving boarder. On his arrival, Jarratt had informed the Moons that he was "concerned for their souls, and did what I could to make them sensible of the danger they were in: *But they made light of it*—turned all off with a laugh—imputing the whole to *new-light cant*—which they had supposed I had catched from Mrs. Cannon." The Moons' reaction was not at all what Jarratt wanted, and he initially dismissed them as ignorant church people who possessed no understanding of heart religion. But their derision forced Jarratt to rethink his views, to probe deeper into the mysteries of God and the divine world. And Jarratt had to admit that he also was not very knowledgeable about God's ways. His understanding of the Bible remained imperfect, as did his knowledge of the Anglican Church. Jarratt responded to this latest epiphany in characteristic fashion. He would study harder, just as he had when he decided he wanted a better education. But how? He remained quite poor. "I had not a single book in the world, nor was I able to buy any books, had I known of any for sale." He borrowed "a little old book, in a smoky condition," containing seven sermons by William Russel, a Baptist minister. Jarratt read the sermons "again and again" in an attempt to grasp their meaning. This modest progress made him more determined. He learned "of a very large book, belonging to a gentleman, about five or six miles distant across the river, which explained all the New Testament. I resolved to get the reading of that book, if possible." Two years earlier, Jarratt would not have had courage enough to approach a member of the gentry. But now, "by my living so long with Mr. Cannon . . . I had worn off some of my clownish rusticity, and had become less shy of persons in the upper ranks of life." So Jarratt went to ask to borrow the book. The gentleman assented, and Jarratt rushed home with his "prize."[15]

Jarratt now had his book, but he had no light to read by and apparently no time to study during the day. He devised a solution: "As I had no candle, my custom was, in an evening, to sit down flat on the hearth, erect the volume on the end of a chest . . . and by the light fire, read till near midnight." Jarratt felt his reading skills improve and his "relish" for books increase.[16]

More important, he "acquired considerable views of the nature and plan of Salvation, through Jesus Christ: but I did not yet think I had attained a living faith in his blood. For some time, I had withdrawn myself from the company of the wicked; had quitted dancing, racing, cards, &c." The combination of a steady albeit small income and frugality enabled Jarratt to save enough money to buy a "small pony and a saddle. I began also to get some credit in a store, and having prospect of getting 13 pounds at the end of that year, ventured to go in debt for a tolerable suit of cloths—my linen, on Sundays, was finer than formerly."[17]

Jarratt believed his fortunes were at last improving. His school was doing better, he was inching closer to a new birth, and his cloudy financial outlook was brightening. Buoyed by this success and enjoying the independence that resulted from owning a pony, Jarratt "determined on a visit to my friends in *New Kent*." His two brothers, along with their wives and slaves, "seemed overjoyed at my coming." It was fall. The harvest was in, and the cellars were "stored with good, sound cider. *These* were set open with great liberality" upon his arrival. The Jarratts, like the Moons before them, greeted Devereux in time-honored Virginia fashion. As he recalled, "They knew I had been very fond of company merriment, and wished to entertain me with frolic and dance." Devereux stood firm and told them why. "This was a disappointment they did not expect, and they soon discovered there was a great alteration in me, and that my mind was turned to religion." In addition to being surprised, Devereux's family pointed out that there "can be no harm in *innocent mirth*, such as dancing, drinking, and making merry." Devereux went to visit other relatives and "discoursed with them on religious concerns." Again, he held firm with his views. But his relatives retained their belief that a little fun was just that—a little fun. Possibly to prove a point, his brother arranged a party while Devereux was visiting his uncle, and Devereux was quite surprised to return and "see such numbers, both within and without doors." Outside, "the tankard went briskly round, while the sound of music and dancing was heard within." The supposedly reformed Jarratt found himself in a tight spot. The revelers urged him to join the party, but that good angel looking over his shoulder whispered different advice. Good briefly won out, but temptation then took over, and Jarratt was "drawn in, once more, to join those vanities and follies, which, I thought, I had forever abandoned." Like Samson, he "soon found myself shorn of all my strength."[18]

Here, in Jarratt's colorful tale, was a Virginia that Puritan reformers would have well recognized and stoutly condemned. A dissolute, irreligious people imbibing all the sins of the world—dancing, drinking, and carousing. Critics aimed their harshest barbs at the church itself, complaining that it did nothing to stem such decadence. One such critic was the pastor of New Kent Parish, Nicholas Moreau, who shared his low opinion of the place in an April 12, 1697, letter to the Lord Bishop of Lichfield: "I don't like this Country at all, my Lord. . . . Your clergy in these parts are of a very ill example, no discipline or Canons of the Church are observed."[19] Thomas Jefferson went further, deriding Virginia's Church of England as intolerant of religious dissenters and tyrannical in its forced tax levies. The ministers, he complained, were indolent, "secure for life in their glebes and salaries." Nor was Devereux Jarratt impressed with the clergyman whom he encountered while growing up in New Kent. "The parish minister was but a poor preacher—very unapt to teach or even to gain the attention of an audience. Being very near-sighted, and preaching wholly by a written copy, he kept his eyes continually fixed on the paper, and so near, that what he said seemed rather addrest to the cushion, than to the congregation."[20]

The Religious Landscape in Anglican Virginia

The real state of affairs in Virginia, as Jarratt's story hints, was far more complex than the critics acknowledged. Virginia's founders wanted not only a colony with a state-established church but a holy colony lording over a society that contained members who said their prayers, attended services weekly, and lived upright lives of Christian rectitude—goals that would have left Thomas Hooker nodding in appreciation. During the seventeenth century, the burgesses repeatedly passed demanding laws outlining a religious society that historian Perry Miller has compared favorably to those of Puritan New England. As early as 1624, the burgesses reconfirmed "THAT there shall be in every plantation, where the people . . . meete for the worship of God, a house or roome sequestered for that purpose." If anyone "whatsoever shall absent himselfe from divine service any Sunday without an allowable excuse," the burgesses continued, he "shall forfeite a pound of tobacco." Most of all, the burgesses said that "there shall be an uniformity in our church as neere as may be the canons in England; both in substance and circumstance, and that all persons yeild readie obedience unto under paine of censure."[21]

These laws were fleshed out over the remainder of the colonial period with the goal of weaving religion into the daily fabric of life. This ambitious task began with the parson, whom the burgesses decided shall have "cure of soules [and] shall preach one sermon every sunday in the yeare." The parsons, moreover, were to "examine, catechise, and instruct the youth and ignorant persons of his parrish, in the ten commandments the articles of the beliefe and in the Lord's prayer." The family, according to the burgesses, also had an important role in religious life: "All fathers, mothers, maysters and mistrisses shall cause theire children, servants or apprentizes which have not learned the catechisme to come to the church at the tyme appointed, obedientlie to heare, and to be ordered by the mynister untill they have learned the same."

If parents and masters failed to fulfill these duties, "they shall be censured by the corts in those places holden."[22]

Drawing on their English heritage, the burgesses gave the parishes—specifically, the church wardens—the task of regulating moral behavior. Wardens took an oath in which they agreed to "make presentments of all such persons as shall lead a prophayne or ungodlie life, of such as shall be common swearers, drunkards or blasphemers, that shall ordinarilie profane the saboth dayes or contemue Gods holy word or sacraments." "Fornicators," "adulterers," and those who "abuse theire neighbors by slanderinge tale . . . or back bitinge" would also be punished.[23]

Virginia's seventeenth-century Anglicans were hardly religious radicals out to remake the world. But they were products of a militant Protestant milieu that sought to counter what it perceived as the pernicious influences of a corrupt Catholicism. While Miller goes too far in arguing that religion was "the really energizing power" in Virginia's settlement, he was correct in noting that the religious impulse was present from the colony's first days. Indeed, in explaining the rationale for establishing a colony in Virginia, Jamestown's founders started with religion: "The Principal and *Maine endes* . . . were first to preach and baptize into Christian Religion, and by propagation of the *Gospell*, . . . a number of poore and miserable soules . . . and to endeavor the fulfilling, and accomplishment of the elect, which shall be gathered from out all corners of the earth."[24]

Virginia's founders came from a society that placed the Church of England at the center of life. Key to this mission was the parish. It was all-inclusive, requiring inhabitants within its borders to be members. Unlike in Puritan New England, people in England did not have to stand before the congregation or church board and prove that they were worthy of membership. Instead, the Anglican Church considered all inhabitants part of the church family. It extended baptism to all infants, a deeply symbolic act that signaled the community's commitment to inclusivity. Dissenters, of course, grew more numerous and important over time, especially after the Glorious Revolution, but they remained an insignificant 5.6 percent of England's population in the early eighteenth century.[25]

The parish became the focal point of community life in the early modern period. The church was often the most important building within the parish. In Hooker's tiny home parish in Marfield, for instance, the church stood on a hill and dominated the landscape. One later visitor captured its allure: "The picturesque old church of mottled gray [stood] on Tilton hill-top, compassed round by the dead of the different precincts of the parish; the wide prospect of alternating woodland and open fields and spire-surmounted hills toward every compass point . . . and the little Marfield hamlet embowered in trees down in the valley . . . approached through rustic gates and stiles in which the visitor opens or climbs as he descends through the sweet green fields." Architectural designers wanted the parish church to inspire. Through its gables without and its altar within, the Anglican chapel was meant to reflect the majesty of church and state. And in its majesty, the church drew parish inhabitants to its pews to pray, to partake in the Lord's Supper, to hear the Word—in short, to share in all the rituals of a loving Christian community.[26]

An intense anti-Catholicism clouded this picture of Christian love. Most Englishmen viewed the Catholic Church as a threat to their church, state, and way of life. They greatly feared "papist" doctrines and wanted them kept out of the Anglican Church. Their fears were fanned when Charles II, a secretly practicing Roman Catholic, ascended to the throne in 1660 and when his openly Catholic brother, James, became king in 1685. Seventeenth-century migrants carried this hatred of Catholicism with them to Virginia. Standard oaths barred Catholics from holding public office: in St. Peter's Parish in New Kent County, church officers had to swear "that I do ffrom my Heart Abhor Detest and Abjure as impious and Heretical that Damnable Doctrine and Position that Princes Excommunicated or Deprived by the Pope or any Authority of the See of Rome may be Deposed and Murthered by their subjects." While swearing off the papists, good Anglicans at the same time "sincerely" promised to "be ffaithfull & bear true Allegiance to his Majesty King."[27]

Shortly after Jamestown's founding in 1607, King James I decreed that "the true word, and service of God and Christian faith be preached, planted, and used . . . according to the doctrine, rights, and religion now professed and established within our realme of England." In such ways, the church became an integral part of a good Englishman's worldview. Church and state—and hatred of Catholicism—became neatly tied together. As Miller observes, during the seventeenth century, "no nation of Europe had yet divided the state from the church; no government had yet imagined that religion could be left to the individual conscience. Society, economics, and the will of God were one and the same, and the ultimate authority in human relations was the ethic of Christendom." God (and the Anglican Church) became an omnipotent presence in homes, fields, and the halls of power.[28]

Jarratt's recollections of colonial Virginia demonstrate the complexity of the religious scene. The Moons certainly did not fit Jarratt's definition of religious. They had not undergone a new birth and were not saved. But as Jarratt conceded, the Moons were *"Church people,"* and they "could listen to nothing but what came through that channel." He added sourly that "in truth, they knew no more of the principles of the *Church of England,* than of any other." But the parish church, as Jarratt admitted, framed their understanding of God and his divine laws. The state church, in fact, framed their understanding so totally that the Moons wanted nothing to do with dissenting Presbyterians and their upstart New Lights. They laughed at Jarratt's New Light leanings and blamed his change on Mrs. Cannon. The Cannons' religious world, meanwhile, was equally complex. The husband was totally absorbed in managing his plantation and was not religious. But the wife was devout. She devoted her days and nights to trying to discern the true light and other evangelical principles.[29]

Jarratt struggled to navigate such confusing religious terrain. When he encountered pious people or teachings during his migrations, he tried mightily to reform his dissolute ways. But he was easily blown off course when he ran into the other kind of Virginian. When Jarratt returned to New Kent, for example, and was presented with a chance to carouse, he regressed from his newfound religious ways. It took a return trip to the Cannons', where he found his *"benefactress* as much engaged in religion as before," to restore his evangelical discipline.[30]

Jarratt's upbringing only contributed to his confusion. As a youth, he hardly ever attended church, although it was located within three miles of his home. Yet religion was a part of his life during these early years. His parents "taught us short prayers, and made us very perfect in repeating the *Church Catechism,"* he recalled. One of the main books Jarratt read as a youngster was the Bible. So even though he did not attend church, his parents introduced him to Anglican ways, in keeping with church doctrine. However, the Jarratts' was not a devout household, especially by Puritan standards. Devereux grew up with only a nodding understanding of Anglican doctrines and no knowledge of evangelical principles. Devereux's older brothers apparently absorbed even less about religion. "During the 5 or 6 years, I continued with my brothers, I do not remember ever to have seen or heard any thing of a religious nature; or that tended to turn my attention to the great concerns of eternity," he observed. "I know not, that I ever heard any serious conversation respecting God and Christ, Heaven and Hell." Instead, when Jarratt lived with his brothers, he settled for watching "a great many people" attending church each Sunday. But he "went not once in a year." One regular churchgoer in St. Peter's during this period was a young Martha Dandridge, who later married George Washington. She grew up in the same parish as Jarratt and learned her catechism

St. Peter's Church, "erected upon the maine Roade by the Schoole house," was completed in 1703; it became the center of parish life in New Kent County, where Devereux Jarratt was born and raised. (Historic American Buildings Survey / Library of Congress)

from the Reverend David Mossom, who was known more for his bad temper than for his skills as a pastor. As one of her biographers recounted, "Martha was punctilious about attending church each Sunday as well about her private devotions. She had a lifelong habit of retiring to her room for an hour after breakfast to read her Bible and pray."[31]

The contrasting experiences of Jarratt and Dandridge reveal the diversity of the religious landscape in a state-established parish. This Anglican community included both the indifferent and the devout. Founded in 1683, St. Peter's was in New Kent, a Tidewater county just northwest of Jamestown that was pocketed by hills, ravines, and rivers. John Broach received the area's first land patent in 1642, and the county grew steadily. New Kent benefited from good soil, close proximity to Virginia's capital, and an abundant water supply provided by the numerous rivers and creeks that coursed through the Chesapeake countryside. By the time Jarratt was born, New Kent had moved beyond the frontier stage. A tobacco economy enabled an elite to build their share of palatial houses, including the "commodious" White House, where George Washington wed Martha Dandridge, and the Chestnut Grove mansion.[32]

With New Kent's population growing in the late seventeenth century, Virginia's General Court created St. Peter's out of Blisland Parish and ran its borders along the streams and rivers that defined the county: the Pamunkey and the Mattaponi Rivers on the northeast, John's Creek on the southeast, and the Pamunkey and Chickahominy Rivers on the southwest. (There was no western border in the parish's early years.) In 1703, when St. Peter's completed its main church, New Kent's 173,104 acres made it the second-largest county in Virginia, trailing only Accomack. Its population, according to Robert Beverley's 1703 census, was 3,374, the third-biggest in the colony.[33]

Like other Tidewater counties, sprawling New Kent created a society that merged the religious and the secular. This marriage of the holy and the profane (to borrow one historian's memorable phrase) was evident in the landscape, where the courthouse and church coexisted peaceably with the tavern to become the center of community life. The first courthouse was erected on a plantation belonging to Colonel William Bassett, a member of one of the county's leading families, and overlooked the York River. The brick courthouse was so imposing that during Bacon's Rebellion, rebel forces under the command of Nathaniel Bacon occupied it in 1676 to prevent a landing by Governor William Berkeley and his troops. In a dispersed plantation society, the courthouse and its dependencies were the closest thing to a village in New Kent. The Bassett family wanted the courthouse on its property so that court days would reinforce its other businesses: a ferry landing, tobacco warehouses, and a tavern.[34]

The second key structure was the main St. Peter's Parish church. Construction began in 1700 and was completed in 1703 for the princely sum of 146,073 pounds of tobacco. The church was a deceptively simple brick rectangular building that featured a massive, Gothic-style tower in front. This church, "erected upon the maine Roade by the Schoole house," became the heart of parish life. It provided relief to the poor, regulated the morals of its members, and took care of the orphaned.[35] Vestry records reveal the parish's importance to those members experiencing hard times. In 1690, for example, the vestry awarded John Lightfoot five hundred pounds of tobacco for "keeping and Cureing a lame woman as by agreement with Mr. Wyatt Churchwarden," while Richard Scruggs received twelve hundred pounds "for keeping Mary fisher being a poor Child & for find of it Cloathes." Such aid was also offered to widows in a region still suffering from a high mortality rate. Thus, the vestry paid Lyonell Morris a thousand pounds "for keeping ye widow faulkner one yeare."[36]

Creating a nurturing church family involved more than providing charity for the needy; for the vestry, it also involved encouraging inhabitants to become good Christians. In 1731, Ann Holt, a "Mullatto Woman," delivered a daughter out of wedlock. When the child turned six, the vestry bound the girl out as a servant to John Lightfoot "untill She Shall attain to the ffull and Compleat Age of Twenty one years from the Day of her Birth." In return, Lightfoot was to "truly and faithfully" employ her and to keep her well housed, fed, and clothed. This obligation included "bring[ing] her up in the Protestant Religion & to give her at the End of the said Time three Barrells of Indian Corn & two suits of Apparell." In such ways did the parish seek to make religion a daily reality.[37]

The vestry also sought to encourage church attendance in at least two important ways. First, in a sprawling parish with bad roads and primitive transportation, St. Peter's erected chapels within reach of most inhabitants. The vestry closely monitored population growth, with prodding from parishioners. One such instance occurred in 1700, when the "upper inhabitants" petitioned the vestry for a new chapel, saying that they found it difficult to attend worship services because "they Live very Remort from the Church." The vestry was sympathetic to their plight, and a new chapel was built.[38]

The erection of a new chapel, however, was only a partial solution, since many people still lived too far away to attend regularly. The vestry tried to resolve this problem by ordering the pastor "to preach a Sermon on Sabath day in Every month at Such Convenient place as the a fore Said inhabitants Shall pleas to apoint." The church, in other words, would go to the members. Improving accessibility also involved redrawing the parish lines. As the population grew, the parish became geographically smaller. In 1691, the burgesses approved an act dividing New Kent County to remedy the "sundry and divers inconveniences attend[ing] the inhabitants of New Kent county . . . by reason of the difficulty in passing the river." The inhabitants of Pamunkey Neck who belonged to St. Peter's were now returned to St. John's Parish, meaning that they would no longer have to cross the Pamunkey River to attend church.[39]

The second important way to encourage attendance was to make the church service as appealing as possible. This effort had begun in England centuries earlier, during the reign of Henry VIII, when the Anglican Church ended Latin masses and increased lay participation to make services more meaningful to members. By so doing, reformers hoped to improve attendees' religiosity. This reform effort was influenced greatly by Richard Hooker, who wanted to advance the Henrician reformation while avoiding the supposed excesses of Puritanism—a middle way. The moderate reformers sought to increase lay participation in church services while maintaining the High Church ideals of order and conformity. Like other European Protestant reformers (most notably Martin Luther), Anglicans began holding services in the language of the people—in this case, English—instead of in Latin. Reformers also shortened the service and ended the Catholic practice of holding multiple services throughout the day. Anglican services revolved around two core rituals, the liturgy and the sermon, both of which sought to instruct listeners in the mysteries of the Bible and of the Lord. Such a reform sounded innocent enough, but it was in fact aimed at removing the "popish" superstitions that Protestant reformers believed riddled Roman Catholic masses. Liturgical services were based on the Anglicans' Book of Common Prayer. Services consisted of the clerk or pastor reading prayers and biblical passages. Services also had responsive readings and psalm singing. Reformers made an important symbolic change as well: pastors became the leaders of fellow spiritual believers, unlike Catholic priests, who were considered privileged individuals with a special relationship to God. These reformers sought to put the congregation on a roughly equal footing with the pastor and thus to increase the congregation's role in the service. These changes did not go as far as Puritan and radical reformers wanted, because the Anglicans did not abolish all differences between the clerics and the people.[40]

The reforms had mixed results in St. Peter's and elsewhere. When John Lang took over as pastor in St. Peter's in 1725, he found "the people here generally very Zealous for our Holy Church as it is established in England." Yet "they are supinely ignorant in the very principles of Religion," he continued, "and very debauch't in Morals." Shortly before Lang assumed the pastorship, his predecessor, the Reverend Henry Collings, had estimated that the parish covered twenty miles and had 204 families. Sunday attendance was strong: "Commonly 170 or 180 souls attended," with 40 to 50 communicants partaking of the Lord's Supper. Collings, however, would have agreed with Lang's assessment that the parishioners were "supinely ignorant." Collings, who had become pastor in 1722, told the Bishop of London in 1724 that he "had as yet done no catechising in the parish, the youth of the parish, through long disuse and neglect of his predecessors, being incapable of receiving that instruction." Baptismal records also reveal a mixed record. On the one hand, 87 percent of white people whose births were listed in the parish register between 1683 and 1700 were baptized into the church. On the other hand, that figure plummeted to 45 percent in 1701–25, indicating that fewer people belonged to the church in the later period.[41]

The common thread in St. Peter's was a constant turnover of pastors and constant complaining about the state of affairs by pastor and laity alike. Following its founding in 1683, the parish went through twenty-six clergymen in fifty-seven years. Not surprisingly, given the turnover, the parishioners complained about their pastors. They had little opportunity to form attachments to their ministers and often dismissed them as boring speakers, indifferent to their charges, or lax in their morals. The pastors, in turn, were nearly as critical of their fellow ministers. Newly appointed ministers continually complained that they were taking over a badly run parish, as when Collings wrote that his predecessors had failed to teach the catechisms. Whatever the reasons for the situation, the Anglican Church was clearly a source of controversy. Everyone had something to say about the church and parish—much of it negative. Yet the church cast a large shadow over the lives of its members. Though members lamented the church's failings and pastors debated whether their flock was religious enough, the church constituted a significant presence in the community in ways that extended beyond charity and the regulation of morals.[42]

On Sundays, groups of parishioners gathered in the yard in front of St. Peter's to socialize. The hour before divine service offered a time to chat with others and occasionally to watch a misbehaving parishioner punished. To better regulate morals, the vestry decided to place a pair of stocks "for the Restraint of licentious and disorderly Persons several such having lately appeared in the Church, to the great disturbance of the Minister and Congregation, during divine service."[43]

Puritan reformers would have found ironic the parish church's important role in Chesapeake society. In early New England, the temporal and the spiritual reinforced each other. The congregation and its covenant formed the basis of civil society. When the Connecticut Valley towns banded together to form the colony of Connecticut in the late 1630s, their representatives declared that they had "enter[ed] into Combination and Confederation togather, to maytayne and presearve the liberty and purity of the gospells of our Lord Jesus." The New England Way was never a theocracy with ministers holding governmental posts. Instead, the government became a partner with the congregational church. In Virginia, the church was also a partner with the state, although not quite an equal one. The church's name itself revealed much about the kind of society that Anglican reformers wanted. The Church of England was a state-established church that became an arm of the government following the reforms of Henry VIII. The monarch was the church's supreme earthly leader, appointing the bishops who ran the church. In Puritan New England, the state wanted the church to encourage people to turn to Jesus Christ. In England and its foreign domains, the state wanted two things—good Christians *and* good citizens. Devout Christians who regularly attended church would make orderly, loyal subjects of the king. The church would reinforce the government's power, and the state would reinforce the church's power. In support of this interlocking mission, the state instituted mandatory attendance laws so that the church could inculcate attendees in the higher purposes of civil society. Catechisms from the Book of Common Prayer explicitly instructed parishioners to "honor and obey the king and his ministers" and to submit to all "masters" and "betters."[44]

In 1660, the link between the monarchy and Anglican Church was reinforced in a very visible way: the state mandated the display of the Royal Arms in all churches. These coats of arms were now hung near plaques listing the Ten Commandments, the Apostles' Creed, and the Lord's Prayer. As parishioners' eyes wandered, they could easily take in the union of church and state. In case anyone missed such a pointed message, pastors frequently preached that good Anglicans must accept the divinely ordained social order.[45]

Early Virginia took the union of church and state even further. The church was not just an extension of the state but an extension of the gentry's power. The state-sponsored church reflected and reinforced the gradations in a hierarchical society, with the gentry at the top, common planters in the middle, and the poor at the bottom, just above enslaved Africans. Historian Dell Upton has ably shown how Virginia church architecture reflected gentry society and its values. "The house of God was not a slave's house or a common planter's house," Upton notes. "It was a gentleman's house." Anglican churches were elegant structures whose symbolism was twofold. First, the church (and the courthouse) were intended to rival the leading planters' mansions in grandeur. They were large, were often built of brick, and featured ornate interiors with elaborate pulpits and pews. Commoners, who lived in far humbler abodes, were to be awed by these monuments to God. Chapels' location strengthened this link between gentry and church. Churches often were built on land donated by a leading gentleman, as was the case with St. Peter's, thereby reinforcing the parish's identification with the gentry. Equally important, as Upton has shown, the church's mission was intertwined with Virginia's culture of hospitality. "At its core," Upton explains, "hospitality incorporated several fundamental virtues. Foremost among them was that selfless quality Virginians called 'good neighborhood.' Good neighborhood recognized the commonality that binds all people together regardless of personal standing." The vestry, in other words, was an instrument of hospitality, with the vestrymen attending to the needs of their "guests" by dispensing relief to the poor and aid to the sick. Not coincidentally, the vestrymen were members of the gentry, betters attending to the needs of their inferiors. Parish social relationships thus mimicked society at large. Vestrymen and laity formed a reciprocal relationship with dual obligations: parishioners followed and offered appropriate deference to their social betters; in return, the gentry took care of the parishioners. Both sides benefited, with these reciprocal relationships helping to bind society together.[46]

Against this backdrop, Sunday services became an elaborate show of gentry power. Ordinary folk would gather in the churchyard to socialize before the service, then wander inside as the hour for worship approached. The gentry would arrive last and would often hold off entering the church until everyone else had been seated. Seating itself reflected society's stratifications. Church wardens—themselves leading citizens—determined seating locations based on the relative standing of parish members. Class, occupation, race, and gender played a role in the seating arrangement. Strangers were placed at the back; the elite received private pews in front or in private galleries. Such arrangements provided a marked contrast to the meetinghouses of evangelical dissenters such as the Baptists, where parishioners were seated by sex rather than by class. In these meetinghouses, all were equal before the Lord. Such was not the case in Anglican Virginia.[47]

Religion and Migration in Anglican Virginia

The complex world of the Anglican parish gets at the heart of what a religious migration was and was not. The Anglican Church promoted order, stability, and deference to betters. It wanted not just good parishioners but good citizens who were loyal to their king and their community. Such a church did not tend to breed intense passion for the Word. Promoting the new birth was not its mission. Instead, Anglican leaders proclaimed that theirs was a "reasonable" faith based on exemplary moral conduct, benevolence, and acceptance of the social order. This religious milieu meant that the church had a different effect on migration than did churches in Puritan New England and elsewhere. The vast majority of Anglicans did not move for overtly religious reasons. They did not migrate to establish congregations untainted by corruption or to venture into the wilderness to convert Indians. Good Anglicans had no need to escape persecution or the unpure. Anglicans usually saw frivolity as an accepted part of Virginia life. King and government promoted, protected, and nurtured Anglican religion. The church provided aid in bad times and spiritual sustenance in good times. Thus, the only true religious migrations in early Virginia were undertaken by dissenters—most notably, Puritans and

Quakers—who moved for the same reasons that a Roger Williams did: to worship in peace, free of persecution.[48]

At first glance, then, religion seems to have had little or no influence on internal migration in Chesapeake Virginia: the colony's population grew rapidly following the disastrous early years of Jamestown, and the movement of people increased as well. In 1607, at Jamestown's founding, the colony had a white population of 105; in 1620, whites' numbers had increased to 900. The arrival of large numbers of immigrants from England and a slowly declining mortality rate subsequently helped the colony's population soar to 8,000 in 1640, 25,000 in 1660, and 85,000 in 1700. As the number of residents grew, settlement spread north and west. In 1620, two years before a devastating Indian attack wiped out nearly 40 percent of the English colony, the tiny white population was huddled along the James River near Jamestown. Settlers then fanned out, and by the 1650s, large numbers of people had settled north of the York River in the Middle Peninsula and on the Northern Neck. The largest population expansion took place between 1648 and 1654, when eight counties were formed in Chesapeake Virginia and Maryland. Another seven were founded during the following decade.[49]

In a tobacco-dominated society, the "noxious weed" exerted a large influence on migration. When the price of tobacco dropped, as in the 1680s, immigration from England fell because the need for labor dropped as well. When prices rose, as in the middle decades of the seventeenth century, transatlantic migration rose, too. This trend continued into the eighteenth century. Migration to Virginia's frontier increased in the 1720s and 1730s when tobacco entered another depression. Poorer families abandoned Tidewater Virginia in an attempt to escape the double whammy of low tobacco prices and expensive, scarce land. By 1740, planters had acquired the best lands in eastern Virginia.[50]

Tobacco exerted another kind of pull on migration. It wore out the land and did so relatively quickly. According to historian Allan Kulikoff, "Tobacco planters systematically exploited thousands of square miles of land during the eighteenth century. They rotated fields rather than fertilizing their land or rotating crops on the same field. After they took fresh land, they cleared a few acres of their holdings, planted tobacco on the parcel until the nutrients in the soil were exhausted, and then moved on to the next piece of land." Planters employed some field rotation, but careless practices and the demands of tobacco meant that the yield and quality of the crop declined. And with the best land—fertile tracts near rivers—in short supply, the land pressures on the Tidewater increased exponentially in the eighteenth century. Thus, the laboring poor moved on during depression years as they searched for better opportunities, and planters moved after the soil's fertility was exhausted.[51]

The population's mobility was abetted by the makeup of the transatlantic migration to Virginia. Unlike the Puritans, who traveled largely in families and even congregations during their Great Migration to New England, indentured servants outnumbered free emigrants to the Chesapeake by about four to one, and young, single men predominated. In the seventeenth century, the Chesapeake welcomed about twenty-five thousand free emigrants and about one hundred thousand servants. These migrants were driven not by idealistic religious motives but by the chance to get ahead, to build better lives for themselves. Contemporaries did not look kindly upon these immigrants, especially the indentured servants, seeing them at best as adventurers and at worst as criminals. The views of Sir Josiah Child were not unusual: "Virginia and Barbados were first peopled by a sort of loose vagrant People, vicious and destitute of means to live at home." The migrants indeed hailed from areas of England that were facing hard times. Like their Puritan counterparts to the north, Virginia's newcomers were pushed out of England by a dearth of economic opportunities. Between 1550 and 1650, England's population grew from about three million to almost five million. As the population rose, so did unemployment and food prices. Real wages, however, dropped. The poor—a category that in some regions amounted to nearly half of the population—felt this tightening vise the most. Most emigrants thus came from these regions, including London, the southeast, and the Thames Valley.[52]

In Virginia, various other secular factors fueled internal mobility. Some people moved to find jobs. Many more moved to obtain land on which to grow tobacco. Regardless of their precise motives, most of these internal migrations were "betterment" moves—that is, people hoped to improve their fortunes. Jarratt's migration to Albemarle, which was unusual because it involved opening a school, was typical in that it involved a young, single person trying to get ahead in life.

Anglicanism's role in internal migration was subtle and of a negative kind. With its emphasis on order and stability, the church tended to act as a brake on members' mobility. Unlike the Puritans, Virginia's Anglicans were not religiously restless. Instead, parish life and church tenets gave the landed and the rooted one more reason to stay. Unlike the Puritans, most Anglicans were not restless souls constantly looking over the next hill for religious fulfillment.

An evangelical bent, by contrast, helped to spur on Hooker's Company and other Puritan divines in seventeenth-century New England. Many Puritans shared this restlessness. Narratives of the first generation reveal an interesting theme: Puritan migrants were idealists who crossed the Atlantic with high hopes. They were leaving behind a "corrupt" England for the New World, where they could establish congregations to their liking. Nathaniel Sparhawk was unhappy in England, where he "had no rest." He moved to New England to enjoy church ordinances "in purity" but had his hopes dashed: "After I came hither I saw my condition more miserable than ever." The theme reappeared in many other conversion narratives, leading one historian to conclude, "A certain emotion begins to be connected with the [transatlantic] migration: a kind of grim, gray disappointment that emerges in conversion stories as an almost obligatory structural element." The drive for purity had set New England Puritans up for failure. They were trying to reform a "false" Church of England, whose corruption they believed disqualified its members from becoming "Citizens in the new Hierusalem." By serving as exemplars, Puritans had hoped to shame their Anglican brethren into reforming but did not do so because of shortcomings in both the Church of England and the Puritan movement. Such disappointments left the first generation of settlers disillusioned and the second generation feeling inadequate.[53]

The conversion narratives show that the Puritans felt their failure on a very personal level. Many migrants came to the New World to save not only society but themselves. They wanted not just purity in the church and society but purity within the individual. Navigating the numerous steps in conversion was tremendously difficult, and Puritans could never be sure that they really were saved. According to Calvinism, God had preordained who was chosen and who was not. But how would a seeker know? Thomas Hooker had conceded that it was virtually impossible for a mere human to know whether someone had been saved; only God knew for sure. Calvinism thus introduced an element of uncertainty into the Puritan movement; indeed, Puritan theologians argued incessantly over exactly how a congregation was to determine who was saved and thus deserving of full membership. And even if sanctification was achieved, it also had to be maintained. According to Goodman Daniel, "Faith hath been wrought more and Christ more revealed more savingly unto me [since my conversion]. I fall short in that obedience that should be, which is my burden when I see how the Lord hath led me."[54]

Roger Williams moved repeatedly in a fruitless search for saints who could live up to his exacting standards. Anne Hutchinson and her antinomian followers were obsessed with a different kind of purity and consequently were forced to migrate. Countless other Puritans possessed the same spirit. If a congregation disappointed them in some way, they moved on. And by moving, they again sought the fulfillment that had so far eluded them.

Virginia's Anglicans could not have been more different. The Book of Common Prayer and a cool rationalism defined their faith. The church's Virginia members found comfort not in the new birth but in the dignity of their church liturgy. In practice, this meant that Anglicans were far more comfortable with who and what they were than were their brethren in New England. Most Anglicans did not worry about whether they were of the elect. Whereas Puritans could attain full church membership only by going before a congregation and convincing the audience that they had been saved, Anglicans merely had to have been born in the parish or have moved there and become residents in good standing. These standards were not terribly high, nor were they meant to be. By design, the territorial church included all inhabitants as part of the church family. For most Virginians, this state of affairs led to a degree of comfort with the church, which became a part of their identity and a comfort in dealing with such exigencies of life as sickness, fear, bad harvests, and death.

Many critics, including Hooker and Jarratt, derided this outlook as smugness. Hooker pointed out with more than a touch of sarcasm that a person could not inherit piety "from his parents, purchaseth it by his money, or receive it by gift or exchange." When Jarratt took over as pastor in Bath in 1764, he was struck by parish members' general indifference to the conversion experience and by their belief that the new birth did not matter. "I found the principles of the gospel—the nature and condition of man—the plan and salvation through Christ—and the nature and necessity of spiritual regeneration, as little known and thought of, as if the people had never [attended] a church or heard a sermon in their lives," he complained. Rather than thinking about conversion, Jarratt believed, they placed their faith in "the great learning and accomplishments of their former *ministers*. From these, I suppose, they had heard little else but morality . . . in no wise calculated to disturb their carnal repose, or awaken any one to a sense of guilt and danger." Jarratt's comments captured what evangelical-minded critics so disliked about the church. Anglicanism valued learning and the Book of Common Prayer and emphasized order and solemnity.[55]

The practical effect of such a religious outlook was apparent in eastern Virginia: religion did not spur Anglicans to move. Instead, it discouraged mobility among better-off church members by inculcating not a drive for purity but an attachment to home and community and state. In a study of Lunenburg County in the mid–eighteenth century, historian Richard Beeman has found that Anglicans were the most stable group in a restless population, while Baptists were the most mobile. Anglicans who stayed tended to be planters from wealthier backgrounds as well as members of the middling class, whom

Beeman characterizes as "individuals who managed to acquire modest hold-ings early in the game and remained content with those holdings." Anglicans resided in Lunenburg longer, had more land, and possessed a larger stake in local society than did members of other groups. Such rootedness combined with religious factors to help slow internal migration for this segment of the population.[56]

This phenomenon also existed in some New England communities. In Windsor, Connecticut, as chapter 1 discusses, the most rooted residents came primarily from two groups—church founders and the most active and devout congregation members. In both New England and the Chesapeake, residents who stayed tended to be those who had adequate land, strong family ties, and a general satisfaction with church. Similarly, in Charles County, Maryland, "acquisition of land did indeed increase the probability that men of unde-termined origins would remain," historian Lorena Walsh argues. "Once na-tives became a majority among adult men in the community, out-migration slowed." Darrett Rutman and Anita Rutman have reached similar conclusions in their study of Middlesex County, Virginia: offspring of the founding gen-eration were more likely to stay than leave. In both places, however, men with few or no local connections were more likely to migrate. Overall, Middlesex residents were not a mobile people, although the exodus from the county was always steady. The Rutmans saw no "driving urge to exploit the vastness" among the area's people; instead, "they were innately conservative, concerned with the mundane affairs of farms, families, and neighborhoods."[57]

Devereux Jarratt's Final Journey

Though he came from a different time and a different place, Jarratt was as restless a seeker as any Puritan in seventeenth-century Massachusetts. In in-triguing ways that paralleled the New England conversion experience, Jarratt sought both spiritual fulfillment and meaningful employment as a school-teacher. His story drives home the new birth's importance to mobility and its unimportance to most Anglicans.

For the "unborn," prerevolutionary Virginia was not the easiest of places to find evangelical religion. The new birth was hardly the concern of the clergy in the Church of England or of the gentry who lorded over the vestry. Jarratt the seeker slipped repeatedly as he traversed such a perilous religious terrain. For years, his resolve was never strong enough to overcome the many tempta-tions he encountered in early Virginia. Still, he kept trying.

After returning from his first interlude at the Cannons', Jarratt informed the Moons "that except we *repent*, we must perish—and except a man be *born again*, he cannot see the kingdom of God. These truths I insisted on . . . especially in the necessity of being *born again*." The Moons, as good Anglicans, disagreed. People can be reborn, they informed Jarratt, only "after we are dead." The Moons' arguments sent Jarratt scurrying to acquire the books he would need to better understand the mysteries of the new birth.[58]

Through study, he learned much about salvation. But Jarratt remained unconverted, unable to make the emotional leap to total acceptance of Jesus that underlay all conversions. Although he had learned much from his examination of books, Jarratt "did not yet think I had attained a living faith in [Christ's] blood," and he looked for ways to take the final steps to justification and sanctification. After he returned to Albemarle from the trip to New Kent where he fell off the wagon, Mrs. Cannon helped Jarratt regain his discipline and focus. So did a Presbyterian minister. Still, conversion was beyond his reach, and he remained consumed by "doubts and fears."[59]

In many ways, Jarratt's experience was not unusual. A sinner's rebirth was long and painful and could not be achieved until after experiencing vocation—the feeling of absolute worthlessness. Jarratt was groping his way to that point. He felt alone, despairing that "my case was singular, and that no man in the world had such trials, oppositions and enemies to contend with, as I had. No book I read, no sermons I heard, seemed to touch my perplexing *case*."[60]

Other Evangelicals often took the step to sanctification after some kind of tragedy—a death in the family, a colossal setback—that left them feeling utterly alone and forsaken, a state in which they were able to open their hearts to Jesus and achieve justification. Not Devereux Jarratt. Instead, his rebirth occurred "with a good *book* in my hand." Sitting at the Cannons', he was reading an account of other conversions. "But not finding my case, I was still thinking it nameless, and altogether singular." However, "at last I cast my eye on Isaiah 62, 12—*Thou shalt be called, sought out, a city not forsaken.*" Those words touched something deep in Jarratt and moved him as nothing else had before. "I was blessed with faith to believe," he recalled in wonderment. "I saw such a fullness in Christ. . . . The comforts I then felt, were beyond expression."[61] About five years had passed since Jarratt had first left New Kent County.

At this pivotal juncture, Jarratt decided to move and open yet another new school, this time in Cumberland County in conjunction with Thomas Tabb. Once again, a religious dimension surfaced during his move. Jarratt lived with Tabb, a Presbyterian, and began performing "the office of a chaplain in the family, morning and evening." Jarratt excelled at the task and "was now more than ever pressed on by my friends, to turn my attention to the ministry." In the spring of 1762, he quit his school and decided to become a man of the cloth, making the surprising choice to join the church of his youth. The decision seemed to amaze even Jarratt, who noted, "My first awakening to any sense of religion, was by means of a *Presbyterian*." After his rebirth, "I scarcely thought there was any religion but among the *Presbyterians*—I imbibed all their tenets," including becoming a "rigid" Calvinist. In the process, his dislike of the Church of England grew: "I had contracted a prejudice against the Church of England, not only on account of the loose lives of the Clergy, and their cold and unedifying manner of preaching, but also by reading some books. . . . By these and other means, I was much set against the *Prayer Book*." But when Jarratt began studying and thinking anew, he concluded that the Anglican Church and its Book of Common Prayer were not as bad as he had thought: "Upon the whole, I thought [the church] contained an excellent system of doctrine and public worship—equal to any other in the world." The church also counted John Wesley and George Whitefield, two of the greatest Evangelicals in the English-speaking world, as members. Jarratt thus chose to become an Anglican pastor.[62]

He was thirty-one years old when he moved into the glebe in Bath Parish, Dinwiddie County. Jarratt had lost none of his youthful idealism or stubbornness as he took to the pulpit for the first time. He was determined to bring the new birth to the church, whether or not it wanted such a rebirth. Jarratt's parishioners were not quite sure what to make of their earnest minister when he began lecturing them about their sinfulness, saying, "We have had many ministers . . . but we never heard any thing, till now, of conversion, the new birth &c.—we never heard that men are so totally lost and helpless." Undaunted by their ignorance, Jarratt remained optimistic about his chances. "My doctrine was strange and wonderful to them," he reported. He was encouraged enough that he embarked on his own Great Awakening in Virginia. He quickly gained many admirers—and critics. During this first year, "I stood alone, not knowing of one clergyman in Virginia, like minded with myself; yea, I was opposed, and reproached, by the clergy—called an enthusiast, fanatic, visionary, dissenter, Presbyterian, madman, and what not." With all the righteousness of a Puritan, Jarratt refused to be cowed. Using the fiery language of a revivalist, he "endeavored to expose, in the most alarming colors, the guilt of sin, the entire depravity of human nature—the awful danger, mankind are in." His fire-and-brimstone sermons succeeded: "A religious concern took place, and that important question, *what shall I do to be saved?* became more and more common. This anxiety was first manifested not among the lowest but rather the middle ranks of the people." Church attendance, he reported with satisfaction, grew not only among parishioners but among "*strangers*, both far and near."[63]

Spurred on by this success, Jarratt then did something even more un-Anglican: he became an itinerant. "As soon as I discovered a religious concern in the parish, I no longer confined my labors to the churches and pulpits, on Sundays, but went out by night and by day, at any time in the week, to private houses, and convened as many as I could, for the purpose of prayer, singing, preaching, and conversation." These wanderings, which began in 1765 and ended in 1783, took him to North Carolina and throughout Virginia, including New Kent, Lunenburg, and King William Counties. Pastoral mobility presented a unique challenge to the territorial church, with its closed borders, state-backed levies, and hierarchically appointed ministers. The presence of outside preachers in a parish threatened to undermine the church's power and to weaken the carefully constructed alliance of church and state. Baptist dissenters and others welcomed itinerancy for precisely that reason: they wanted an open system that stressed the dynamism and fluidity of their religious creeds. They believed, in short, that the new birth rather than the state-established territorial church should stand at the center of a voluntary religious fellowship. This profound difference went to the heart of what a church was or should be.[64]

By leading the life of an itinerant, Jarratt seemed to be aligning himself with these dissenters, traveling to other parishes and in effect challenging his fellow pastors. He was, his fiercest critics complained, hitting the Church of England at its very core. Jarratt denied any disloyalty. At heart, he was a Pietist, someone who wanted to work within the mother church to reform it. He praised the Methodists for their Pietistical fervor and denounced the Baptists for working outside and thereby harming the church.[65]

Jarratt's crusade demonstrated just how foreign most Anglicans found the new birth. His efforts showed just how sanguine most parishioners were in the years before the Great Awakening and the arrival of evangelical dissenters. Anglicanism, as Jarratt understood all too well, was rooted in a different world than was Puritanism or evangelicalism. Religious migrants sought *something*—the new birth, a godly community, or both. Devereux Jarratt came to identify with this longing. His journey from New Kent County began for typical Virginia reasons, but by the 1760s, he had very different motivations for taking to the road.

CHAPTER THREE

Ethnicity and Mobility

Scotch-Irish Presbyterians in
Eighteenth-Century America

Maine. The ultimate borderland. Rocky, thin soil. Thick pine forests. Fierce cold. Spring came late; summer departed early. Devastating Indian wars. A frontier far removed from Boston and the sweet virtues of Puritan divines. Farther south, in the Shenandoah Valley, was another borderland, this one a world away from Williamsburg and the gracious living of Tidewater Virginia. The land on this western frontier was rolling, the soil was fertile, the climate warmer than in Maine, but in 1720, the Shenandoah Valley was raw, remote, and largely uninhabited, even by Indians.

Two frontiers, two extremes.

One bordered Puritan New England in the north, the other Anglican eastern Virginia in the south. Scotch-Irish Presbyterians, the ultimate border people, gravitated to both places, and their presence along the margins of the British empire was hardly surprising. They were fiercely religious, stubbornly independent, and extremely mobile. New Englanders never knew what to make of these migrants from Northern Ireland (were they Scottish or Irish? Catholic or Protestant?), nor did colonists to the south. One contemporary dismissed the Scotch-Irish as "the very scum of mankind." Another, watching a group of Scotch-Irish passengers disembark in Delaware following a transatlantic voyage, described them as "mostly poor beggarly idle people [who] will give trouble to the inhabitants." Yet others saw them as criminals who "love to drink and to quarrel."[1]

Stereotypes, mostly. What the Scotch-Irish were was the largest white immigrant group in prerevolutionary America, with some 225,000 of them coming to the New World between 1718 and 1775. The vast majority of these Scotch-Irish were not drunkards but stout Presbyterians who valued education and embraced a church that emphasized discipline and conformity. Their reputation as footloose frontiersmen was well deserved, though. The Scotch-Irish were among the most restless of the restless, a highly mobile people who sought prosperity in the British Atlantic world by venturing to remote, often hostile locales—places such as Ulster, Ireland; Boothbay, Maine; and Augusta County, Virginia.[2]

Their mobility presents an interesting challenge in the effort to understand Protestant migrations in all their complexity: What lay behind such restlessness? After all, unlike their Puritan counterparts, Presbyterians from Ulster did not move to the next valley in an effort to find their own version of a Canaan. Nor were they troubled seekers like Devereux Jarratt, wandering about in a search of religious fulfillment and a chance to be reborn. Ironically, however, they shared some common ground with their English cousins, with whom the Scotch-Irish often feuded. Both groups belonged to state churches whose identity was intimately tied to conceptions of nationality and politics. To be a Scot from the Scottish Lowlands was to be Presbyterian, while to be English was often to be Anglican. Yet Anglicanism's impact on mobility differed greatly from Presbyterianism's; as the previous chapter shows, the English church helped to anchor devout members to their parishes. Such a contrast to the Scottish experience raises the question of whether something within Presbyterianism propelled its members to move about.

Not exactly.

The story of Scotch-Irish migrations in eighteenth-century America did not involve land or kinship or even religion, although all of these elements were present and were important to varying degrees. Instead, the Scotch-Irish story involved the role of ethnic/religious identity in mobility. Certain immigrant groups developed an ethnic identity through their religion. Ethnicity reinforced religious identity at the same time that religion reinforced ethnic identity. Church services thus became, in the words of one historian, "a symbolic rite of affirmation to one's ethnic association." Scottish and Scotch-Irish Presbyterians were classic examples of this phenomenon, but plenty of others existed in early modern Europe: Dutch Calvinists, German Lutherans, and Spanish Catholics, among others.[3]

Ethnicity could be a potent force in the movements of religious pilgrims. It gave shape to underlying cultural trends and channeled powerful currents that coursed through history, nationalism, economics, and religion. Ethnicity entangled religion with cultural and economic developments and thus encouraged migration. The intertwining of these diverse currents helped determine when and why Scottish Presbyterians moved. The first great exodus of

Lowland Scots occurred in the seventeenth century, when nearly one hundred thousand migrated to Ulster in Northern Ireland, a Catholic land hostile to Protestantism and the English in general and to Presbyterianism in particular. In 1718, Scottish colonists began leaving Ulster for British North America. Then came a third phase, migration within America, which began as early as 1719, gathered momentum in the 1740s, and mushroomed in the 1750s.

Each migration had its own internal dynamics. Economic factors loomed larger than religion in the Ulster and transatlantic migrations. But in America, religion and ethnicity became more important than had previously been the case. Everywhere in the New World, the Scotch-Irish moved to the frontier in kinship groups or as individual families, where they established Scotch-Irish communities and Presbyterian congregations. Religion was especially important to internal mobility within Puritan-dominated New England. There, Scotch-Irish Presbyterians found themselves in a place nearly as hostile to their religion as was Catholic and Anglican Ireland. Presbyterians were dissenters in Ulster, and dissenters they remained in Puritan New England. Thus, the Scotch-Irish moved and moved again when faced with hostility from their Puritan brethren. They repeatedly sought out places along the far reaches of settlement where they could farm and worship in peace as Presbyterians, away from the meddling of congregational churches. The Scotch-Irish who abandoned Pennsylvania's frontiers for the southern backcountry in the 1730s and later had subtler motives. Land, kinship, and community were some of the factors behind their wanderlust. But like their brethren farther north, they wanted to form communities centered on Presbyterianism and their Scotch-Irish heritage.

This journey to a new life could be quite bumpy, however. Building Scotch-Irish Presbyterian communities in a harsh New World environment entailed undertaking sometimes difficult migrations and confronting numerous obstacles ranging from finding ministers to overcoming internal divisions. Such was the case in Boothbay, Maine, and Augusta County, Virginia.

Two frontiers. Two stories. Similar outcomes.

The New England Frontier: Boothbay, Maine

Boothbay was a harbor town some two hundred miles north of Boston. In the late 1730s, this settlement populated mostly by Scotch-Irish Presbyterians clung to a narrow neck of land off the Gulf of Maine, sandwiched between the Sheepscot River to the west and the Damariscotta River to the east. Dense forests ran to the water's edge. Boothbay's founders quickly learned about the site's numerous drawbacks. One settler described the place as "an inhospitable desert, in the midst of Savage beasts." Maine, quite simply, was far colder than what these new arrivals had experienced in Europe. Frigid winters and late springs left farmers with a growing season that was a month shorter than that in southern New England. The thinness of the soil posed another serious problem. New England's landscape was notoriously rocky, and Maine's was no exception. In Boothbay, the prospects for farming were so unpromising that the early Scotch-Irish Presbyterian settlers relied on fishing for much of their sustenance. To earn a little cash, they sold firewood to Bostonians.[4]

The second threat was human. Indeed, the same settler who complained of "an inhospitable desert" noted that "Savage beasts" were only half of the inhabitants' problems. Residents also faced constant threats from even "more savage" Indians. Between 1689 and 1713, the region saw nearly continuous fighting between whites and Indians during King William's War and Queen Anne's War. The Indians nearly wiped out Maine's eastern settlements and drove off the white inhabitants, who numbered roughly six thousand in 1700. The 1713 Treaty of Utrecht settled large issues of state between the French and English but brought only a brief respite to eastern Maine. Settlers and tribes fought again between 1722 and 1725, forcing those few whites who had returned to flee anew.[5]

The small band of Scotch-Irish Presbyterians had ended up in such a difficult place as the result of happenstance. David Dunbar, a colorful but shady Irish-born adventurer, was a colonel in the English army when he arrived in Maine in 1729 as surveyor general of the "King's Woods," charged with protecting the white pine forests for the Royal Navy. His commission also awarded him the grand title of governor of the Sagadahoc territory, a large tract that ran between the Kennebec and St. Croix Rivers. On his arrival, Dunbar found himself in the middle of land speculators' spirited contest for control of eastern Maine, and he did not shrink from the competition. From its earliest years, the Massachusetts government had wanted to settle colonists on its exposed Maine frontier, then part of the Bay Colony. Massachusetts officials hoped to establish a buffer that would prevent attacks by the French and their Indian allies. Land speculators were eager to help Massachusetts achieve this goal, competing to lure colonists back to this remote and dangerous frontier. At least eight proprietary companies claimed rights to the Boothbay region. Dunbar himself may have been an agent for English interests based in Nova Scotia that wanted to expand south after the English conquest of that former French colony.[6]

Regardless of whether he was acting alone or as an agent, "Governor" Dun-

Maine, 1730s: Scotch-Irish Presbyterians from Ulster started a settlement between the Sheepscot and Damariscotta Rivers that came to be called Boothbay.

bar saw an opportunity to make money by coaxing settlers back to the region. Security, of course, was essential to any hopes of building a thriving colony. He started, therefore, by rebuilding Fort Frederick, which had been damaged in earlier Indian warfare and which he garrisoned with troops from Nova Scotia. Luring colonists to return to his territory would be a larger and more difficult task, however, and Dunbar used land as his bait. The colonel envisioned establishing two towns on each side of the Damariscotta. The future Boothbay, which until 1764 was called Townsend, in honor of English secretary of state Charles Townshend, would be located between the Sheepscot and the Damariscotta. Dunbar wanted Townsend to be a true farm village despite the challenging terrain of rocks, trees, and river. Under his ambitious plan, settlers would receive small, narrow lots measuring twelve rods wide and two acres deep. If a settler built a house eighteen feet long and cleared his two acres within three years, he would receive two additional lots, one of forty acres and one of one hundred acres.[7]

Within two years, Dunbar had attracted about sixty people to Townsend, nearly all of them Scotch-Irish Presbyterians. This modest success had resulted from another happenstance. An early leader of the Scotch-Irish contingent was Samuel McCobb, who had been born in West Ulster, probably in County Tyrone, in about 1707. In 1728, he and his brother, James, decided to try their luck in the New World. In Londonderry, Ireland, they boarded a Philadelphia-bound ship with other Scotch-Irish families. Probably as a result of some combination of bad weather and fickle winds, the ship landed at the mouth of the Kennebec River in Maine, far to the north of its intended destination. After learning of Dunbar's offer of land in Townsend, the McCobb brothers convinced other Scotch-Irish settlers at Arrowsic, the settlement at the Kennebec, to move as well.[8]

Between 1718 and 1720, some twenty-six hundred Scotch-Irish migrants, led by Presbyterian ministers, had arrived in Boston. The new arrivals anticipated receiving a warm reception from the Puritans, since they were fellow Calvinists and sometime allies in the fight against popery. However, the New England Puritans saw the Presbyterians not as allies but as wild Irishmen, foreigners from a "papist" land long hostile to England. The Puritans also feared that these Irish were paupers who would tax Boston's charity rolls and clean out its tenuous food supply.[9]

In the face of this unexpected hostility, the Scotch-Irish left Boston as soon as possible. Most of the migrants had come to farm and thus headed to western Massachusetts and to New Hampshire, where good land could be had at affordable prices. But Puritans in the rest of New England were not any happier to see the Presbyterians from Ulster. The harshest reception ultimately came in Worcester, Massachusetts, where fifty families traveled directly from Boston in 1718. Worcester, on the western fringes of the Bay Colony, remained a frontier with Indian troubles of its own. Its Puritan residents at first welcomed the Ulster Presbyterians, seeing them as reinforcements in the battles against Native Americans. Religious differences quickly surfaced, however. According to one historian, "When the Presbyterians lost their first minister, they were persuaded to give up their own church and unite with the Puritans, upon the clear understanding that the pulpit might occasionally be filled by a Presbyterian." The Puritans failed to keep their end of the bargain; as an added insult, they required the Presbyterians to pay a tithe to support the Puritans' congregational church. The Scotch-Irish protested, to no avail. The newcomers then began constructing a Presbyterian meetinghouse, but a mob tore it down, burned the timbers, and carried off the remaining building materials.[10]

Most of the Scotch-Irish in Worcester moved on, some to Scotch-Irish settlements in Nutfield and Londonderry, New Hampshire, others to Pelham, Massachusetts, and the colony of New York. The bitter experience in Worcester reinforced an important lesson for many of these Irish expatriates: to worship in peace, Scotch-Irish settlers needed to settle with their compatriots whenever possible. This desire became explicit in Pelham. Two men who had attempted to settle at Worcester, Robert Peoples and James Thornton, bought thirty thousand acres and drew up an agreement for settling the tract. Pelham's founders would seek "Inhabitants of the Kingdom of Ireland or their Descendents being Protestants and none admitted but such as bring good and undeniable Credentials or certificates of their being Persons of good conversation and of the Presbyterian Persuasion as used in the Church of Scotland and Conform to the Discipline thereof." The town consequently was settled primarily by Scotch-Irish farmers, and the migrants built a Presbyterian congregation and recruited a minister from Ireland.[11]

In 1718, another unhappy band of Scotch-Irish in Boston headed to Maine. Religion again played a role in their decision about where to go. Massachusetts's governor had given the migrants a choice. They could settle anywhere in the colony and gain full citizenship if they became members of the established (congregational) church, or they could go to the frontier and receive a "township right" that would enable them to settle land twelve miles square. That option presumably would have permitted them a measure of religious freedom. The governor recommended they head to Maine's Casco Bay, near present-day Portland.[12]

Many of the Presbyterians chose the frontier despite its grave risks. The climate was challenging, and the Indians remained hostile. But on the frontier, the Scotch-Irish Presbyterians would have the chance to acquire more land and to worship as they pleased, prospects so beguiling that they apparently outweighed other factors. The families departed Boston by ship in late fall, arriving in Casco Bay and attempting to build a settlement in the harshest winter they had ever seen. The weather was so cold that several families never left the warmth of their ship at anchor in the bay. Three shivering months later, the members of this vanguard headed south, where it was warmer. One group founded Londonderry, New Hampshire, while the rest scattered throughout New England, remaining there until Dunbar enticed a small group of them back to Townsend in 1729.[13]

Like the hapless Casco Bay party years earlier, these settlers did not know what they were getting into when they accepted Dunbar's land deal. Samuel McCobb claimed his one hundred acres, built a log house at Lobster Cove, and started a family but soon ran into trouble. Years later, he looked back at the difficulties of the founding years with wonderment. For starters, the terrain was "naturally broken and poor [and in a] wild uncultivated State." The migrants, McCobb lamented, were "utterly unacquainted with the Mode of managing Lands in that State." This unfamiliarity, combined with their generally "low Circumstances" and the incessant Indian wars, meant that the settlers struggled to extract a living from the soil. Unable to grow enough food, "their whole living depended on cutting firewood and carrying it to Boston and other Towns more than one hundred and fifty miles from them." In 1745, McCobb continued, Indian attacks during King George's War (called in Europe the War of the Austrian Succession) forced Townsend's residents to flee westward, "where they were Scattered in a strange Country at near 200 miles distance from their homes for four years." With peace, the settlers returned and tried to rebuild their lives. But, McCobb recounted, "they had scarce finished the Repairs of their wasted Cottages & Improvements when in a year or thereabouts, the Indians, tho' in a Time of Peace fell on their Neighbourhood, burnt Barns, killed many Cattle, attacked the little Garrison kept by the People and carried away a Number of Men, Women & Children into captivity."[14]

McCobb and the others again fled the town. Their exile was short but nevertheless costly: the Indians destroyed the settlers' crops and the provisions they had set aside for the coming winter. "Horrors of Famine were in prospect—Many were obliged to live by Clams only," McCobb recalled. The settlers struggled along until the French and Indian War broke out in 1756. Maine was truly on the fringes of this transatlantic conflict, and McCobb complained that the settlers' pleas to British authorities for protection and economic aid went unheeded. Indeed, the settlement received not even "a Morsel of Bread." The residents thus "lived in continual Terrors and Alarms from the Savages who ranged the Wilderness all around till the late Peace was concluded." Peace meant another chance to rebuild, and "new Comers from the Western Parts" of Massachusetts bolstered Townsend's population.[15]

The town of Boothbay was thus born in chaos, amid war and deprivation. It was no planned religious community of neat streets and handsome meetinghouses, founded by visionaries setting out to establish a well-ordered society for the worship of God. It was founded by an army colonel out to line his pockets who managed to entice a few people to come try their luck at farming on the frontier. That a few settlers accepted resulted from a wayward sailing ship's wrong turn and from the poor treatment of Presbyterians elsewhere in New England. Despite such chaos, however, an important pattern was at work: a Scotch-Irish family migrated to a frontier and persuaded other Scotch-Irish families to follow. Banding together on the frontier, these families then began to establish a Scotch-Irish Presbyterian community.

Doing so was never easy. The troubles of the early years led to repeated delays. As the settlers explained, "The inhabitants of this town having long been harassed and distressed by the natural difficulties of settling a new country without any considerable resources of wealth, and more especially by the frequent wars with the Savages on the border by which the settlement was repeatedly broken up, and the whole place laid waste; had hardly recovered strength for the settling the gospel amongst them and therefore had long been languishing under the heavy infliction of silent Sabbaths."[16]

The settlers also faced other difficulties in their efforts to start a congregation. Presbyterian ministers visited Townsend from time to time, but the lack of a meetinghouse kept the settlement from obtaining the full-time services of a pastor. To build a meetinghouse and sustain a congregation, however, the settlers needed to incorporate as a town and pool their resources. They succinctly explained their motives in their incorporation petition to the Massachusetts General Court: "We have a desire of settling the Gospel among us." McCobb, too, cited this sentiment: "When desirous of obtaining the benefit of order and the enjoyment of the gospel, [the settlers] applied to the Gen'l Court of the Province and were legally incorporated into a town by the name of Boothbay."[17]

Church records reveal the settlers' motivations even more plainly. The Scotch-Irish settlers wanted a *Presbyterian* town. Boothbay, the first two articles of incorporation stipulated, was to be placed "upon the following fundamental articles, viz: Article 1. That the town of Boothbay shall be deemed to be under the ecclesiastical constitution of Presbyterians as to worship, ordinance, discipline and government. Article 2. That into whatever number of Parishes or districts said town be divided, it shall always be considered as one Church, and shall be regulated by one Consistory."[18]

The decision to incorporate as a Presbyterian town formed part of a careful strategy to win the services of a Presbyterian minister from Ireland. Like other faiths in the New World, the Presbyterian Church had too few ministers. The Presbyterian shortage was especially severe because the church insisted on a well-educated ministry, refusing to lower its standards despite the rapid increase in the number of members in America. Boothbay, a small town on the far fringes of empire with both Indian and economic troubles, faced daunting odds in attracting someone from Scotland or Ireland to fill its pulpit.

The task became even more challenging when the residents of Boothbay focused their search on John Murray, a talented minister with a reputation as an inspiring speaker. In 1763, inhabitants met at the house of John Beath and "unanimously voted to give [Murray] a call to be the stated Pastor of this Town." They offered Murray ninety pounds sterling per year, an especially impressive salary in light of the town's relative poverty. The town would also award him a two-hundred-acre lot, clear the lot, and provide him with firewood. Murray was pleased with the offer but worried about how Townsend would fulfill its conditions. Because of these concerns, Murray went to Boston.[19]

Boothbay's inhabitants responded by appointing a committee to travel to Boston to plead with Murray. He declined to reconsider his refusal, explaining that he wanted to return to Ireland, but promised "that if ever he returned to settle in America, and [if the position was] vacant still, and [the town] should renew their application to him Townsend should be the place of his settlement. Elated with having thus far gained their point they returned to report their successes." Murray headed to New York City, where he planned to board a ship to Ulster. Before he could depart, however, he received offers of pastorships from the Presbyterian congregations in New York and Philadelphia.[20]

Murray put his plans to return to Ireland on hold and informed Boothbay's Presbyterians of this turn of events. Unsure about what to do, Murray told the Philadelphia presbytery of his three suitors and asked for advice. Not surprisingly, the presbytery persuaded him to settle in Philadelphia, convincing him that his promise to Boothbay was "null and void" because he had never returned to Ireland. This reasoning struck Boothbay's residents as spurious, and they renewed their efforts to force Murray to return to Maine. The town received its charter in late 1764, satisfying one of Murray's initial conditions for accepting its call.[21]

In February 1765, Boothbay's inhabitants informed Murray "that we were incorporated as a town by the name of Boothbay, had voted to build a meetinghouse . . . and was hastening all preparations for his settlement; that their affections were unanimously fixed on him" and again asked him to keep his promise. They also warned that they would "push on all possible claim" to ensure that he fulfilled the agreement. In case Murray missed the point, two follow-up letters soon arrived, signed by Boothbay's "principal settlers" and two of the town selectmen.[22]

The entreaties must have given Murray pause, because the pastor paid a surprise visit to Boothbay, preaching several sermons and "inform[ing] us of the particulars of his settlement at large"—he intended to remain in Philadelphia. He asked Boothbay to release him from his promise. The town refused. In fact, inhabitants drew up a new "supplication" for Murray's services and reminded both Murray and the presbytery in Boston that "for a course of years" they had "had cause to lament the want of the Gospel of Christ, having long been destitute of the ordinary means of Grace whereby the knowledge as well as the lively influence of the great truths of our religion is greatly decayed among us." The document emphasized that "we cannot but trust [that Murray] will see this as a loud call from divine providence for him to come over and help us." The town then raised its offer to 120 pounds. Murray again said no.[23]

Still, the settlers refused to give up. On March 13, 1766, they again petitioned the Philadelphia Synod, noting the latest rejection and repeating their determination to pursue the matter "until it is issued in his transportation to us." To demonstrate to the synod that Murray's promise to Townsend was valid, three witnesses vouched for the truth of the inhabitants' claims. This tactic worked. The synod finally agreed that Murray and the town had reached a valid agreement. Boothbay's inhabitants then formally renewed their offer to Murray in writing, and the Philadelphia presbytery agreed to release Murray from his duties there. Boothbay had won, but one final delay still awaited: "bodily indisposition" prevented the minister from traveling to Maine until late July. Soon after his arrival, which was greeted with "great joy [by] the inhabitants," the selectmen convened a town meeting and installed Murray as the town minister.[24]

The episode was extraordinary on several levels. The settlers displayed great persistence in their pursuit of Murray's services, procuring them despite the competition from congregations in more comfortable locales and with far larger memberships and resources. Even more important, the long, difficult courtship demonstrated the value that the settlers placed on building a town on the foundation of Scottish Presbyterianism. Like a jilted lover, Boothbay's Presbyterians responded to the indignities of repeated rejections by increasing their ardor for a minister.

On the Maine frontier, a functioning church would give structure to the settlers' lives and allow them to solidify their identity as a Scotch-Irish community. Murray's initial actions as minister revealed the importance of these goals. According to Beath, who left a detailed account of the congregation's early years, Murray first undertook "pastoral visitations, in which he went to all the inhabitants, at their houses, catechized and conversed with every one, old and young, separately, and one by one, concerning the state of their souls and the great work of salvation." The minister then organized Monday evening prayer sessions and established a rotation so that the meetings were held at every house "about the harbour." On Wednesdays, he conducted "lectures at the several quarters of the town in their turns; to this he added a public catechizing at each place at the same meeting." For the catechisms, Murray divided the inhabitants into three groups: people under age fourteen; unmarried people fourteen and older; and heads of families. He also created four divisions for the town and assigned a central place in each division where lectures and catechizing would take place. Such sessions began "with prayer and singing, then [the minister would] call over the names of all in that division that belonged to that class to be examined that day." Murray concluded with a sermon and additional prayer and singing. The rotating schedule ensured that although the settlement's houses were far apart and travel was difficult, every person was catechized at least once every three months.[25]

Murray's larger goal was to bring together the scattered members of his flock and unite them under the banner of Scotch-Irish Presbyterianism. Inhabitants would find common ground not in their fields or homes but in a Presbyterian church whose tenets derived from the Scottish national church and its elaborate rituals. The Presbyterian faith had roots deep in Scottish and Ulster history, and its reformation ways held great cultural significance for these settlers on the Maine frontier.

The Scottish Kirk

The Protestant Reformation in the Scottish Lowlands was largely the work of one man: John Knox (1513–72), a brilliant preacher who had survived exile in Geneva, an imprisonment for his reformist beliefs, and a stint as a galley slave for the French. Like other Protestant reformers, Knox had an intense hatred of and disdain for the Roman Catholic Church. In the sixteenth century, the Catholic Church in Scotland was a corrupt and indolent backwater of the Rome-based universal church. The church owned more than one-third of Scotland's land and a staggering 50 percent of the nation's wealth. As in other pre-Reformation European countries, priests faced no competition and made little effort to win popular affection. Parishioners saw the clergy as venal and lazy. Moreover, earlier reform movements had not reached Scotland. The Catholic Church thus had few defenders in the tiny country far from the European Continent.[26]

Change came from an unlikely source. On New Year's Day 1559, a revolutionary manifesto known as the Beggars' Summons was found on the gates of every church in Scotland. The summons, written anonymously for the "blind, crooked, lame," and others, condemned the church's wealth and corruption and demanded "restitution of wrongs past": "Let him . . . that before hath stolen, steal no more; but rather let him work with his hands that he may be helpful to the poor." Knox chose this auspicious moment to return from his Geneva exile, where he had become a friend and colleague of the great reformer John Calvin. Knox, an eloquent speaker known for delivering spellbinding sermons, then led a thorough and radical reformation in the Lowlands that resulted in the Scottish Parliament voting on July 10, 1560, to end the Catholic Church's status as the national church. (The Catholic Church, however, remained entrenched among the Gaelic-speaking population in the sparsely inhabited northern region known as the Highlands.) Parliament followed up by approving three acts that rejected the pope's leadership, condemned Catholic practices as inimical to Protestantism, and forbade the saying of Mass. In Catholicism's place, legislators made Presbyterianism the established *kirk* (Scottish for church) of Scotland. Presbyterian ministers then drew up the First Book of Discipline, which would govern the new church. This book, along with the Book of Common Order (1564), placed the Bible at the center of Presbyterian worship with the goal of following Jesus' teachings as closely as possible.[27]

The overthrow of Catholicism was an act of political revolution as well. Presbyterianism's ascendancy meant the end of a long alliance between Scotland and Catholic France, two countries that shared a hatred of the English; the treaty of Leath, signed in July 1560, stipulated that all French troops had to leave Scotland. In addition, the Scottish Reformation signaled a declaration of religious independence from Anglican-dominated England.

These neighbors shared an enmity that took several violent forms. Warring parties from both sides repeatedly conducted raids inside enemy territory. As one historian has written, "For seven centuries, the kings of Scotland and England could not agree who owned [the border region], and meddled constantly in each other's affairs. From the year 1040 to 1745, every English monarch but three suffered a Scottish invasion, or became an invader in his turn. In the same period, most Scottish kings went to war against England, and many died 'with their boots on,' as the border saying went." The fighting could be particularly brutish. One of the most infamous incidents occurred in 1297, when legendary Scottish leader William Wallace invaded Cumberland in an attempt to recapture the Lowlands from the English. Wallace's troops flayed the bodies of their English foes; the English, in turn, captured Wallace and impaled his head on a pike. When the attention of the two countries' monarchs was occupied elsewhere, warlords carried on the fight, and "the region never enjoyed fifty consecutive years of quiet" until 1745, thirty-eight years after England and Scotland had formally ended hostilities through a political union.[28]

The incessant border fighting became central to the formation of a Scottish national identity. Lowland Scots rallied around the common cause of defeating the English invaders. Hatred of the English ran so deep that it influenced the Scottish Reformation. Presbyterianism flourished in the Scottish Lowlands not only because of unhappiness with Catholicism but also because the movement took on an anti-Anglican and anti-English tone. Religion—specifically, Presbyterianism—became an important way for a Scot to declare his disdain for all things English.

The religious antagonism had its ironies. Both Anglicans and Presbyterians wanted to rid Western Christianity of the Catholic devil. In 1643, the two faiths even codified this alliance through the Solemn League and Covenant, a document that approved of the religious reformation in England, Ireland, and Scotland. But the English never took the covenant seriously. In Scotland, the National Covenant of 1638, drawn up as part of the Scots' revolt against the ecclesiastical policies of Charles I, assumed far greater importance. The National Covenant was designed to uphold the Scottish kirk against English attempts to bring the two national churches closer together. These attempts dated to the reign of James I, a Scot who had become king of England. James's son, Charles I, alarmed the Scots even further in 1637, when he sought to impose a version of the English Prayer Book in Scotland. Scottish nobles and ministers responded a year later by drawing up the National Covenant, which announced that "none shall be reputed as loyall and faithful subjects . . . who shall not give their Confession and make their Profession of the said true religion"—Presbyterianism. "The taking of the covenant represented an act of resistance that was represented through ritual," historian Ned C. Landsman notes. "Covenanting was a public performance in which participants were obliged not only to accept the approved doctrines of the church, but to do so publicly, before the whole congregation. . . . Covenanting was thus an explicit rejection and renunciation of innovation and foreign ideas." More broadly, the document equated Presbyterianism with Scottish citizenship.[29]

In Ireland, Presbyterianism assumed equally great importance for Scottish colonists. The transplanted Scots not only lived among a Catholic majority that despised all Protestant interlopers but also had to coexist with their ancient English foes, who had made Anglicanism the national church of Ireland.

Presbyterians were thus reduced to dissenters, an inferior status that made Ulster's Presbyterians even more protective of their church and heritage. Colonists maintained close contact with nearby Scotland, and Scottish-born and -educated ministers filled the pulpits.

On several occasions in the seventeenth century, the native Irish attempted to drive the English and Scots out. The most serious uprising occurred in 1641, when Catholics killed thousands of foreign settlers in a failed attempt to win back their land. Another crisis occurred in 1685, when James II became king of England and placed a Catholic in charge of the Irish army. The new commander promptly ousted Protestants from the ranks, raising fears that the new regime would next target Protestants' land. Ireland soon found itself a central actor in the drama known as the Glorious Revolution of 1688. When James, a suspected papist, was forced to flee to the Continent, he chose to fight in Ireland to regain his throne. James and his main ally, Louis XIV of France, believed that by capturing Ireland, James could force his successor, William of Orange, to abdicate. Not surprisingly, James's plans met with fierce resistance in Ulster, most notably in the port town of Derry. The deposed king's troops besieged the Protestant—and Presbyterian—stronghold for 105 days until William's forces finally relieved the suffering city and drove off the Catholic army.[30]

In addition to the bloody Catholic challenge, Scottish Presbyterianism in Ireland faced a serious challenge from the English. Confronted with an armed rebellion by Irish Catholics and the refusal of Ulster's Presbyterians to support Oliver Cromwell during the English Civil War, the Cromwellian protectorate invaded Ireland in 1650. Cromwell's forces ruthlessly crushed the Catholic revolt and put the Presbyterians in their place. Over an eleven-year period, famine, plague, and fighting killed approximately 504,000 of Ireland's 1,450,000 natives. Although Presbyterianism survived this dark period, Cromwell's campaign did nothing to endear the English to the Scots in Ulster, and the Scots redoubled their efforts to build up the Presbyterian Church in Ireland. By 1690, Ulster had a synod, nine presbyteries, three subsynods, and 120 congregations.[31]

At the same time, Scots continued to resist all English efforts to Anglicanize their church. King James I may have been a Scot, but he was unsympathetic to Presbyterianism and was wary of Puritanism. Radical Presbyterian reformers, he correctly believed, were hostile to Anglican episcopacy and the king himself. Thus, James set out to introduce English bishops into the Scottish church, one of several measures he pursued with the goal of Anglicanizing the church. Scottish Presbyterian resistance took several forms, including rioting. In 1637, English efforts to alter Scotland's prayer books led to violence in Edinburgh and elsewhere. Presbyterians also held revivals, known in Scotland and Ulster as "Holy Fairs." For ministers trying to fend off the English, this popular evangelical tool became an effective way to solidify the church's hold on Scottish society and to rally followers.[32]

An early leader of the revival movement was Robert Bruce, a famed preacher whose career lasted from 1587 to 1631. He built a large following among Presbyterians resisting King James's religious reforms. The monarch tried to silence Bruce by periodically confining him to jail, but the intimidation had little effect on the fiery evangelist. Bruce continued preaching in southwest Scotland and in Inverness and Edinburgh, sparking an awakening that swept through Scotland and Ulster during the 1620s.[33]

The Holy Fairs combined religious holy day, secular holiday, and political act of resistance, becoming the center of an evangelical Presbyterian culture that helped to define a Scottish religious / national identity. Each parish typically held an annual Holy Fair, making the four-day event the highlight of the year for participants. In addition to the political benefits, Bruce and other reformers saw revivals as a way to inspire piety and religious passion. In particular, these leaders saw revivalism as a way to fill the void left by the elimination of Catholic festivals and holy days. But unlike America's nineteenth-century camp meetings, which concentrated on sparking conversions through emotional preaching, the Scottish revivals centered on the Lord's Supper. By administering this most solemn sacrament, reformers pursued a larger goal: "to renew Presbyterian communities, to invigorate flagging saints, and to transform flagrant sinners." The migration of Scottish evangelical ministers to Ireland ensured that the revival movement became popular in Ulster and ultimately in America.[34]

Across the Atlantic, however, the revivals' had a slightly different impact. Holy Fairs became a way for Scottish groups to come together in a foreign land to affirm who they were and what they believed. Boothbay was a prime example. Murray, it turns out, was an ardent evangelical minister, and one of his first actions after assuming the Maine pastorship was to schedule communion and to prepare the community to receive it. He announced his intentions from the pulpit and informed members that in the ensuing weeks he would be "entirely" devoting his time "to the business of examining candidates at his lodgings." Twenty members applied to take the sacrament, and Murray got to work ascertaining whether they deserved to participate.[35]

Passing muster with Murray in these private interviews was only the first step for candidates. They then had to face the scrutiny of the church community. Murray informed the congregation that a day would be "set apart for that purpose, that all objections against [the candidates] might be discussed before" the congregation. Candidates who cleared this hurdle then had to show that they understood the covenant of grace, "in answer which they all solemnly . . . declared their taking God the divine for their Father in Christ Jesus, God the Son, as Mediator for their Saviour in his three fold character of prophet, priest and King."[36]

Anticipation within the congregation built as communion day neared. Catechisms instructed members about the ritual's importance, and a larger group met at the home of William Fullerton for prayer and instruction. On the Sunday before communion, Murray conducted a "preparation Sabbath," devoting both the morning and afternoon services to sermons and instructions on communion and its significance. In homes across the settlement, families prayed together and examined their members in further preparation for the big day. On Saturday afternoon, Murray preached on "the dying love of Christ." Near the close of the service, he left the pulpit and "poured out on the [communion] table a great number of small square pieces of lead on which the initial letters of his name were stamped in capitals." Murray then called up the members who qualified for communion one by one to receive their token, which would admit them to the Lord's table the following day. Like the service itself, the tokens carried great meaning for Presbyterians. Murray stressed to the congregation that the tokens belonged to the "custom of the Presbyterian Church." Holding one not only entitled a congregant to the "privileges of Christ's disciples" but also carried the "great obligation" to "seek with renewed earnestness the inward tokens of his being a member of the Church invisible." Conversely, the unworthy did not qualify for tokens. With great solemnity, therefore, Murray handed out the tokens. The ceremony included a short exhortation, a solemn prayer, the singing of a psalm, and the dismissal of the congregation with a blessing. In all, the communion revival was an elaborate dance that carried deep cultural significance for the Scotch-Irish and that featured rituals that had been carefully worked out in Scotland and Ireland in the seventeenth century.[37]

John Beath described communion as transformational, producing "such symptoms of the powerful and special presence of God of grace as every one might discern and we can never enough be thankful for; it was a solemn, sweet and glorious season; many of God's children were filled with the joys of the Lord and many poor souls brought to see their need of that Saviour they had shamefully neglected, and wickedly crucified." Murray wanted the communion to be grand and solemn and festive. Many people traveled great distances to watch or participate. In one sense, the journey resembled a pilgrimage, with people enduring rough roads, bad weather, and poor food to participate in a most holy event. The sacrifice involved—studying, fasting, and penitence—only brought people closer together, as did their affirmation of the bonds that made them a community in the Maine wilderness. For Beath, "It had been very observable that through the whole of Winter a very unusual seriousness and solemnity appeared amongst the generality of the people here, accompanied with an insatiable desire after the word, and several people awakened to an anxious concern for their souls." The revival thus simultaneously strengthened the settlers' identity as Presbyterians and reinforced the community's cultural heritage as Scots.[38]

The Southern Frontier: Augusta County, Virginia

In many respects, Augusta County was a long way away from the world of Samuel McCobb and John Murray. In war-racked Boothbay, all was love and harmony. In peaceful Augusta, all was conflict and divisiveness. The ironies of this situation were many. Augusta's Scotch-Irish, led by a vanguard from Pennsylvania, found themselves in a place that Boothbay's settlers would have praised as positively Edenic. Augusta County, founded in 1738, was warmer. The spring planting season was longer and more temperate. The soil was better, too, and farmers thrived. The religious climate was equally encouraging. No Puritans lived among Augusta's lush hills and vales, and the Anglican Church's presence on the frontier was weak. Moreover, the Scotch-Irish Presbyterians pretty much had this Eden to themselves, with the exception of a few German-speakers and Anglicans.[39]

Yet unlike their coreligionists who found spiritual contentment in the unforgiving harshness of Maine, the Scotch-Irish of Augusta County bickered among themselves, creating divisions that threatened to tear apart their community. Given the Scottish history of confronting common foes, what caused such internal divisiveness? More important, how did this conflict affect mobility and the creation of a Scotch-Irish community?

In one sense, Augusta's divisions were not terribly surprising. Boothbay's long fight against the Indians and poverty helped to keep the settlers unified in their quest to find a minister and build a congregation. But settlement of the southern backcountry in the mid–eighteenth century coincided with a religious earthquake known as the Great Awakening that produced fissures within Presbyterianism, as "New Side" preachers pressed to reform their supposedly more staid "Old Side" rivals. In Maine, evangelism helped to build a

Scotch-Irish Presbyterian identity and unify Boothbay, with Murray enjoying almost universal support. In Virginia's Shenandoah Valley, however, New Side clashed with Old.

The first Presbyterian minister to settle in the Augusta area was John Craig, an Old Side follower. Although he became a prominent target of the evangelical reformers, Craig was a devoted Presbyterian who dedicated his life to building the church in the American wilderness. But he frowned on American-style revivals and what he considered their excessive emotionalism. The New Side, in turn, saw him as hopelessly staid. Born in 1709 in Antrim, Ireland, and raised by parents whom he described as "pious," Craig recalled receiving "early instructions in the principles of religion . . . which had strong effects on my young and tender mind, (being then about five or six years of age,) and engaged me to fly to God with prayers and tears in secret." This was no Devereux Jarratt who grew up in a spiritual wilderness, surrounded by apathetic churchgoers who valued a good horse race over the Good Word. Craig described the parish of his youth as "Remarkable for the Modest Sober Religious Conduct of the people inhabiting that place." Unlike Jarratt, Craig also had warm praise for his minister, describing the Reverend Alexander Brown as "faithfull able & Diligent" and his "Name [as] Ever Dear to thee." Craig believed from a young age that he was destined to serve God, and by age nine, "God was Graciously pleased to lay ye happy foundation of virtue & piety in thy mind." After several detours as a young adult and an appropriate period of soul-searching, he concluded that God did indeed want him to become a minister and that he was most needed in America, where "Service would be most pleasing and acceptable."[40]

So in 1734, having had "America . . . Much in my mind," Craig set sail for New Castle, Delaware. He had no firm idea about where he would go next. "When I Came ashore I mett with an old acquaintance the Rev'd Benjamin Campbell then Minister of New-Castle." Craig asked his friend for advice, and Campbell "gave me an account of the Ministry & of men of parts among them which turn'd out greatly to my advantage."[41]

Craig sized up the Philadelphia Synod through the stern gaze of an Irish-trained conservative: "It Gave me both Grief & Joy to See that Synod, Grief to See their Small Number & mean appearance, Joy to See their Mutual Love and Good order, & men of Solid Sense among them & Steady in their Presbyterian Principles & against all innovations which began to appear at this Synod from an overture Read publicly by the Rev'd Gilbert Tennent."[42]

Craig's arrival in Philadelphia had placed him in the middle of a brewing controversy between Tennent's New Side devotees and the Old Side. Craig dismissed the New Side as upstarts and lamented that the evangelical attacks on the ministry divided the Presbyterian Church in America and "put ye Church of God here into ye utmost confusion." Craig took up the life of a young Presbyterian minister, spending five years as an itinerant for the presbytery of Donegal in Pennsylvania, preaching to frontier Presbyterians happy to hear the Word. In 1739, Craig moved to another frontier, Augusta County, Virginia, becoming the first full-time Presbyterian minister assigned to the Virginia backcountry. His primary responsibility was Augusta, but his territory was huge, covering ten thousand square miles. He ranged over mountains, streams, and valleys to visit a total of thirty-six isolated settlements. Like their Maine counterparts, Virginia's Scotch-Irish Presbyterians at first were thrilled to have Craig among them, receiving him "in the Most friendly manner." Craig had his work cut for out him, though. Augusta, he noted, "was a New Settlement, without place of worship, or any Church order. A wilderness in a proper Sense and a few Christians settled in it, with Numbers of the Heathen [Indians] traveling among us, but Generally Civil."[43]

In building a congregation, Craig's task resembled Murray's. Achieving this mission entailed teaching Augusta's Scotch-Irish inhabitants "how to Act So as to maintain Presbyterian order & Rules of Government in our Church." Two congregations—the Tinkling Spring meetinghouse and the Augusta stone meetinghouse—became the center of Craig's sprawling pastorship. Tinkling Spring was established first and became far more troublesome to Craig. "That part Now Called Tinkling Spring was most in Number & Richer than the other," he recalled, but "their leaders [were] proud Selfinterested Contentious & ungovernable." The congregation, according to its unhappy pastor, "Could Not agree for Several years upon ye place or Manner where & how to build their meetinghouse, which Gave me very Great trouble to hold them together." Two wealthy members of the congregation, John Lewis and James Patton, jockeyed for power and feuded about where the meetinghouse should be built. Despite Craig's best efforts, he was unable to "Bring them to friendship with Each other," and the dispute "Continued for 13 or 14 years till Col. Patton was murdered by the Indians." Even then, the congregation's "wicked Devices" persisted, and "the old Contentious Spirit Still Remain[ed] amongst them."[44]

The divisions among Augusta's Scotch-Irish Presbyterians went far deeper than personalities and arguments over the location of the meetinghouse. The real problem involved theology. Craig's huge territory split into feuding evangelical and antievangelical camps. Craig was a proud and almost defiant Old Sider, and his opponents, in his words, ridiculed him as a "poor, blind, Carnal,

Scotch-Irish congregants at the stone meetinghouse in Augusta County, Virginia, were far more supportive of their embattled Old Side minister, John Craig, than were the parishioners at Tinkling Spring. (Historic American Buildings Survey / Library of Congress)

hypocritical Damn'd wretch," mocking his version of the Lord's Supper as "Craig's Frolick." Craig was hardly cowed. "Not Instantly, I attain'd Clearness of Mind to Join in ye protest against these New and uncharitable opinions and ye Ruin of Church Government." But his decision to oppose the New Side "Gave offence to Some two or three families in my [Tinkling Spring] Congregation; who then Look'd upon me as opposer of ye work of God." At the Augusta stone meetinghouse, in contrast, he enjoyed significant support.[45]

Nevertheless, this conflict did not harm the Scotch-Irish community and weaken its members' sense of belonging to an ethnoreligious group. For all the thunder of revivalism and the New Side's attacks on the Old Side as insufficiently saved, the two groups shared much. The revivalists remained loyal to Presbyterianism and their Scottish heritage. The center of Presbyterian revivalism in the New World was New Jersey, which was also a bastion of Scottishness. In 1738, under the guidance of Scottish ministers, Presbyterian congregations in Freehold, New Brunswick, Basking Ridge, and elsewhere held their first revivals, which subsequently spread to Scotch-Irish and Scottish churches in South Jersey, eastern Pennsylvania, and Delaware. In Virginia, New Side revivalism gained its first foothold in Hanover County, spread west to the backcountry, and quickly found common cause with its northern variant in New Jersey. The catalysts for the New Side were the members of a Scotch-Irish family, the Tennents. William Tennent Sr., an immigrant from Ulster, founded "the Log College" in Neshaminy, Pennsylvania, in the mid-1730s to train young men for the ministry. The Presbyterians, he well understood, were struggling to fill their pulpits in the New World and badly needed a seminary on this side of the Atlantic. Despite the shortage of candidates for the cloth and the great need for more ministers, the church still insisted on a highly educated and trained ministry, which meant that congregations recruited ministers from Scotland and Ulster. Young congregations in such out-of-the-way places as Boothbay, Maine, had to go to great extremes to attract qualified ministers. Tennent's college sought to fill this void. But he had another goal as well. He wanted regenerate ministers thoroughly versed in traditional Scottish Presbyterianism. The Log College curriculum stressed the Westminster Catechism and other mainstays of the Scottish national church.[46]

His revivals thus had a decidedly Scottish accent. As in Boothbay and Ulster, they centered on the Lord's Supper and the exhausting cycle of preparation, penitence, fasting, conversion, and communion. Unlike their American counterparts at Cane Ridge and elsewhere, Scottish revivals lasted six months or longer. One Freehold, New Jersey, revival began in 1730 and did not end until 1733. The elaborate rituals were one cause; another was that ministers rather than laity controlled the revivals. Anglican Devereux Jarratt, for example, became reborn after careful individual study and reflection—a solitary journey. In Scottish and Scotch-Irish congregations, by contrast, the minister led the unconverted through the steps needed to become reborn. This journey involved extensive consultations, usually at the sinner's house over many months. During these pastoral visits, ministers instructed their charges in correct Presbyterian doctrines and tested their knowledge. William Tennent Jr. compared ministers' task to that of doctors, visiting the unsaved and dispensing "as much care as a physician would." The Log College graduates understood the role of emotion in the conversion experience but believed that conversion could not occur until the rebirth had occurred in a "right-gospel way, including both a change of manner and an acceptance of proper doctrine." Thus, the ministers expected the reborn to give "rational and scriptural" accounts of their conversions. The process took time.[47]

Many good Scots frowned on the participation of Anglicans and others in revivalism. When George Whitefield joined a revival at the Cambuslang parish, outside of Glasgow, the centuries-old antagonism between Anglican and Presbyterian was renewed. The presence of an Anglican minister clashed with the goals of those New Side reformers who wanted a specifically Scottish Presbyterian revival. The American revivals' emphasis on ecumenicalism also came into conflict with that goal. Whitefield and many other revivalists cared little about ethnic and denominational distinctions and gladly ignored parish and ethnic boundaries in their efforts to lead people of all persuasions to a new birth. As Whitefield told one audience, "Don't tell me you are a Baptist, an Independent, a Presbyterian, a Dissenter—tell me you are a Christian, that is all I want." For many Scottish and Scotch-Irish Presbyterians, that statement constituted blasphemy. As the revival movement spread in the 1740s, adherents of this point of view saw the Great Awakening through the wide cultural lens of their Scottish cultural and religious heritage. Historian Ned C. Landsman has likened Presbyterian revivalism to nativism. That is, Scottish revivalism did not emphasize "the integration of diverse persons, customs, or values" from many nationalities or ethnic groups into a coherent movement. Instead, it emphasized a separate cultural identity. It stressed the traditional. Scottish Presbyterian colonists, Landsman observes, "would enter into the heterogeneous inter-colonial revival movement only after identifying it firmly with Scottish traditions. And, for many of those settlers, the revival would play a major role in the formation of an explicitly Scottish-American identity."[48]

Craig and other Old Side ministers found little to argue about here. Revivalism, after all, was a Scottish tradition dating to the early seventeenth century. But the American New Side carried its reforms one step further, attacking Old Side ministers as orthodox, out of touch, and unsaved. The most famous salvo was lobbed by William Tennent Sr.'s son, Gilbert, in 1740. In "Danger of an Unconverted Ministry," the younger Tennent compared Old Side ministers to "Pharisee-Shepherds" who were ignorant of the new birth and unfit to lead their congregations. The Old Side fought back, accusing the New Side of espousing "anarchical principles" and delivering overly emotional, terror-laden sermons that inflamed the "passions and affections of weak minds." The battle was waged in, among other places, the Philadelphia Synod, which expelled the New Side in 1741 after hearing an appeal from Craig and others. In so doing, the synod reaffirmed its allegiance to the Westminster Confession of Faith, the Catechism, and the Directory. The New Side then formed its own synod, the Synod of New York, in 1745, formally dividing American Presbyterianism. The heart of the evangelical movement remained New Jersey, where the Log College graduates operated and where Scottish Presbyterianism thrived among its evangelical followers.[49]

The New Side also thrived in Virginia, led by Samuel Davies. Davies, an orthodox Calvinist who loved a good argument, criticized the Anglican Church but avoided the excesses of many of his New Side brethren, and he could sound positively ecumenical by stressing the universality of the new birth.

Born in 1723, Davies was ordained in 1747 and arrived in Hanover County a year later. He soon earned a reputation as an outstanding preacher. Davies focused on the afterlife, since in his view, his real mission as a minister was "to save my country, and which, is of much more consequence, to save souls—from death—from that tremendous kind of death a soul can die." As one of his biographers put it, "The preparation of souls for imminent death was in fact the core of Davies' theology. To better prepare his listeners for the ultimate event, Davies demanded a unity of Christian life—a unity of inward belief and outward action." Like other Evangelicals, he attacked those lacking proper religious zeal—those who professed to be good Christians but were in fact hypocrites.[50]

The New Side, aided by the ministries of Alexander Craighead (the first New Side minister to settle in the Shenandoah Valley) and John Brown (the second), enjoyed strong growth in the Virginia backcountry at the expense of Craig and his Old Side brethren. The New Side was so successful that the Synod of New York agreed in 1755 to create a New Side presbytery in Virginia. The new Presbytery of Hanover's territory extended all the way down to the Carolinas. The Old Side struggled to meet this growing evangelical competition. Lacking enough ministers to send into the backcountry, the Donegal presbytery sent itinerants to tour the frontier settlements for two to six months. This plan enjoyed only limited success. The Presbytery of Hanover had seven ordained ministers in the field to Donegal's three.[51]

In 1758, the two sides finally made peace. One catalyst for unity was the French and Indian War. The reality that the Virginia frontier was exposed to attack by enemy forces forced the two sides to cooperate in the face of a common danger. Davies led the way, delivering a sermon on "The Curse of Cowardice" that called for cooperation to fight those who "would enslave the freeborn mind [and] ravage our frontiers, butcher our fellow-subjects, or confine them in a barbarous captivity." The fact that the Old Side was losing badly to the revivalists in the competition for souls also spurred the traditionalists to make peace. A failure to compromise would put the Old Side in danger of falling into complete irrelevance. But the biggest reason for the détente was that the two sides had so much in common. Both groups shared a belief in Holy Fairs, grounded in a Scottish Presbyterian identity, as well as an insistence that ministerial candidates be well educated. In the Hanover presbytery, an applicant was examined not only "as to his religious Experience" but also "in the Latin and Greek Languages." The New Side presbytery, in brief, wanted scholarly ministers in the Scottish tradition who could still deliver thunder from the pulpit. In 1752, Davies advised the Hanover presbytery to strike a balance between "the wild reveries of *enthusiasm* and the droning Heaviness and serene Stupidity" of the scholar. The New Side, in accepting the conventional tenets of Presbyterianism, would closely question candidates to ensure that they subscribed to the "Confession of Faith . . . and conformity to the Directory, and [that they promised] Subjection to the Presbytery in the Lord."[52]

Finally, both sides agreed on the need for a disciplined laity. Improving members' behavior was an early goal of the Scottish church, and this concern was carried across the Atlantic in the eighteenth century, as Jon Canachan could attest. The Donegal presbytery of Pennsylvania judged him "guilty of Some rash Expressions, profane swearing, and odious imprecation, which we hereby reprove him for, and Exhort him to a serious repentance." The presbytery also rebuked Thomas Thomson, "lately from Ireland," for the "sin of adultery with Mary Alison, a young woman of this Congregation." Thus, the divisions between Old Side and New Side did not last. Sharing so much, the two sides reunited in 1758.[53]

A People on the Move

Augusta's Scotch-Irish Presbyterians viewed the world through the same unique prism as those in Maine, and the Virginians' decisions regarding migration—when, where, and how to go—thus followed the same pattern found to the north. A vanguard would scout out a new location to settle and would purchase a large tract. Members of the vanguard would then recruit fellow Scotch-Irish Presbyterians—often neighbors and members of the same congregation—to join them as part of a larger kinship and religious network. The migrants moved onto individual family farms clustered together and built a Presbyterian meetinghouse. The settlers then constructed a community centered on church, ethnicity, kinship, and land.

The examples were numerous. In 1780, Robert Witherspoon described how Ulster emigrants had begun a Scotch-Irish settlement years earlier along the South Carolina frontier. Presbyterianism, a Scotch-Irish heritage, and hostility to all things Anglican and Catholic infused the settlers' efforts. The Witherspoons settled in Williamsburg Township, along the Black River about a hundred miles from Charleston. As in Maine, the settlers struggled to deal with the isolation of wilderness and other hardships. They particularly feared "being massacred by the Indians, or bit by snakes, or torn by wild beasts, or . . . being lost and perishing in the woods." To instill a sense of community amid the stresses of frontier life, the settlers moved quickly to organize a congregation. In late 1736, within two years of the settlement's founding, "the people began to form into a religious society, built a church and sent to Ireland for a minister," Witherspoon wrote. The first person buried in the church graveyard was Witherspoon's grandfather, whom Witherspoon described as a devout Presbyterian: "He was well acquainted with the scriptures—had a voluability of expression in prayer and was a zealous adherent to the reformed protestant principles of the church of Scotland." A "great aversion to episcopacy"—the Church of England—infused the elder Witherspoon's beliefs, as it did for other members of the family. "They were servers of God," Witherspoon noted. "They were well acquainted with the scriptures and were much in prayer. . . . In a word they studied outward piety and inward purity. God blessed this settlement at first with a number of godly pious men."[54]

In Augusta County itself, Presbyterian John Lewis and his family served as the vanguard. In 1738, he claimed a 2,071-acre tract on Lewis Creek near the headwaters of the south fork of the Shenandoah River, and numerous Ulster families followed him from Pennsylvania. So many Scotch-Irish settled in the area that it became known as the Irish tract. The process was much the same in other parts of the Shenandoah. Although German-speakers also lived in the area, sometimes on neighboring farms, Scotch-Irish Presbyterians clustered together. They soon erected a Presbyterian meetinghouse, which became the focal point of community life.[55]

In behaving so uniformly, the families replicated earlier events in Pennsylvania. The Reverend Samuel Blair, who accepted a call to serve as pastor at Faggs Manor there, was struck by the fact that the migrants from Ulster had stayed together in the New World. He described his congregation as "a new Settlement, generally settled with People from Ireland (as all our Congregations in Pennsylvania, except two or three, chiefly are made up of People from that Kingdom)." In Pennsylvania's Paxton Township, for example, more than a hundred Presbyterian migrants from Ulster had settled by 1730. James Magraw, who arrived in 1733, recalled building his cabin "on a level peese of ground near the road or path in the woods at the fut of a hill." The Magraws soon had company. "We have 18 cabbins bilt here now and it looks like a town but we have no name for it."[56]

Land certainly provided a major spur to all this internal migration. Many Scotch-Irish left Pennsylvania because farms were becoming too expensive there. By leaving, they were joining a massive mid-eighteenth-century migration to the southern colonies that saw a "greater Pennsylvania" spread to Virginia, the Carolinas, and Georgia. Virginia's population jumped from 120,000 in 1740 to 200,000 in 1760, while North Carolina's nearly doubled from 41,000 to 77,000 during that time. The Shenandoah Valley offered cheap land and fertile soil, much of which did not need to be cleared because of Indian burning practices that created "old fields." In Maine, settlers confronted a thicket of trees; in the Virginia backcountry, "large and rich Meadows" abounded, with "good Grass on the Uplands." The desire to acquire bigger and better farms in the Shenandoah was thus irresistible. Craig's Presbyterian parishioners, among others, became major landholders. Adult members of the Augusta stone meetinghouse owned an average of 2,363 acres. In the Tinkling Spring congregation, landholdings averaged 394 acres, still far larger than members could ever have aspired to in Scotland or Ulster.[57]

But as the next chapter shows in detail, land acquisition underpinned religious and cultural needs. Presbyterian migrants sought a better and more secure place to raise their offspring, a Scotch-Irish version of the English "competency." Many migrants were newly married couples looking to build their holdings. Yet they moved as part of a larger kinship and religious network. New arrivals settled near former neighbors and near relatives. In Craig's stone meetinghouse congregation, a core group of families—the Allens, Andersons, Givens, and Poages—clustered on the lower Middle River and the North River and took the lead in securing Craig's services while finding a temporary place to worship until the community could build the stone edifice on 27 acres donated by John Poage. The meetinghouse then became the physical centerpiece of a sprawling backcountry community of individual family farms. At the Borden Tract, which was southwest of Tinkling Spring on the James River, the McDowell and Greenlee families secured control of 3,000 acres, and they would gain even more land for every cabin they built. Members of the two families acted as land agents for the Bordens, recruiting kinsmen and former neighbors from Pennsylvania and Ulster. At Tinkling Spring, the leading families "appointed Commissioners to chuse & buy a plot of ground to build a meetinghouse upon it." One goal, according to a later petition, was to found a church based on "ye Constitution of the Established kirk of Scotland." The leaders attempted to find a central location for the rectangular log meetinghouse, which measured twenty-four feet by fifty feet. Located on a 110-acre tract, the church sanctuary was carved out of a large plantation owned by William Thompson. The earliest settlers—James Patton, John Lewis, and others—had taken out land patents along the Cowpasture and Calfpasture Rivers. Similarly, at the Opequon settlement in Frederick County, Virginia, north of Augusta, these Scotch-Irish settlers "worshiped together in a single Presbyterian congregation," according to historian Warren R. Hofstra. "The inner workings of the Opequon community were dependent on a complex of interrelated factors: family, kin, ethnicity, land, and congregation."[58]

The importance of an ethnoreligious identity to internal migration in pre-revolutionary America becomes even clearer when these migrations are compared with earlier ones in Scottish history. Scotland in 1603 was one of the poorest countries in Europe. Approximately the size of Maine (30,405 square miles), it was a small nation with a population of only 500,000, and it had few towns. Samuel Davies, who visited Scotland in 1754, was well aware of the country's poor reputation, and he expected little as he toured the country-side. "Scotland makes a better Appearance on the Way that we travelled than I expected," he offered, adding, "tho' there are a great many of the poorest Huts that I ever saw." John Ray also was not impressed: "The ordinary country houses are pitiful cots, built of stone and covered with turves, having in them but one room, many of them no chimneys."[59]

Scotland's soil was poor, and farming was difficult. While English husbandmen in Kent and East Anglia were enclosing their farms and modernizing their methods, Scottish farmers clung to their old "infield-outfield" system. The infield, as the name implies, was closest to the farmhouse, and it was the most intensively cultivated, usually for oats and bere, a form of barley. Farmers used the outfield for pasture and to grow oats, a crop that placed fewer demands on the soil. Landholders plowed fields until the soil was exhausted and then moved on to another area of the infield until the infield itself was exhausted.[60]

Scottish farmers often teetered on the brink of ruin. One bad harvest brought hunger and financial calamity. Moreover, farmers' precariousness was increased by the fact that most did not own their land. One historian described the dangers of tenancy in Scotland: "The meliorating features of the English common law—common lands, common rights, copyholding, and customary tenancy—all were lacking in Scotland. Tenants held their lands only at the pleasure of the proprietors. Leases were rare and, where they existed, quite short, often lasting only a single year." Such a system meant that farmers had little or no incentive to invest in their farmsteads. They worked the soil until it was exhausted. When the infield was used up, the farmer would literally move on to greener pastures, often taking his house with him. Cottages were small and flimsy so that they could be put up or taken down in just one day. Living in such conditions, farmers rarely formed any attachment to their homes. In England and America, by contrast, the homestead became the family seat, with members showing great attachment to it. Fathers lovingly passed on houses and farms to their eldest sons.[61]

Mobility in Scotland was also encouraged by family structure. Unlike the English, the Scots favored a collateral rather than lineal inheritance system.

The English system of primogeniture enhanced paternal authority and emphasized the nuclear family. The Scots preferred partible inheritance, with all children sharing equally. High mobility rates and collateral inheritance practices led to wider kinship networks that strengthened social bonds. "Instead of forming lineal families with strong attachments to particular farms," historian Ned Landsman has observed, "Scottish families moved frequently from farm to farm, estate to estate, and parish to parish, maintaining ties to a wide group of kinsmen throughout their regional communities." Economic incentives and cultural norms thus loomed large in the initial migration to Ulster. From 1603 to 1700, one hundred thousand Scots made the approximately twenty-five-mile journey to Ulster. By 1630, they constituted 60 percent of Ulster's population of forty thousand, with particularly high concentrations in Counties Donegal and Tyrone.[62]

Economic matters also played a prominent role in the transatlantic migration to British North America, which began in earnest in 1718. But these problems were of a different nature than the ones of a century earlier. In Scotland in 1603, poverty induced struggling farmers to migrate to Ulster. In Ireland in 1718, the success of the Ulster plantation ironically helped lead to migration. Ulster and its Scottish inhabitants had mostly thrived. The region now had successful woolen- and linen-manufacturing industries, leading England's mercantile interests to fear their Ulster rivals. In 1699, the merchants persuaded the Irish Parliament to pass the Woolens Act, which barred the exportation of Irish wool and woolen cloth to anyplace except England and Wales. The act greatly hurt the linen trade as well and made it even more susceptible to downturns. The English Parliament, meanwhile, was steadily backtracking on the free-trade provisions of the 1660 Navigation Act. For example, with two exceptions, the Staple Act of 1663 barred Ireland from directly exporting any goods to the colonies. In 1671, Parliament further restricted Irish exports.[63]

Ireland's foreign trade suffered, and a depression followed. Between 1717 and 1718, linen exports to Britain fell from 2.4 million yards to 2.2 million, while yarn exports dropped by 25 percent. For all its success, Ulster still had a fragile and underdeveloped economy that was not strong enough to withstand the whims of foreign markets. At the same time, rents and tithes were rising, and a 1714–19 drought led to poor harvests. Food prices soared, while the supply of flax used to make linen cloth dwindled, adding to weavers' already great troubles. On top of these local problems, the kingdoms of England and Scotland merged in 1707, opening the door of the British empire wider to Scots and Scotch-Irish, who could now more readily migrate to

British North America. "There emerged," in the words of one historian, "a sense of new and creative intersections of the Scottish world with the worlds of England and America."[64]

The first large exodus to the New World occurred in 1718 and 1719; later waves came in the 1740s and the 1760s. During the early years of the transatlantic migration, some 80 percent of the Scotch-Irish paid their own passage; nevertheless, this migration shared some important characteristics with the later internal migration in America. In both movements, most migrants left with their families. And in both, migrating Scotch-Irish relied on kinship and religious networks. A vanguard led the way to the New World, sending back positive reports and encouraging kin to cross the Atlantic. One historian has found that more than half of the migrants aboard one ship, the *Newry Pacquet*, were related, and she concludes "that all immigrants, once they were established in the New World, were under strong family obligations to facilitate the subsequent transfer of relatives in Ireland across the Atlantic and to assist them after they landed."[65]

Religious motives also were present in the transatlantic migration. For complex reasons, numerous Presbyterian ministers were encouraging their congregants to undertake the ocean crossing. As the research of historian Patrick Griffin has shown, Ulster's Presbyterian community was struggling in the early eighteenth century. One small but important group of Presbyterians concluded that the growing market economy was leading to a decline in godliness and a loss of discipline among the laity. For these Scotch-Irish, the drought, the depression in the linen and woolen trades, and the general privation of the 1710s constituted a sure sign of God's displeasure. They thus linked economic hardship and religion and saw migration as a solution to these interlocking problems. Many ministers advised their congregants to leave Ulster's decaying society for the New World, where Presbyterians could get a fresh start in a land of toleration and plenty. The influence of ministers in the transatlantic migration was most apparent in the early popularity of New England as a destination. James McGregor, pastor of a parish in Ulster's Bann Valley, led his flock to Boston to "avoid oppression and cruel bondage, to shun persecution and designed ruin." Another minister promised Connecticut authorities that he would lead a hundred families to that colony if he could be assured that his charges would enjoy religious freedom. Many other congregations followed. In all, some twenty-six hundred Ulster Presbyterians migrated to New England in 1718 and 1719.[66]

However, the bulk of the migrants went to Pennsylvania, with the largest concentration of Scotch-Irish found in the Cumberland Valley. In this branch of the Scotch-Irish migration, commercial ties loomed far larger than congregational connections. The migrant trade to the middle colonies was an extension of the linen and flax trades, with ships carrying goods and immigrants. Humans thus became another cargo for merchants looking to make their runs between Irish and American ports as profitable as possible. New Castle, Delaware, at first served as the most popular port of debarkation but was overtaken by Philadelphia by 1750. Philadelphia then became a base from which new arrivals from Ireland fanned out into the interior. But regardless of where they first stepped on American soil, most Scotch-Irish migrants welcomed the chance to settle in Pennsylvania. One potential migrant from County Tyrone neatly summarized the colony's attractions: "The good bargains of your land in that country do greatly encourage me to pluck up my spirit and make ready for the journey." Another Scotsman in Ulster complimented his brother on his "safe Arrival [in Pennsylvania] with your Family out of A Land of Slavery into A Land of Liberty and freedom." Pennsylvania's reputation as a place where all could worship in peace was important to Presbyterians in Ulster. Migrants saw this colony, in the words of Patrick Griffin, "as a perfect Ulster, one where opportunity coexisted with religious freedom."[67]

By 1775, Scotch-Irish settlements had spread from their Pennsylvania base to the Delaware Valley, the Shenandoah, and the Carolinas, especially western North Carolina, where they comprised more than 60 percent of the population. As Scotch-Irish Presbyterians moved about, their church scrambled to keep up with them. Between 1750 and 1780, the number of Presbyterian congregations in America doubled from 250 to nearly 500. In 1774 alone, Presbyterians established eighteen churches in Virginia. In 1789, as a consequence of the geographically diffusing membership, the church divided into several synods: New York / New Jersey, Virginia, and the Carolinas.[68]

IMPULSES DEEP WITHIN the Scottish character—family structure, farming practices, religious beliefs—encouraged the Scotch-Irish to move about in America. Being a Presbyterian from Scotland or Ireland carried with it a host of cultural assumptions. In Scotland, English efforts to unify the national churches of the two nations only caused Lowlands inhabitants to cling ever more fiercely to their Presbyterianism. Their kirk became a way to resist their ancient foe to the south. In Ulster, Scottish colonists occupied a shaky middle ground between a hostile native Catholic population on the bottom and a tiny Anglican elite at the top. Once again, religion served as a defining marker for the Scots, and they carried this marker across the Atlantic. Although the experiences of Scotch-Irish settlers differed in the northern and southern colonies, the church again helped define who they were in the midst of great stresses (challenges from Puritans in New England) and internal conflicts (attacks by New Side evangelicals in the middle and southern colonies). These stresses only strengthened the migrants' ethnoreligious identity as Scotch-Irish Presbyterians.

Other faiths, in contrast, could dampen ethnic identity. Certain Evangelicals such as George Whitefield and ecumenical groups such as the Moravians discouraged ethnicity, instead preaching the overwhelming importance of becoming reborn. In creating strong communities of believers, they downplayed and even ignored nationality. Admittance was open to all who pledged allegiance not to a king or a nation but to Jesus Christ.[69]

The Scots and Scotch-Irish were different, tending to turn inward for complex religious and cultural reasons. They migrated within America not just to establish a new settlement but to establish a Scotch-Irish Presbyterian community. This desire linked seemingly diverse migrations within America. Even in Augusta County, the New Side / Old Side split was not enough to dampen this desire. The intertwining of ethnicity and religion meant that Presbyterians moved often, albeit for sundry reasons, including for more and better land.

In the end, all groups of Scotch-Irish Presbyterians thrived on the peripheries of empire. All sought a better life but did so among a widening kinship and religious network. Migrants settled near other Scotch-Irish, where they built their meetinghouses—log edifices in distant borderlands that were monuments as much to their mobility as to their God.

Land and Family

The Pietist Migration to North Carolina
in the Late Colonial Period

The Freys rode into Wachovia, North Carolina, on June 10, 1765, after a four-week journey from Pennsylvania. A wave of emotion likely engulfed them as the party—twenty-one people in all—surveyed the hilly countryside of their new home. These migrants surely felt tired after a monthlong trip that had subjected them to bad roads, swirling rivers, steep hills, and lonely wilderness stretches. And they surely felt relief that the most vulnerable among them—seventy-five-year-old Peter, the family patriarch, and fifteen-month-old Tobias, the youngest member of the Frey clan—had safely come through the journey. But they also must have entered Wachovia with heavy hearts: one member of their party, a single man accompanying the family, had drowned a few weeks earlier while helping them cross the treacherous waters of the Potomac River into Virginia.[1]

The strongest emotions may well have belonged to Peter. The father of this large brood had traveled the longest and farthest to reach North Carolina, and he had undertaken this journey at an age when most men would have been enjoying the quiet comforts of a porch rocking chair. Peter was born in Wingen, Alsace, on September 27, 1689, and had brought his wife and seven children to the New World in 1734 when hard times struck his native land. Frey settled his family in eastern Pennsylvania, in Berks County, where he and his sons took up farming.[2]

The Freys had arrived in Pennsylvania as religiously indifferent Lutherans but had seen the light after hearing a Moravian bishop preach on the saving grace of Jesus Christ and the liberating power of the new birth. The Moravian message struck them with the force of a thunderclap. It jarred and "awoke" them. The alarming message that they were unsaved and that their souls were in mortal danger carried such force that the Freys abandoned the cabin they had so recently built and moved to Heidelberg, a farming hamlet where they could participate in a growing Moravian congregation and learn how to be reborn.[3]

Picking up and moving for a third time must have been difficult for Peter. He was entering the final stage of his life (indeed, he died only a year after arriving in Wachovia), and he had already endured the rigors of a transatlantic ocean crossing. Yet he moved south to join a community belonging to a church of which he had never even heard a few years earlier.

His behavior raises several questions. One is quite basic: Why do such a thing? The Freys, after all, could have saved themselves the bother of a difficult migration and remained in Pennsylvania to farm and to worship at the Moravian congregation in Heidelberg. Or they could have moved to a farm near another congregation in Pennsylvania (as they had done before). But they rejected those options, instead heading south to begin life anew. What was it, exactly, about land that made the Freys pick up and move to the southern frontier? Their decision seemed to run counter to accepted notions of what a good Pietist should do. In the canon of Pietism, worshiping the Lord and reforming Christianity were always to come first. For the reborn Christian striving to lead a life of discipline and piety, didn't land represent something selfish—the desire of its holders to get ahead to make money? And didn't land represent individualism—a grasping for personal wealth at the expense of faith?

The Moravian experience provides insights into these questions and the complex role that land and family played in the migrations of religiously minded people in early America. As with Scotch-Irish Presbyterians and others, obtaining land was a means to achieve religious ends: migrants sought to provide for their families both economically and spiritually. These Pietistic migrants had joined the Moravian movement in the northern colonies and Maryland, had undergone (or had attempted to undergo) a new birth, and had become active members of this German-based group. Yet despite their decision to join a devout religious movement, they retained their family-based cultural values. They did not renounce marriage, as did some religious radicals, most notably at Ephrata. Nor did they turn their back on the world, as did some separatist Anabaptists. Traditional family life remained important to these Moravian converts.

Their views on family and land were critical in the decision to migrate to North Carolina. Generous land deals, intricate kinship connections, and Wachovia's unique religious community pointed them southward, as did complex conditions in their home congregations up north. Spiritually restless, land hungry, and deeply religious, the migrants did not hesitate to move in the two decades before the American Revolution.

Wachovia and the Moravian Movement

Land and the farmers who work it have long held an exalted place in the American imagination. For Thomas Jefferson, the real heroes of the republic were not presidents or senators or manufacturers or bankers but tillers of the soil. "Cultivators of the earth are the most valuable citizens," he wrote to John Jay in 1785. "They are the most vigorous, the most independant, the most virtuous, & they are tied to their country & wedded to it's liberty & interests by the most lasting bonds. As long therefore as they can find employment in this line, I would not convert them into mariners, artisans or anything else." Most Americans would have agreed with him about the importance of farm-ers. Land's strong hold on Americans cut across regions, ethnicities, and cen-turies. Indentured servants in seventeenth-century Virginia wanted it. So did Scotch-Irish Presbyterians in eighteenth-century Maine and westward-bound pioneers in the nineteenth. In between, Americans of all stripes looked long-ingly and lovingly at the frontier, where land could be had for the taking. In the great expanses of the North American continent, they would farm.[4]

Land dazzled the Freys, too. They crossed an ocean in the mid-1730s for the opportunity to purchase it. And purchase it they did: in Heidelberg, Penn-sylvania, they became major landowners, with the eldest son, Valentine, for one, owning 587 acres. They moved to Wachovia so that the next generation of Freys could partake in the bounty as well. But Jefferson's ode to land and farming would likely have puzzled them. The members of this Moravian fam-ily did not view land through the prism of enlightened Whig political philos-ophy and its benefits to a young America; they viewed it primarily through the prism of religious faith. Their move to Wachovia represented the opportunity to get land in one of the most unusual religious communities in early America. Puritan New England had its ordered villages, with steepled meetinghouses dominating town squares. Eastern Virginia had Anglican parishes, with stately brick chapels huddled on country roads near taverns or plantation houses. The Scotch-Irish Presbyterians had their log meetinghouses surrounded by family farms. Wachovia was something altogether different.[5]

Founded in 1753 by the Moravian Church, Wachovia was a well-defined ninety-eight-thousand-acre enclave in backcountry Carolina. The land it-self was quite beautiful. Rolling hills and streams dominated the landscape. Three major creeks and their tributaries snaked north through the heart of

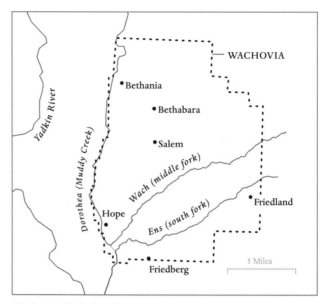

Wachovia, North Carolina

Wachovia—Muddy Creek to the west, the Ens (or South Fork) to the east, and the Wach (or Middle Fork) in the center. Well-ordered farms congregated around these waterways, with three European-style villages (Salem, Bethabara, and Bethania) off in the distance.

But what really made Wachovia unique was not any geographical feature but rather its inhabitants' commitments to "heart" religion and the sophisticated community that they had constructed. Wachovia featured an arresting blend of settlement types that reflected the complex goals of a religious movement pursuing a dual mission to reform Christianity. By the American Revolution, this Moravian colony consisted of approximately one thousand inhabitants living in six settlements scattered about seven miles apart—enough distance that each settlement had its own distinct personality, yet close enough together that they maintained a strong sense of community. Three of the settlements were congregation towns, known as *Ortsgemeinen*, that the church itself had founded: Bethabara (the staging area for colonization of the tract) in 1753, Bethania (a farm hamlet with stores and mills) in 1759, and Salem (the spiritual and economic capital) in 1766. In these ordered villages, with their quiet streets and Germanic architecture, the church restricted residency to the most devout members and instructed them to fully devote their lives to Jesus and the *Gemeine*. These "closed" congregation towns have enchanted modern tourists and given the Moravians a misleading reputation among historians as religious utopians who sought to keep some distance from the outside world. The church itself organized the migration to Bethabara from Pennsylvania, selecting who went and when. Once in Wachovia, members of an *Ortsgemeine* lived under strict rules: single members bunked together in choir houses; married members did not own their homes; and tradesmen practiced crafts regulated by the church.[6]

The bulk of Wachovia's population, however, did not live in the *Ortsgemeinen*. About 55 percent of Wachovia's inhabitants lived in the three *Landgemeinein*, an evocative German term that translates loosely as "farm congregations" and that hints at the complex mix of piety, land, and brotherhood that defined them. The Moravian Church did not begin the three settlements ringing the congregation towns; migrants from Maine, Pennsylvania, and Maryland, respectively founded Friedberg in the 1760s, Friedland in 1771, and Hope in 1772. In contrast to the *Ortsgemeinen*, these places were "open" congregations that served a critical role in the Moravian movement as missionary outposts that could introduce the Gospel to the "unborn," regardless of a sinner's church affiliation, ethnicity, or skin color. Here, seekers could choose whether to affiliate with the Moravian movement as Society (partial) members or as full members.[7]

The Moravians belonged to a Pietist movement that sought to spark a second Protestant reformation in the early modern period by leading adherents to a new birth. Based in early modern Germany, Pietism was a transatlantic phenomenon in which converts were expected to shed their worldly ways and turn instead to piety. Some of the reborn belonged to small radical sects that sought to save Christianity by separating from it, while others remained at their home churches to lead a reformation from within. The largest number of adherents could be found within the Lutheran and Reformed churches.[8]

The Moravian movement was the biggest, most influential Pietistic sect in the eighteenth century and one of the most ecumenical. Based in Herrnhut, Germany, the Unitas Fratrum (as the Moravian Church was formally known) was led by Count Nicholas von Zinzendorf until his death in 1760. The count espoused heart religion and pursued an aggressive missionary program. In 1727, the Moravians began sending missionaries to the Caribbean, Greenland, Africa, South America, Europe, and North America to work among blacks, Indians, and whites. In addition to trying to Christianize "heathens," Zinzendorf established the Diaspora, where Moravian missionaries worked to win over Christians of other sects and churches to heart religion with the very Pietistic goal of awakening spiritually dead worshipers. The count's highest hopes for this Diaspora were in the religiously diverse milieu of America, specifically in

Pennsylvania. In 1741, Zinzendorf crossed the Atlantic to oversee the development of the Moravian town of Bethlehem, Pennsylvania, and to help launch his American Diaspora. Twelve years later, the Unity founded Wachovia as a refuge for its European members and to generate income. Wachovia thus had a complex mission from the start. It was to make money; it was to provide a safe haven for the devout; and it was to pursue missionary work among both Indians in Georgia and unsaved Christians in backcountry Carolina.[9]

This mission appealed to awakened Society members in three places: former German Lutherans in Pennsylvania; former German Lutherans and Reformed in Maine; and English-speaking former Anglicans in Maryland. These Society members founded the three *Landgemeinen* and helped turn Wachovia into a vibrant place. The migrants came in family groups on their own initiative and at their own expense, unlike in the church-led migrations to the *Ortsgemeinen*. The settlers in the *Landgemeinen* established strong communities that featured centrally located meetinghouses—communities that said a great deal about why these people had chosen to migrate.

Life in the Landgemeinen

On January 7, 1770, Moravian minister L. C. Bachhof learned that "the dear Savior" had chosen him to serve as pastor of the new congregation that would soon be called Friedberg. Bachhof was then the minister at Bethania, a handsome congregation town in the far northwest corner of Wachovia. Bachhof's new assignment represented a return to a familiar place. In the 1750s, he had served as a missionary in the region, conducting services for white settlers interested in affiliating with the brethren. Ten days after learning of his new assignment, Bachhof and his wife arrived at Friedberg "to the heartfelt joy of the people waiting for us." With their arrival, the Bachhofs had reentered the intimate world of the *Landgemeinen*.[10]

Life there rested on the twin pillars of the plow and the pulpit. A visitor entering Friedberg by road from the south would have found no village center; the settlement had but one store and one tavern. Instead, he would have come across a sprawling backcountry community of family farms hugging the Ens, eventually spotting a modest meetinghouse in a small clearing near the center of the settlement. Friedberg's economy was based on agriculture (wheat and corn were the main crops) and the trades needed to support farming: blacksmithing, milling, teamstering. Water—and religion—helped define the landscape. The choicest settlement spots were along the river and near the meetinghouse. Sites along the Ens gave Friedberg's farmers the water they

In 1771, migrants from Maine established Friedland, a "long" village consisting of nine farms arrayed in a row. Each family received a rectangular strip measuring two hundred acres. (Courtesy of Friedland Moravian Church)

needed to grow their wheat and corn and easy access to the meetinghouse, which they often reached by canoe.

Hope, the settlement bordering Friedberg to the north, looked much the same, though it was even smaller, with no store or tavern. The inhabitants of Hope, too, lived on family farms along a river, this one known as Muddy Creek. A meetinghouse of logs and clapboard, built in 1775, stood sentinel on a hill. Both places could have passed for frontier Methodist or Presbyterian settlements: scattered farms clustered near a central meetinghouse. Not so Friedland, located several miles north of Friedberg and southeast of Salem. A visitor entering the third farm settlement would have been struck by its unusual appearance. Farms were not plopped haphazardly along a river; migrants from Broadbay, Maine, had constructed a true farm village. Wachovia's administrator, Frederick Marshall, admiringly described the place as a "long" village consisting of nine farms arrayed in a row. Each family received two hundred acres in one rectangular strip, with regularity intended to facilitate the creation of community. As Marshall explained, the settlers' had bought "adjoining farms, laid out in the form of a village, so that none shall be more than a quarter of an hour from the center, where they want to have a schoolhouse or church."[11]

Meetinghouses served as the spiritual heart of all three communities. Surrounded by a garden, picket fence, and God's Acre (the cemetery), the *gemeine Haus* was where members sent their children to be educated, their parents to be buried, and their families to be inculcated in God's ways. Built of logs and covered in clapboard, the meetinghouse also served as the pastor's residence and a community center—at least twice a week, on Thursdays and Sundays, settlers congregated to worship, to meet, and to talk, and other gatherings were held there throughout the year. On December 31, settlement members assembled for a general worship service, where prayers were invoked, songs were sung, and the past year was reviewed. In summer, farmers gathered for harvest love feasts, skillfully blending faith and work and allowing members to thank the Lord for the bounty he had provided. The *Landgemeinen* also held choir festivals, celebrated milestones such as the anniversary of the congregation's founding, conducted Easter services, and organized prayer meetings.

Schools were a spiritual home and place of learning for the youngest Moravians. Students devoted their mornings to learning how to read, write, and do math and spent their afternoons outdoors. Friedberg and Friedland's schools met four days a week from October to Pentecost, while Hope's met every day. In all the schools, pastors held biblical instruction at least once a week on "the saving truths of religion."[12]

Unity boards expected both Society and full congregation members to "wholeheartedly concern themselves with being cleansed of all sin through the Blood of Jesus. . . . They must constantly rely on the dear Saviour." *Landgemeine* members were expected to undergo the new birth and to devote their lives to Jesus. Brotherly Agreements, or codes of conduct, for each settlement cemented this requirement and specified that a settlement was to be a "living congregation of Jesus."[13]

Land, Family, and Migration

Religion, including a commitment to Lord Jesus, was thus the main glue that held the *Landgemeinen* together. But kinship and family were vital, too, underpinning the religious mission and influencing the actions of the *Landgemeine* settlers in complex ways. Kinship helped determine where migrants settled. It helped influence who joined the church and when. And, most of all, it helped determine who came to Wachovia. The strongest motivation to migrate belonged to parents, who wanted to raise their children in a tight-knit religious community where they could teach their sons and daughters about heart religion and pass on to them a love of the evangelical experience. Parental efforts to achieve this ambitious goal were overarching and involved a multipronged strategy that included migration to Wachovia from colonies north of North Carolina; carefully devised inheritance practices; and education.

At bottom, migration was a way for parents to securely anchor their children in the religious haven of a Pietist sect. Families migrated to the three *Landgemeine* settlements and then assiduously built up their landholdings in the late eighteenth and early nineteenth centuries. Parents needed land in or near Wachovia to give to their sons and in many cases daughters. Landholdings, as a result, were large, averaging 200 acres and up in the *Landgemeinen*. In Friedberg, the largest landholders averaged just over 1,000 acres, while the overall average was 265 acres; in Friedland, the average was 224 acres. In Hope, the largest holdings averaged 705 acres, and the overall average was 181 acres. Moravian fathers believed that proper bequests of land could help keep their children nearby. This reasoning resembled that followed by Quaker parents in the Delaware Valley. The families of both religious movements sought to avoid the experience in Puritan New England, where younger sons were forced to move to start families and get farms of their own.[14]

That families in the *Landgemeinen* followed this strategy is evident from comparing the actions of those brethren with children and those without. Abraham Hauser (1761–1819) worked as a farmer, mason, and tavern hostler. He married in 1786 and by 1799 had five children, including four sons. In August 1800, less than a year after his last son, Martin, was born, Abraham bought 126 acres on Peter's Creek in Wachovia for the boy. In 1813, Abraham purchased a 198-acre plantation on Brushy Fork. He held the property for three years before dividing it and selling halves to two of his sons, Jacob and Timothy, for six hundred dollars apiece. With the exception of a 212-acre tract that he bought in 1805 and sold in 1809 at a hundred-dollar loss, all his purchases were for family purposes. The timing of the purchases was telling. The Brushy Fork plantation was purchased just a few years before the two middle sons reached their majority; when Abraham sold them the tract, Timothy was twenty-one and Jacob was twenty-three. In contrast, another member of the Hauser clan, Frederick Hauser (d. 1807), had no children and purchased no land, unlike the rest of the large family. He bequeathed his entire estate to his wife, Elizabeth. Although other factors may have played a role, the absence of children appeared crucial. Childless brethren of middling means lacked the incentive to participate actively in the land market.[15]

An ethnically diverse Wachovia had two types of inheritance systems, partible and impartible, both of which rested on conceptions of the "perennial family" that sought to tie the generations to land and family. German-speaking Moravians in the *Landgemeinen* tended to favor partible inheritance, while English-speaking settlers preferred impartible inheritance, but members of both groups shared the desire to provide sufficient incentives for their children to stay on family land. Under the impartible system, the home place became the property of one heir, while other children received bequests in the form of cash or "movable" property. Under partible inheritance, the land and movable property were divided equally among the heirs, although in America, one heir would often get the home place. Both systems sought to keep family farms running efficiently while allowing parents to retire comfortably. In southwestern Germany, where the movement was strong, Pietism did not make significant inroads into these traditional practices. One of the family's essential functions in an agrarian society remained the transfer of assets between generations.[16]

The abundance of land in America meant that German-speaking Moravians could maintain the principle of partible inheritance yet avoid the problem of having family farms divided until they became so small that they were no longer economically viable. Parents in Wachovia bequeathed the home place to one of their children while helping others obtain large farms of their own. In only 19 percent of cases did estates in Wachovia sell the main farm at the death of the father.[17]

Jacob Miller of Friedland was a typical German-speaking Moravian settler. During his lifetime, he gave his eldest son, John, 250 acres, while his other three sons received tracts of about 218 acres. One daughter received 203 acres as a dowry. When he died in 1796, his will decreed that the rest of his property be sold and the proceeds divided among the three remaining daughters. The children with land were to pay the other three money if the sale failed to raise enough cash for division among the heirs. All of Miller's children received equal portions, but the sons and the daughter who married were favored with land. In most instances, daughters received money or livestock as a dowry or inheritance.[18]

By bequeathing land to their offspring, parents tied their children to a strong religious community that stressed an all-absorbing commitment to Jesus Christ. Young brethren would go to Moravian schools, attend Moravian church, socialize with Moravian neighbors, and marry Moravian spouses and farm Moravian land. The important role of land and family in the *Landgemeinen* made Unity leaders nervous, however. They feared that the pursuit of land could undermine religious commitment by encouraging materialism. And they feared that by amassing large landholdings and becoming active in the land market, members could stray from the church and from the Lord, as was occasionally the case. The church never resolved this dilemma. Understanding that the *Landgemeinen* rested on land and family and knowing full well that Wachovia needed to succeed economically, Wachovia's leaders decided to make land affordable by offering generous lease-purchase agreements to cash-strapped buyers and by allowing individual family farms. Unity leaders had initially planned to restrict settlement in Wachovia to thirty-five European-style "villages of the Lord" populated by full church members, but the sect abandoned those plans in the early 1760s.[19]

At the same time that they were encouraging the purchase of land and the economic development of Wachovia, leaders repeatedly admonished members to put Jesus first and preached that the family was an extension of the *Gemeine*, "a little church of Jesus." In the battle to remain true to the Savior, families were to serve as one of the first lines of defense. Spouses were to support each other and to keep one another from backsliding. Most of all, parents were to help instill a love of the Savior in their children and to teach them to be good Christians. "The main Matter in the Children's Education is chiefly this," Unity elders agreed in 1775, "to let the Children from their Cradle know nothing else, but that they exist for Jesus." Count Zinzendorf stressed that families existed for the sake of children. Although schools played an important role in young Moravians' religious education, Unity leaders placed far greater responsibility on the shoulders of parents. Wachovia's pastors and church boards expected parents to serve as exemplars for their children and to inculcate in them a love of Jesus.[20]

The home thus had to function as a small church, where devotions and prayers were to be as important a part of the family's day as chores in the morning and meals together in the afternoon and evening. With its formation in September 1780 to oversee the *Landgemeinen*, the Land Arbeiter Conferenz took on the encouragement of home worship as one of its first tasks. "Since there is a great lack of home devotions in the families in the country, it should be explained to them that they . . . are expected to hold the Morning and Evening Blessings in devotions with their families." The conference expected *Gemeine* families to show even more "faithfulness and diligence therein so that they set an example for the others."[21]

Most of all, the church expected households in the *Landgemeinen* to adhere to strict standards of conduct. Parents were not to allow young boys and girls to mingle or to permit such worldly activities as dancing and drinking in their homes. In addition, parents were to avoid quarrels, slander, and other signs of an "irregular life." The institution of the family, congregational pastors concluded, represented one of the best ways to counteract such temptations.[22]

Cultural and religious imperatives exerted fairly intense pressure to construct strong families in the *Landgemeinen*. Men were expected to marry and set up farms, and women were expected to serve as their husbands' "helpmaids." Both the Unity and individual brethren in the *Landgemeinen* viewed marriage as an important stage in the life cycle. When young men turned twenty-one, fathers owed them the chance to set up independent households, and those who did not do so faced criticism. Wachovia's Land Arbeiter Conferenz was upset to learn in 1780, for example, that "Peter Pfaff [of Friedberg] for various selfish reasons has not made up his mind to establish his son, who is already twenty-six years old." This failure, the board continued, involved more than the rights of a child to land; it threatened the piety of the Pfaff family, since the presence of an adult child at home could upset the entire household's morals.[23]

Kinship networks and the church became intertwined and mutually supporting. The selection of baptismal sponsors, or godparents, for children became an important way to strengthen kinship and thus the family and the congregation. Parents in the *Landgemeinen* selected neighbors or friends to serve as spiritual complements, using godparenthood as another layer of support to help them raise their children in the Lord's ways.[24]

An analysis of Friedberg's baptismal sponsorships from 1774 to 1778 shows that adult siblings often turned to each other. In 1774, Peter Frey, the son and namesake of the seventy-five-year-old who had made the long journey to Wachovia, and his wife, Catharina, named their son after Peter's brother, George, and chose him as a baptismal sponsor. Three years later, Philipp Rothrock chose his brother, Peter, and his wife as godparents for his newborn son, George. Such decisions acknowledged the love between family members and tied relatives closer to the stem family by giving them a vested interest in their nieces' and nephews' welfare.[25]

Most parents chose two to five sponsors, relying on a mix of kin, friends, and immediate neighbors to create a dense network of fictive kinship that radiated across Wachovia. In numerous instances, Friedberg's families selected godparents from Salem, Bethania, and other congregations. Closer to home, expatriates from Yorktown, Pennsylvania—the Pfaffs, Rothrocks, Hahns, Eberts, and others who settled on Friedberg's upper farms—turned to each other for support when their children were born, routinely selecting their neighbors as godparents. Such a step further drew together these families and provided a fitting recognition of their already deep ties.[26]

The selection of baptismal sponsors also helped to tie together migrants of different origins, including bridging the ethnic gulf between English and German, and thereby tightened the bonds of community. The families from Heidelberg, Pennsylvania, including the Freys, Volzes, Graeters, Holders, and Staubers, mingled regularly with the Hartmans, Spachs, Mullers, and others living in southern Friedberg near the *gemeine Haus*. Close working relation-ships in the congregation, as well as intermarriage between families, made such alliances normal and natural and created enduring friendships.[27]

These ties of family and kinship played a large role both in the migration to Wachovia and the settlement process. Close contacts with former family and friends sustained the exodus to this *Landgemeine*. Friedberg residents regu-larly sent wagons to Heidelberg and other Pennsylvania communities, usu-ally in late fall, after the harvest had been brought in. These wagons carried agricultural goods, letters, and encouragement. Returning travelers brought Friedberg residents "many cordial greetings from Pennsylvania, not only from brethren and sisters but also from their friends, and told them many stories." One wagon from Yorktown groaned under the load of nine packages of let-ters and German newspapers.[28]

The Freys traveled as a family unit and financed their migration by selling their Pennsylvania lands. Their plans to leave elicited no offers of help from authorities in Bethlehem or from their congregation pastor. Indeed, church authorities in Pennsylvania barely took notice of the Freys' departure. Con-gregational diary entries recording the family's departure were, without ex-ception, brief and to the point: "The old Peter Frey and his son Valentine Frey, with their wives and eleven children, along with their son-in-law and daughter, left for North Carolina," read one entry. When the family arrived in Wachovia in 1765, settling in Bethabara or Bethania was never a realistic option. They instead looked to the South Fork, where their former neighbors from Pennsylvania were congregating. Migrants to Friedberg sought tempo-rary shelter with relatives or old neighbors while they hunted for a home site in Wachovia. And they initially asked kin and friends for assistance in find-ing land. Former neighbors showed arrivals the area, advised them regard-ing a tract's availability, and explained the financing options available from the church. Networking in the *Landgemeinen* resembled the process common among Lutherans and other German-speakers in the New World: settlers in Friedberg followed a collective strategy, with fellow brethren providing vari-ous kinds of advice and assistance.[29]

In choosing farm sites in Friedberg, Marylanders tended to settle near other Marylanders, and Pennsylvanians near Pennsylvanians. Former Yorktown residents lived on Friedberg's "upper farms," a group of at least five farms covering the settlement's northern reaches.[30] In the lower farms, the earliest arrivals to southern Wachovia—a group of former Lutherans from Mono-cacy and Heidelberg, including the Freys—dominated the area just outside the Wachovia line. George Hartman, Adam Spach, John Muller, and Peter

Frey owned tracts of at least two hundred acres south of the site where the Friedberg congregation constructed its meetinghouse in the late 1760s. Moravian authorities observed the settlement process with some wonderment. "The settlement of the Tract and its Lots is a difficult proposition," Wachovia administrator Frederick Marshall said in the mid-1760s, "but I must say this: the migration of men are like the movements of a flock of sheep, where one goes the flock follows, without knowing why."[31]

George Hahn arrived in Friedberg in September 1770 and pondered his options. Needing advice, he turned to Christian and Peter Frey, acquaintances from Pennsylvania, to learn about the availability of land in that settlement. The Freys sent Hahn to Salem to meet with Marshall. Hahn explained his needs—accessibility to water, church, and friends—and Marshall promised Hahn and his family that "a homesite with a spring would be picked out for them near the meetinghouse." On October 14, Friedberg's pastor showed the Hahns the various available tracts, and "they chose the one closest to the *gemeine Haus*, on Wachovia's land," the pastor reported. The Hahns immediately went to work carving out a farm. Only one day after choosing a site, the Hahns began "blocking up" their log house; with help from neighbors, the dwelling was finished by October 19, allowing the Hahns to move out of the "little private" room in which they had been staying at the meetinghouse.[32]

On another occasion, Johann Bockel approached pastor L. C. Bachhof after the conclusion of a *Singstunden* (singing hour) "and expressed his regret that he lived so far from the schoolhouse and therefore could not always take part in the worship services. Therefore . . . he was firmly resolved to leave his place immediately, just as soon as he could get another piece of land near the schoolhouse."[33]

The Migration to Wachovia

Land, family, and religion combined to produce the prerevolutionary migration to Wachovia. The 261 settlers who traveled to the North Carolina *Landgemeinen* in the 1760s and 1770s moved as extended families, linked by kinship and religious ties. They hailed from three locations: Carrollton Manor in Maryland (whose English-speaking settlers founded Hope); Broadbay, Maine (whose German-speaking settlers founded Friedland); and southeastern Pennsylvania (whose German-speaking settlers founded Friedberg). In those three places, the *Landgemeine* settlers were introduced to Moravianism, developed Moravian identities, and became devout members. Religious and economic conditions in their home congregations contributed to their decision to come to Wachovia.

All the migrants were products of Count Zinzendorf's ambitious Diaspora, which formally began on July 15, 1742, when Bethlehem sent out its first wave of missionaries—ten itinerants in all—with the goal of bringing "unchurched men and women to a saving knowledge of Jesus Christ." Traveling on horseback, Moravian missionaries visited remote and scattered German- and English-speaking settlements, where they performed baptisms, held worship services, and preached. Moravian itinerants during this first decade concentrated on Lutheran, Reformed, and other church settlers because of suspicions about the Moravians' intentions. Under the supervision of Bishop Augustus Spangenberg, the Diaspora produced swift results. By 1748, the Moravians had established strong presences in at least thirty-one Pennsylvania and Maryland communities, gaining more than a thousand adherents.[34]

In Berks County in the early 1740s, Zinzendorf helped spark interest in heart religion among German-speakers and others. Lutheran settlers at Heidelberg were especially impressed, and in 1742 they asked the Unity to supply them with a preacher. A member of the count's traveling party, Gottlob Butner, agreed to remain and work with the Lutherans and others, including members of the Reformed Church. In March of that year, Butner delivered his first sermon to a large gathering, an event that the congregation marked as its beginning. In 1743, the Lutheran settlers formally requested that a brother and sister "be sent to live with us here, to administer to our needs, and the school." Bethlehem dispatched Anton Wagner and his wife in January 1744, and they opened a school and began holding religious services. Diaspora members began clearing a site for a meetinghouse in August, and in November, they asked the synod for permission to organize a Moravian congregation, stressing to the elders that "while they were Lutheran and Reformed, they had a desire to be a congregation of Jesus without name." By 1745, the fledgling congregation enjoyed a membership of seventy-six, including fifty-three children. In the 1750s, the Frey family joined the group when the struggling Moravian congregation at Muddy Creek disbanded.[35]

Farther south, the same process was occurring among English-speaking Anglicans at Carrollton Manor, in the Monocacy Valley in western Maryland's Frederick County. Carrollton Manor was part of a substantial empire amassed by Charles Carroll the Settler, who accumulated money, slaves, and property after emigrating from Ireland in the late seventeenth century. Carrollton Manor was one of the family's largest and most lucrative holdings. Charles the Settler's son, Charles of Annapolis, inherited the manor in the 1730s and decided to develop the 12,553-acre tract not by deploying slave labor but by using tenants to farm individual tracts of about 100 acres. That way, the Carrolls would see their lands developed and improved without the family incurring the massive expenses involved in acquiring and maintaining a large slave force. Charles recruited tenants from as far away as Ireland and Germany, but most came from eastern Maryland. As one chronicler concluded, the strategy proved "enormously successful," with the son negotiating nearly two hundred leases and putting more than 19,000 acres into production.[36]

The manor constituted an English-speaking enclave in the German-dominated Frederick County. Before 1773, German-speakers constituted less than 10 percent of the manor's population, while the county itself was about 50 percent German. Most Carrollton tenants were Anglicans, but a recent historian of the manor found none of their names on the All Saints Parish register. Other faiths did little better. The Quaker community north of the manor had stagnated, and only a handful of tenants were Friends. Many of the tenants who affiliated with the Moravians recalled having spent childhoods in a religious wilderness. Mary Padget, for one, told a Moravian chronicler that as a child, "she did not get the least learning or any instruction in the Christian faith . . . but had grown up in the greatest ignorance and stupidity." Culturally, the area was a complex mix of the Chesapeake, with its slave-oriented tobacco plantations, and the grain-based family farms of Pennsylvania. The typical Moravian family owned a slave, grew tobacco, and cultivated several grains on a family farm of about 100 acres.[37]

That these families got to hear the brethren preach at all on the manor largely resulted from the efforts of the longtime steward at Carrollton, Joseph Johnson. Johnson, who was responsible for collecting rents and enforcing leases, had been raised in England, where he was exposed to evangelical religion and "awakened." He subsequently "lost this received Grace by being enamored with this World" but became "stirred up again by reading Mr. [George] Whitefield's evangelical sermons" and began to worry anew about the salvation of his family and servants. Unsure what to do, Johnson talked with a member of the Moravian congregation in northern Frederick County that became known as Graceham. Johnson asked the brethren to send missionaries to the manor and offered the use of his house for preaching. The Moravians accepted the invitation, but the pastor at Graceham, J. M. Zahn, spoke only German. Bethlehem had no trouble finding English-speaking missionaries who could converse with Carrollton's tenants, however, sending in these early years more than ten missionaries, including Bishop Spangenberg, Richard Utley (who later pastored the fledgling Hope congregation in North

Carolina), and George Soelle (who later pastored congregations in Maine and in Friedland). In 1762, the Provincial Synod in Bethlehem assigned Francis Boehler to visit the manor about once a month, a task he performed for the next four years. As the Moravians' popularity grew, Bethlehem granted the manor a formal congregation in 1766 and sent Joseph Powell and his wife to minister full time to its members.[38]

For the Moravian church, a worldwide organization engaged in missionary work among Christians and non-Christians alike, Carrollton Manor represented yet another opportunity to spread the word of Jesus' saving grace. The prospect of ministering to an English-speaking population did not trouble the German-based brethren. Instead, it was appealing, because they viewed the manor as a religiously apathetic place. Establishing a congregation at Carrollton would shine "a Light in a dark place, that thousands by Her light may See and joy in Her, and with Her find Shelter, Covert [Comfort], and Refuge in Jesus' Wounds." Powell viewed his mission in similar terms. After four years of careful work on the manor, the reverend described his congregation as a "Candle on a Hill," drawing the unconverted to the Savior by setting an example and teaching them how to be saved.[39]

The arrival of these evangelists from a German-based church aroused intense curiosity on the English manor and, in time, some hostility. Curiosity drew William Barton Peddycoard, to a sermon given by a missionary from the Moravian *Gemeine* at Lititz, Pennsylvania. The missionary, Brother Sydrich, preached from John 1:9–12 on the true light. With little exposure to organized religion, William found the missionary's message intriguing, although it stirred up a host of conflicting emotions in him, ranging from excitement over the prospect of attaining eternal salvation to fear that he would be unable to achieve a new birth: "The discourse made a great impression on my heart, yet I did not understand all the phrases." The concept of a "true light" especially puzzled him. But William's curiosity was so aroused that he returned to hear more about his lost state and how he could escape it by turning to Jesus.[40]

On a small manor with a weak church structure, the Moravians rapidly became a force with their radical message that all true followers of the Savior could achieve salvation. During their first few weeks on the manor, the Powells stayed with a tenant named Zimmerman and held meetings at the man's house. Listeners crammed the front room, and Powell marveled at the diversity of attendees—Baptists, Anglicans, Catholics, and Reformed Germans. The pastor described one such gathering as "very extraordinary," with "the power of God truly attending the Gospel word." Powell traveled throughout the valley, both on and off manor lands, holding meetings wherever inhabitants expressed an interest in hearing him preach. In late August 1766, when a large crowd gathered in Frederick for court, someone sent word that the visitors wanted to hear Powell preach. He arrived promptly at the house of Noodley Masters along the Potomac, about twelve miles from his residence on the manor. The crowd was so large that Powell had to move the meeting outdoors, where Masters set up a "table under a large Tree in the field under which they sat close together on the grass entirely filling the shade." From a rustic pulpit by the tree, Powell preached from Kings 2:5–13 on God's judgment of Ahaziah. By September, Powell believed that he was making good progress: "One perceives a moving and awakening by Some, by others love and good will desiring to be better acquainted with us." Within a few years, the Moravians had become the most successful church on the manor, and about one-fifth of all tenants had become converts.[41]

For many manor residents, congregational life was a family affair. When one family member joined the Moravians, others in that family followed. The Peddycoards were typical, with William, the oldest son, taking the lead in bringing religion to his kin. With his encouragement, his mother and siblings joined, as did other members of the growing Peddycoard clan. Sophia Elisabeth Peddycoard, the wife of William's brother, Basil, was raised as a Quaker but learned of the brethren through the activities of her husband and brother-in-law. "The gospel of the atoning sufferings and death of the Savior for us soon made such an impression upon her that the Holy Ghost was able to convict her of unrighteousness." In 1767, she became quite worried about her unsaved state, approaching Powell "in tears, desiring we'd visit her" to satisfy her "earnest desire" to be baptized for the first time. Such feelings had begun "at her first awakening about four weeks prior."[42]

Powell tried to make the Moravian presence felt in tangible ways by becoming involved in tenants' daily lives. He helped residents raise barns, build houses, and husk corn. He regularly crisscrossed the manor, visiting members and nonmembers alike, offering advice or lending a sympathetic ear to the troubled. Powell also turned his attention to building a meetinghouse that would enable the congregation to function properly and give him and his wife a place to live in some comfort—eighteen people lived at the Zimmermans' house. In August 1766, the Powells moved into a home owned by congregation member Matthew Markland, and other congregants donated furniture for the couple, enabling them to escape their cramped circumstances at the Zimmermans'. Although the new accommodations offered the Powells more room, Markland's house was relatively isolated, "not lying so convenient for the people as hithertofore." Ironically, the Powells now lived among the manor's tiny German-speaking population. The reverend promptly introduced himself to his new neighbors, but, in a further irony, none expressed an interest in participating, "all as yet seeming satisfied with thare Religion."[43]

Despite the improvements to his living circumstances, Powell still reasoned that a meetinghouse was badly needed as a concrete symbol of the Moravians' commitment to the manor. Moreover, a commodious and centrally located meetinghouse would presumably allow the pastor to build a more durable congregation, since it would have sufficient space to preach the Word and to conduct school and meetings. In 1768, Powell and Johnson turned to Charles Carroll for help. Johnson and fellow member John Padget hand delivered a letter to the esquire in Annapolis that laid out the need for a meetinghouse and asked Carroll to donate a tract. Carroll rejected the plea, dismissing the two messengers with the declaration that "there was Religion enough already in the world." Undaunted, Powell authorized construction on the desired tract without Carroll's permission.[44]

On September 27, twelve men gathered to begin building a meetinghouse that was to be thirty-two feet long by twenty feet wide. The men felled and squared fifty-eight logs, and Powell noted that they "all labored with such love and willingness as one likes to see." In early October, Powell suspended construction while Johnson again pleaded with Carroll to donate the tract for Moravian use. This time, Carroll was in a friendlier mood, although he peppered his steward with questions about the German evangelical sect that was proselytizing on his manor. On October 3, Carroll finally agreed that the brethren could use the ten-acre tract "for the consideration of a rose per year" for twenty-one years. The men resumed work the next day, laying the bottom logs for the building just a week later. Sixteen men, with supportive female congregants in attendance, then "raised the Chapel in readyness for the frame of Rafters." The roof, two chimneys, and fireplaces were finished on November 13, and on December 3, the Powells moved into their new home, using Markland's wagon to haul their furniture. Powell described the meetinghouse as "finely Situated on a Town Road, with each necessary convenience." Carroll, too, approved, telling Powell that "through your Industry, it by far is the neatest, prityest on my Manner."[45]

Some county residents, including Daniel Smith and Elizabeth Goslin, found congregational life so appealing that they moved to the manor solely to be closer to the brethren. Smith, a fisherman and a tobacco farmer, lived along the Potomac about eleven miles from the manor. He became acquainted with the brethren well before Powell's arrival in 1766, likely having heard a

NORTH ARKANSAS COLLEGE LIBRARY
1515 Pioneer Drive
Harrison, AR 72601

missionary preach in the area. According to Powell, Smith was a "loving friend" who persuaded the pastor to come and preach before deciding "to move from thence and settle near us." In January 1767, Smith kept his promise, and Powell helped the family raise its new house. Goslin, a widow since 1763, also attended Moravian preaching in her neighborhood and underwent a new birth that saw her develop "trust in her heart." She told Powell that she wanted to "leave the Dark neighborhood wherein she lives and move here amongst us." In November 1770, she relocated to the manor with her family, "purely to be nearer the sound of the Gospel."[46]

Despite all these positive developments, however, congregational life at Carrollton Manor was suffering by 1772. Powell was tired after a lifetime of missionary work and was eager to retire and return to Bethlehem because his wife was dying. In May of that year, Powell, himself in bad health, asked elders in Bethlehem to let them return to Pennsylvania. After six years at the manor, he explained, "we not only are become quite Old, and near the close of our Days, but seem also to have become something Old to our hearers." Powell hoped that a change in leadership "might Occasion a fresh stir, or an awakening in the Neighborhood." Our auditors, he noted sadly, were "becoming fewer." The dampening of congregational enthusiasm, combined with the Powells' impending departure, influenced both the vanguard's decision to emigrate and its timing. A move to Carolina represented a chance to recapture the spark that had brought the founding families to Moravianism. Led by Daniel Smith and the Goslin family, four families left in the spring of 1772 to begin an English-speaking settlement in Wachovia that bordered Friedberg.[47]

Land, of course, was critical. In Wachovia, these Maryland tenants would have a chance to own farms in a more religiously stable environment and to acquire enough land to bequeath holdings to their heirs. In late 1772, Wachovia's administrator, Marshall, helped Smith select tracts and arrange financing that allowed his family and the other Marylanders to purchase farms. Smith, who lacked the cash to buy land, took out an indenture with Marshall on December 21, 1772, for 221 acres. Marshall offered Smith the standard terms for leasing land in Wachovia with an option to buy. Smith was to pay an annual rent of 6 pounds, 2 shillings, 9 pence sterling. The purchase price for the land was to be 110 pounds. The leases for Smith and the others allowed the Marylanders to apply 1 shilling per 20 shillings toward the purchase price, plus 5 percent interest. Marshall gave the Marylanders ten years to come up with the purchase price instead of the usual three or seven years. As a further incentive, the Marylanders could clear as much land as they wanted for building and fencing, "together with full Liberty of hunting and ranging upon the Premises."[48]

In contrast, leases at Carrollton Manor contained no options to buy. After 1750, tenants leased their tracts "at will," meaning that they relied on oral, probably annual, agreements that were renewable at the will of the landlord. Rents had risen steadily, increasing from 8 shillings, 4 pence sterling for every hundred acres to more than 6 pounds in the 1760s. Not surprisingly, the Moravian tenants found Wachovia's lease-purchases enticing. Church chroniclers explicitly noted that John Jacob Peddycoard, for one, moved his family to North Carolina not only for religious reasons but so that "they might also get Land on better terms."[49]

The Marylanders moved south both as a congregational unit and as extended families: kinship linked three of the four original families. Goslin was Smith's mother-in-law, and Smith's sister had married into the third family that traveled to Wachovia. Blood ties induced less enthusiastic family members to make the trek south, since staying with family was preferable to being left behind in Maryland. Other congregation members soon followed the Smiths and Goslins, and with each departure, the struggling Carrollton Manor congregation weakened. With membership and interest declining, Bethlehem decided not to send a missionary to replace the Powells, to the great disappointment of the remaining congregants. The decision sealed the congregation's fate; its demise in 1773, in turn, forced others to leave.

The migrants stressed different aspects of these related developments. John Padget moved to Wachovia only because all of his neighbors had left. A leader in the congregation since its founding in 1766, Padget had deep Maryland roots. In August 1772, he and several others in the congregation wrote plaintively to Bethlehem's elders, imploring them to send replacements for the Powells: "We trust and hope, Dear Brethren, that your compassion and tender love will still reach us, furder favoring us with a Brother and Sister, who shall continue the ministration of the blessed, saving Gospel." Padget and the others characterized the departure of the members to North Carolina as a blow. But the bigger setback, they pointed out, was "to have the saving power of the blessed Gospel withdrawn from us."[50]

With no missionary on the manor, Padget felt he had no choice but to go south so that his children would not be left abandoned in a religious wilderness. In addition, the news that former neighbors were building an English-speaking Moravian settlement in Wachovia increased the appeal of a move to the south. The first four families were augmented by three families in 1774 and seven in 1775. By 1780, when Bishop Johann Friedrich Reichel stopped at the old meetinghouse at Carrollton Manor, he found a desolate scene. The building was in "ruin," and Johnson and the Schau family were "the only Brethren still living at Carrollton Manor, the rest have moved away."[51]

For Moravians in Broadbay, Maine, a move to Wachovia represented a chance for their children to grow up in a safe haven where they could prosper materially and spiritually. In Maine, the settlers lived on the Waldo Patent, near the Medomak River, which widened at one stretch into a "broad bay." In 1732, Samuel Waldo, the Boston agent for a Hamburg merchant house, had sent his son to Germany to seek migrants to settle on their patent, promising one hundred acres to every man who made the treacherous transatlantic journey. By 1760, one thousand settlers had accepted the offer. In 1742, the first Moravian in the area, George Hahn, a single man from Herrnhut, arrived at Broadbay, where he found a mixed population of Scotch-Irish and Germans. Hahn was not a missionary, but he became one because of the barren religious scene he encountered. "At the place where we lived there was neither school nor church, so a group gathered around me of those who were concerned for their own and their children's salvation," he recalled. He held prayer meetings and love feasts and preached in the parlor of his home. As a result of Hahn's efforts, "the desire of the people to come under the care of the Moravian Church grew daily stronger."[52]

The response to Hahn's impromptu evangelizing was so strong among the Germans (but not the tight-knit Scotch-Irish) that the Unity dispatched missionary George Soelle to begin ministering to the settlers; in 1762, he became their regular pastor when the settlers formed a congregation and built a meetinghouse. Soelle's tenure on the Maine frontier was difficult, however. Some Society members of the Reformed persuasion had hired a pastor from New York to minister to them. When the pastor arrived, he objected to Soelle's presence. Settlers divided over the two pastors, and the dispute became so fierce that the followers of the Reformed pastor had Soelle and Hahn arrested in May 1762.[53]

Poverty also bedeviled the struggling and divided congregation. The people, Soelle wrote, "are as poor as church-mice, and the land is not rich. . . . They all have large families: they cannot plow, and if they wish to sow rye, they must use the hoe to stir up the soil." To add to the settlers' misery, they learned in the 1760s that their land titles from Waldo were worthless and that their leases were nonbinding. Congregation members concluded that their prospects were poor on all fronts.[54]

In 1767, a discouraged Soelle and other Unity leaders debated abandoning Broadbay and urging the congregation members to relocate elsewhere in New

England. They considered establishing a congregation on the Kennebec River, but the plan held little appeal to Broadbay's members, who feared that they would not be able to acquire secure land titles. Bishop John Ettwein of Wachovia visited Broadbay in May 1767 and told congregation members of North Carolina's virtues, including "its genial climate and fertile soil." Soelle returned from a trip to Bethlehem to "find a large number of them bent on removing" to Carolina because of its powerful religious and economic attractions. Soelle advised congregation members to move cautiously because of the need to plan carefully and thoroughly for a difficult move south. Ettwein could offer encouragement but no practical assistance. Nevertheless, persuaded that moving to North Carolina was in their best economic and spiritual interests, the settlers pressed ahead with their plans in 1768.[55]

Migrants left Broadbay in two main waves. In 1769, a vanguard including Hahn and six families bought passage on a ship headed to Wilmington, North Carolina, and hurriedly departed. Their journey was harrowing. Their schooner sank off the Virginia coast during a storm, and the survivors became ill after reaching the port of Wilmington. Several died. Moreover, Wachovia's administrators were not expecting them. Because of their lack of planning, the first arrivals waited for the second group to arrive in Wachovia before making any moves. The second group, which included fifty settlers and was led by Soelle, arrived in 1770. The Broadbay settlers then decided to stay together, although several families opted to move to other settlements within Wachovia. The migrants chose a site several miles north of Friedberg and southeast of Salem, where they built their "long" village, whose heart was the centrally located meetinghouse.[56]

Hahn spoke for many when he succinctly described his motivations: "Our children are going to ruin; we want to live near a congregation of Brethren." Similarly, Catharine Rominger's parents moved her family to Wachovia because they were "desirous of seeking the salvation of their souls and mindful of the everlasting happiness of their children." The settlers chose to name their new community Friedland (the land of peace) because they hoped to be free of the hostility of their neighbors. According to Soelle, the migrants "honestly wish to be farther from the tumult and temptations of the world, that in quiet they may learn more of Him." Of the three North Carolina *Landgemeinen*, the settlers who began Friedland had the strongest desire to live and farm in a Pietist haven apart from the world.[57]

The settlers who created Friedberg did not suffer from the internal congregational problems that plagued the founders of Carrollton Manor and Broadbay. Nevertheless, religion, land, and family stirred the Pennsylvanians in nearly identical ways, as the wanderings of Lutheran Matthias Wesner demonstrate. Wesner was born in Stuttgart, Germany, in 1730, came to Pennsylvania in 1758 for reasons that are unclear, and later joined the Moravian congregation at Emmaus after hearing the brethren preach. Wesner worked as a tailor, started a family, and constructed a house in Emmaus but struggled financially. In 1771, he decided to move his wife and five children to North Carolina "to improve his outward circumstances." But family and religious factors were also decisive: he turned down an offer of land from his brother because it was sixty miles from Wachovia—too far for his family to worship with the brethren. Instead, Wesner settled in Friedberg, where he planned to work as a farmer and tailor "until he could turn the farming over to his son Jacob." The move to Wachovia thus represented a chance to worship with like-minded Pietists as well as to obtain enough land to provide for his heirs.[58]

Although the migration from Pennsylvania to North Carolina was dominated by family, the congregation also played a role in the founding of Friedberg. Word of Wachovia's virtues spread among members of congregations in Pennsylvania, especially at Heidelberg and Yorktown, and some of the migrants had served as missionary helpers in Pennsylvania, accompanying the pastor during his rounds, talking with people in the field, and regularly conversing with congregants. Much information about conditions in Carolina was exchanged during these visits. Future migrants also observed firsthand the passing of *Ortsgemeine* travelers. For instance, Bernhard Adam Grube and a small party of brethren left Bethlehem for Wachovia on October 8, 1753. Their first stop was Heidelberg, where the congregation "rejoiced to greet us once more," providing food, clean beds, and companionship. These encounters increased Pennsylvania Moravians' awareness of events beyond their borders and helped pique their interest in emigrating.[59]

Friedberg's settlers moved in six waves: 5 migrants left Heidelberg, Pennsylvania, in 1755, and the numbers grew quickly, peaking in 1774, when 40 left from York, to bring the total to 111 migrants in nineteen years. Emigrants came primarily from two Pennsylvania congregations, York and Heidelberg. Although the migrants traveled without formal church assistance, they took advantage of the elaborate Moravian network that had been developed in 1753 to facilitate the long journey from Bethlehem when the church founded Bethabara.[60]

Moravian congregations served as stopping points in Pennsylvania and Maryland. In Virginia, where the Moravians had failed to establish a presence, travelers relied on friends of the Unity for food, lodging, and other as-

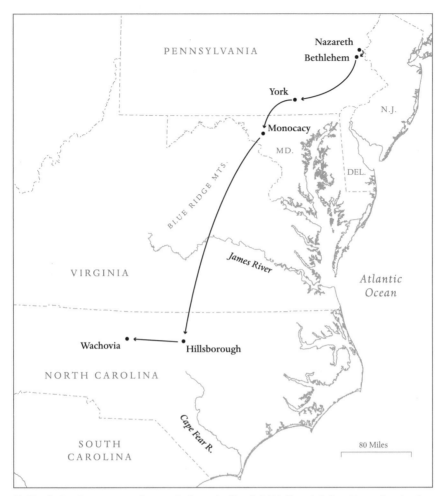

To North Carolina, 1760s and 1770s: Settlers who founded Friedberg left from Pennsylvania; they stopped at Moravian congregations as they headed south and traveled east of the Blue Ridge after entering Virginia.

sistance. The Freys' route to North Carolina was typical. From Heidelberg, they headed to the Moravian congregation in York and then on to Monocacy, where a German-speaking Moravian congregation existed near the Carrollton settlers. From there the Frey party crossed the Potomac River and headed south through Virginia. Unlike other backcountry migrants, the Moravians did not travel the Great Wagon Road that ran just west of the Blue Ridge Mountains to Salisbury, North Carolina, the seat of Rowan County. Moravian travelers followed an easterly route that took them through Leesburg and across the Rappahannock, James, and other rivers farther south. The trip took the Freys four weeks: they departed Heidelberg on May 10 and arrived at the South Fork of the Yadkin River on June 10.[61]

For most Moravian migrants, Wachovia represented the final stop in a restless search for spiritual and familial fulfillment. Before arriving in Wachovia, Friedberg's settlers had been the most restless: 86 percent of its prerevolutionary residents moved at least twice, and 46 percent moved more than three times. In Hope, 23 percent of the settlers moved more than twice during these years. In the smallest of the three congregations, Friedland, only 8 percent of settlers moved more than twice.[62]

Pennsylvania's Moravians exhibited greater mobility as a consequence of the greater number of religious and economic options available to Society members there. During the 1740s and 1750s, Pennsylvania was the center of American Moravianism, giving members great choice in joining congregations. Friedberg's founders thus moved periodically to establish closer ties to neighboring congregations, to improve their economic opportunities, or for both reasons. Broadbay's residents had lower mobility because they had few options as a result of the paucity of Moravian congregations in New England. Settlers from Carrollton Manor fell into the middle because they had more choices available than Moravians in Maine but fewer than Moravians in Pennsylvania. Brethren who moved did so to be closer to the congregation or to head to York County, the site of another strong Moravian presence.

With such a robust local Moravian presence, why did Marylanders and Pennsylvanians opt to go to Wachovia? The answer is land. Wachovia's leaders abandoned plans to restrict development to thirty-five European-style villages populated by full church members in an effort to create a vibrant Pietist community that could reach its fullest potential as a religious and economic enterprise. Because the original concept proved both unworkable and unpopular, the church decided to allow both full and Society members to purchase land on individual farms. In addition, during the 1760s, administrators began offering generous land deals to spur development, enticing would-be migrants with the pitch that they could get farms on easy terms in a religious community endowed with abundant land, water, meadows, and woodland. Although the Unity did not directly help migrants move, it welcomed their arrival as a boon to Wachovia's economic and spiritual development, and it encouraged settlers to relocate to North Carolina.[63]

These land deals clearly underlay migration. Settlers in Heidelberg could have remained with that congregation or chosen to move to a neighboring Moravian village, like so many other Moravians of the time. Broadbay's settlers could have started a new congregation elsewhere in New England or relocated to Pennsylvania. The bulk of Carrollton Manor's residents could have followed the handful of their neighbors who went to nearby York. Yet all of these settlers spurned their local options in favor of Wachovia at precisely the time when Wachovia's administrators offered land deals to newcomers and when land prices were rising in Pennsylvania and Maryland.

PARENTS' DESIRE TO ANCHOR their children in a religious community contrasted sharply with those of "secular-minded" migrants. The Moravian migrations to North Carolina did not involve landless sons heading to the frontier on their own in search of farms; it involved parents and their children moving to a religious community where they could participate in religious life. Families did move around before settling on Wachovia, but it was not a mindless search for land or riches or personal "independence." Nor were these Moravian migrants middle-class "liberals" who placed material gain over a greater public good. They belonged to a religiously motivated movement consisting of an ethnically diverse people who had primarily been members of the Anglican, Lutheran, and Reformed faiths.[64]

The reborn of all faiths shared a restlessness. Like Devereux Jarratt and other seekers, these Moravians wanted to experience the new birth and then lead the disciplined lives that being regenerate required. Land and family dampened this restlessness: when parents acquired enough land to provide for themselves and their heirs in the religious community of their choosing, they tended to stay.

The motivations of most Anglicans in eastern Virginia more closely resembled those of nonreligious migrants than of the Moravians and Puritans. Poorer Anglican Church members moved constantly to get land, but they lacked religious motivations for doing so. Many were former indentured servants struggling to gain financial independence who did not particularly care where that land was located, in large part because of their different religious environment. Virginia's Anglicans belonged to the state church, established by law and enjoying the backing of the civil government. Chapels existed across the colony (although the church struggled to keep up with population growth), and migration entailed leaving one state-established parish for another. Thus, unlike the Moravians in the *Landgemeinen*, Anglicans lacked the incentive to move to a more appealing religious community.

Historian Susanne Mostelle Rolland has noted that mid-eighteenth-century Pietism served as a unifying force among German speakers in Pennsylvania. Migrants to western North Carolina, she concludes, relied on networks of kinship, religious inclination, and friendship in establishing new communities. These Germans' moved south primarily to acquire land.[65] Mennonites, too, treated land, family, and religion holistically, moving from southeastern Pennsylvania to the Virginia frontier in the mid- and late eighteenth century in search of cheap, fertile land where they could establish new congregations and safely raise their children. Similarly, Quaker families in southeastern Pennsylvania used land as a tool of religious commitment.[66]

The dynamics of inter-American migrations varied somewhat among different religious groups. The pull of a unique religious community played a greater role in the *Landgemeinen*, for example, than it did for Pietistic settlers moving to western North Carolina. Despite these differences, land, family, and religion worked together to produce migrations both near and far.

CHAPTER FIVE

Reform and the Missionary Drive

Methodists in the Ohio Country

In an 1802 letter to his brother, Philip Gatch sounded the trumpet call for Ohio. "The Countrey is beautiful in its situation and promices every advantage," he began. "I am settled about Ten miles distance from the Ohio [River] and about Fifteen from Cincinnatta a Flourishing Town. . . . I believe we shall not want for trade in this Countrey." The land was rich and the water supply was superb for both milling and farming. But Ohio's greatest virtue, in Gatch's view, was its labor system. "We have no Slavery as yet among us. Some whish for it but I hope God will never permit it. I Pray against it, and talk against it."[1]

Gatch's crusade against slavery had begun years earlier, in the 1780s, when he was living in Virginia. He manumitted his nine slaves and urged his neighbors in Buckingham County to follow his example. Most did not, and Gatch and thirty-five others decided to migrate to the Ohio Country in 1798. Their departure signaled the start of a small but telling migration that saw several hundred Virginia Methodists move to Ohio to escape the stain of slavery and to establish Methodist societies on a free-soil frontier. These migrants believed, as Virginian John Sale put it, that the Ohio Country was a "Garden of God," a place where pilgrims could cultivate the Lord's ways, free from the soul-wrecking phenomenon known as slavery. Conversely, they viewed Virginia as "a land of oppression" and scolded those who stayed behind for "tarry[ing] in Sodom." For Gatch, the move represented a chance to save his children. He loved Virginia, he confessed to his brother, "but I felt unwilling to lay my Bones there, and leave my Children whom I tenderly loved in a land of slavery."[2]

As this band of Virginians was making its way to the midwestern frontier, Ohio was attracting another kind of Methodist migrant exemplified by Alfred Brunson. In 1808, he set out alone for the Ohio Country to escape his sinful life in Connecticut. Like Devereux Jarratt, the Anglican itinerant in mid-eighteenth-century Virginia, Brunson was young and a bit naive when he departed for the western frontier. He was only fifteen and had no money saved for the six-hundred-mile journey, and he had no firm plans about what he would do once he arrived in the Northwest Territory. However, he did possess a desire to change his life. Methodist itinerants had convinced him that he was a sinner badly in need of reform. By migrating to Ohio, Brunson concluded, he could get a fresh start and a chance to turn his life around. He would quite literally embark on a new path that he hoped would carry him to a new birth and to a career as a Methodist itinerant.

James Finley could have identified with Brunson's travails. But Finley was not a New Englander; rather, he was a child of the western frontier who, from an early age, ranged between Kentucky, where he was born in 1780, and Ohio, where he escorted his father's freed slaves, drove cattle, and hunted bears. Finley was the offspring of a strict Presbyterian minister who put the fear of God into his questioning, sometimes rebellious son. From a tender age, Finley asked probing questions about God, faith, and salvation but found no easy answers. Instead, his search resulted in a peripatetic existence that carried him to Ohio, to Methodism, and, like Brunson, to a new life as an itinerant.

These migrations involved Methodists from different states and entailed journeys undertaken for different and quite personal reasons. Yet varied as they were, the migrations arose out of a common impulse: a reforming spirit that sought to transform antebellum society in some way. Itinerants such as Brunson and Finley sought religious fulfillment on a personal and societal level—they wanted to save themselves and the people around them. Itinerants lived on the road in a relentless effort to convert people, to spread the Methodist faith, and to lead a reformation of behavior. At the same time, Methodist reformers were tackling a host of causes, including temperance and slavery. The Virginia migration was part of this effort; when Methodist abolitionists failed to change the slave system in their native state, they moved.

The experiences of Brunson, Finley, and the Virginians thus highlight another important aspect of the Protestant migratory experience: the impact of reform on religious migrations after the American Revolution. Reform spurred mobility much as land and ethnicity had previously done for the Moravians, the Scotch-Irish, and others. In essence, the itinerants and the Virginians moved to the frontier to get a fresh start, just as Thomas Hooker's Company did in 1636. But important differences distinguished these migrations. Mobility grew in importance in the early national period, and its relationship to reform became more complex than in earlier periods. Seventeenth-century Puritans feared separation and moved only as a last resort because they believed that migration would harm religious life in their home communities; nineteenth-century Methodists had no such worries. Instead, they saw mobility as a way to achieve reform both for themselves and for their evangelical cause. A reformist drive and mobility, in other words, combined to propel Methodism in the years following the American Revolution; itinerants and individual members alike led a vigorous expansion that saw Methodism become the largest Protestant church in America.

Methodism was quite literally a church on the move. It prospered in a mobile world, and it fed off the massive movements of people and ideas that accelerated in the early nineteenth century. The sources of this heightened mobility were not hard to find. The Revolutionary War had ended. Land west of the Appalachian Mountains had opened to settlement. A new national constitution had been approved, ushering in a new era of democratic and economic expansion—Thomas Jefferson's famed Empire of Liberty. The Midwest—specifically, the Ohio Country—profited from this expansion: Ohio's population rose from 45,365 in 1800 to 230,760 ten years later to nearly 1,000,000 by 1830. Neighboring Indiana enjoyed a population increase nearly as dramatic, from 24,520 in 1810 to 343,000 in 1830.[3]

Methodists—most notably their horseback-riding itinerants in Ohio and elsewhere—were products of this nomadic world and understood it intimately. Churches still grounded in a colonial-era ethos struggled to keep pace with a bustling and growing nation, especially as population spread to the vast North American interior. Methodists moved quickly to fill the void left by other churches, understanding that itinerancy and reform provided the keys to meeting the needs of a frontier people hungry for spiritual comfort and community. They grasped the idea that the opposite of mobility was stasis: to stay still, anchored to a home church, was to wither as a reform movement and die.

Mobility, as a result, enabled Methodism to expand to unprecedented heights, both benefiting from and contributing to migration. Taking to the road, Methodists spread their Arminian message that salvation was available to all. The path to salvation and a new life, they said repeatedly, was there for the taking. All one had to do was to get moving.

The Reforming Spirit, Part I: The Antislavery Impulse in Virginia

Philip Gatch served faithfully in the Methodist ranks as a preacher and deacon, winning praise for his talent, leadership skills, and devotion to the evangelical cause. He went on to become a justice of the peace, a judge, and a delegate at

Ohio's Constitutional Convention. But his two most memorable accomplishments were ones he undertook with a heavy heart: he was an early leader of the antislavery cause in Virginia, and he was one of the first Methodists to protest slavery by migrating to the Ohio Country. Born in Baltimore County, Maryland, in 1751 on a 130-acre farm, Skidmore's Last, he became a Methodist in 1772 and a "local" preacher in 1773. He married Elizabeth Smith a few years later, settled down in Powhatan County in southeastern Virginia, and took up the harried life of a planter and preacher. Gatch, who inherited nine slaves from his wife's family, grew cotton and corn; he preached, according to a friend, twice on Sundays, "attended many funerals, [and after becoming ordained as a minister] frequently administered the ordinance of baptism and the rites of matrimony," turning his house into a "retreat" for fellow Methodist ministers.[4]

After about five years in Powhatan, Gatch moved to nearby Buckingham County for a mundane reason: a neighbor wanting to create a millpond had built a dam, causing the stream that crossed Gatch's property to pool near his house. "My wife, fearing it would cause sickness, and the danger of the children being drowned, became dissatisfied, and we moved two miles to a place I had purchased," he recalled. This move represented an "inconvenience, as it was farther from the Church than our late residence." Yet "our new neighbors were principally Baptists, and were very friendly. During our stay at this place, we were favored with a gracious revival of religion, both in the Methodist and Baptist Churches." Gatch thus tried to make the best of the situation. His new home was located on a thousand-acre parcel; he farmed five hundred acres and made "such other improvements as were calculated to render my family comfortable." He hoped, he said, to live out his days in Buckingham.[5]

Living in a slave society gnawed at Gatch, however, and he was particularly embarrassed that he had come to possess slaves through his wife's family. Gatch's discomfort with slavery resulted from his strong religious bent as well as the lofty ideals of the American Revolution. In the 1780s, he manumitted his slaves, drawing on the language of the Declaration of Independence and the Enlightenment to explain his decision: "Know by these presents, that I, Philip Gatch, of Powhattan county, do believe that all men are by nature equally free; and from a clear conviction of the injustice of depriving my fellow-creatures of their natural rights, do hereby emancipate" them. Beyond the humanitarian act of freeing nine enslaved human beings, Gatch hoped to set a good example to his neighbors. "I never felt favorable to slavery," he stated in his memoir. "Two of my brothers-in-law and myself liberated our slaves. I believe it caused others to reflect on the evil."[6]

Gatch was part of a small but growing antislavery movement in the South during the revolutionary period. The southern effort to abolish slavery was undergirded by the ideals of the revolutionary movement as well as evangelism. The contradictions of the times were obvious to contemporaries. Many Americans took seriously Thomas Jefferson's ringing declaration that all men had been created equal, arguing that the ideal should apply to enslaved blacks as well. A number of evangelical Protestants, including Quakers, Baptists, Methodists, and a few Anglicans, were among those who questioned why slavery should survive in a land dedicated to democracy and human rights. A Quaker, Robert Pleasants, was instrumental in founding the Virginia Society for Promoting the Abolition of Slavery, a group modeled on a similar organization in Philadelphia. Gatch and his brother-in-law, James Smith, joined, with Smith serving as secretary.[7]

Other Methodists were equally outspoken opponents of slavery. John Wesley, the English founder and leader of Methodism, published a 1774 antislavery tract, *Thoughts upon Slavery*. In 1780, the Methodist Church in America held a conference in Baltimore at which it declared that "slavery is contrary to the laws of God, man, and nature." Five years later, the church's first discipline included a plank denouncing slavery as a violation of "the unalienable Rights of Mankind." The Virginia Society, meanwhile, met twice a year, petitioned Congress, and issued condemnations of slavery as "not only an odious degradation but an outrageous violation of one of the most essential rights of human nature, and utterly repugnant to the precepts of the gospel." The drive for freedom during the Revolutionary War and the evangelical assault on slavery achieved modest results. In 1782, Virginia legalized the manumission of adult slaves under the age of forty-five, and the free black population there totaled 31,570 by 1810, a tenfold increase since 1776.[8]

But the economic, social, and political forces opposing the nascent abolitionist movement were too great for the antislavery effort to make great headway in Virginia and other southern states. Planters in Virginia attacked the Methodist Church as pro-British and its members as enemies of property rights and persuaded the church to suspend the discipline's section on slavery. Back in Powhatan and Buckingham, Gatch's crusade against what he called "the evils of slavery" met with both hostility and indifference. Slavery was firmly entrenched, especially in Powhatan, where the black population outnumbered whites by approximately two thousand in 1790. None of Gatch's neighbors justified the practice," he lamented, "but most of them held the truth in unrighteousness." For Gatch, the 1780s and 1790s were a bittersweet time. Religion was spreading—"A gracious revival took place, and Zion was greatly enlarged," he reported with satisfaction—but he was making little headway on the antislavery front. Such a contradictory state of affairs left him in a quandary. Successful revivals, in Gatch's view, signaled the Lord's pleasure. His neighbors were gaining religion, and the church was harvesting souls. Yet these neighbors refused to do their Christian duty and act against slavery, a failure that left Gatch stricken and worried. The survival of slavery, he strongly believed, cast a dark shadow over all of Virginia society and threatened to bring divine retribution down on everyone. On a personal level, he feared for his soul as well as the souls of his eight children if he remained in Virginia. Gatch alluded to both fears when he exclaimed, "I could not feel reconciled to die and leave my posterity in a land of slavery."[9]

Gatch saw migration as the only way out of his dilemma. Moving to the Northwest Territory would remove his family from a slave society, and he could continue doing the Lord's work as a preacher while fighting the spread of an evil institution. Gatch's choice of destination was telling. Well before the Underground Railroad began operating and the intense sectional controversies had erupted, Gatch saw the Ohio Country as a place of freedom. The national government had barred slavery there, and the territory served as a dividing line between the free labor system of the North and the slave system of the South. Observers as varied as novelist Harriet Beecher Stowe and Frenchman Alexis de Tocqueville came to share Gatch's perception. Kentucky and Ohio "differ only in a single respect: Kentucky has admitted slavery, but the state of Ohio has prohibited the existence of slaves within its borders," Tocqueville wrote in the first volume of Democracy in America, published in 1835. "Thus the traveler who floats down the current of the Ohio [River] may be said to sail between liberty and servitude; and a transient inspection of surrounding objects will convince him which of the two is more favorable to humanity."[10]

Gatch had had his eye on the Northwest Territory for years, but until American troops took control of the immense territory from the Indians in late August 1794, he considered it too dangerous a place to take up residence. With the Indians' defeat at the Battle of Fallen Timbers, Gatch began planning in earnest for the migration. He had a willing partner in James Smith, another fierce critic of slavery who freed his slaves and wanted to leave Virginia. In the fall of 1795, Smith traveled to the Northwest Territory to begin scouting locations for settlement. In August 1797, he returned for a second scouting visit. With help from Methodist acquaintances in Ohio, Smith focused on the Little Miami River, just above East Fork, and the Virginia Military Reserve and its main town, Chillicothe. He reported glowingly on both areas. The

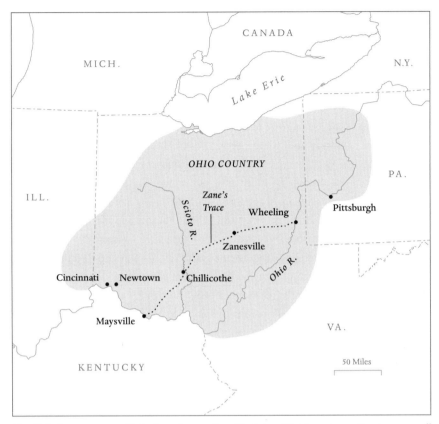

The Ohio Country, 1790s: Methodist migrants from Virginia settled in and near Newtown as well as on tracts north of Cincinnati.

land was spectacular, Smith told Gatch, and the soil excellent for farming. Fish were so thick in the rivers that schools of them could be spotted from fifty yards away. The forests teemed with bears, buffalo, and turkeys. Smith's report convinced Gatch that it was time to move his family to Ohio. "O what a country this will be," he wrote. "What a Paradise of pleasures, when these fields shall be cultivated and the Gospel of Christ spread through this rising Republic."[11]

In 1798, Gatch made one last-ditch effort to get his neighbors to join him. "Before setting out I met with a large assembly of my neighbors and acquaintances," preaching from Acts 20:25 ("And indeed, now I know that you all, among whom I have gone preaching the kingdom of God, will see my face no more"). The reception was chilly: "My neighbors opposed [migrating to Ohio] warmly. They stated to me, in glowing colors, the difficulties of the journey and settlement." Thus rebuffed, Gatch finalized his plans to leave, determined to press on without them.[12]

The Reforming Spirit, Part II: An Itinerant's Life

James Finley, too, ended up in Ohio, working for the Methodist cause. But he took a far more circuitous route to this frontier than did Philip Gatch. A frontiersman, hunter, and drover, Finley loved the good life and engaging in bone-jarring brawls. Yet he knew that such behavior was wrong, and he believed that he was risking the ire of a higher being. The son of a strict Calvinist Presbyterian minister from Kentucky, James had heard numerous lectures on the dangers of eternal damnation. "I was taught the catechism," James recalled of his childhood. "From this I learned that God, from all eternity, had elected some men and angels to everlasting life, and passed by the remainder, ordaining them to eternal death. This election and reprobation was unconditional." Such a cruel doctrine bothered him greatly. "Though young, I could not see the reason or justice of such a procedure on the part of God, and it gave me a very unfavorable impression in regard to the character of the Supreme Being."[13]

This questioning nature made him a dissenter, albeit a polite one. When his minister father asked whether James prayed, he responded no. Pressed to explain why, he defiantly said, "Because I do not see any use in it. If I am one of the elect, I will be saved in God's good time; and if I am one of the non-elect, praying will do me no good, as Christ did not die for them." Finley was unable to keep his doubts to himself, and word spread through his father's Cane Ridge congregation "that the pastor's son had become a renegade from the faith of his fathers. This brought me into a new field of conflict with older and wiser heads." Finley did not back down, however, engaging in sometimes heated debate with congregation elders. For his trouble, "I became very obnoxious to the high-toned Calvinists, and they looked upon me as very dangerous to their young people."[14]

Despite his outward assurance and defiance, Finley was scared "and harassed with doubt." He fell into despair; "sometimes I was led to doubt the very existence of God." Finley was not yet fifteen. His spiritual condition, he lamented, was "wretched." Thus, like Brunson, he embarked on an intense period of soul-searching and study. His conclusion must have upset his father: "If God had brought me into the world, without my consent, for his own purposes, it was no concern of mine, and all I had to do was be honest, enjoy life, and perform the errand of my destiny." In practice, this meant that Finley embarked on a carefree existence that surely must have further appalled his parents: fighting, dancing, carousing. If he was not saved and could not be saved, the minister's son reasoned, why bother to live a godly life?[15]

Yet Finley remained miserable. He knew he was sinning and living a life that, in his own words, was "thoughtless and wicked." He attempted to change his behavior but failed. Like Jarratt and other seekers, such unhappiness created a restlessness that carried Finley to Ohio, to Kentucky, and back to Ohio, working at various tasks, including surveying, along the way. But no matter what he did during these early years, he was unable to reform. Instead, he found himself drawn ever deeper into the Ohio Country and its endless forests. Finley was mesmerized by the Ohio frontier. "The clear and beautiful rivulet creeping through the grass . . . the gentle zephyrs freighted with nature's incense, pure and sweet, regaled our senses, and filled us with delight," he wrote. "All nature had a voice which spoke most impressively to the soul; and while all the senses were pervaded with an unutterable delight, the solemn stillness seemed to say, *God reigns here.*"[16]

By age twenty, Finley was a grizzled veteran of the wilderness. Accompanied by John Cushon, a Tuscarora Indian, Finley hunted bears, deer, and other animals, immensely pleased by the tracking and killing of game. He took to this life so completely that his "parents feared I would go off with the Indians and become connected with them," and they insisted he come home to Kentucky.[17]

Finley agreed to return to his father's academy, "enjoy[ing] the advantages of a thorough drilling in Latin and Greek." This bow to filial duty was just that—a bow to please his father. He never intended to practice medicine; instead, "my recreations were with the gun in the woods, or the gig in killing fish in the river. . . . At all the sports of these days I considered myself a full hand." After finishing his studies, the rebellious son returned to the woods in Ohio, "where I joined with three others and purchased a drove of fat cattle, and we started, in October, with them for the Detroit market."[18]

Finley might have continued on this path for a long time. He had married Hannah Strane over her parents' objections and seemed to be enjoying life in a dense wilderness as a hunter and part-time farmer, with his nearest neighbor three miles off. But try as he might, he could not shake off his conscience as he partook in the pleasures of the world. When Finley learned in August 1801 that a huge revival was under way at his father's old congregation in Cane Ridge, Kentucky, he decided to go. Finley had never been to a revival, but he had heard many wondrous things about them. "The excitement," he explained, "was one of the most intense and astonishing character." Some ministers ordered their congregations not to attend, warning that the revival "was the work of the devil." Such warnings "only increased the desire of thousands"— including Finley—"to go and see for themselves," he remembered.[19]

Finley told himself that he was going only to watch, vowing not to be swept up by emotion. He remained confident that his "manhood and courage" would keep him from "being overcome by any nervous excitability, or being frightened into religion." When he arrived at Cane Ridge, Finley nevertheless marveled at the scene before him. The crowd, which he estimated at twenty-five thousand, made a noise like "the roar of Niagara." Seven ministers were preaching at one time, and their exhortations had aroused "the vast sea of human beings." Finley immediately felt his resolve weakening and became overwhelmed by the scene before him. "I became so . . . powerless that I found it necessary to sit down. Soon after I left and went into the woods" in an attempt "to rally and man up my courage."

Appropriately bucked up, Finley returned, only to find the crowd worked into an even greater pitch of excitement. "At one time I saw at least five hundred swept down in a moment, as if a battery of guns had been opened upon them, and then immediately followed shrieks and shouts that rent the very heavens." Trembling, Finley fled again into the woods to compose himself.

His efforts failed, and he next went to a tavern for a shot of brandy. There, he found a hundred men "engaged in a drunken revelry, playing cards, trading horses, quarreling, and fighting." Finley was appalled, not just because of the men's behavior but because of the realization that he had always behaved just as badly. Finley left in a daze, trying to figure out where to go. The arrival of night brought no relief. "At times it seemed as if all the sins I had ever committed in my life were vividly brought in an array before my terrified imagination, and under their awful pressure I felt that I must die if I did not get relief."[20]

He had hit bottom. In the language of the seeker, Finley was undergoing vocation, the feeling of being utterly forsaken: "Then fell the scales from my sin-blinded eyes, and I realized, in all its force and power, the awful truth, that if I died in my sins I was a lost man forever." Despite this awful realization, Finley recalled his vow to avoid being swept away by the revival and decided to leave Cane Ridge altogether.

Though Finley returned home, he could not so easily return to his old life. He prayed and wept and read and talked as he struggled to deal with his inner turmoil. He retreated to the woods, where he felt most at peace. "O what a day it was to my soul!," he recalled of his moment of rapture. "The Sun of righteousness had arisen upon me, and all nature seemed to rejoice in the brightness of its rising. The trees that waved their lofty heads in the forest, seemed to bow then in adoration and praise. The living stream of salvation flowed into my soul."[21]

James Finley's rebirth changed his life in several ways. The hunter who had preferred the solitude of the forest now craved Christian companionship. His formerly idyllic frontier existence suddenly looked lonely: "There [were] no religious persons in the neighborhood, and no religious meetings to attend." Worse, "persecution began to be waged against me, and difficulties rose up on every hand." Feeling alone but in need of group support, Finley started family prayer and Bible study, but this remedy provided only a limited measure of relief. "I sighed for Church privileges, and communion with the people of God."[22]

He sought a church but "could not join the Presbyterian Church; for I did not believe in the doctrine of unconditional election and reprobation." The revival-minded New Lights turned him off, as did the Shaking Quakers, whose "worship seemed to be so ridiculous." Finley found himself "back sliding" into his sinful ways. Severe bouts of insecurity only added to his distress. Having undergone a rebirth, Finley felt the call to preach but he was too unsure of himself to try. He again retreated to the woods to pray, telling his "Maker, if I must preach the Gospel, or go to hell, that the latter must be my portion, as I had not the least qualifications for the work. Just then all comfort and hope left me." Three years passed before Finley emerged from this funk, time he spent "pursu[ing] the way of sin, seeking happiness in its guilty pleasures."[23]

In the fall of 1808, however, he nearly killed his brother, John, when James's gun accidentally discharged while they were riding on a narrow path. John fell from his horse, and James assumed the worst, but John was not hurt. The incident so scared James that he questioned his very being: "All my sins crowded upon me like so many demons of darkness; my disobedience to God, my backslidings all rose before me, and it seemed to me that hell was at just at hand, and that soon I must plunge into its dismal abodes."[24]

Depressed and plagued by thoughts of suicide, Finley received a visit from his brother, telling him that "I did not know what was the matter with me; but ever since the gun had gone off in the morning, I felt as if [my brother] should die and go to hell." Praying and reading the Bible produced no comfort. "My wife and friends became alarmed at my condition. . . . I thought I had committed the unpardonable sin." At this low point, a friend "put into my hands 'Russel's Seven Sermons.' This book I read with the most thrilling interest. . . . [I]t proved a balm to my wounded spirit. Hope again sprung up in my heart." And at this critical juncture, his wife persuaded him to attend a

Methodist prayer and class meeting, where he experienced a further awakening. The Methodists gave Finley a place to worship and the support to achieve and sustain a second rebirth.[25]

Finley had previously known little of the Methodists, but he saw their arrival in his life as providential. Intrigued by their powerful message of redemption for all, he first invited them to hold prayer meetings at his house and then began holding meetings on his own, drawing crowds of neighbors and relatives. Finley's meetings were so successful that a Methodist "circuit preacher came into our neighborhood, and formed us into a class or society," with Finley as the leader. Fighting nervousness and self-doubt, Finley called for a meeting at his house the next Sabbath. "When the day arrived, the whole surrounding country appeared to be on the move," he recalled. "The people came from every direction, and filled the house and the yard, and the lane leading thereto." Finley led the large crowd in a hymn and shared "what God had done for my soul, and how happy I was in religion." A few weeks later, Finley delivered his first sermon.[26]

Gatch's Journey and the Virginians' Migration to the Ohio Country

On a swath of the frontier several rivers and mountains removed from the Virginia countryside, the worlds of Philip Gatch and James Finley converged. In early October 1798, Gatch, Smith, and thirty-four members of their families and friends, including four former slaves previously owned by the Gatches, began the approximately 450-mile journey to Ohio. Gatch worried about the challenges ahead: "The way was truly a difficult and dangerous one. Many gloomy valleys, rugged mountains, and deep and rapid streams were crossed in our journey," he recalled. The migrants traveled in three wagons, each drawn by four or five horses; a "stage" drawn by four horses; a carriage pulled by two horses; and three horses for individual riders. The migrants took an overland route, moving northwest through Virginia's Campbell, Bedford, and Botetourt Counties before crossing the Blue Ridge and Allegheny Mountains, where steep and narrow paths forced the migrants "to use ropes to save our carriages from being dashed to pieces by the frightful precipices and jutting rocks which obstructed our path."[27]

After two weeks of travel, the party reached Boatyard, in western Virginia, where the migrants planned to buy a flatboat that would carry them north on the Kanawha River to the Ohio River and then west on the Ohio to Newtown. The migrants were unable to buy a flatboat, however, a development that Gatch considered a blessing in disguise because the river was low from the

Flatboats were a common sight on the Ohio River because of their popularity with migrants. The smaller ones were about thirty-five feet long, while the bigger ones could top one hundred feet. (Bettmann/CORBIS)

lack of rain and a flatboat would have been unable to traverse it. The settlers instead purchased two small boats and split into two groups. The women and children, along with some of the families' goods, rode on the two boats, while Gatch led the rest of the party, including their horses and their provisions, on an overland route that carried them north of the Ohio River to Chillicothe and then west to Newtown.

When the settlers in the two boats arrived at the Ohio River town of Point Pleasant, they purchased a flatboat for the final leg of the journey on the Ohio. These vessels, also called Kentucky boats, were flat bottomed and homely. The smaller ones were about thirty-five feet long, while the bigger ones could top one hundred feet. One traveler likened the flatboat to an ark made "of a clumsy construction. . . . Its foundation consists of sills like those of a house, and to these is trunneled a floor of plank. The sides are loosely put together, and the top is covered in the same way." A passerby was startled when he saw a flatboat for the first time. "I was alone upon the banks of the Monongahela, when I perceived, at a distance, five or six of these barges, which were going down the river. I could not conceive what these great square boxes were," he reported. "As they advanced, I heard a confused noise, but without distinguishing any thing, on account of their sides being so very high. However, on ascending the banks of the river, I perceived in these barges several families, carrying with them their horses, cows, poultry, waggons, ploughs, harness, beds, instruments of agriculture, in fine, everything necessary to cultivate the land, and also for domestic use." Clumsy as the flatboats were, they provided a modicum of comfort to their passengers. "Our floating houses," one migrant stated with some satisfaction, contained a shelter "divided into two apartments, [which] formed a very comfortable habitation for our family."[28]

The broad and serpentine Ohio River served as a natural highway for thousands of migrants. One early chronicler advised that the best time to traverse the river was in the spring and fall, when the water was at its highest and swiftest. "The banks of the Ohio are high and solid; its current is free from a thousand obstacles that render the navigation of the Mississippi difficult, and often dangerous," he wrote. "On the Ohio persons may travel all night without the smallest danger."[29]

The Gatch party was not so lucky, however. Early on, most likely because the Ohio was running low, the flatboat became impaled on a rock, a potential disaster that could have sunk the vessel and sent its passengers scrambling to shore and its goods to the river bottom. But Providence was with them: the boat was speared in the center and settled on the rock and did not sink, and the party members extricated themselves and proceeded. Gatch and his land companions had an uneventful trip, reaching Newtown a few days before those on the flatboat. When he learned of the boat's safe arrival, Gatch's "heart was dissolved into love and gratitude to God for his care over us on our journey, and bringing us safely into this desirable and distant land."[30]

The Gatches rented a house in Newtown, east of Cincinnati on the Little Miami River. They had arrived in Ohio with about seven hundred dollars, which Gatch invested in several tracts of land. He also owned another parcel that he "had taken in exchange for [his] farm in Virginia."[31]

Over the next decade or so, several hundred Methodist migrants from Virginia, as well as a few from Kentucky, the Carolinas, and Tennessee, followed the Gatches to Ohio. These newcomers settled primarily in the Little Miami River Valley, including Clermont and Greene Counties. The Methodist migrants were linked by their strong distaste for slavery.[32]

Born in Virginia in 1769, John Sale became an itinerant in 1795, acquiring a fierce devotion to Methodism and an equally fierce hatred of slavery. In 1807, he reported to his brother in Virginia that Ohio's residents "have a fertile soil & Sallubrious Air that is not contaminated with *Slavery*." Another staunch Methodist and critic of slavery, Peter Pelham, made the "tedious and fatigueing" nine-week migration from southeastern Virginia to Greene County, Ohio, in

1807. He saw his arrival there as a deliverance: "You have something of my happy feelings on setting my feet on a Land of *Liberty*. If ever you arrive here my dear brother," he continued, "may you and yours feel at least [what] I felt on that happy Day." The same year, Frederick Bonner saw the Ohio Country in biblical terms, writing that the call to come there was "LOUD. I know there are difficulties not only in preparing to start but also on the way; but thanks to the Lord there is no red Sea in the way; no phar[aoh]'s host to pursue us while traveling to the American Canaan." He likened the Ohio River to "our Jordan." Once the river is crossed, "our children are saved from the harmfull practice of trading on their fellow creatures."[33]

Most of the Virginia migrants came from Buckingham, Powhatan, Dinwiddie, and Greenville Counties, which arced across southeastern Virginia to the North Carolina border. Several migrants, including Bonner (b. 1759), were personally close to Gatch. The two men rode together on the Sussex circuit in the late 1770s. Another Gatch intimate, Bennett Maxey, attended the Powhatan revival, converted, and became an itinerant in 1788 before moving to Ohio in 1803.[34]

At least five families were from Dinwiddie County, and they all settled together in Greene County in the upper Little Miami Valley. In fact, the Virginians' closeness invited comment among visitors. When Methodist leader Francis Asbury spent the night with the Pelham family in 1807, "he reckoned he must come this way again it looked so much like old Virginia." Frederick Bonner, for example, had sold his land in Dinwiddie County in 1802 for two thousand dollars and used the money to buy two thousand acres in Ohio. In April 1803, the family set out for its new home in the Northwest Territory, joined in a group of at least thirteen people that included members of two other families. The party traveled in two large covered wagons drawn by eight horses, which carried their household goods and carpenter's tools; a smaller wagon carried the provisions. The Bonners settled near another relative on a tract two miles south of Xenia, where they hired young men to build a one-room cabin. In the fall, when the cabin was finished, "the family and four of their Virginia neighbors, who came west with them . . . moved into it," Frederick's son recalled. Intermarriage further linked these families when Peter Pelham's eldest son married a Bonner, a Pelham daughter married a member of another prominent migrant family, the Dromgooles, and so on.[35]

The migrants expended considerable time and effort trying to persuade other relatives and friends to join them in Ohio. They took two tacks. One was to tug at their fellow Virginians' consciences—they should leave behind a land tainted by slavery for a place where they could lead fulfilling lives under the watchful eyes of God and Methodism. In July 1807, Bennett Maxey urged his brother "in the Name of the Lorde" to come to Ohio; "you live in a land of Slavery and have your doubts whether it be right in the sight of God for you to die there and [leave] your children and grand children In that land of oppression, When there is a fare [far] more excellent place provided." Ohio, he noted pointedly, was a "good land Where That evil is not."[36]

The second tack was to stress the practical. As a newly opened frontier, Ohio offered unlimited opportunity. Maxey stressed that Ohio was "a helthy country. We have had but little or no sickness since I moved to the state." He added, "I'll tell you that there is the largest body of good land in this state that I ever saw anywhere and it is [of] a superior quality. You may do well by keeping a retail store in this country." Gatch concurred, telling his brother that "we shall not want for trade in this Countrey; . . . our Countrey is good for every kind of produce. . . . [T]he land is in common Rich and a great deal of it richer I expect than you ever saw." Pelham conceded that the migration to Ohio entailed "great sacrifice" but quickly added, "My wife, and our children *do wonderfully*, we had our Dinner yesterday, our supper last night and our breakfast this morning on a neat Cherry 4 foot square Table, and in neat and [much] better order than in old Virginia, and that *too without one black person to wait on us*. We Rest in peace, we Eat in peace & Glory to God we, in general, live in peace."[37]

The migrants also came to Ohio to spread Methodism and establish Methodist societies. After arriving in the Ohio Country, Gatch resumed his Methodist ministry, preaching in Newtown "and at two places on the west of the Miami river." But to Gatch's dismay, Newtown's residents "cared little for religion," and he decided to look elsewhere to settle; he wanted to be near other Methodists. His preaching tours brought him into contact with an acquaintance of James Smith named Francis McCormick, a Methodist preacher from Virginia who had come to Ohio in 1797 to escape slavery. McCormick had begun farming on a site on the Little Miami in Clermont County and formed a Methodist society there, and he invited Gatch to come to an adjoining tract. In February 1799, Philip and Elizabeth Gatch left Newtown and built a cabin and plunged into Methodist life in Clermont County. "Other considerations" involving land also helped induce Gatch to leave Newtown.[38]

Gatch had bought twenty-six hundred acres outside of Newtown sight unseen and discovered that they were "unsuitable for settlement. The land was covered with dense forests, inhabited by wolves, bears, and panthers, and the nearest neighbors were at least eight miles away." Thus, Newtown had proved unsatisfactory in terms of both religious life and land. For Gatch and the other migrants, the ideal settlement spot required both good land and proximity to friends and the Methodist meetinghouse. Another migrant, Edward Dromgoole Jr., described the importance of these factors in explaining his decision to move on from the first tract he had acquired in Ohio: "I was well pleased with this land in High land County but had by far rather live" on Brush Creek in southern Ohio. "The land is excellent here, good neighbours, christian friends meet[ing] convenient & this part of the country healthy and [we]ll watered. I shall next week close a bargain for land[;] the land contains 450 acres has two log cabbins on it and about 16 acres clear." He then declared himself content with his new home, reassuring his parents that "I expect to start to a Camp Meeting on Friday next within 4 miles of Bro. Bonners. I still feel bound to find my way to heaven and do what good [I can]. Pray much for me."[39]

Like James Finley, who no longer wanted to be alone after his rebirth, the migrants craved Methodist life and its elaborate support system of classes, preaching, and revivals. They moved to acquire it; once settled, they worked hard to build up a Methodist community, even when their mobility outpaced church expansion, which happened frequently in early Ohio, as Gatch described: "While we were without circuit preaching, we continued to exercise ourselves in matters of religion to the best advantage," he began. "The family of the Hills had moved to this country, and they were a praying people. Brother Ward, and also brother Whitaker, who afterward became a preacher, and others who were steady members, came to the country and settled among us. We kept up meetings similar to our quarterly meetings."[40]

These informal gatherings, Gatch said, led to a "great revival" within the settlement, "and a considerable number were converted, and our little Church rejoiced in the God of our salvation." Gatch hosted numerous meetings. In 1805, Asbury reported, "We held a meeting of four hours at Philip Gatch's: Brother Whatcoat's subject was 'Repent and be converted.' . . . We felt quickened and comforted in God." Gatch also hosted a camp meeting at which Asbury "saw many whom I had not seen for years—how delightful to see our old friends after a separation, and to find them still on the Lord's side!"[41]

The Lure of a Missionary Movement

In migrating to the Ohio frontier, in holding class meetings and revivals on their own, and in building Methodist communities, the Virginians were helping to spread the faith. Their activities brought them into close contact with

Methodist itinerants such as Finley and made them an important part of an energetic movement in which mobility and religion went hand in hand.

Such energy was the result of a remarkable religious phenomenon known as Methodism. Two English brothers, John (1703–91) and Charles Wesley (1707–88) founded the movement in the mid–eighteenth century. The Wesleys were Anglicans who displayed a religious bent from an early age. As students at Oxford University, they became inspired by the example of English Pietists and began holding prayer groups that sought to teach the ways of "holy living." In 1728, John was ordained as an Anglican minister and was elected to an Anglican missionary movement known as the Society for the Promotion of Christian Knowledge. Until the mid-1780s, he maintained close ties with the Anglican Church, but he was heavily influenced by the Pietist movement, particularly the Moravians. During the 1730s, the Wesleys learned much about heart religion and the structures that could nurture it: love feasts (special meals to promote brotherhood and love of Christ); choirs (bands of fellowship organized by age, sex, and marital status); and missionary work (most notably among wayward Christians). In the summer of 1738, John Wesley spent two weeks at the Moravian settlement of Herrnhut in Saxony studying the brethren and especially their communal living arrangements.[42]

Based on these and other experiences, John Wesley began developing ideas for his movement, which he envisioned as a reform conventicle that would work within the Anglican Church. Two ideas were central to his thinking: the need to conduct missionary work among the unchurched of England, Ireland, Wales, and later North America, and the importance of stoking enthusiastic religious experience throughout Christendom. Wesley, as one historian of Methodism has observed, "became a people's preacher, speaking and publishing in terms accessible to his frequently unchurched, poor, and laboring-class 'hearers.'" And speak he did, delivering some forty thousand sermons over the next fifty years, traveling nearly a quarter of a million miles in the process.[43]

Unlike their Anglican ally, George Whitefield, who was a Calvinist, the Wesleys retained the Arminian belief that salvation was open to anyone who sought it, and they developed a network of itinerant preachers to spread this message. To supplement the work of itinerants, the Wesleys borrowed the Moravian institution of the society and adapted it to their own purposes. These societies rested on the core Arminian belief that religious association was open to any and all seekers. As John Wesley put it, any one who shared "a desire to flee from the wrath to come, and to be saved from their sins" was free to join a Methodist society.[44]

The Wesleys' innovations paid dividends throughout the British Atlantic world, especially on the American frontier. Finley's experiences reveal why. This young man found himself drawn to the Methodists after hearing the Wesleys' simple but hopeful message of salvation; attending revivals and night meetings helped pique his interest in the church. At the first meeting Finley attended, the Methodist leader adroitly isolated the doubters by having repeat attendees leave the room. He then shared his experiences with those who remained before "inquiring into their spiritual prosperity; addressing to them such language of instruction, encouragement, or reproof, as their spiritual states seemed to require." Finley was deeply moved by what he witnessed. "It was a time of profound and powerful feeling; every soul seemed to be engaged in the work of salvation." For Finley, the Methodist leader's handling of the meeting was extremely effective: "I never heard more plain, simple, Scriptural, common-sense, yet eloquent views of Christian experience in my life." When the leader asked about the state of Finley's religious condition, "I could only reply in tears and sighs; for I felt as if my very heart would burst with an overwhelming sense of my wretched state."[45]

Preaching was another effective weapon in the Methodist arsenal. For sinners and the saved alike, sermons graphically highlighted humans' sinful states. The key to the Methodists' success, Gatch observed, was that ministers aimed their appeals "more at the heart than the head." Finley quickly figured out that his sermons were most effective when he preached from personal experience. He described taking "a passage of Scripture which led me to speak of the new birth, and this opened up the way for me to give a relation of my experience, and to show the goodness and power of God, as manifested in my conversion." Although many preachers spoke spontaneously, Methodist sermons normally followed a prescribed format, opening with the reading of a text such as "John 10:9: 'I am the door; by me if any man enter in he shall be saved.'" The preacher then fleshed out the full meaning of the text. The primary theme was often the new birth and the need for the unsaved to embrace Jesus. Gatch saw the goal as showing "how we are to enter into these privileges by Christ, the door. It is through faith." Other sermons sought to refute the doctrine of predestination. Individuals, pastors stressed, had the power to be saved by embracing Jesus Christ and by shedding their sinful pasts. "The Methodist preachers of that day," Gatch explained, "believed if the heart were made right, it would influence the life and conduct of the individual."[46]

The Methodists' most potent weapon was likely the revival, or camp meeting. Finley had good reason to fear them before his arrival at Cane Ridge: revivals converted thousands to Jesus Christ and brought thousands more into the Methodist fold. As one Methodist observer noted about this Presbyterian-inspired tool, "No church can live without revivals. They are as necessary to its existence and prosperity as the April shower to the autumn vintage, the warmth of spring to the golden fruits of harvest." Indeed, Asbury saw them as a tremendous recruiting tool, proclaiming after one particularly successful 1808 revival, "I rejoice to think there will be perhaps four or five hundred camp-meetings this year; may this year outdo all former years in the conversion of precious souls to God!"[47]

The revival combined the exuberance of a festival with the solemnity of a church service. These gatherings could last anywhere from one day to several weeks. Many were quite elaborate. Peter Cartwright, an Ohio itinerant, described how participants would "erect their camps with logs or frame them, and cover them with clapboards or shingles. They would also erect a shed, sufficiently large to protect five thousand people from wind and rain." Workers also built stands from which preachers could deliver their sermons. Then came the crowds—people "from forty to fifty miles around," according to Cartwright. The largest revivals, like the one at Cane Ridge, drew throngs of upwards of twenty-five thousand. Revivals only grew in importance after 1800, spreading beyond Cane Ridge and leading to a phenomenon that became known as the Second Great Awakening.[48]

Revivals allowed people starved for community and Christian companionship to gather, a particularly important function on the frontier. In Cartwright's Ohio circuit, for example, church members were few and scattered. A spontaneous revival broke out one year; participants "got happy and shouted aloud for joy, and joined in and exhorted sinners. . . . Between twenty and thirty professed religion, and joined the church; and fully as many more went home under strong conviction and in deep distress," Cartwright said. "Many of them afterward obtained religion, and joined the Church."[49]

An army of Methodist itinerants—3,587 in 1840—worked assiduously to bring in members for the Methodist Church. The itinerants were mostly young, single men from middling and artisan backgrounds. Few had advanced degrees or much education at all. But, like Finley, they were extremely dedicated men who had undergone difficult conversions and knew how to connect with their audiences. John Kobler, one of the first Methodists to preach on the Ohio frontier, gained an impressive reputation. According to Gatch, Kobler was "tall and well proportioned; his hair was black and he wore it long, extending over the cape of his coat. . . . He had a most impressive countenance. It showed no ordinary intellectual development." Gatch saw Kobler sermonizing before an attentive audience in a two-room cabin: "His manner was very deliberate at the commencement of his discourse, but as he progressed he became more animated, and his words more powerful. He awakened in himself and in his Christian audience a sublimated feeling in the contemplation of heaven, and, in those who had a foreboding of future ill, unspeakable horrors." John Strange, another Ohio itinerant who worked with Finley, made an equally good impression, but for different reasons. Strange was "unassuming and modest in all his deportment to his superiors; kind and conciliatory in all his bearing to his equals," but Finley most noted the "unusual sweetness, compass, and power" of the preacher's voice. "He was one of nature's orators. . . . When he described heaven, which he always did in the beautiful and impressive imagery of the Bible, the mind seemed transported to that bright world." One impressed observer also believed Gatch to be "truly a very fine sample of primitive Methodist preachers, simple, plain, and powerful."[50]

Itinerants, missionary work, meetings, preaching, and revivals all played a role in the growth of Methodism in late-eighteenth-century America. In 1781, the movement had only 10,000 members in America, its growth stymied by the American Revolution (John Wesley sided with the British, making his movement suspect to rebels battling the king's forces) and the hostility of the Anglican Church (the bishop of London dismissed Methodist itinerants as fanatics). Wesley had tried to avoid a breach with the Anglican Church, and the Methodists remained part of that institution until 1784, when Wesley concluded that the time had come to form a separate church. Independence from the mother church meant that the Methodists could ordain their own ministers and send more and more evangelists into the field. That decision sent the Methodists and their circuit riders galloping into an era of explosive growth. The number of American Methodists soared from 15,000 in 1784 to 64,000 in 1800; by 1860, one-third of American church members were Methodist. Thus, within seventy-five years, Methodism became the largest Protestant church in the United States.[51]

The bulk of this growth came in the South and Midwest. In 1800, New York, New Jersey, and Pennsylvania totaled only about 12,000 Methodists; Virginia alone had nearly as many. The western frontier, with its virgin religious landscape and growing population, presented fabulous opportunities for the Methodists. The movement began forming circuits in Kentucky and Tennessee in 1782, and by the turn of the nineteenth century. more than fourteen circuits existed west of the Allegheny Mountains, including six in Kentucky. In 1800, the church had 2,307 white members in Kentucky and Tennessee. The Methodists formally entered Ohio in 1798, establishing first the Miami circuit and then the Scioto circuit. They formed two more circuits in 1804. In 1803, the

Scioto and Miami circuits had a mere 354 and 414 white members, respectively. In 1805, those numbers had grown to 474 and 722, and by 1810, Scioto had 744 members, and Miami (now called the Mad-River circuit) had 826.[52]

Itinerants and Mobility

Itinerants' wanderings represented an almost perfect fusion of mobility, migration, and reform. "Far from being backward-looking traditionalists, most early Methodist preachers were products of post-revolutionary America and felt comfortably at home among its rising middling classes. In particular, they knew the importance of mobility in an era of unprecedented expansion," notes one historian.[53]

And what a mobile world it was. Foreigners were astonished by how often Americans of this period moved. In the new republic, "all is circulation, motion, and boiling agitation," exclaimed one Frenchman. "The Americans are a restless, locomotive people: whether for business or pleasure, they are ever on the move in their own country," commented a British officer. "Wandering about seems engrafted in their Nature."[54]

In the colonial period, the British had restricted white settlement to territory east of the Appalachian Mountains; when that prohibition was lifted at the end of the revolution, settlers began heading west to the Northwest Territory and to points south. Eight states joined the Union in two waves. First came Kentucky in 1792, Tennessee in 1796, and Ohio in 1803; Louisiana followed in 1812, Indiana in 1816, Mississippi in 1817, Illinois in 1818, and Alabama in 1819. Migration was so massive that by 1810, approximately one-third of all Americans lived somewhere other than where they had been born.[55]

The Ohio Country ranked among the most popular destinations. Whites had long eyed this fertile region that lay just west of Pennsylvania and north of Kentucky. The landscape was diverse—it ranged from rugged hills to dense forests to open prairies—and won the praise of observers. Tocqueville was especially impressed by the mighty Ohio River; the Indians, he noted had dubbed it "the Beautiful River," and it "waters one of the most magnificent valleys which have ever been made the abode of man. Undulating lands extend upon both shores of the Ohio, whose soil affords inexhaustible treasures to the laborer." Asbury echoed these sentiments, exclaiming, "Beautiful indeed!" during an 1810 visit. "How rich the hanging scenery of its wood-crowned hills!" Migrants, too, were enchanted by the Ohio and its surroundings, but they took a more practical view of the Ohio Country as an inviting place to farm, a longing that became known as "Ohio fever."[56]

Several factors made the large-scale settlement of Ohio possible beginning in the 1790s. The first was the settling of the Indian question. In January 1785, the Wyandot, Delaware, Ottawa, and Ojibwa agreed to cede most of their lands in Ohio to the United States in a treaty negotiated by Richard Butler, Arthur Lee, and George Rogers Clark at Fort McIntosh.[57]

At the same time, Congress was drawing up the 1785 land ordinance whose goal was to ensure a smooth settlement process by regulating the surveying and sale of western lands ceded by the eastern states or acquired from Indian tribes. The ordinance established townships six miles square, with land set aside for public schools and veterans of the Revolutionary War, and it allowed the sale of 640-acre tracts to individuals. Two years later, Congress passed another milestone, the Northwest Ordinance, which created a territorial system of government for the western lands—a governor with broad powers and, when the population reached five thousand, the creation of a legislature.[58]

The 1785 Indian treaty, however, did not bring immediate peace to the Ohio Country because the powerful Shawnee and Miami refused to sign. Instead, under the leadership of Joseph Brant, the Shawnee formed an Indian alliance to defend land against white encroachment. The Indians sought to retain control of their lands north of the Ohio River, a claim that the United States found unacceptable, especially since large numbers of squatters had begun moving into the area following the conclusion of the treaty. The government wished to avoid war, though, instructing the territory's new governor, General Arthur St. Clair, to pursue negotiations with the confederacy. He reluctantly complied, doing so only because relations between white settlers and Indians were worsening. Through bribery and intimidation, St. Clair got several tribes to sign the Treaty of Fort Harmar, which affirmed the land cessations in the 1785 treaty.

The Shawnee reacted angrily to this development, stepping up their attacks on white settlers. In the fall of 1790, the new federal government sent General Josiah Harmar and 1,453 troops on an expedition to punish the Indians. Harmar's ragtag force of militia and regular army troops burned some Indian villages but was mauled in October by warriors under the command of Little Turtle, a Miami war chief. A year later, St. Clair led another expedition against the Indians and was routed in one of the worst defeats suffered by American forces at the hands of Indians. General Anthony Wayne received the unenviable task of avenging the losses and pacifying the Ohio frontier. After intense training of his troops and extensive maneuvering, he defeated the Indians at the August 1794 Battle of Fallen Timbers. The Treaty of Greenville, signed in February 1795, did little more than ratify the Treaty of Fort Harmar, but it was monumental nonetheless: the United States now effectively controlled the Ohio Country.[59]

With the Indians finally subdued, Ohio fever spread in earnest. Rising land prices and population in the East, combined with the lure of cheap, fertile land in the Ohio Country, drew settlers to the Northwest Territory from as far away as Maine. Wrote William Parkman of Camden, Maine, "As to the times they are very hard. The District of Maine is going [to] wreck as fast as ever a country did. Farms can be purchased for less than half of what they could [have] been 5 or 6 years ago. A great many is moving away to Ohio." The territory grew quickly as a result. Ohio's population jumped from a few thousand in the late 1780s to 230,760 by 1810 and nearly a million by 1830. According to geographer Hubert G. H. Wilhelm, the settlers came primarily from Virginia (which supplied 81 percent of the migrants from the South and 17 percent of the total migrants), Pennsylvania (which supplied 38 percent of all migrants to Ohio), and New York (15 percent).[60]

Methodists converged on this frontier, sensing the chance to spread religion and lead a reformation of behavior. Alfred Brunson was one. He was born in Danbury, Connecticut, in 1793, and endured a somewhat troubled childhood that saw his family move to New York and back to Connecticut because of financial setbacks and his father's drowning. The Brunsons' Puritan forebears left England during the Great Migration of the 1630s; one brother settled in Hartford, the town founded by Hooker's Company, while the other established himself in New Haven colony. The family prospered for a time, but Brunson's father, "who was fond of good living, and the higher class of society," squandered a sizable inheritance and in 1800 was forced to move his family to Sing Sing, New York, where he opened a public house and brickyard and operated a ferry.[61]

While in Sing Sing, young Alfred learned of the Methodist Church and its small local following. His family did not think much of this upstart group. "My father was opposed to them, in common with others of a worldly cast of mind," Brunson recalled, "and, like other children, I imbibed his prejudices." Alfred paid the Methodists little mind despite the full-time presence of a Methodist minister and the building of a camp meeting ground in nearby Sommers. However, Brunson began to hear tales of strange doings at these camp meetings—events, critics warned ominously, where "all manner of evil" occurred. These stories made him suspicious of the Methodists and their revivals, leaving him with the impression that "Methodists were nothing but demons incarnate."[62]

But Brunson also noticed that neighbors who went to the revivals returned home changed people. Intrigued, he decided to attend an 1806 camp meeting held about four miles from Sing Sing. Brunson was immediately struck by the large crowds: "Such a multitude of Methodists! Where did they all come from? The world must be turning upside down, and all running after this strange people." He also noticed the participants' unusual behavior—"a ring of men holding hands, within which I judged there were two hundred persons some standing, some kneeling, some sitting, some praying, some singing, and a large number lying on the ground helpless. . . . Some were apparently in the greatest possible distress."[63]

Brunson did not begin looking inward at the state of his soul until his father drowned in the Hudson River in 1806. At the funeral, Brunson "felt the first sense of my own sinfulness, and the need of a Savior." His father's shortcomings contributed to his angst: "My father, not being a professor of religion, like other worldly men indulged in sin. This circumstance gave more pungency to our loss, and gave us the more alarm for our safety." Brunson's mother decided to move her children back to Danbury, where her relatives still lived. There, Brunson found himself face to face with postrevolutionary New England in all its religious complexity. His mother was a faithful Puritan Calvinist who turned to the congregational church for comfort following the death of her husband; her brother remained a proud deist and a "disciple" of Tom Paine. Methodists were nowhere to be found in Danbury.[64]

Times were difficult for Brunson. He still grieved over his father's death and worried about the state of his soul. Yet the Calvinism of his mother and its harsh doctrine of predestination left him cold. As a result, when Methodist itinerants finally rode into Danbury, Brunson found himself attending their meetings. He was struck anew by the Methodists' energy and enthusiasm, their services full of "life and animation." Frequent attendance at informal night meetings convinced him of the need to get religion, but taking the next step toward conversion proved elusive—Brunson's resolve departed almost as soon as he left the meetings.[65]

Brunson decided that the only way he could change would be to pick up and move. "I could see no chance for saving my soul without a change of residence—the enchantment of young company had such a control over me," he explained. He had an uncle living in Cincinnati, and he "promised the Lord that if I ever got away from the enchantment or incubus thus hanging upon me, I would seek religion." He also wanted to migrate to "study law and rise, if possible, with the young State to whatever distinction merit might entitle me to." This newly opened territory thus offered Brunson opportunity on both spiritual and practical levels.[66]

As Brunson made his way west, he had to stop periodically to make money to continue his journey, and he struggled continually with his conscience. When Brunson's money ran short in Carlisle, Pennsylvania, west of Philadelphia, he lodged with and attended a meeting with a Methodist family. The minister delivered his sermon, and a stricken Brunson felt that the words were directed right at him, that the preacher was recounting Brunson's each and every sin. He "concluded that the Divine Spirit must have led him to discourse thus," he recalled, "and took it as a warning from God."[67]

God was not done talking to young Brunson. A voice later scolded him, "Now you are away from your youthful companions, who so hindered you from seeking religion, and you have not formed new acquaintances to keep you back, and you have repeatedly promised God [to] seek religion; and this is the last call you will have." The message ended with a dire warning: "If you refuse to obey this, you will never have another." Brunson understood. Broke and alone, he returned to Connecticut chastened and determined to reform his behavior and even to become a minister. He had just turned eighteen.[68]

Because of his youth, the Methodist conference rejected his application to become a minister, leaving Brunson discouraged, and he again considered becoming a lawyer. But he remembered the warning. "I had not the vanity to think that I could go alone, or without the church," he said. "Nor could I think of changing my Church relationship. I was then, and still am, a Methodist, and could be nothing else." He married in August of that year and "entered into business to make stock-work for the New York market." By taking on a wife, Brunson greatly damaged his chances of becoming an itinerant, because the church favored unencumbered single men who were free to roam the frontier and who cost less to support. Brunson subsequently resurrected his old dream of migrating to Ohio to start a new life. The War of 1812 had harmed his fledgling business, and the move again represented a chance to improve his prospects in both the business and spiritual realms. He reasoned that his chances of getting a circuit would improve on the frontier, where so much opportunity beckoned.[69]

Loading a wagon with their clothes, bedding, and provisions, the Brunsons headed west, passing through New York City and Easton, Pennsylvania, before crossing the Alleghenies through Blair's Gap. The six-hundred-mile journey to the Connecticut Western Reserve in northeastern Ohio saw only a few minor mishaps—their wagon got stuck in the mud several times and overturned once.[70]

Success nevertheless remained elusive. The Methodist conference again rejected Brunson's application to become an itinerant, this time because of his marital status, and Brunson despaired anew. He was ready to resume his study of the law when the voice returned, "whisper[ing] so loudly that I *must* itinerate, that I could not possibly content myself in anything else." Members of his circuit encouraged him to persevere, and Brunson continued preaching on a fill-in basis. One sermon was so well received that it nearly landed him a circuit: the quarterly "Conference was ready to vote my recommendation to the Annual Conference," he recalled, "but the presiding elder put in the old plea of the poverty of the circuits, and their inability to support married men, and said he could not advocate my reception at the Conference if I was recommended." The conference "dropped the subject."[71]

Brunson nevertheless persevered, buoyed by the support and loyalty of the people in his circuit, who "now almost unanimously favored me in this matter," and by his unswerving belief "that I was called of God to the itinerancy." In 1817, the clamor for Brunson's appointment was so loud that the conference finally gave in, assigning him a circuit in Huron County, some 150 miles from his home. To reach it, he had to travel "through an almost impossible wilderness."[72]

But Brunson was not really complaining. Constant motion and effort had at last produced results: he had left behind his old ways, moved to Ohio, and become an itinerant, serving the Lord, spreading the Gospel, and aiding the Methodist cause.

MOBILITY AND REFORM PROVED a potent combination, spurring on migration as well as Methodism. The two impulses worked in tandem to allow the Methodist movement to thrive in Ohio and beyond. Itinerant Methodist preachers well knew that mobility was the springboard to their success. "Localize the ministry," Peter Cartwright warned, and ministers become "secularize[d]; then farewell to itinerancy; and when this fails we plunge right into congregationalism, and stop precisely where all other denominations started." Staying still, in other words, would signal that Methodism was atrophying and becoming like other churches, including most notably the Episcopalian Church (the name adopted by the Anglican Church in the United States after the revolution).[73]

The Methodists who left Virginia also were motivated by the desire for reform—in this case, by their dislike of the ever-more-entrenched slave system. Unlike the Moravian migrants to the *Landgemeinen* in the 1760s and 1770s, these Methodists were not pushed out of Virginia by problems in their home congregations or drawn by the opportunity to worship in a religious enclave.

And in Ohio, the Virginia migrants continued to try to lure friends and family away from a society they saw as dangerously corrupt and to work to establish Methodist societies.

The Methodist and Moravian migrations also differed in that the former was far more involved with the outside world than was the latter. In a very real sense, the Methodists' mobility was a product of the times. The church operated in an environment where migration was commonplace and geographical expansion was the norm. With thousands and thousands of people moving about, the church tried hard to fill a religious void, and the frontier proved an especially fertile recruiting ground. Frontier settlers hungered for the Word of God, living as they did in a rugged wilderness beyond the reach of the eastern-based churches. In the years following the American Revolution, the frontier was virtually a blank canvas which an energetic, growing Methodist movement could exploit. The Moravian migration to the *Landgemeinen*, by contrast, was more insular, having little to do with outside forces and even less to do with reform.

Both movements were evangelical and missionary oriented, and both attracted new adherents from across national, ethnic, racial, and class lines. German-speakers joined the Methodist Church, English-speakers became Moravians, and enslaved blacks joined both faiths (although far larger numbers of blacks became Methodists). The Wesleys studied Moravianism carefully and built on many of the practices the brethren developed in Germany. But Methodism took a far more aggressive approach to seeking converts in the backwoods of America.

James Finley could testify to that. In the early 1800s, he got lost in the woods and ended up at "the cabin of an old Irish gentleman, a Roman Catholic." Finley could not resist talking religion with someone who qualified as Protestantism's most hated enemy. Finley asked how his host "got along without his confession. At this he became visibly agitated, and informed me he had not seen a priest for years; but that he was laying up money to go to Pittsburg to obtain absolution." When Finley asked the Irishman if he had been reborn, the man responded that he had "never heard of such a thing in all my life." He became alarmed at the prospect of spending eternity in hell and called his son into the room. According to Finley, the whole family soon became agitated, and the preacher tried to reassure them that he meant no harm. Taking out his Bible and reading from "the third chapter of John," Finley "spent an hour in explaining to them the nature and necessity of the new birth," before spending the night with the family members and praying with them. In the morning, "the old gentleman invited me to preach for the neighborhood when I came round the next time, which I promised to do." When Finley returned, a large crowd awaited him, and his sermon on salvation had the desired results: "Many were awakened, and a good work begun."[74] In such ways, in such times and such places, did Methodism spread in Ohio and elsewhere. Its success rested on the tired legs of a worn-out horse, carrying a lone itinerant to the next cabin in the next clearing over the next hill.

PART THREE

Journeys of the Pure

CHAPTER SIX

The Dissenters

Baptists and Congregationalists in a Separatist World

Two groups of migrants, some seventy-two people in all, gather at Clay Pit Creek in Middletown, New Jersey. It is September, still hot and a bit dry. The leaves have not yet turned, but fall is approaching. A wagon train loaded with supplies and the migrants' belongings is forming in a grove a relatively short ride from Shrewsbury, where most of the migrants have been living. The oxen swish their tails languidly, while the children exchange excited glances about the journey ahead. The atmosphere is hopeful, almost festive. Friends are arriving to bid the migrants good-bye, bringing food and drink for the enjoyment of all. This will be the last meal before the fifteen wagons pull out. But before the departure and the good-byes, there will be a farewell sermon.[1]

The picture is idyllic and quintessentially American, repeated countless times since the first settlers arrived on the shores of the New World. The picture has a Protestant tinge, too—an entire church congregation is picking up and moving en masse from Shrewsbury, New Jersey, to western Virginia, some four hundred miles away. Beneath this placid farewell scene, however, lurks something harsher: a group of religious dissenters is struggling with life in the new American republic. The year was 1789.

The Shrewsbury church, founded by a group of Seventh Day Baptists in the 1740s, had suffered through eight years of the American Revolution and another eight years of postwar economic turmoil. Moreover, it had long struggled with dissension within its ranks. By migrating, these Seventh Day Baptists were seeking to start anew on the frontier—a timeless motivation in American history.

A century earlier, something similar occurred, and it occurred in a surprising place: the Hartford congregation of Thomas Hooker. Reverend Hooker had led his followers out of Massachusetts Bay to the Connecticut frontier in

1636, and, through the force of his charismatic personality, he had succeeded in building a strong congregation in the years that followed. But appearances were deceiving there, too. When Hooker died in 1647, serious divisions came to the fore. The fissures that surfaced were so deep and irreconcilable, a dissenting faction decided to abandon Hartford to start a new congregation in western Massachusetts.

The religious causes of the exodus were far more overt in Hartford than in Shrewsbury, but the two episodes highlight an important theme in migration history: the role of a dissenting culture in Protestant mobility. Earlier chapters in this volume touch repeatedly on this theme, showing the numerous ways that conflict contributed to migration. In addition to the problem with the "withdrawers" who left for Massachusetts, Hartford faced a challenge from "outlivers"—congregants who lived a distance from the meetinghouse and were unhappy about it. A restless and peripatetic Devereux Jarratt, searching to become reborn, took on the staidness of the Anglican Church and its followers. Scotch-Irish Presbyterians split into feuding camps colorfully known as New Lights and Old Lights, while southern Methodists divided over slavery. Despite their diversity, these conflicts share a common thread: in a dissenting world, Protestant believers did not hesitate to speak up for what they believed was right or needed.

Such impulses were present from the earliest days of colonization, as the story of the Hartford congregation reveals, but they strengthened during the revolutionary era. Imbued with republican notions of freedom, common people seized on the heady promises of the period to reshape Christianity in their own image. Evangelism, already a potent force in America, benefited the most. The expansion of a dissenter culture in the late eighteenth century was a messy process, filled with conflict and volatility as people pressed ahead with their vision of what popular religion should be. As the Shrewsbury incident shows, the conflicts could take many forms. The disputes bedeviling the Seventh Day Baptist Church arose out of complex internal congregational dynamics involving religious, political, economic, and social forces.

The complexity of the conflicts in Shrewsbury contrasts sharply with those in Hartford. In the latter migration to Massachusetts, the disputes emanated from theological and personal clashes with the minister, with the unhappy dissenters fully explaining their reasons for leaving. In the Shrewsbury migration, however, the internal problems were more opaque and more layered. Religious conflict intertwined with family relationships and with powerful outside forces, including the American Revolution.

A Baptist Dissenter's Career

The dissenting world of Protestantism produced important theologians such as John Knox and Thomas Hooker. It also produced colorful characters such as William Davis. Davis, who was born in Wales in 1663, was first a Baptist, then a Quaker, and then a Baptist again. He was argumentative, passionate, difficult, eccentric, and restless. Equally interesting, he passed on many of these traits to his children and to the church that he and his family helped found. As the patriarch of the leading family in the Seventh Day Baptist Church in Shrewsbury, New Jersey, Davis was, in the words of one contemporary, "the spiritual and almost natural father of the church." His offspring formed not only the core of the membership but also the nucleus of the leadership.[2]

Davis was the product of an officious English family that counted a high sheriff, a deputy sheriff, and a county recorder among its members. His parents sent young William to Oxford with orders to become a clergyman. In a sign of things to come, the son instead joined the Quakers after learning of George Fox and his plain-speaking followers. Davis later quit school, crossing the Atlantic in 1684 to settle in the Quaker colony of Pennsylvania. Within seven years of his arrival, Davis had joined a separatist faction led by George Keith, a schoolteacher who disavowed the central tenet of Fox's movement: the idea that every individual possessed the inner light and the power to achieve salvation. Instead, Keith believed, only Jesus could award salvation to individuals. Keith established a rival Quaker meeting in Burlington, New Jersey, across the river from Philadelphia, but before long, the new society turned on Keith and ousted him. Davis soon left the Keithians, joining the Baptist church in Cohansey, New Jersey, around 1696 before abruptly leaving to affiliate with the Pennepek Baptist Church near Philadelphia. He served as pastor there until his unique take on theological matters landed him in trouble: in 1698, the congregation banished him for arguing that Jesus Christ was neither human nor divine.[3]

Despite this rebuff, Davis decided to remain a Baptist, in part because of the influence of Abel Noble, a former Keithian who had arrived in America in 1684; purchased land in Bucks County, Pennsylvania; and become acquainted with the Baptists through the efforts of missionary Thomas Kellingsworth. Noble, now ensconced in the Baptist camp, convinced Davis that Saturday, the seventh day of the week, was the true Sabbath. Davis was so persuaded by the rightness of this tenet that he became a Seventh Day Baptist and published a tract defending Sabbatarian beliefs. His efforts prompted a spirited response from the pastor at the Pennepek church. Davis responded by founding a Seventh Day Baptist Church in Pennepek in 1699. All of his first followers were former Keithians.[4]

Keith himself came back to haunt Davis's efforts to build the Seventh Day Baptist congregation in Pennepek. After losing the support of his own society, Keith had returned to England and become an ordained Anglican minister. The church's Society for the Propagation of the Gospel in Foreign Parts decided to send him back to the New World as a missionary. His return set off a "fierce" ideological struggle between Keith and his supporters and Davis and his allies. Davis published a tract under the title *George Keith Disabled*, and an ally of Keith responded by having the property deed for the Seventh Day Baptist meetinghouse turned over to the Church of England. A discouraged Davis sought to move to Newport, Rhode Island, but because of his reputation as an eccentric, the Seventh Day congregation there rejected his application for membership. He tried again four years later in Westerly, Rhode Island, where the church admitted his wife but not him. In 1711, the congregation finally agreed to admit Davis; two years later, it made him a minister with authority to administer the ordinance of baptism. Davis had taken a step toward respectability and apparently toward stability, but in 1716 he had a falling out with the congregation. He moved back to Pennsylvania a year later and remained there for more than a decade before settling in Stonington, Connecticut.[5]

Davis's dissenting ways thus carried him to Pennsylvania, New Jersey, and New England and back again. Wherever he went, he feuded with those who questioned his beliefs. But his volatility created a network of family and religious supporters. The Shrewsbury church was founded in the early 1740s by members of Davis's family from Pennsylvania and acquaintances from Stonington. By this time, Davis was in the twilight of his career and in bad health. He migrated to Shrewsbury sometime in the mid-1740s and died in 1745 at age eighty-two.[6]

The Baptists of East Jersey

Sired by a troubled and peripatetic dissenter, the Seventh Day Baptist Church in Shrewsbury came of age in a dissenting world. Its founders—five men and eight women—were part of a far larger religious migration to East Jersey that saw Puritans, an assortment of Baptists, and numerous Presbyterians push into the region from Long Island, Connecticut, and elsewhere in New England beginning in the mid–seventeenth century. Puritans from New Haven, led by Robert Treat and Jasper Crane, founded Newark along the Passaic River in

1666. Other Puritans from Massachusetts and New Hampshire settled in what became Woodbridge and Piscataway. Monmouth County in central New Jersey, where Shrewsbury is located, was formed in 1683 following the arrival of migrants from Long Island and Newport who included a large contingent of Baptists. One historian has concluded that Puritans and former Puritans were so numerous in East Jersey that the New England Way permeated the region, with church-dominated villages serving as "the farthest southern extension of the New England town system." The Seventh Day Baptists were late arrivals to this dissenters' haven, founding their first church in Piscataway in 1705. The Shrewsbury church, led by the Davis and Maxson families, was the colony's third Seventh Day church.[7]

New Jersey attracted Protestant dissenters from the colony's earliest years because of its congenial religious climate. East Jersey's founding charters—the Concessions and Agreement of 1665 and the Concessions and Agreements of the Proprietors (1677)—promised full toleration to nonconformists. Such towns as Shrewsbury, Piscataway, Middletown, and Woodbridge consequently became havens for Baptists, Quakers, and other dissenters dealing with a myriad of troubles in New England and Europe. Quakerism predominated in West Jersey, and New Jersey quickly became nearly as well known for its religious pluralism as its larger, more famous neighbor to the west, Pennsylvania.[8]

In Shrewsbury, small farms surrounded a village core that consisted of two intersecting streets with churches, houses, and shops. Established about 1665, Shrewsbury lay in the northeastern reaches of the Monmouth patent, a vast tract covering more than six hundred square miles along New Jersey's coastal plain, bordering the Atlantic Ocean from Sandy Hook in the north down into what is now Ocean County in South Jersey. Much of the land was low-lying, flat terrain broken up by occasional small hills. This benign landscape changed abruptly to the south, where plains and meadows gave way to a sandy "Desart" dominated by oak and pine trees—the Pine Barrens. The acidic soil was notoriously poor for farming and was shunned by early settlers; the pine forests were dotted with swampy marshes and brackish rivers. The Seventh Day Baptists settled well north of this area, mostly in Shrewsbury but also in Middletown, on lands that one visitor described as "remarkably good." Most of the migrants were small farmers living along the Manasquan, Squan, and Shark Rivers, where they carefully tilled holdings averaging one hundred acres. A few settlers engaged in the manufacture of salt, and local tradition states that the Maxson family owned a shipyard.[9]

The Troubled Revolutionary Years

During the congregation's first thirty years, New Jersey's warm embrace of dissenting Protestantism enabled the Seventh Day Baptists to settle in their new home and build a durable church. Membership remained at about fifty in this prewar period, and the congregation was both close-knit and disputatious. The founders from Connecticut and Pennsylvania had bonded around the pledge to "uphold the public worship of God at appointed places on the Sabbath Day with the help of the ministering brethren amongst them, by joining in prayer, reading the Scripture, preaching and expounding the Word of God one to another." A broad consensus existed on the need for piety and discipline. But the arrival of the revolutionary crisis in the 1770s turned the Baptist world upside down in numerous ways. The war disrupted church services, led to the death of at least one member of the Seventh Day flock, harmed the economy, and intensified splits within the congregation.

Yet the revolutionary crisis also provided the church's leaders with an opportunity: with war on the horizon, they saw the chance to reform members' behavior and to create a resurgence of piety, a broad and ambitious effort that involved the appointment of a new pastor, the building of a meetinghouse, and the reemphasizing of Sabbatarian Baptist beliefs. The reform effort began in December 1773, when a church meeting appointed three members to visit "straying brethren, and bring them into the fold from whence they have strayed." Follow-up meetings during the winter months of 1774 sought "to reconcile differences between brethren and sisters and in particular the difference between William Brand and Brother Babcock."[10]

The meeting also issued a detailed statement of faith, a document designed to educate members about the main tenets of their church. These Sabbatarians constituted one wing of a diverse Baptist movement that had been born in England at the dawn of the sixteenth century, amid the dissension and controversy created by the Puritan movement and its sustained assaults on the Church of England. Indeed, many scholars consider the Baptists an offshoot of Puritanism: both movements sought to purify Protestantism by placing the authority of Scripture over church traditions. The Baptists differed from the Puritans in the belief that only true believers could be baptized—that is, the Baptists, like their Anabaptist cousins in the Netherlands and elsewhere, rejected the baptism of infants and young children because only people who had accepted Jesus as their savior could receive the sacrament. The issue of when to baptize someone went to the heart of how these dissenters defined the church. In the words of a leading Baptist historian, the church could include only "baptized believers [who possess] all the authority and gifts from Jesus Christ." The visible church, therefore, was a voluntary gathering of true believers. Such a gathering could be as small as two people or infinitely large.[11]

The Baptist definition of church carried several important ramifications. For one, membership was open only to those believers who joined voluntarily. God granted people the freedom to choose to join or found a church. Second, all believers—not just university-trained educated leaders—were free to interpret the Scriptures in any way they saw fit. The Baptist movement, as a result, placed virtually full autonomy in the hands of the local congregation (or more accurately, the "church"). And by doing so and by basing its beliefs on an individual's interpretation of the Bible, the Baptist movement almost guaranteed that it would split into various branches with differing views and emphases. Several distinct groups of Baptists quickly formed in England and America as a result. General Baptists, also known as Freewill Baptists, were Arminian in outlook, maintaining that salvation was open to all. Particular Baptists were Calvinistic, like the Puritans, believing that Jesus died for a particular group—the elect. The Seventh Day Baptists believed that the Scriptures showed that Saturday was the true Sabbath.[12]

In 1774, as the revolutionary crisis was spreading throughout British North America, Shrewsbury's meeting attempted to reconnect with its Baptist past while educating its members on the movement's core principles. The first tenet of the Shrewsbury statement of faith, or covenant, was the most basic and important: members pledged "in the presence of God [to] give up ourselves to the Lord." This commitment entailed a promise "to walk in all Holiness, Godliness, Humility and Brotherly Love." Only those who accepted Jesus as Lord and "the Holy Ghost [as] the Spirit of God" could be true members. To cement one's relationship with the church and the Lord, an applicant had to be "baptized in water by dipping or plunging after confession made by them of their faith in the above said things." The members defined their church as "a company of sincere persons being found in the faith and practice of the above said things." The covenant concluded with a "promise to watch over each other's conversation and not suffer sin upon our brother . . . to warn, rebuke, and admonish one another with meekness according to the rules left to us of Christ in that behalf." Forty-two members—most of the church—signed.[13]

The meeting then moved to strengthen the church's leadership. On Christmas Day 1774, members decided that "there should be ruling elders appointed to take charge . . . and to endeavor to go to any brother or sister out of the way to admonish them." They appointed one member from Middletown, Joseph Maxson, and one from Shrewsbury, Thomas Babcock, to fill the posts.[14]

In February 1775 came the ordination of a new minister, twenty-eight-year-old Jacob Davis. Davis was ideologically compatible with his charges: one contemporary observer described him as "a strict Calvinist, as all his church are." He also had family connections—he was a grandson of the church patriarch, William Davis, and succeeded another family member as pastor. Davis also brought youthful energy to his new position, promising to "preach the word in and amongst them; . . . administer the holy ordinances, amongst them, exhort and rebuke them with all long suffering and patience." Davis wasted no time in pursuing change. The congregation had gone thirty years without a meetinghouse, convening instead at members' homes, but only one month after his ordination and only one month before the Revolutionary War began at Lexington and Concord, Davis convened a conference at his house to discuss building a meetinghouse. Participants agreed to undertake the project, voting to build the meetinghouse on the southeast corner of Zebulon Maxson's property, "commonly known by the Great Branch." Thus, as a war was getting under way, the Shrewsbury church began the momentous and expensive construction of a house of God.[15]

As Shrewsbury's Seventh Day Baptists intensified their soul-searching in 1775, outside events began crowding them. New Jersey was about to become a battleground. After the American army's decisive defeat on Long Island in August 1776 and the British capture of New York City in September, the Redcoats invaded New Jersey. George Washington's reeling and rapidly diminishing Patriot army retreated across New Jersey before crossing the Delaware River into Pennsylvania in early December. New Jersey's militia broke under the stress of retreat, outraging Washington and leading Thomas Paine to lament the dangers of summer soldiers and sunshine patriots. The king's troops, settling in for what they confidently expected would be a long occupation of New Jersey, established a main base in New Brunswick and sixteen outposts throughout the state. Believing that the rebel forces would be vanquished in the Jerseys, the British hoped that their military presence would push the neutrals into their camp while bucking up the loyalists.[16]

The plan made sense on paper. New Jersey was a reluctant rebel that had no real quarrel with the king and Parliament. The acts on stamps and tea that had so angered the other colonies generated only mild protests in New Jersey. Although the Whigs enjoyed significant support in both East and West Jersey, loyalists and neutrals comprised about half of the population. Monmouth County was a stronghold of loyalism, making it an especially volatile and violent place. In 1769 and 1770, debtors rioted. During the war, Patriot forces suppressed at least six counterinsurrections in Monmouth. Although the Association of Shrewsbury declared in May 1775 that it would "join the Rest of our Townships in Uniting our force for our Just Defence and Protection," backers of the revolution were in the minority. Both Middletown and Shrewsbury, home to members of the Seventh Day Baptist Church, were hotbeds of loyalty: according to historian Dennis P. Ryan, 24 percent of Shrewsbury's population was loyalist, while another 40.5 percent was neutral; in Middletown, loyalists comprised 25.5 percent of the population, although neutrals constituted only 3.6 percent.[17]

Most loyalists actively opposed the Whigs, and Monmouth's proximity to New York City further encouraged resistance. Some Monmouth residents enlisted in the British army or in loyalist regiments, while others harassed the Whigs by plundering their supporters' farms, supplying produce to the British, or providing intelligence and havens for the king's troops. Such activities vexed the new state government from the start. The war had barely begun in New Jersey and Governor William Livingston could be found complaining, "I have authentic Information that some of the most malignant New York Tories have seated themselves in Shrewsberry, a very improper place on Account of the facility it affords for keeping up a Communication with the Enemy." He later expressed exasperation with New York's "Villainous traffic" with Shrewsbury. In fact, Livingston considered Shrewsbury the most troublesome town in a state that was engaged in a virtual civil war.[18]

East Jersey's intense political divisions quickly acquired religious overtones. Anglicans saw the American Revolution as a crusade by nonconformists to overthrow the king and his church, specifically blaming Presbyterians and other leading dissenters. "It is a certain truth that dissenters in general . . . were the active Promoters of the Rebellion," declared one Anglican clergyman. And indeed, dissenting ministers throughout the state used their pulpits to encourage their followers to defeat the "Friends of Mammon," as some sarcastically called the loyalists. Jacob Green, a Presbyterian minister from Morris County, published a broadside deriding conservatives' attempts to reconcile with Great Britain: "What obliges us to submit to British government? . . . She has endeavoured to crush us." By becoming independent, he preached, "we shall avoid tyranny, and oppression."[19]

The revolutionary crisis exacerbated and politicized divisions within the Seventh Day Baptist Church in Shrewsbury by forcing members to choose sides. In one sense, the church's ranks mirrored Shrewsbury's at large: a few rabid revolutionaries, an outspoken backer of the king, and a significant number of neutrals. Church leaders—specifically, Davis, who enlisted as an army chaplain—actively backed the Patriot cause, but few congregants followed. Prewar attempts to discipline members apparently won the meeting few friends; at the very least, the reform effort did not enable the church to present a unified front to the outside world.

The vocal loyalist was Simeon Maxson, who was nearly forty-nine years old when the Continental Congress voted to declare independence in July 1776. Maxson was a member of a distinguished Baptist family. His father, Joseph, a New England minister, had led the migration from Stonington to Shrewsbury three decades earlier; his older brother, Zebulon, had donated land for the meetinghouse and was a respected voice in the congregation. Simeon, however, was a gadfly—a perennial thorn in the leadership's side. His first recorded offense was for "straying" from the church. More seriously, the meeting condemned "his life and conversation"—his habit of challenging key Baptist doctrines. The meeting was so unhappy with Maxson that it considered excommunicating him on January 30, 1774, but settled for a warning. This threat got his attention, for in December the meeting reported that he "hath given full satisfaction to this church by a hearty acknowledgment of those things wherein he has been astray."[20]

The truce was short-lived. A few months later, Maxson challenged "several principles of faith, in particular the eternal judgment" and how God punishes humankind. He then asked the meeting for a recommendation to preach. Given the animosity between the two sides, the request can be viewed as either daring or laughable. The members' reaction most likely leaned toward the latter: the meeting not only denied him permission to preach but voted to bar him from communion until "such times [as] he makes suitable acknowledgment according to the word of God." In August, Maxson again appealed to the meeting for the right to preach, but this conference went little better; the following month, the meeting declared that "the said Simeon Maxson has had not a call to preach the gospel, and therefore the church votes the said Simeon Maxson not to preach any more till further reconciliation with this church." Maxson finally compromised, admitting he was "in error" over his views on eternal salvation, but vowed to preach despite the church's objections.[21]

There things rested in September 1776, when General William Howe's troops began their hot pursuit of Washington's forces across the New Jersey countryside. Maxson continued to absent himself from church services. When he showed up at meeting to confront his critics that month, he bitterly condemned the war effort and those who backed it, declaring that these church members were "children of the Divell." He also blasted the leadership for teaching "carnall war," a stance that was bringing "sickness" upon the congregation. Maxson saw the revolution as morally wrong and as risking God's wrath and the consequent ruin of the Shrewsbury church. Yet his harsh attacks on the meeting's stance also likely resulted from individuals' personalities and his ongoing feud with the meeting: the leaders' decision to back the revolution was merely an additional point of disagreement between the meeting and Maxson.[22]

Most members were less vocal about their views of the war. As the military engagements moved closer and closer to Shrewsbury, the neutrals within the congregation remained largely silent, a dangerous proposition in 1776. New Jersey's Whig authorities under the leadership of Governor Livingston and the Council of Safety demanded that the state's citizens take loyalty oaths, threatening those who refused with fines, loss of property, and worse. Howe, too, issued proclamations requiring New Jerseyans to declare their allegiance to the king. Both sides viewed neutrals with suspicion, even branding them traitors. Within the state's dissenting churches, leaders often pressured members to take sides. The Presbyterians were the most fervent backers of the revolution and had the lowest proportion of neutrals. The Quakers were equally adamant on the other side. Under no circumstances was a brother to bear arms, supply substitutes to the militia, or even pay war taxes.[23]

The Baptist record was more mixed. The Middletown church barred loyalists from communion and summoned those with wavering allegiances to explain their views before the meeting. The Seventh Day Baptist Church in Piscataway, where the British encamped for a time, was rent by political divisions. As a church pastor later observed, "The inhabitants . . . differed among themselves in relation to the justness of the war. . . . A few of the members of this church left their friends and joined the British; but most of them were patriots, and some of them were officers in the army. For a number of years their house of worship was nearly forsaken."[24]

The splits within the Shrewsbury Seventh Day Baptist Church had complex causes. One likely was the makeup of the church membership: some, including Simeon Maxson, were former Quakers with pacifist leanings. Family dynamics played another possible role: several Davises enlisted, while the Maxsons and others did not. The war's timing may also have been a factor: The British invasion of New Jersey in 1776 coincided with church leaders' push for piety. When Jacob Davis came out in favor of the war, the strayers did not follow his lead, and the gulf between the leadership and a sizable proportion of the membership consequently widened. Demonstrating independence in the mold of patriarch William Davis, dissenting members did not blindly follow their leaders. Yet the split contained an irony: Jacob Davis was not a hotheaded radical who put heavy pressure on the membership to back the Whigs, nor did he punish those who defied him. The minutes of the church meeting make no mention of the war, apparently because leaders did not overtly pressure members to take sides. Unlike more radical ministers in other churches who circulated fiery sermons and broadsides exhorting people to support the revolution, leaders of the Shrewsbury church did not publish any polemics for or against the war. But Jacob Davis and a few other members, including Joseph and Moses Davis, did enlist. In so doing, the pastor made a clear statement about where he stood in the political contest, and his stance obviously upset Simeon Maxson and worried the neutrals.

There was nothing abstract about these fears. The American Revolution exacted a heavy toll on New Jersey's residents. Those churches that sided with the Whigs became targets of British retaliation. British raiding parties burned Presbyterian churches throughout the war and on at least one occasion killed a Presbyterian minister. The Quakers, too, paid a price for their pacifism. The Whig government forced Friends in Shrewsbury to pay more than one thousand pounds in fines in 1779 alone. Indeed, given the great number of loyalists in Middletown and Shrewsbury and the violent activities of the Whigs, neutrals within the Seventh Day congregation were taking a courageous stance by trying to stay out of the war.[25]

In November 1776, Livingston dispatched militia "at or near Shrewsbury to intercept & put a Stop to the Intelligence said to be carrying on between the Tories and Lord Hows fleet." The governor also issued a proclamation against those in Monmouth who "have committed divers Robberies, Violences and Depredations on the Persons and Property of the Inhabitants thereof." Monmouth's Patriot supporters formed a group of "Retaliators" to act against "Detestable Persons" aiding the enemy. These vigilantes so aggressively assaulted the loyalists that they earned a rebuke from the state assembly, which complained that the Retaliators' violent acts were "Leading to Annarchy and Confution."[26]

For four long years, the war's main theater was not the South or New England but the Middle Atlantic, especially New Jersey. By one historian's count, more than 296 battles and skirmishes took place in New Jersey between October 1775 and April 1783—the most of any state. Camping in New Jersey or the neighboring states of New York and Pennsylvania, both armies repeatedly called on farmers for grain and foodstuffs. Monmouth offered "great Quantities of Grain," and its proximity to New York City further increased its value to the British. Livingston warned General Washington, "From Shrewsbury Middletownpoint & Amboy, I believe, New York receives considerable Supplies; and it is not in our power to secure by our Militia those places from that infamous traffic." The state and local militia attempted to cut off trade with the enemy: on at least one occasion, the governor "dispatched orders for the removal of live stock & provisions from those parts of Monmouth where they are most in danger of falling into the enemy's hands." Yet even when the militia managed to slow illicit trade, foraging parties from both sides simply took what they wanted from farmers. Much property was burned in raids or destroyed during the incessant clashes between American and British forces. The British targeted almost anything that could be of military value, including saltworks and supply depots. To lower civilian morale, Redcoats also burned houses, destroyed churches, looted stores, and carried off livestock.[27]

The Seventh Day Baptists had front-row seats to the ugly theater that was the Revolutionary War. In mid-June 1778, Sir Henry Clinton, the new commanding general of British forces, withdrew his troops from Pennsylvania and crossed into New Jersey. Washington followed. Harassed by the Marquis de Lafayette's cavalry and the New Jersey militia, Howe halted near Monmouth Courthouse, just eight miles from the Seventh Day Baptist meetinghouse. General Charles Lee attacked Howe's forces on June 28. When the British brought in reinforcements, Lee began withdrawing his troops. An angry Washington arrived as Lee was attempting to retreat. The two men clashed, with the commander berating his subordinate as "a damned poltroon" before relieving him and attempting to salvage the situation. Fighting raged all day, with the Americans solidifying their position. The battle, the longest continuous engagement of the war and the revolution's fiercest artillery duel, took place in one-hundred-degree heat, and both sides were exhausted as the sun went down. Casualties were heavy: the British lost some 500 men, the Americans about 360. Clinton decided to withdraw. Another casualty was the Reverend Davis's father, James, who had ridden a horse to the battlefield to watch the fighting and was struck by a stray shot.[28]

The revolution disrupted church services across the state, and the Shrewsbury congregation apparently was not exempt, as the minutes indicate that no meetings were held between August 9, 1778, and May 13, 1781. In the days leading up to the Battle of Monmouth Courthouse, the church had struggled to maintain some semblance of normalcy. The meeting continued to discipline wayward members: on June 13, two weeks before the British and American armies fought at the courthouse, Margaret Wilson was chastised for living "contrary to the rule of God's word." The meeting also decided to

The Battle of Monmouth Courthouse took place only eight miles from the Shrewsbury Seventh Day Baptist meetinghouse, and the Reverend Jacob Davis's father, an onlooker, was killed in the fighting. (Bettmann / CORBIS)

excommunicate "our straying brethren . . . at one and the same time." In July, the meeting harshly rebuked three members, declaring that it will "deliver those persons mentioned before by name to Satan, according to the apostles directions . . . till God of his infinite mercy brings them to the light of his blessed truth." The war also slowed progress on the meetinghouse. Although construction began in 1775 and a roof was in place in late 1776, the building remained unfinished two years later, and the congregation was still trying to raise enough money to complete the structure.[29]

The cessation of the war brought no real peace to the congregation. Six years of conflict had left church members even more divided, with the most outspoken loyalist heatedly condemning the leaders and a large number of neutrals refusing to follow the church elders.

Daunting challenges lay ahead, too. New Jersey's economy suffered during the 1780s, as the fighting had badly damaged East Jersey's villages and farms. One English visitor on a postwar tour of the United States pointedly noted that the region "suffered extremely by the ravages of war." In addition to rebuilding their homes and businesses, East Jersey residents struggled with high taxes, hyperinflation, and foreclosures. Money and credit were scarce. The illicit trade with New York City, ironically, had represented an economic boon to the area, but the war brought such prosperity to an end, and British creditors restricted credit and demanded payment in specie. Population increases between 1772 and 1790—more than 20 percent in Monmouth alone—added to the problems. The presence of more people, especially young people, meant that land became scarcer and more expensive. Farm sizes consequently fell: in 1780, according to Ryan, landholdings averaged 71.7 acres in Shrewsbury. By 1789, however, that number had fallen to 64.7 acres. The number of landless in the area rose to 27.1 percent of taxpayers, while those holding less than 50 acres constituted another 23.6 percent. Conditions were harshest for the young, who had fewer opportunities to become landholders. Farming thus became "a less attractive career for the young man."[30]

The troubles affected the members of the Seventh Day Baptist Church, middling farmers of modest means who now faced onerous postwar taxes. In the Davis family, Jacob had the largest taxed holdings, with 200 acres, but only 100 acres were improved. According to a 1785 list of tax ratables, a later James Davis had the clan's largest working farm with 170 improved acres, while William Jr. had the smallest holdings—only 40 improved acres. These were small, family-run operations; no Davis owned any slaves, and each farm had only about three cattle. (By contrast, each of Shrewsbury's larger farms covered more than 300 acres and had more than twenty cattle.) The ruinous inflation during the 1780s and the state's pressing need to pay its war debts further darkened the congregation's picture. Tax assessors levied three taxes on Shrewsbury's residents: a "revenue tax," which was the largest of the three; a "support tax"; and a "tax to Sink the bills of Credit," which equaled the support tax and effectively raised a payer's tax burden by one-third. Some church members thus struggled with debt during the 1780s, sparking occasional disputes among members over bonds.[31]

In 1781, faced with such an array of problems, Pastor Davis and the Seventh Day Baptist meeting decided to resurrect their strategy from the 1770s. They would again lead a revival of piety. The first sign of rebirth was small but tangible: the meeting resumed keeping minutes. And the church again began gaining new members: the first entry after the hiatus noted that "Margret Newman is received into this church. Also this day Elezabeth Gifford is received into full communion." The church gained thirty-seven new members between 1786 and 1788 and nearly forty members during the decade as a whole. Religious activity also quickened, with the meeting reemphasizing discipline and commitment to the Baptist faith. In June 1782, the meeting read and explained "our rules of faith and practice . . . and every member of the church [was] definitely examined about their advances in practical holiness, and prayer in particular." This effort, the meeting proclaimed, "caused great conviction in the minds of some, and great joy and gladness to others."[32]

The revival of faith, however, did not end members' argumentative ways. The meeting continued to chastise strayers and slackers. Mosher Maxson and his wife, Tacy, communed with Quakers, giving rise to accusations that the Maxsons were heretics who were "going contrary to the commandment of God and denying all Gospel ordinances." Simeon Maxson reappeared in the records, this time charged with having "spoken against the Elder," a transgression for which "he confessed his fault." The meeting accused three other members of breaching the Sabbath.[33]

Personal animosities, especially within and between families, continued. Membership remained at about eighty even with the influx of new members. Davises and Maxsons still dominated both the membership and the leadership; Jacob Davis remained ensconced in the pulpit. The church's clannish nature thus added another layer of tension to the congregation's religious, political, and economic conflicts. Gossiping became a problem, and the meeting had to step in to mediate "some unhappy differences subsisting between" Thomas Babcock and William Brand, who was delivering "hard speeches" against the other man. Similarly, Simeon Maxson accused James Davis of maligning Maxson's son as "idle and negligent in his business."[34]

Animosity also arose between the Davises and the Maxsons on the one hand and different congregation families on the other. In 1774, when the meeting wanted to "bring [sinners] to their duty," for example, it sent William and Jacob Davis to accomplish the task, thus conflating religion and familial power. Members' challenges to the meeting took on a personal component. When Margaret Miller and William Brand told the meeting that they were "offended with the church," leaders sent William Davis and Zebulon Maxson to deliver "an invitation to come and give us a visit in love and fellowship." Intrafamily feuding also broke out, as when Rebecca Davis went before the meeting to face accusations of "speaking against the body of the church." On another occasion, James Davis and his wife were barred from communion "till there could be some acknowledgment to pacify the matter of difference between them and the church." And in 1783, James Davis and his wife accused Jacob Davis of being "no better than a thief & a robber," though the meeting concluded that the charge "appears to be false."[35]

Such was the state of affairs as the 1789 migration neared. Although the revolutionary era had brought great turmoil and division to the congregation, it also presented tantalizing opportunities. Its success meant the opening of new frontiers and the possibility of allowing the congregation to get a fresh start elsewhere by migrating. However, the church minutes are silent about why the congregation decided to abandon New Jersey. The pastor delivered no ringing exhortations on how the membership could rekindle the faith by migrating. Nor did the leadership discuss how the congregation's bickering contributed to the decision to leave its home of some forty-four years. Instead, to understand more fully about the ways that a dissenting culture fueled migration, we need to return to a familiar figure from a familiar place.

Discord in the Garden of God

Thomas Hooker's final years were relatively happy. With the 1636 migration behind him, he took to his study to read and write and to the pulpit to preach. His last decade of life was among his most productive, as Hooker the polemicist churned out pamphlet after pamphlet detailing his vision of the New England Way. Hooker the mediator also repeatedly traveled to Massachusetts to defend Connecticut's interests in negotiations with the Massachusetts Bay Colony, all the while tending to the needs of his Hartford flock. But the growing workload took a toll on his health. "My years and infirmities grow so fast upon me, that they wholly disenable to so long a journey," he confessed in a 1646 letter. A year later, Hooker was dead. His passing badly shook his congregation and led a grief-stricken Samuel Stone, Hooker's associate, to lament, "God refused to heare our prayers for him, but tooke him from us July 7, a little before sunne-set. Our sunne is set, our light is eclipsed, our joy is darkened."[36]

For Stone, life was about to become even darker. His mentor's strong leadership skills and personal charm had enabled the Hartford congregation to remain unified. Magistrates in Connecticut and Massachusetts Bay never had to mediate any disputes within the new settlement, an astonishing feat at a time when Puritans throughout New England were bickering over the larger goals of their reform movement. Things were so peaceful in Hartford, according to Cotton Mather, that the congregation had to excommunicate only one person and admonish one other during Hooker's fourteen-year tenure as pastor there. But Hooker's death led long-simmering disputes to boil over and caused unhappy dissenters to depart for the upper Connecticut Valley in 1659.[37]

Part of the dissenters' unhappiness was caused by personality conflicts. According to contemporaries, Hooker combined a great intellect with a warm personal touch and an engaging personality. Observed Mather, Hooker had "lively Sparkles of Wit. . . . His Natural Temper was cheerful and courteous;

but it was accompanied with such a sensible *Grandeur of Mind . . .* that he was born to be *considerable.*"[38]

Stone, however, was his predecessor's opposite in many ways. Where Hooker was warm and engaging, Stone was cold and stern. Where Hooker was a moving speaker, Stone was dull. The two men had been together since Hooker returned to England following his short exile in the Netherlands. Stone, then a lecturer at Towcester in Northamptonshire, helped Hooker evade Archbishop William Laud's minions. When Hooker boarded the *Griffin* in 1633 for America, Stone was with him. And Stone accompanied Hooker on the 1636 migration from Newtown to the Connecticut Valley. In Hartford, Stone served as "teacher," a post equal in importance to that of pastor in the congregational system. A graduate of Cambridge, Stone was nearly Hooker's equal as a thinker. Mather praised Stone as "Learned" and "accomplished" but also described him as "both a *Loadstone*, and a *Flint-stone*," a not-so-flattering reference to Stone's leadership style in the controversy that erupted following Hooker's death.[39]

Hooker's view of the ministry differed fundamentally from Stone's, and while Hooker was alive, the revered pastor's leadership and popularity muted these differences. Hooker believed in a preaching clergy, seeing the minister's job as to "wooe and win the soule to the love" of Jesus Christ and the new birth. "When the Soul is truly brought to Christ," he observed in *A Survey of the Summe of Church-Discipline*, "the Pastor must endeavor by heat of exhortation to quicken it, strengthen and incourage the soul in every holy word and work." This emphasis on salvation and the minister's role in it cut to the heart of Hooker's conception of the congregation. Unlike some other Puritans, he did not want the congregation to become an island of a small group of the elect surrounded by a sea of the unconverted. Instead, Hooker believed that the congregation should be the base for conversion and that the minister bore responsibility for leading the congregation. Through an energetic ministry and enthusiastic preaching, he would bring Christ's "subjects"—that is, the visible saints—into the church.[40]

Hooker's views reflected his experience in England. In Essex, he and other Puritans were reformers who came to see the institutional church, which was built on the parish system, as an empty shell devoid of true believers. He particularly criticized the territorial parishes that girded the institutional system. "Parish precincts," he declared, "doth not give a man right, or make him matter fit for a visible Congregation." A man, he continued, cannot inherit piety "from his parents, or purchaseth it by his money, or receive it by gift or exchange." In Hooker's view, an evangelical ministry would awaken the spiritually dead to the glories of Jesus Christ and the new birth.[41]

By 1650, however, few Puritan clergy shared Hooker's views. Stone and other seventeenth-century preachers in the Connecticut Valley believed that Hooker's beliefs tipped too far in the evangelical direction. But in true dissenter fashion, these leaders did not agree on the proper role of the minister and congregation. The rigid congregationalists emphasized not the winning of souls but the providing of a proper spiritual environment for the elect. They saw the church as a haven for the faithful, who would strive to maintain their purity and continue their spiritual growth. The moderate congregationalists sought to institutionalize evangelism in an effort to keep church membership growing but nevertheless wanted to keep the church itself as the gathering place for the saintly, restricting communion to full members. Nonmembers, however, could be baptized and participate in church life. They would, in other words, be halfway members. These moderates thus envisioned a Pietistic future for Puritan congregationalism: a small church, or conventicle, within a larger church that would consist of only full members.[42]

Stone was a moderate congregationalist who sought to achieve a middle way in the wake of Hooker's death. Stone first attempted to loosen the requirements for joining the church. Hooker had believed in "saving grace"— the idea that people had to have private conferences with their ministers to demonstrate that they had been saved. Stone concluded that such a requirement was too difficult, suggesting instead that a simple profession of faith before the congregation would suffice. Stone also believed that Hooker had allowed the laity too much latitude in congregational government. He wanted to strengthen the clergy by establishing something akin to a "speaking aristocracy" of ministers. More broadly (and somewhat paradoxically), Stone sought to fortify the church by increasing membership and tightening discipline through stronger clerical controls. In 1657, he laid out these ideas in forceful language that could hardly be misconstrued by those with opposing viewpoints. His first proposition declared baldly, "The Church of Christ at Hartford doe bynde themselves in the presence of God to Samuel Stone their teacher, to submitt toe every doctrine which he shall propound to them, grounded upon the sacred Scriptures." For his part, Stone added, the teacher had to rule with justness and reason and persuade the laity to follow "by scripture, convincing argument, and right reason." But assuming that the minister was such a person, "the Church must then follow, and not oppose."[43]

Stone's imperious tone likely confirmed his opponents' long-held suspicions that he was high-handed and arrogant. On a deeper level, they feared that their pastor was pressing for a "presbyterian" system of governance that would effectively remove power from the congregation and place it in a synod of clergy led by people such as Stone. Stone's efforts to loosen church membership while tightening clerical control also drew bitter protests from those who wanted to maintain high admission standards. Members of this faction especially objected to efforts to introduce a "halfway covenant" into the congregation under which children of partial members could be baptized. These dissenters were committed to Hooker's high standards, although not necessarily to his evangelical vision. In some ways, therefore, these dissenters were even more strict than Hooker had been, seeing the congregation solely as a haven for the elect. They remained committed to the Cambridge Platform and opposed changes being introduced by church councils in Boston in favor of an ideological past that no longer existed.[44]

The dissenters represented a minority of congregants but nevertheless remained firmly convinced of the rightness of their position. So, in the 1650s, they continued battling Stone, splitting the congregation into two camps and landing Hartford's affairs in the highest councils of both Connecticut and Massachusetts Bay. As in 1634, the pressure to avoid a split was enormous. Authorities in both colonies attempted to reconcile the two sides. In June 1656, ministers in Massachusetts Bay even cited Hooker in a vain attempt to heal the rift: "We hope yet we sometimes heare ye sounding of your Christian bowels at the remembrance of your late pastor's voice, who being dead yet speakes alowde to Hartford at such a time."[45]

Three years later, Puritan leaders convened a council in Boston in a final attempt to settle the "long, sad, and afflicting controversy" between Stone and the dissenters. Stone characteristically took the offensive, arguing that separation was an "exceeding scandalous" sin that would lead to the "destruction" of the church. As members of First Church, he maintained, the dissenters were obligated to remain and to fulfill the terms of the covenant. The dissenters countered by criticizing Stone's "irregular" conduct and his "rigid handling of divers brethren." They had previously cited the deep divisions within the congregation as precisely the justification for their withdrawal. They likened the dispute between the two parties to having "long lived in the fire of Contention," which left them "scorched more and more." Facing such heated divisions, "we have been forced . . . to flee from that which wee could neither quench nor beare." The council blamed both sides for the dispute and declared that it wanted them to reconcile: "We expect [the dissenters] will hold communion with the church at Hartford, and the church with them." But the council's admonitions against separatism carried little force with the warring parties. The religious divide was simply too wide. In fact, the dissenters had concluded before the council convened that the chasm was too wide to be overcome, and they proceeded with plans to "flee" upriver to western Massachusetts, near Springfield.[46]

Two Congregations, Two Migrations

The congregations in Shrewsbury and Hartford shared a history of conflict, but the nature of the conflict differed substantially in the two places. The two congregations thus followed different strategies in deciding where to go. By leaving Hartford, the "withdrawers" believed they were defending a purer, more stringent form of Puritanism than was being practiced in Connecticut under Samuel Stone. So, instead of heading west to Long Island or New Jersey (as did so many Puritans), they decided to return to the main Puritan colony, a decision that Hooker surely would have found ironic. A party of men set out in 1658, proceeding north up the Connecticut River to scout potential settlement sites in western Massachusetts. Despite their small numbers and lack of support within the community, the dissenters did not lack for resources. Their party included several prominent residents of Hartford, including John Cullick, a prosperous landowner, and William Goodwin, a respected congregation elder. They also had the full backing of Thomas Hooker's son, Samuel, who served as pastor of the congregation at nearby Springfield and may have influenced the selection of the settlement site. And the dissenters received significant help from sympathetic Puritans in neighboring Windsor.

In late May 1658, Cullick and Goodwin traveled to Boston to hand deliver a petition seeking land within Massachusetts Bay Colony. Momentum for the move then quickened. The General Court agreed to the dissenters' request within five days, granting them "liberty to inhabit in any part of our jurisdiction . . . provided they submit themselves to a due and orderly hearing of the differences between themselves and their brethren." The dissenters selected a site on the east side of the Connecticut River belonging to the town of Northampton and entered into negotiations for the land, including a much prized meadow known by its Indian name, Capawonk. In October 1658, Northampton agreed to award the land to the Hartford faction on generous terms, stipulating only that the new settlers maintain a fence for their cattle and hogs; pay ten pounds annually in wheat and peas; form two plantations on each side of the river; and commence their settlement by May 1659.[47]

On April 18, 1659, five months before the council of Puritan leaders met in Boston to mediate the dispute, the dissenters gathered at the Hartford home of Goodman Ward to solemnize their separation from First Church. Fifty-eight men and two widows, including a few supporters from Wethersfield and Windsor, attended and signed the resulting document. It was all very Puritan: the dissenters pledged in their covenant to "engage ourselves mutually one to another, that we will, if God permit, transplant ourselves and families to the plantation purchased." The migration and town building were to be a joint undertaking—"We will raise all common charges . . . upon the land that men take up; mow, plow land and house lot, according to the proportion of land that each man takes of all sorts." Most of all, "no man shall have liberty to sell any of his land till he shall inhabit and dwell in the town three years; and also to sell it to no person, but such as the town shall approve on."[48]

A few weeks later, in May, the colony's General Court appointed a committee of five, including the influential William Pynchon of Springfield, to lay out the boundaries of the town, to be called Hadley. The committee reported back at the end of September with its plan, and a vanguard of approximately seven people commenced building on the river's east bank that fall and winter. Within a year, enough people had moved to the site for the village to hold its first town meeting in October 1660. Fittingly, the problem of dissent was already on inhabitants' minds. The twenty-eight or so participants at the meeting agreed that settlement of the west bank could commence but noted "that all who sit down on the west side of the river, shall be one with those on the east side, in both ecclesiastical and civil matters."[49]

Although they split from the Hartford congregation over theological disputes and unhappiness with Stone's leadership, the settlers did not deviate from the New England Way in constructing their village. Church and covenant stood at the center of the settlers' lives. The inhabitants built their houses in a row, on small lots ranging between one and eight acres. In building their congregational village, the Hartford dissenters gained a powerful ally from Massachusetts in Pynchon. In addition to serving on the founding commission, the wealthy merchant loaned Hadley money to buy additional lands from the Indians. He also invested in the town, constructing grist- and saw-mills that greatly aided Hadley's economy.[50]

The members of the Hartford congregation who chose to leave came from a broad section of the congregation, forming a bloc that coalesced around specific theological disputes. Family dynamics and economics played little role. The amount of available land in Hadley was roughly the same as in Hartford, and some of the dissenters walked away from large holdings in Connecticut: William Goodwin, for example, owned 1,822 acres in Connecticut, a huge total by New England standards, and Andrew Warner owned 517 acres. Migrants' landholdings in Hartford averaged 110 acres. The migration was also quite costly, as the dissenters had to buy the land and finance the cost of the move. They left Hartford even though their community was thriving economically and had become the political seat of the Connecticut colony.[51]

The Baptists in Shrewsbury, by contrast, did not return to the familiar when they sought their fresh start. Instead of going back to Connecticut or Pennsylvania, they looked west to the Virginia frontier. It was a curious choice in many ways. The new state was not exactly hospitable to those with unorthodox religious views. On the eve of the revolution, as historian Rhys Isaac has observed, the colony's powerful Anglican gentry viewed Baptists as crude upstarts intent on disrupting traditional culture, and evangelical-minded dissenters such as Devereux Jarratt were far from welcome. During the war, however, the Anglicans lost their privileged position as the established church. In 1786, moreover, the legislature passed Thomas Jefferson's act on religious freedom—a milestone, the Enlightenment apostle observed with satisfaction, that "wiped away" statutory oppressions in religion. Yet Evangelicals still had their critics, and Virginia was one of at least thirteen states with "blue laws" mandating that religious services be held on Sunday, an oppressive and offensive measure for a Seventh Day church.[52]

The selection of western Virginia was curious for another reason: it remained a dangerous place. Mountainous and thickly timbered with white oak and maple, the frontier district of West Augusta occupied a plateau west of the Allegheny Mountains and south of the Ohio Country. After surveyors and trappers demonstrated the region's potential, it began attracting settlers from Virginia and Maryland as well as from New England, New Jersey, and Pennsylvania, but population growth remained slow into the 1780s. Even after the American victory in the Revolutionary War put an end to the British ban on settlement west of the Appalachians, the Indians, who were prepared to fight to keep possession of their ancestral lands, posed another barrier for would-be residents of the region. The establishment of Clarksburg and Morgantown in western Virginia shortly after the revolution sparked a fierce response from the Indians, part of a broader effort by chiefs of the Eastern Woodlands tribes to unify their members and lead a spiritual reformation of their peoples. Many Indians were alarmed by the British defeat, well understanding that American expansionism would now proceed unchecked. The Ohio Country and western Virginia, as chapter 5 discusses, became especially contested as Chickamaugas and others began harassing the border regions of the new United States. Three years before the Seventh Day Baptists left New Jersey, warfare resumed

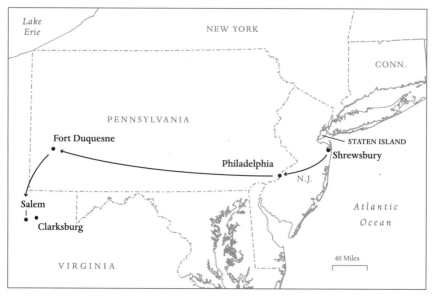

To Western Virginia, 1789: Shrewsbury's Seventh Day Baptists made the four-hundred-mile journey from New Jersey to western Virginia. They used Forbes Road from Philadelphia to Fort Duquesne, then turned south to the Virginia frontier, eventually settling in Salem in Harrison County.

in earnest along a broad front stretching from Georgia through Kentucky, western Virginia, and into the northern Ohio Country.[53]

Free-soil Methodists from Virginia waited until the Indian threat was ended before moving to the Ohio Country in significant numbers; the Shrewsbury Baptists came to a different decision. On August 8, 1789, they voted to sell their church building. Only a month later, a train of roughly fifteen wagons pulled out of Monmouth following a farewell sermon by the Reverend Jacob Davis. Seventy-two members from ten families were making the trip. No account of the migration survives, but the group probably stopped first at Middletown before pointing their wagons west. The migrants likely took the Forbes Road, a wagon trail running from Philadelphia to Fort Duquesne. After more than four hundred bumpy miles, the train lumbered into the sylvan expanse of western Virginia.[54]

The migrants first settled on land owned by John Reed on White Day Creek in Monongalia County. Apparently because the land was of poor quality, the Seventh Day Baptists moved on two years later after receiving a better offer from a fellow believer. Samuel Fitz Randolph, a Seventh Day Baptist originally from Piscataway, New Jersey, had learned of the migrants' unhappiness and persuaded them to relocate to New Salem, a village he was founding in nearby Harrison County. Randolph had bought a 256-acre tract between the Ohio River on the west and the Monongahela River on the east for 132 pounds (Virginia money) in November 1790. The Shrewsbury contingent's arrival in the neighborhood was thus quite fortuitous, allowing him to combine affairs of the purse and of the pulpit.[55]

Leading congregation members from Shrewsbury, including Jacob Davis and Zebulon Maxson, became trustees of the new town, which was incorporated in late 1794. New Salem was a simple village that formed a partial triangle, with a main street running through the center and a front street to the south and a back street to the north. Such an arrangement represented a way to mitigate the Indian threat, as did a blockhouse erected on a "high plat of ground." With the Indians no longer an issue in the mid-1790s, the settlers began to spread out, primarily along the Middle Fork of Ten Mile Creek, several creeks to the west of New Salem, and Pattersons Fork, to the south.[56]

The Dissenting World and Migration

The Hartford migrants lived during a time of heady religious experimentation, members of a vibrant Puritan movement that was determined to reform western Christendom. Shrewsbury church members lived in a pluralistic middle colony that became engulfed in an epic war for national independence. Both congregations were products of a dissenting Protestant culture that encouraged spirited religious debate and fostered internal conflict in diverse ways. Fed by religious, economic, and social factors, dissent nipped at the Seventh Day Baptist Church almost from the start. The Revolutionary War and its aftermath added to the stresses on the church. Dissent had a more subtle and complex impact on migration in Shrewsbury than in Hartford. The Shrewsbury church did not split into competing factions. Rev. Davis remained popular, and no ideological thread tied together the strayers. Simeon Maxson's episodic challenges to Baptist creeds apparently drew little or no support from other members. Those malcontents who sniped at the leadership and the meeting did so as individuals, not as a coherent opposition.

Nor did dissent directly influence who migrated and who did not, which was not the case in Hartford. Most Shrewsbury congregation members—even those who had clashed with the meeting—moved to western Virginia. The people who remained behind were the members with the shallowest ties to the church. They lacked a shared history with longtime members. Church members whose ties dated as far back as the 1740s were clearly tired of the environment in New Jersey and wanted a fresh start somewhere else. Part of this desire was economic, but such motivations were not decisive, as newer members' decision to remain behind demonstrates.

Family ties also played a role in the migration. In one sense, this Seventh Day Baptist Church resembled congregations founded by Scotch-Irish Presbyterians in eighteenth-century America and by the Moravians in Wachovia in the 1760s and 1770s. Family and religious ties were virtually inseparable. Kinship helped define the Shrewsbury church and helped determine who joined the migration westward. None of those who joined the church during the 1780s and who were not named Davis or Maxson migrated. Eight of the ten departing families were either Davises or Maxsons, while another family's matriarch was a Maxson. The dominance of just a couple of families was not unusual in the Baptist movement: the leading historian of the Seventh Day Baptists, Don A. Sanford, has observed, "During the years of the westward migration, most of the new churches established on the frontier involved a clan type movement of two or more generations." Strong family ties apparently motivated even Simeon Maxson to set aside his long-running feud with the church meeting and join the migration. Thus, while kinship rivalries likely intensified Maxson's animosity toward the leadership, they also kept him in the church, contributing to the church's endemic volatility.[57]

In addition, the dominance of those two families probably left those members not named Davis or Maxson feeling like outsiders. Again, the Shrewsbury church was not unique in this regard. Sanford recounts the story of a young Seventh Day Baptist minister who "enter[ed] his first parish in a rural area [and] was informed that 'the Crandalls sat on one side and the sinners sat on the other side of the church.'" In Shrewsbury, the Davises and Maxsons were likely perceived as the most devout, looking across the aisle at the "sinners."[58]

The American Revolution added yet another dimension to the church's tangled web of conflicts. Historian Nathan O. Hatch has written that the revolution "dramatically expanded the circle of people who considered themselves capable of thinking for themselves. . . . Respect for authority, tradition, station, and education eroded." In Shrewsbury, such an expansion of individualism preceded the war, but the revolution moved the process along—members had to make personal decisions about whether to support the loyalists or the rebels. The conflict thus further encouraged independent thinking among members of a religious movement with an already demonstrated propensity for independence.[59]

The Shrewsbury migration, as a result, demonstrates the Protestant dissenting world in all its variety and complexity. Internal congregational dynamics greatly affected the behavior of members and helped determine who went and who stayed. When it came time to decide whether to migrate, the "outsiders" remained behind. The "insiders" left.

The internal dynamics of the Hartford congregation were far clearer. The withdrawers came from a broad section of the congregation, and they formed a bloc whose unhappiness can be traced to specific theological disputes with the Reverend Samuel Stone following Thomas Hooker's death. This migration had nothing to do with the stresses of war, and it had little to do with family dynamics. Nor was it about land. Religious concerns trumped economic ones—a quite typical decision in a volatile, and mobile, dissenting world.

CHAPTER SEVEN

God's Chosen Sojourners

The Inspirationists of Amana, Iowa

God said move, and they did. The exodus from Ebenezer, New York, began in 1855. When it ended ten years later, some eleven hundred members of the Society of True Inspiration had made the pilgrimage to Iowa, where they were to start life anew in a remote colony they called Amana. This migration was hardly the first for the Inspirationist movement. Society members had originally been scattered across Europe, mostly in Germany and Switzerland, before the Lord bade them to gather at select estates in Germany. Then, in 1842, he informed them that it was time to cross the Atlantic for the United States, where they would be beyond the reach of Germany's meddling princes and could construct a religious community on sturdier and purer foundations. In Ebenezer, a collection of four villages that the society built in upstate New York, five miles from Buffalo, the Inspirationists thrived. Their members prospered. Materialism rose. And membership grew.

Christian Metz witnessed these developments with alarm. Prosperity might make for comfortable living, but it threatened to undermine the society's mission. The Inspirationists were religious utopians who shared the radical dream of trying to live the perfect, godly life. They sought to recapture the purity of early Christianity by leading exemplary lives that placed the glory of God first. Metz became convinced that Ebenezer's rampant materialism risked all that the society had achieved by leaving Germany.

Someone very important agreed with Christian Metz: God. In the Inspirationist movement, Metz enjoyed a unique relationship with God because of his status as the Lord's spokesman. Metz was *der Werkzeuge* (the instrument), the member with a direct pipeline to God. This reliance on revelations helped define Inspirationism and set it apart from other utopian movements. Members saw inspiration as a divine gift, and the person who possessed it served as the de facto leader of the Inspirationists. When Metz spoke, he was conveying the will of the Lord. And in May 1854, God wanted the Inspirationists to move to the American Midwest. Many members grumbled, and some even argued that they had arrived in New York only a few years earlier and that it was too soon to move again. Metz rejected these arguments—the Lord had spoken, he reminded his followers, and all must obey God's wishes or leave the society.

After the American Revolution, Protestant utopians migrated for two basic reasons: to escape persecution (for example, the Mormons) or to keep a distance from the world so that they could better pursue religious reforms (the Shakers). The Inspirationists belonged in the second camp. Having arrived in the United States as a small part of a massive migration from Germany and Europe in the 1840s, the Inspirationists had miscalculated by settling near Buffalo in the Burned-over District, a region famed for its religious intensity. Buffalo's strong population growth soon left the Inspirationists feeling hemmed in, and the city and the world it represented—materialism, greed, and lust—had become too close for comfort. By moving across the country to an isolated site along the Iowa River, the Inspirationists would again regain their discipline. Or so the Lord commanded.

Rekindling the Faith in Ebenezer, New York

Christian Metz was struck by the beauty of the land and the wretchedness of its human occupants. In 1842, when the prophet first laid eyes on the five-thousand-acre tract in upstate New York that was to become Ebenezer, he was traveling with three other church members. They had arrived in New York City on October 26 of that year after thirty-eight storm-tossed days at sea. Before Metz and his companions left Germany, the Lord spoke to Metz in a revelation, offering guidance on the task before them: "You are to migrate . . . a great distance to a destination I will disclose. Look to where the land is open and to where, through the Spirit, My Hand shall direct. . . . Obtain a space for you and your children to live." During the Atlantic crossing, the Lord dropped further hints about the location, alluding to Ohio and Wisconsin, two midwestern states with open land available at low prices. When the four Inspirationists met with a land agent after arriving in New York, however, he discouraged talk of purchasing government land in the Midwest because of its distance from markets. Instead, he recommended a fifty-five-thousand-acre tract near Lake Erie in Chautauqua County, New York.[1]

On November 3, intrigued by the potential of the Chautauqua land and reassured by a revelation that the Lord gave his "complete consent" to this change of plans, the Inspirationists boarded a steamer bound for Albany. They then took a canal boat to Buffalo, a growing city that was the western terminus of the Erie Canal. Metz and his companions took rooms at the Mansion House, a three-story hotel owned by Phillip Dorsheimer, a well-connected German immigrant who was Buffalo's postmaster and a man quite knowledgeable regarding the local real estate market.[2]

Dorsheimer passed along an interesting tip: the Ogden Company had bought the Seneca Indian reservation outside of Buffalo and was looking to sell it. He advised the Inspirationists to go see the tract. The next day, Dorsheimer led them to the site, where he introduced them to tribal chief John Seneca, who showed them around. Metz was intrigued by all that he saw. The land was relatively level, dominated by a "great virgin forest" that was thick with majestic trees, including oak and pine. Streams coursed through the wide, mostly uncultivated countryside. The soil appeared quite fertile—a rich, thick black loam. The weather was in fine, upstate New York form: raw, gray, rainy. Metz and his companions were soon cold and wet, but as they trudged through the deepening mud, Metz felt a spiritual connection with the land, "a deep feeling of joy and innate well-being" that the Lord wanted them to move here. He made no decision that day, however. The Lord had not yet confirmed Metz's feelings about the Seneca tract. Besides, the Inspirationists realized that they faced a potential obstacle: Indians still resided on the tract. Impoverished members of the once-powerful Iroquois tribe were reluctant to leave the land of their ancestors.[3]

Lacking a confirmatory revelation and recalling the Lord's previous instructions, the Inspirationists decided to go see the Chautauqua tract. The Lord confirmed the wisdom of their decision in an *Einsprache* (a speaking) that evening. Thus, in mid-November, Metz and Wilhelm Noe boarded a steamer that would carry them across Lake Erie. The visit did not go well. A "raging storm" sunk nine ships during the crossing—a bad omen, indeed. Once safely at Chautauqua, Metz and Noe toured the site and came away unimpressed. "Even though we were physically on this land, our spirits were not here," Noe recalled. "Rather, it seemed as though our thoughts were always of that place which we saw first, namely the Indian Reservation near Buffalo." Metz and Noe returned to Buffalo by carriage and entered into negotiations for the Seneca tract. Ogden's agent agreed to drop the asking price by nearly $2.00 an acre to $10.50. Metz was pleased, and so was the Lord, who revealed on November 27 that he had selected the Seneca tract for the Inspirationists, pledging "that I am a God who can help you overcome every difficulty through which I have led you and will continue in doing so."[4]

Despite the Lord's blessing, Metz and his band of Inspirationists faced numerous hurdles in closing the deal. For one, the discounted price remained far higher than they had expected to pay—in the Midwest, the government was selling land for $1.25 an acre. In addition to haggling with the land company over the final price, the Inspirationists needed to agree with the seller on the location of the eastern boundary; the company pushed to set the boundary farther east than the Inspirationists wanted. The Inspirationists also needed to determine exactly how much land they could afford. Metz did not know how much cash they could raise back in Germany. Ideally, he wanted ten thousand acres, enough land to give the group room to grow as well as provide the isolation they required. But his colleagues warned that the higher price meant that the community could afford only four thousand acres. The group compromised on five thousand, at $10.00 an acre, and Ogden reluctantly went along.[5]

Although the Senecas were to be paid for their land, Ogden allowed them to stay on the tract until June 1, 1844. The stipulation was more than an annoyance for a communitarian group with plans to erect a community isolated from the outside world. The Senecas' presence also meant increased difficulty for the German migrants in clearing fields and planting crops. And Ogden's concession meant that the Senecas had an excuse to dally. Indeed, many of the Indians refused to leave, threatening lawsuit after lawsuit.[6]

The Senecas' continued presence forced the Inspirationists to negotiate with individual tribal members. As a Seneca accepted cash to move out of a hovel, an Inspirationist quickly moved in to prevent the Indian or one of his tribesmen from returning. Metz moved into a shack that lodged a team of horses at John Seneca's sawmill.[7]

During these troubled early days, the Lord reassured Metz and his followers with revelations that they had his full support and that the undertaking would succeed. He provided tangible signs as well: members arrived steadily from Germany—nearly 240 in 1843, 217 in 1844, and 118 in 1845, raising the group's total to more than 800.[8]

Despite Metz's organizational efforts, the migration from Germany was quite chaotic. After Metz and his vanguard had begun preparing the site for settlement, he wrote back to Germany, urging leaders there to send the most useful members first—those brethren who could handle a saw, hammer, or hoe. But the departures followed no set plan. Members left when they could, so the vanguard was never quite sure who would arrive and when. Metz was startled one day to run into a newly arrived group of brethren in Buffalo; he also was annoyed at the amount of baggage they brought. As a result, early arrivals were forced to construct housing as quickly as they could, and they hired an outside contractor to build the colony's first large structure, a building that would serve as a community kitchen, meetinghouse, and dorm. Migrants were usually housed in the Senecas' old sheds, one-room shacks built of logs; elders then assigned families to individual houses as they were completed.[9]

Given the arrival of eight hundred people within a few years, Metz and the vanguard had to work fast. As early as 1845, Ebenezer had momentum and a sense of permanency. Metz selected the settlement's name from Samuel 1:7–12: "Then Samuel took a stone, and set it between Mizpeh and Shen, and called the name of it Ebenezer, saying: Hitherto the Lord helped us." If that reference was not clear enough, Metz composed a hymn that further explained his reasoning:

> Ebenezer you shall call it
> Hitherto our Lord has helped us
> He was with us on our journey
> And from many perils saved us
> His path and way are wondrous.[10]

In 1846, Metz seemed satisfied with what his group had achieved within only four years. In addition to building upper, middle, and lower villages, the Inspirationists had cleared a thousand acres for farming and had constructed numerous shops. By Metz's reckoning, the two largest villages had thirty-five houses each, while the third had about eight houses. In addition, there were numerous barns, granaries, mills and sawmills and large herds of horses, oxen, cattle, and sheep. In a letter to Germany, he cited this progress as evidence of "God's Work and Hand. . . . [T]he dear Lord did not forsake us."[11]

An 1848 visitor to the villages agreed that the Inspirationists had made impressive progress. "Since purchasing their estate, these enterprising Germans have cleared completely and put in the best order, nearly five thousand acres of their land, erected a great many miles of durable fences, planted twenty-five thousand fruit trees of various sorts, [and] settled three compact villages." The villages were attractive and reminiscent of the Inspirationists' European homeland; houses hugged a main street, and gardens abutted the residences. "Dutch" gates and extensive fencing enclosed their lands. Housing styles varied. Some residences were two stories, others were one and a half, while yet others were cottages. Timber-frame construction was common, but brick could be found, too. Charles Nordhoff, who visited Ebenezer after the Inspirationists had departed for Iowa, described the former colony as a garden located on a wide plain, with "large, substantial" houses.[12]

Christian Metz, the Inspired One

By most measures, the Inspirationists' first decade in upstate New York was a rousing success. Ebenezer thrived, a testament to the settlers' dedication and hard work. Things were going so well, in fact, that Christian Metz decided in 1852 that the Inspirationists should construct a fourth village, New Ebenezer, located between Middle and Upper Ebenezer, a backbreaking undertaking that involved digging a millrace, building wool and cotton mills, and erecting houses. With Ebenezer's population still expanding, the elders had already purchased an additional four thousand acres, bringing the society's holdings to nearly nine thousand acres, and were contemplating buying even more.[13]

In May 1854, however, Metz met with the society's elders and had a sudden revelation: "You will have to leave your property and go to a place where it is bare and scant." God was telling them to migrate again. As word of *der Werkzeuge*'s latest pronouncement spread, opposition arose. The Lord had not given Metz a specific destination, merely telling the Inspirationists to head someplace into the wilderness, presumably in the West. A summer of discontent followed, but Metz and the Lord held firm. A series of revelations in late August 1854 confirmed God's instructions to "leave this place which the Lord has given you and . . . take your staff and wander on."[14]

Metz's followers faced a stark choice: obey his (and the Lord's) wishes and migrate, or leave the movement. It forced members to reexamine their commitment to the Inspirationist movement. They could stay behind in upstate New York, or they could move and abandon all that they had painstakingly built. But why should Ebenezer's residents have believed the prophet? Where did Metz get the authority—or the audacity—to speak for God and to issue commands in his name? How could he compel his fellow Inspirationists to undertake yet another migration?[15]

The man responsible for this upheaval was sixty years old. He had no great oratorical gifts, nor was he physically imposing. Contemporaries described Metz as heavyset with brown hair and eyes. He had been born in 1793 to an Inspirationist family in Neuwied, Prussia. The Society of True Inspiration, whose proclaimed goal was "the glory of God and the salvation of man," had been founded in 1714 by a group of Pietists, and the society's beliefs were tied firmly to Pietism. The Inspirationists and their fellow Pietists, including the Moravians, sought to shake up the staid religious formalism of Europe's state churches, stressing a thorough reformation that would return these churches to the primitive Christianity that existed in the days following Jesus Christ's resurrection. But as one historian of the movement has noted, Inspirationism had a twist: "Central to the emergent Inspirationist dogma was the idea that now, as in the days of the prophets, God would speak directly to humankind through chosen individuals."[16]

Movement members were not alone in believing in the existence of prophets. Revelation had been an important part of Christianity from the very beginning, and the idea enjoyed a renaissance in nineteenth-century America, where prophets such as Joseph Smith were wandering the hills and valleys of a religiously charged landscape during the tumultuous years of the Second Great Awakening. Inspirationism drew on a mysticism personified by the beliefs of German Pietist Jakob Boehme, who saw inspiration as a visit from the Holy Ghost; those so inspired often shook violently as they conversed with the Lord. Others entered a trancelike state, pacing back and forth with their eyes closed and issuing a steady stream of divine commandments.[17]

In these early years, Inspirationism faced the challenge of separating the "true" instrument from the outright fraud or the merely mistaken. No fewer than eleven members claimed to possess the divine gift. The task was further complicated by the fact that many people gained and then lost the gift of prophecy. Of the eleven people who claimed to be instruments, six possessed inspiration for less than two years, and only one kept the inspiration for longer than five years. This man, Johann Friedrich Rock, born in 1678 to a clergyman and his wife, staked the strongest claim to leadership and, after intense maneuvering and bickering within the movement, emerged as the society's leader.[18]

With help from Eberhard Ludwig Gruber and others, Rock led the Inspirationists through a period of robust expansion. Gruber drew up "the Twenty-One Rules for the Examination of our Daily Lives," while his son developed a companion set of twenty-four rules. The key theme in both sets of regulations was self-denial. Members were to put God first. They were to not lie or pursue wealth; they were to be honest and sincere and to "fly from the society of women-kind as much as possible."[19]

When Rock died in 1749, no prophet arose to take his place. Lacking a leader, the society foundered and entered a long period of decline in the late eighteenth and early nineteenth centuries. Contributing to the crisis was a changing European religious climate. Pietism had fallen out of official favor, with political leaders instead embracing the Enlightenment. By 1814, Inspirationism was confined to a few estates in France and Switzerland. And with Rock long gone, the few surviving congregations were mere shells—elders oversaw them, and people came to worship services on Sunday, but they lacked the fervor and commitment of the movement during Rock's heyday.

Into this void stepped Michael Krausert, an obscure tailor who in 1817 had a mystical experience in which he spoke with God. But he could make little sense of what had happened to him. Feeling confused, he headed to an Inspirationist congregation in Alsace to learn about his apparent gift. Most of the congregation elders greeted Krausert's story with skepticism, but two of them believed him, and Krausert took to the road to preach, attracting a small following. At the same time, Metz and other young men were engaged in a separate attempt to revitalize the Inspirationist movement. Metz met Krausert and was impressed. A woman, Barbara Heinemann, emerged as a second instrument before Metz had his first inspiration in May 1819, fulfilling a prediction made by Heinemann.[20]

The existence of three prophets set off a period of infighting, especially among Heinemann and Krausert. Under intense pressure and facing great skepticism, Krausert began to waver and question whether he truly was inspired. Metz quickly lost his gift and blamed himself for this setback, concluding that God was punishing him for becoming involved in the bickering. Krausert left the community in 1819, and four years later, Metz regained his gift and Heinemann lost hers. He consolidated his position as *der Werkzeuge* and emerged as the society's leader in the 1830s and 1840s.[21]

Metz thus derived his authority to lead from his status as an instrument. Serving as God's spokesman was an awesome responsibility; indeed, the burden had broken Krausert and helped lead to his departure from the society. Anyone claiming such a fearsome power could count on being greeted with intense skepticism and hostility from within the movement and sometimes by violence from without. Metz thus noted that his gift was "born out of anguish and [was] only possible by hurling oneself into and losing oneself in the depths of the unfathomable." An instrument had to sacrifice a great deal on a personal level. "God must propel us through fear," Metz explained. "We are flung into the darkness of faith. In this state, our self-will must be completely negated."[22]

The vain and the power-hungry, Metz declared, could not serve God; an instrument needed to be completely humble. "It is no simple matter to be God's instrument. . . . I have often discovered how God's grace has been hindered because of subtle self-love and personal thought," he wrote in his diary. "Those who believe having such a talent might give them certain enjoyment and advantage, are entering into yet the gravest spiritual danger." Metz never lost his gift. In all, according to his biographer, he delivered 3,654 revelations from 1823 until his death in 1867. Some revelations ran thirty-four pages and could take hours to deliver.[23]

For all his experience and assuredness, Metz worried at times that he might be delivering a false inspiration, a "revelation [that] did not originate in God but was an expression of the instrument's personal feelings and opinions," according to his biographer. "This was highly unsatisfactory and could not be permitted, for it indicated that the *Werkzeuge* was no longer spiritually pure." Metz had no patience for those who falsely claimed the power of inspiration, darkly describing such people as having "no understanding of the secret wisdom of God . . . the wrong key to the door."[24]

Assuming that the instrument enjoyed the Lord's grace, Metz and his followers were convinced that revelations came directly from God and had to be followed. In fact, revelations constituted one of the chief attractions for members. They became closer to God by virtue of their association with *der Werkzeuge*. This reliance on revelation separated the Inspirationists from other churchly Pietist groups, including the Moravians. The two movements had considered merging during the 1730s because they shared so many beliefs. But Moravian leader Count Nicholas von Zinzendorf backed off when Rock refused to temper his claims to being *der Werkzeuge*. Zinzendorf saw such claims as false, even outlandish, while Rock believed that inspiration was "nothing with which to trifle or compromise. It is God's and so it shall remain."[25]

Troubles in the Garden of Ebenezer

In the 1850s, Christian Metz was the leader, the interpreter, the guide, the seer. Although he believed that he was undertaking the migration to Iowa at God's behest, Metz also clearly believed that the Lord wanted the Inspirationists to move as a way to force change on a movement that again seemed to be losing its way.

Inspirationism was at heart a reform movement. It sought to alter the behavior of its members and ultimately of society. The Inspirationists had come to upstate New York primarily to unite the scattered European congregations in one place and reinvigorate the faith. The Inspirationists also sought to escape mild persecution in Europe, where princes had for years harassed them with tactics that ranged from levying onerous taxes to denying citizenship to new arrivals in Germany. A revelation on the eve of the transatlantic migration told members, "You are to live in accordance with your faith as originally presented. . . . Egotism has also arisen and often still arises. It is a paramour, proud, sullen, unbridled, and willful." By migrating to America, society members could "live in integrity, in pure brotherly love, in divine compliance. . . .

To this He has summoned you—all of you—to live and work not for yourselves but for Him and for the Community."[26]

Thus, on New Year's Day 1846, the faithful gathered in Lower Ebenezer for a Covenant Service. Some 150 people sat on the wooden benches in the unadorned meetinghouse to watch new members be received "into the blessed bond of brotherhood in accordance with the 24 Rules." The assembled sang a hymn, "Wach auf, du Geist der treuen Zeugen." The Lord, through a revelation delivered by Metz, reiterated the movement's raison d'être: "A pure-intentioned, wholehearted offering and sacrifice of love in everything . . . is what the Lord wanted and required," recalled the *Inspirations-Historie*, a contemporary account of the society compiled by a colleague of Metz's. "If you no longer want to belong to the Lord then take what is yours and care for yourselves. But woe until the soul that does this after having acknowledged the summons that it was indeed the pure will of God."[27]

As Ebenezer took shape, with members clearing fields and erecting houses and shops, Metz instituted a community of sharing that had two purposes. One was practical. To finance the purchase and development of a fairly large, expensive tract in a new country, Metz decided that the community should pool its resources. The society needed to tap into the cash reserves of its wealthier members, and Metz expected these members to help cover the society's costs; poorer members were to contribute their skills and labor to the greater good. Second, communal sharing would help society members develop a sense of religious mission, making tangible the Pietistic notion that all believers should devote their lives to the Lord.[28]

The communalism that Metz envisioned meant that all members would surrender their property and capital to the society. In return, financial contributors would receive interest for the money they handed over to the capital fund. The society was to pay all wages, which members would use to buy food supplied by the society. The society would own all shops, industries, and farms and provide all the community kitchens, gardens, and houses for individual families. Metz saw communal sharing as a temporary expedient, to last but two years: "In our early years here we must live communally," he declared in a revelation. "It is not possible otherwise." But Metz and other elders decided that the arrangement worked so well that it should be permanent; communal sharing constituted "the spirit of self-interest. . . . The bond of brotherhood is much more pure and close here than it was" in Germany. Metz, for his part, believed that continuing the communal arrangement represented the fulfillment of God's wishes. On January 29, 1845, the Lord told him, "Hear this, My people, you are to do your work and carry your responsibilities joyously! . . .

You do not labor for money, as do the unbelievers—the necessities shall be your portion."[29]

Many other utopian groups also cited this classic rationale for sharing. The Hutterites, an Anabaptist group from Russia that came to North Dakota in the 1870s, shared all goods and lived communally, stressing the need for members to surrender themselves completely to the Lord. Members of this group believed that sacrificing for the community (and for God) represented a way to achieve salvation. The Oneida Community of New York, founded by John Humphrey Noyes in the early 1840s, sought to regenerate society by practicing a form of primitive Christianity. In an attempt to eliminate selfishness, Noyes instituted a radical version of communalism that went well beyond what the Hutterites and Inspirationists practiced: Oneida members lived together in communal housing and practiced "complex marriage"—every woman was the wife of every man. In Noyes's view, love confined to one couple was unsocial, was selfish, and threatened the communal interests of the gathered saints. By living under one roof and sharing both property and love, members would give themselves completely to God and overcome the individualism that Noyes and other critics saw as rampant in nineteenth-century America.[30]

The Inspirationists were much less radical. Metz never questioned the nuclear family. He merely saw communalism as an expedient that would allow a movement with limited financial reserves to pull off a complex colonization while strengthening members' religious commitment. With assistance from Wilhelm Noe, Metz drew up a constitution codifying the communal arrangement. Land was to be held in common, with all members bearing their burden according to their ability. The decision to make communal sharing permanent was not universally popular, and the writing of the constitution thus took on a secondary purpose, making "Community members recognize that they have a mutual responsibility for protecting and securing the Community against disloyal Elders and members." Those who opposed the constitution and communalism should leave Ebenezer; only the committed should stay. The vast majority stayed, ratifying the slightly modified constitution in January 1846. Members would receive a yearly allowance instead of wages, and the society would pay no interest to members who withdrew from the community.[31]

The migration to Ebenezer, the permanent adoption of communal sharing, and the forcing out of the dissatisfied proved no cure-all, however. As the 1840s wore on, Metz saw disturbing signs all around him. Creeping materialism. Religious indifference. Misbehavior, especially by the young. The problems were interrelated and were exacerbated in the late 1840s by outside economic pressures. Buffalo's population jumped from 5,141 in 1825, when the Erie Canal was finished, to 74,214 by 1855, reducing Ebenezer's isolation. Ebenezer, too, was growing. Its population topped one thousand in part because of an unexpected development—former members in Germany heard of the community's success and chose to join the New York settlement. Two challenges arose: members were becoming too concerned with affairs of the world, and the society was running out of room. All of these problems steadily worsened.[32]

Metz initially responded to waning religiosity by using his revelations to chastise individual members and the community as a whole. In 1849, for example, "a very serious testimony was presented in Lower Ebenezer concerning the total state of the Community and the command was issued for a day of fasting and repentance." When a cholera epidemic broke out in Buffalo that summer, Metz interpreted the event as a divine warning and used the opportunity to castigate members for "taking their secure life all too lightly and not showing humility before their all-powerful God." When fever struck the community a year later, killing eight people in Upper Ebenezer, Metz told the society that the illness constituted God's punishment. He called for another day of repentance and prayer while issuing a soothing revelation: "Whosoever believes with all his heart and obeys will not die for I am a God of the living and not of the dead. Therefore arise to a new life and the mercy of your God will conquer all adversity."[33]

Metz had less kind words for Ebenezer's young people, who were spending too much time in Buffalo. "They run off to the city to make love," der Werkzeuge complained, "to have intercourse with the untrue and the deviant, with the world. [This] has become an abomination before the Lord." Metz also deplored members' growing materialism. Inspirationists were becoming too interested in books, alcohol, cigars, and other sinful pleasures, all of which abounded in Buffalo.[34]

Metz's complaints about the encroachments of the outside world were ironic. The vanguard of Inspirationists, including Metz, had agreed with the land agent that upstate New York was preferable to the Midwest because of the Erie Canal and the proximity to New York City and the Atlantic Ocean. In New York, the Inspirationists would be closer to markets. The Inspirationists had also turned aside the opportunity to purchase more land, leaving them with a tract that was too small for their numbers and causing a crisis for a communitarian society that sought to keep some distance from the outside world. Metz concluded that his group needed more land, preferably in a more isolated place.

The Migration to Iowa

It was now 1854, and the Lord again stepped in with a revelation: "There is one more remedy against the decline, namely to change the place of abode so that there will be struggle and hardship—a separation. You will have to leave your property and go to a place where it is bare and scant." This stark declaration told the Inspirationists that they would have to leave New York, migrating across the country to regain their focus and commitment. God likened the exodus to the ancient trials described so graphically in the Old Testament: "Like the children of Israel in the desert," the Inspirationists would have to wander "on account of your disobedience, dissatisfaction and ingratitude." Migration, in short, was a punishment.[35]

In late August 1854, just three months after the initial revelation about the need to migrate, Metz announced that the decision was final: "You will have to leave this place which the Lord has given you." But even Metz was unsure about where the Inspirationists would go. The Lord had said only to look to the wilderness. As Metz's biographer observed, "The whole affair was a great surprise to all, and the undertaking must have seemed at first like sheer folly." A revelation explained that a committee of four, including Metz, was to find a location and act as a scouting party. Relying on word of mouth, the committee quickly turned its attention to Kansas.[36]

On September 8, Metz and the other committee members departed for Buffalo, where they boarded the steamer *Northern Indiana* for the voyage across Lake Erie to Monroe, Michigan. The *Northern Indiana* would have to navigate Lake Erie, "the most tempestuous and choppy of the Great Lakes," one chronicler noted. "The wide frontal storms roaring down over Lake Huron from upper Canada and Hudson's Bay strike Lake Erie with great force. . . . All through its maritime history Lake Erie has been unpredictable. Uncounted numbers of disasters, tragedies, and shipwrecks have overtaken men who have sailed over her blue surface." Metz knew firsthand of the dangers; a great storm had arisen during his first crossing of Lake Erie, sinking a staggering nine steamships.[37]

Stepping ashore in Michigan, the Inspirationists thanked the Lord for their safe arrival before boarding a train for Chicago and then a second train to Alton, Illinois. The heat and mosquitoes, Metz complained, were awful, although the scenery was enchanting, "a boundless prairie, mostly level land with high grass on which graze large herds of cattle, horses, and sheep. . . . It looked like a field of flowers where also countless pigeons find their feed."[38]

After spending the night in Alton, Metz and his companions rode yet another train to St. Louis, arriving on September 12. Metz, who was then sixty years old and in tenuous health, felt ill from gastric and intestinal disorders and needed to rest. The Inspirationists spent the night at the Friedrichs Haus before steaming north on the Missouri River aboard the *Admiral*. Four days later, the Inspirationists found themselves in a small, dusty town, Parkville, Missouri. As they proceeded west, Metz remained in poor humor. He still felt ill, and he derided the accommodations in Parkville as "gloomy and expensive." Moreover, "the people in the state of Missouri . . . are very crude and have many slaves," Metz reported. "All of their cooks are slaves. The women folks of the white men are ladies and are dressed in silk and veils and do not work."[39]

As a religious utopian, Metz could not have uttered a more damning indictment of the South. The region, in his view, was inhabited by a pampered, lazy people who sought riches by relying on the labor of slaves. Metz's comments pointed to a larger, looming problem. The Inspirationists were headed for ground zero of the tempest known as slavery. A great collision between northern opposition for slavery's expansion and southern support for it was unfolding in Kansas just as Metz and the Inspirationists were contemplating buying land there. Under the auspices of the New England Emigrant Aid Society, northern settlers who opposed slavery were streaming into the territory, hoping to thwart efforts to make Kansas a slave state. Southerners, especially Missourians, were equally determined, and in 1855 and 1856, the competition turned ugly.[40]

Widespread violence, however, had not yet broken out when Metz and his companions entered Kansas on September 25, 1854. They approached the territory in horse-drawn wagons with the assistance of an Indian guide, Charles Journeycake. Several other Indians headed to a buffalo hunt also accompanied the party. When Metz and the other members of his group entered the broad flat plain known as the Great American Desert, they were not impressed. Metz summed up the Kansas prairie's shortcomings: "There is not much timber . . . except on both sides of the river, for when the tall prairie grass is so dry in the fall it is usually destroyed by fire and the young trees are destroyed with it." The lack of water was a second serious problem. Growing wheat and corn would be difficult in such a dry climate. Metz was so discouraged that he concluded that a further search to the west would be pointless. So on October 1, the Inspirationists broke camp and headed east to explore other options. They considered buying land from the Delawares and working with a land agent, but success remained elusive. Metz had had enough: on October 23, he received a revelation that the community should postpone leaving Ebenezer, and on November 7, the scouting party returned to the settlement.[41]

The society concluded that Kansas was not the Lord's choice. Members, Metz included, reasoned that God wanted to make the move as difficult as possible as punishment for their shortcomings. In a November 13 revelation, the Lord told Barbara Landmann, "You should not drop the matter. . . . I will draw out the process for the sake of your weakness." Nearly a month later, Metz added specificity to Landemann's proclamation: the Lord had defeated the Kansas expedition because of the worldly weaknesses of one of the scouting-party members. The elders soon decided that the Inspirationists had to look elsewhere for land. In early December, they dispatched Johann Beyer and Jacob Wittmer to Iowa, though no supporting revelation directed the pair there. They returned on December 23 with the news that they had found a suitable spot some twenty miles west of Iowa City.[42]

Iowa may have seemed a curious choice. "Manifest Destiny" was carrying droves of Americans to Texas, California, and Oregon. In 1849, when gold was discovered in the Sierra Nevada range, more than 100,000 people flocked to California, many of them to San Francisco, which saw its population skyrocket from 1,000 in 1849 to 50,000 in 1856. In 1854, 231,164 migrants headed to California, Oregon, and Utah. But, of course, following the crowds was precisely what Metz did not want to do. Instead, the Inspirationists fell back on a very utopian impulse: they looked for something a little more isolated.[43]

Iowa was part of the Louisiana Purchase, the immense western territory that Thomas Jefferson's administration bought in 1803 from France for fifteen million dollars. White settlement in Iowa did not begin until thirty years later, when the federal government began removing the native Indians. The territory's population had reached only 10,531 in 1836 but soared thereafter, totaling 96,088 ten years later. Settlement moved east to west, determined in part by topography. Eastern Iowa resembled the Northeast, with trees and hills and rivers and lakes, the welcome legacy of prehistoric glaciers. The land was so rolling and picturesque that white settlers came to call the area the Switzerland of Iowa. Rainfall was abundant, and the soil was fertile, making the area suitable for farming, while ample timber provided building materials for houses and other structures. Central Iowa, too, had trees (oak and hickory, mainly), but only along the rivers. As in Kansas, tall prairie grasses dominated here. Bluestem sod grass, for example, averaged five feet in height but could grow as tall as eight feet. The terrain in northwestern Iowa was flatter and drier, with fewer trees, and this region was the last to be settled. Overall, settlement in Iowa followed a fairly orderly if not rapid pattern. The fastest

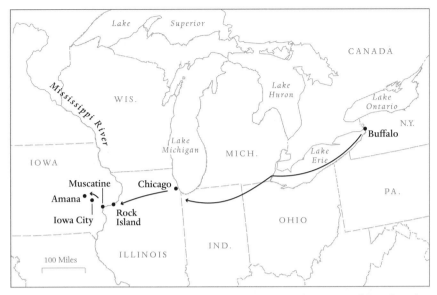

To Iowa, 1850s and 1860s: The Inspirationists' exodus to Amana began in Buffalo, where they boarded a steamer to cross Lake Erie. They landed at Monroe, Michigan, and boarded a train to Chicago. Another train then took them from Chicago to Rock Island, where they got on a steamer to Muscatine.

growth came in the 1850s, precisely when the Inspirationists were scouting out the area. Land sales peaked in 1855, when 3.7 million acres changed hands.[44]

The Inspirationists, as a result, were late arrivals to a region that was experiencing steady growth. Nevertheless, although Iowa was filling up, they hoped to avoid repeating their New York mistakes. Metz and his followers believed that the western fringes of eastern Iowa offered both isolation and adequate land on the one hand and access to markets on the other. The scouting party especially favored a scenic valley along the Iowa River, describing it as "the only place we have found so far where there is water, stone and wood found together in combination with very good farm land." Equally important, the tract was fairly cheap. The federal government was selling land in the vicinity for $1.25 an acre. By mid-June 1855, the Inspirationists had purchased nearly five thousand acres from the government and private landowners, and the group's holdings ultimately came to twenty-six thousand acres, nearly triple their land in New York.[45]

A vanguard of thirty people left Ebenezer on July 9, 1855, following a route similar but not identical to the one that Metz had taken to Kansas. The migrants rode a steamship from Buffalo to Chicago, where they boarded a train for Rock Island, Illinois. From there, they traveled on another steamship down the Mississippi River to Muscatine, Iowa. Wagons brought them the final fifty miles to Amana. In all, the journey from Ebenezer to the Midwest took nearly ten days, making it far faster than eighteenth-century migrations.[46]

The decision to leave Ebenezer was made so quickly that Metz and the Inspirationist elders had not yet lined up a buyer for their New York land. Since the plan called for funding the migration with the proceeds from such a sale, leaders began scrambling to unload the tract, placing advertisements that stressed Ebenezer's "remarkable" virtues, including its proximity to Buffalo, the "richness and variety of soil," and the Inspirationists' hard work: "The Lands offered embrace farms in the highest state of cultivation; lands unrivalled for gardening and fruit cultivation; wood and timber lots, with a variety of timber, which always meets with a ready sale in Buffalo." In July 1855, two men from Lancaster, Pennsylvania, offered to buy nearly the entire tract—7,636 acres—for nine hundred thousand dollars, but the deal fell through when the buyers could not raise the necessary cash. A second, less lucrative offer from a still-forming land company also came to naught. The Inspirationists and their legal adviser, George Babcock, concluded that they would have to sell Ebenezer piecemeal, a strategy that Babcock assured Metz would raise at least $700,000. In the interim, the Inspirationists covered their expenses in settling Amana with a loan from the Oliver Lee Bank.[47]

In Amana, the vanguard of thirty began the laborious task of establishing a new colony. A second party of eight men and three women arrived in September. Metz did not make the cross-country trek until April 17, 1856, and he returned to Ebenezer several times to oversee the sale of the New York land and to deal with those members who were unhappy about moving. Overall, the migration of the remaining members went smoothly, despite the latent discontent and the outbreak of the Civil War in 1861. As Amana's main historian has noted, "The relocation of members followed a fairly definite pattern. Elders were drawn from all of the main villages at Ebenezer and sent to Amana where they were distributed among the villages there. Members followed, a few from each of the Ebenezers, but the villages there were given a planned phasing out." Members thus moved in relatively steady waves after the first year: 41 in 1855, 166 in 1856, 95 in 1857, and approximately 100 annually over the next four years. They traveled in groups as small as 5 and as large as 50. The 1861 migration was so large that the society dissolved two of the New York villages. During the decade of the migration, 1,156 members traveled from New York to Iowa, including 230 people aged twenty or younger in 1865 and 56 people aged seventy or older. The migrants were evenly split between men and women. When the final migrants arrived in 1864, Amana's population reached 1,228.[48]

As Amana's population grew, the society erected more villages. The first expansion occurred in the fall of 1856, when the population of the central village of Amana reached 200, and South Amana and West Amana were started. The following summer, a fourth village was built between West Amana and Amana. Two more had been created by 1862, when the final village, Middle Amana, was inaugurated. Amana had the largest population, 364, while East Amana was the smallest, with 94; the other five villages ranged between 133 and 227 people.[49]

The careful, decadelong migration enabled the society to build the Iowa settlement as financial and human resources permitted. It also allowed members to develop the lands they would need to grow wheat, corn, barley, and potatoes to support the growing population. The construction process was as carefully thought out as the migration. A vanguard to a new village would first erect a kitchen house that contained living quarters for the early arrivals and space for a meeting hall. Residences and stores followed. To avoid a repeat of the New York experience, Metz wanted members to stay out of Iowa City as much as possible, a goal furthered by the presence of stores in Amana.

After leaving upstate New York in a well-planned series of migrations that covered ten years, the Inspirationists erected seven bustling villages at their new home in Amana, Iowa. (Amana Heritage Society)

Each village was relatively self-contained, with farms, shops, blacksmiths, and community kitchens.[50]

Most Inspirationists quickly adapted to Iowa. "Spring wheat and oats stand like a wall," exulted one member. "All that is possible comes out of the soil. We have never seen anything like it." Most important, the site felt spiritually right. "There is something good at this place where we have found anchor," the same member wrote. "It is by itself and not many strangers come to Price Creek."[51]

Amana as a Migration of the Pure

In its attention to detail, the Inspirationists' move to Iowa resembled the migration organized by the Moravian Church from Bethlehem, Pennsylvania, to the congregation town of Bethabara in Wachovia, North Carolina, in the early 1750s. These were not family migrations to the *Landgemeinen* composed of Society members; they were led and organized by the church. Moravian brethren moved to the *Ortsgemeinen* at the behest of the leadership. The Moravian Church balanced religious and economic considerations in deciding who moved when. And, as with the Inspirationists, the Moravians placed a premium on planning to avoid straining financial resources. The Moravian vanguard was mostly male, as befitted the rugged work of establishing a colony in the southern backcountry—clearing land, building houses and shops, and establishing church-run farms. But after a foothold had been established in the wilderness, Moravian planners became more concerned with demographic balance and began sending women and children. Regardless of the practical needs, though, Moravian leaders expected migrants to Bethabara, Bethania, and later Salem to be devout followers of the Lord who were willing to leave behind the comforts of Bethlehem for the rigors of the frontier. Although the Moravians never forced settlers to move against their will, leaders instructed members to "always keep the pilgrim spirit and whenever they could be used at any place to be ready and prepared immediately."[52]

Both migrations thus shared something elemental: pilgrims were to move when God wanted them to do so. They were embarking on a divine mission in which they would help build a new colony where the religious society could prosper and grow. By moving, pilgrims were sacrificing for the Lord, with the act of migrating a dramatic symbol of this commitment. Yet significant differences also existed between the two migrations. By issuing orders through the prophet's revelations, God played a far more direct role in the Inspirationists' migration than in the Moravian move. And reform motives assumed a far more prominent role in the Inspirationist migration: Metz repeatedly warned his followers that they had wandered from the correct path.

Utopians wanted distance from the world so they could worship God more fully, and the Inspirationists shared this motive with the Shakers and others. As evangelical Pietists, however, the Moravians had a mission to engage the world and to convert others to Jesus Christ's ways. They never sought to set themselves completely apart from the world (although they did want some distance, especially in the *Ortsgemeinen*). As a result, the Moravians' underlying motivations for migrating differed from those of the Inspirationists. The Moravians did not abandon Bethlehem because of a faltering mission; they wanted to expand into the South, where they could convert more people to Jesus and make money to support an ambitious global missionary network.

Other differences were more mundane. The Moravian migration occurred a century earlier. The journey from Bethlehem to Wachovia covered approximately 485 miles, considerably less than the 800 miles that separated Ebenezer and Amana. Yet the Moravians' challenge was harder. Eighteenth-century pilgrims lacked the transportation advantages available in the mid–nineteenth century, making the earlier journey much more time-consuming and difficult even though it covered fewer miles.

The challenging conditions and the greater time involved forced the Moravians to rely on internal networking, using other congregations as rest and resupply points. According to one historian of the migration to Bethabara, "Moravians migrat[ing] overland to North Carolina . . . received a great deal of support from their fellow members who lived along the trail. Indeed, most were able to stay overnight at the homes of other Moravians nearly every day of the journey." The Inspirationists had no need for such assistance, although later arrivals benefited from the experiences and help of their predecessors.[53]

Both the Moravians and the Inspirationists were old hands at the migration game. Their groups originated in Germany, made transatlantic crossings, established villages in the American North, and embarked on secondary migrations in America. The migration from Europe taught the Moravians a great deal, and they used that expertise in organizing their subsequent migration. But the Moravians' transatlantic crossings were elaborate affairs, with migrants organized into "sea congregations" that traveled on ships chartered by the Moravian church and manned by Moravian crews. The church carefully selected who was to go and when, and church members could not migrate unless they were selected.[54] The Inspirationists, by contrast, migrated from Germany far more haphazardly, with members choosing whether and when to depart based on such factors as their ability to raise cash for the crossing or to get out of leases and as family circumstances permitted. The relocation to Iowa from Ebenezer was better planned and executed. Elders led the way, and members moved only when Amana was ready to accommodate them.

The Inspirationists' migration to Iowa is a classic example of the second migration type outlined in the introduction—that is, mobility with the goal of strengthening the group's religious mission. As with Metz's followers, that task at times involved seeking greater distance from the world; other times, as with Hartford's "withdrawers," it meant starting in a new place in an effort to achieve a more pure religious society. In yet other cases, migration provided a way to overcome conflict, to refocus members' flagging piety on something larger, more important than themselves—motives that were implied in the Seventh Day Baptists' migration from New Jersey to western Virginia but that became explicit elsewhere. For the Hutterites, for instance, migration offered a potent way to keep a utopian movement invigorated and to avoid stasis and complacency. By migrating repeatedly and starting new villages, the Hutterites sought to rekindle zeal for both communal living and the church, especially among members of the younger generation, who would learn about sacrifice and about how to build a community from the ground up. The group's leaders thus instituted a simple but effective strategy: when the population in one of their villages in North Dakota reached about 110, they founded a daughter colony, where the renewal process began again.[55]

Similarly, the Shakers viewed other humans as hopelessly corrupt and human society as a lost cause of greed, lust, and violence. Adherents of the faith saw but one solution: to withdraw from the world. Thus they formed their own communities where they could pursue their vision of perfection. In such places, men and women were to be equal, "selfish" impulses such as sex were prohibited, and the Lord reigned supreme. Revelations played an important role in Shaker history, too. The movement's founder, Mother Ann Lee, was in an English prison in 1770 when Jesus appeared to her in a series of visions. These visions enabled Lee to develop the doctrines that came to define her movement, including celibacy. In 1772, the Lord instructed Lee and her small group of followers to move from England to America and establish a new Eden.[56] God, in essence, told Lee to move, and she did.

An American Exodus

Mormons and the Westward Trek

For Joseph Smith, the end came on a muggy June day in 1844. The Mormon prophet, beset by jeering mobs and facing punishment from hostile civil authorities, was in jail in Carthage, Illinois, along with his brother, Hyrum. Illinois's governor had promised to protect the Smiths, instructing all but one of the various local militias to disband: the Carthage Greys, however, had orders to keep Joseph and Hyrum Smith alive. It was not an easy mission. Threatening crowds repeatedly gathered outside, and the nervous town jailer moved his two prisoners to his own quarters on the second floor, where they would presumably be safer.

These efforts to protect the Smiths accomplished little. On June 27, some 125 former militiamen assembled outside the six-room jail and prepared to enter. They had an important ally—the Carthage Greys, derided by Joseph Smith's father as "our bitterest enemies." Only seven members of the Greys were on hand to guard the front entrance, and they loaded their weapons not with bullets but with blanks. When the mob approached with blackened faces, the Greys fired into the crowd, then stepped aside to let the attackers through. The men forced their way upstairs and began firing into the bedroom where the Smiths and two visiting Mormon apostles readied to defend themselves. Hyrum Smith was the first to die. A bullet fired through the door hit him in the neck, severing his spinal cord. As the militiamen entered the room, Joseph retreated to the window and prepared to jump but was struck by four bullets. Crying "O Lord, my God!" he fell through the window and toppled to the ground below, where he was shot again and bayoneted.[1]

Brigham Young was half a continent away when the attack occurred. He did not learn of Smith's murder until mid-July, nineteen days later. Stunned and horrified by the news and fearing for Mormonism's future, Young rushed back to the Mormon capital of Nauvoo, Illinois. His first task was to gain control of the church that Joseph Smith had founded fourteen years earlier. The second, more daunting challenge was to ensure that Mormonism would survive. Young, president of the powerful Quorum of the Twelve, never doubted that he was the man to achieve both tasks. On August 8, six weeks after the storming of the Carthage jail, Young stood before the Saints in Nauvoo and confidently explained why he was the best person to succeed the beloved prophet. At first glance, his confidence seemed misplaced, for Young bore little resemblance to the charismatic prophet. Smith was handsome and trim; Young was short and doughy. Smith was a dreamer and impulsive; Young was a methodical organizer. The gathered Saints were familiar with these differences—Young had been a church member and a respected leader since 1832. Given the great differences between the two men, Young delivered a performance that astonished his audience.

"Brigham Young arose and roared like a young lion, imitating the style and voice of Joseph, the Prophet," one witness recalled. "Many of the brethren declared that they saw the mantle of Joseph fall upon him. I myself . . . imagined that I saw and heard a strong resemblance to the Prophet in him, and felt that he was the man to lead us." Another witness proclaimed, "As soon as [Young] spoke I jumped upon my feet, for in every possible degree it was Joseph's voice, and his person, in look, attitude, dress and appearance; [it] was Joseph himself, personified; and I knew in a moment the spirit and mantle of Joseph was upon him."[2]

Having gained control of the church, Young turned his attention to saving Mormonism. The assassination left the faithful angry and bitter, the last straw for a movement that had faced repeated persecution since the church's earliest days. Mormons were not pacifists. Smith's burly bodyguard, Porter Rockwell, was one of the first to lash out against Mormonism's tormentors. On September 16, 1845, he shot and killed Frank Worrell, the lieutenant who commanded the Carthage Greys. A few days later, a party of Mormons captured a man suspected of burning Mormon homes and "castrated him, cut his throat, sliced off one of his ears, and shot him two or three times." These acts of revenge may have been emotionally satisfying, but Young well knew that they only further imperiled the Mormon faithful. Young proposed a deal to Illinois governor Thomas Ford: the Mormons would leave the state in the spring of 1846 if the "Gentiles" (as members of the faith referred to nonmembers) would agree to a cease-fire. On October 1, 1845, the agreement was finalized.[3]

With Joseph Smith's assassination, the Mormons realized that they had to get as far away as possible; migrating to a neighboring state or territory would no longer do. The Mormons had already migrated five times in search of a refuge, and five times they had failed to find it. Instead, trouble and violence followed them wherever they went. This time the Saints would head west across the Great Plains and the Rocky Mountains. After months of intense preparations, the first Mormon wagon train pulled out in early February 1846. When the opening wave of migration ended in October 1848, some forty-six hundred Mormons had journeyed to the Salt Lake Valley in what became the territory of Utah; by 1852, nearly sixteen thousand had made the trek.[4]

This massive internal migration, unprecedented in American religious history, preceded the Inspirationists' exodus to Iowa by a few years. Both groups were utopian. Both wanted to be left alone. Both compared their westward exoduses and the accompanying trials with those of the ancient Israelites. Both relied on revelations (although the Inspirationist movement did so to a far greater degree), and both viewed their migrations as a chance to reenergize their movements. But a fundamental difference between the two groups' migrations lay in the fact that the Mormon exodus was fueled by intense persecution, while the Inspirationists' was not. Mormonism, a faith that offered believers a chance to enter the "celestial kingdom" as gods, was born amid controversy and forged in misunderstanding and violence. As a result, persecution, not a revelation from God, determined the timing and scope of the migration. It also determined the Mormons' destination. Persecution helped define who the Saints were as well as the meaning of the exodus to Utah. In 1847, one migrant explained why he and his fellow brethren abandoned Nauvoo, the capital they had so painstakingly built only a few years earlier: "I started, with eight of the twelve apostles, together with one hundred and forty-three other persons, to search out an advantageous spot to be able to worship God according to our conscience, where we could rest from persecution, violence, and the cruelties we suffered for so long."[5]

A History of Persecution

From the earliest days of Mormonism, members of the faith had been on the move—from upstate New York to Ohio, to Missouri, to Illinois, and finally to Utah. All of these migrations occurred when the local populace turned on them.[6]

The source of this hostility was no mystery. It resided in the spare figure of a charismatic visionary named Joseph Smith Jr. and the controversial—many would say outrageous—doctrines he espoused. The founder of one of the largest modern religious movements in the United States arose from humble origins. He was born two days shy of Christmas in 1805, the third son of a struggling Vermont farmer, Joseph Smith Sr. The family had moved five times by the time Joseph was eleven, when the Smiths settled down in the upstate New York town of Palmyra and established a cake and beer shop. The Smiths also worked as day laborers and peddled various goods—pies, boiled eggs, root beer, tablecloths—in the countryside. Joseph Sr. and his wife, Lucy, did well enough to take out a mortgage on a hundred-acre farm in east Farmington, only a few miles from Palmyra.[7]

During these formative years, Joseph Jr. became a conjurer who claimed to possess the ability to locate stolen property and buried gold and silver. The boy had learned this talent from his father and a neighbor, using three seerstones that he unearthed. One night in the fall of 1823, Smith experienced a vision that changed his life. Others in the household had gone to bed, and Smith was alone, praying for forgiveness for his sins. The room grew as bright as daylight, he testified, and a spirit appeared, wearing "a loose robe of most exquisite whiteness." The visitor was an angel, Moroni, who assured Smith that his sins had been forgiven and told him about a book written on gold plates that were buried in a nearby hill. Buried with them "were two stones in silver bows fastened to a breast plate . . . called the Urim & Thummim."[8]

According to the angel, "God had prepared" the stones "for translating the book." Moroni then withdrew, only to reappear twice more, warning young Joseph that he was to use the plates not to get rich but to glorify God. Smith found the plates quite easily; a vision had revealed the location as a hill about three miles south of the family farm. He "dug away the earth and pried up the stone with a lever. Under the top stone was a box made of five stones set in cement with their flat sides turned in. Inside lay the plates, the Urim and Thummim, and the breastplate."[9]

Finding the plates was one thing; removing them was another. On September 22 of every year from 1823 to 1826, Smith visited the hill and attempted to lift the plates; each time he failed. Moroni explained that Smith was "tempted to . . . obtain riches and kept not the commandment that I should have an eye single to the glory of God." Smith subsequently discovered that he could not obtain the plates until September 1827, when he would be twenty-one years old and presumably would possess the maturity and the wisdom to undertake such an important task.[10]

Accompanied by his new wife, Emma Hale Smith, Joseph Smith returned to the hill on the evening of September 21, 1827. As midnight came and the calendar turned to September 22, Joseph at last extracted the plates, hiding them in a birch log. Smith later brought the sacred plates home and locked them in a cherrywood chest. Working behind a curtain, Smith began the laborious task of translating the ancient texts, although he had no formal education or knowledge of ancient languages. He relied instead on the Urim and Thummim. As he worked with the seer-stones and read the passages aloud, trusted associates wrote down the translations. According to one associate, "Now the way he translated was he put the urim and thummim into his hat and Darkned his Eyes then he would take a sentance and it would apper in Brite Roman Letters." Smith likened Urim and Thummim to "spectacles" provided by the Lord that enabled him to read the book. According to one recent biographer, Smith "saw twenty to thirty words at a time, dictated them, and then waited for the next twenty to appear. . . . By any measure, transcription was a miraculous process." Translating the book took nearly three years, and Smith overcame numerous setbacks, including the permanent loss of 116 pages when the disbelieving wife of one of the scribes threw the manuscript into a burning fireplace.[11]

The story unearthed by Joseph Smith, which became known as the *Book of Mormon*, was a fantastic one, leaving skeptics sputtering and admirers awestruck. It recounted the thousand-year tale of an ancient Hebrew tribe, led by a prophet named Lehi, that fled Jerusalem on the eve of the Babylonian captivity and came to North America by ship about 600 B.C. Lehi's family was riven with dissension, which eventually turned violent after Lehi selected Nephi, his "good" son, to succeed him as tribal leader. The decision angered the "bad" son, Laman. After Lehi's death, the family formally split into two tribes: the Nephites, who were righteous and fair skinned, and the Lamanites, whose divine punishment was to become dark skinned. The two factions never got along, and the quarrels were serious enough that Jesus Christ felt compelled to visit both groups in North America after his resurrection. His mediation worked for a time, but the Lamanites were unable to reform their ways, and the two tribes resumed warring. The climactic battle between them occurred around 400, with the Lamanites wiping out all 230,000 of the Nephites. Thus, when Columbus arrived in the Western Hemisphere in 1492, he found no Nephites, only the Lamanites' descendants—American Indians.[12]

The name "Mormon" refers to the last leader of the Nephites, a military leader and general. Mormon compiled most of the history in the *Book of Mormon*, and Mormon's son, Moroni, wrote the final chapters, hid the gold plates in the hill near Palmyra, and returned as an angel fifteen hundred years later to guide Smith to the buried treasure.[13]

Smith published his *Book of Mormon* in 1830, and critics wasted no time in deriding it. The derision actually began even before Smith had finished translating the plates. He could not resist boasting that he had an unearthed a "Gold Bible," and as word of this miraculous find spread, people demanded to see it. Those wanting to view the plates included fellow conjurers, who brought their own seer-stones in an unsuccessful effort to locate the magic plates. When Smith failed to produce the plates, claiming that he had hidden them during the translation phase and that Moroni had taken them back after the translation was finished, many people became angry, accusing Smith of taking "that which belonged to them." According to Smith, during this period he and his followers were "threatened with being mobbed, from time to time."[14]

The skepticism and hostility worsened after the *Book of Mormon*'s publication on March 26, 1830. The Smiths' Presbyterian congregation barred members of the family from communion and censured them. Critics pressured the printer to halt publication, and he temporarily did so. Newspapers savaged Smith as a money-hungry charlatan, and a minister denounced the *Book of Mormon* as "the greatest fraud of our time." With the ridicule mounting, Smith received a revelation commanding him to relocate the church to the friendlier confines of Kirtland, Ohio.[15]

Kirtland was a seemingly suitable choice. A small town east of Cleveland, not far from the shores of Lake Erie, it was the home of an early Mormon convert named Sydney Rigdon, who had been a leader in the Campbellite movement and was a Baptist minister until 1824. Unlike Smith's leering neighbors in Palmyra, Rigdon was quite impressed by the *Book of Mormon*, and in October 1830 he and his entire congregation converted to this controversial new movement. Smith, for his part, "rejoiced" at Rigdon's conversion, "believing that the Lord had sent him to this great and mighty man Sydney Rigdon, to help him in the work." So with opposition rising in upstate New York, and with the Mormon following growing in Kirtland, Smith and the fledgling church's quarterly conference concluded that relocating to northern Ohio would be prudent. The move would also allow scattered church members to "gather" in one place, where they could conduct missionary work and begin the task of strengthening the church. Smith and his fervent followers quickly got to work; in early August 1831, the Mormon prophet dedicated the temple site and commenced construction.[16]

Kirtland, however, proved to be no sanctuary. As their numbers grew, the Mormons faced external opposition, just as they had in New York. On March 24, 1832, a mob tarred and feathered Smith and beat Rigdon. The Saints also struggled with internal dissension and a slew of economic problems, including a failed bank scheme that brought more opprobrium on the movement. Once again, with opposition growing, Smith received a revelation telling him that the Mormons should move. The true gathering place, this revelation proclaimed, was farther west, in Jackson County, Missouri, one of Earth's holiest places, the former site of the Garden of Eden. This revelation also said that Jesus Christ would return there before the century ended. This second Mormon exodus lasted from 1831 to 1838, and the church began building its New Jerusalem. The motivations for this move closely resembled those for the departure from New York. In Missouri, the Saints could again gather and build a magnificent city. This New Jerusalem, one revelation exclaimed, was to be "a land of peace, a city of refuge, a place of safety for the saints of the most high God."[17]

When Smith visited in mid-July 1831, Independence, the seat of Jackson County, Missouri, was a raw frontier settlement only six years old. The town consisted of twenty-odd houses and a few traders and trappers who traversed the Santa Fe Trail and the Missouri River. The Mormon exodus quickly transformed the place; by the end of 1833, twelve hundred Saints had already come to the area. And as at Kirtland, Smith's followers, buoyed by millenarian expectations of Christ's imminent return, proved industrious colonizers. The symbolic heart of the Mormons' Zion was to be a temple complex consisting of three public squares and twenty-four temples that would serve as meetinghouses and schools. Equally important, the temples would constitute the center of a religious community where converts would worship God and missionaries would learn the skills needed to go out in the world and convert the masses to the only true religion. Smith hoped that the city would grow to nearly twenty thousand people.[18]

These ambitious plans alarmed Jackson's non-Mormon residents, and the continual arrival of more Saints only further darkened the mood. As one historian has noted, the Saints arrived in Independence proclaiming that "they were God's chosen people [who] had been granted a divine right to claim northwestern Missouri as their Zion." The Mormons thus came across as arrogant, self-righteous, and clannish. In addition, most of the Mormon migrants were from the North and were hostile to slavery and its spread; and they aggressively bought land, so that by the summer of 1833, they held more than twenty-four hundred acres. The locals also worried that the Mormons' large numbers and penchant for voting as a bloc would enable the brethren to take over the region's political realm, a plausible fear considering that the Saints constituted one-third of the county population within two years of their arrival.[19]

Tensions rose quickly between established residents and the newcomers, and within two years after the first Mormons arrived, Jackson County inhabitants formally demanded that the Saints depart. Residents backed up these demands by throwing rocks and bricks at Mormons' houses and by tarring and feathering a Mormon bishop and burning another leader's house. In November 1833, the Mormons reluctantly agreed to leave Jackson County. Smith was aghast at this turn of events, "driven nearly to 'madness and desperation' . . . not understanding why the grand plan for Zion, the heart of the whole restoration movement, had been set back."[20]

Despite their pledge to leave, the Mormons did not abandon Jackson County. Too much was at stake. Instead, they turned to Governor Daniel Dunklin for help and protection. He responded that no troops were needed, and he urged the Saints to take their grievances to the courts. The Mormons agreed to do so, hiring four lawyers. But this decision merely angered the Jacksonians, who accused the Mormons of going back on their word and again attacked Mormon homes, beat church members, and ransacked a Mormon store. The incidents led to an exchange of gunfire, killing one Mormon and two Missourians.[21]

In late 1833, the Saints were finally forced to retreat to neighboring Clay County. Residents of Clay, however, were just as unwelcoming. In the summer of 1836, they, too, demanded that the Saints leave. The Mormons asked the residents of Ray County for permission to move there but were denied. The Mormons again appealed to the governor for help, but he rejected their overtures. A lawyer representing the Mormons who served in the state legislature devised a clever solution: the assembly would divide Ray County and create a new county, Caldwell, for the Mormons. Smith's followers would live in Ray's sparsely inhabited northern section on prairie lands that no one else wanted and would be able to form their own government. The proposal became law on December 19, 1836. A relieved and rejuvenated Smith got busy making plans to build yet another city that would replace Independence. Migrants, including some from Kirtland, flocked to the area, believing that they at last had a safe refuge. Smith lyrically proclaimed that the church would provide "solitary places to bud and to blossom, and to bring forth in abundance." By May 1837, this new city, called Far West, had grown to 150 houses.[22]

But the shortcomings of the new refuge soon became apparent. The Mormon migrants occupied all the best lands in Caldwell, forcing later Mormon arrivals to move to neighboring counties, again stoking tensions with neighbors. This time, however, the Mormons resolved to stay and fight. On July 4, 1838, at an Independence Day celebration in Far West, Rigdon delivered a bellicose address: "That mob that comes on us to disturb us; it shall be between us and them a war of extermination." An admiring Mormon press distributed his comments and highlighted Rigdon's more inflammatory statements. Missourians took notice. Zion was rising again, being rebuilt by a growing and belligerent Mormon contingent. When the Mormons refused to support a local Whig politician for election, the angry candidate, William Peniston, urged non-Mormon residents to keep the Saints from voting, and he lambasted the Mormons as "horse thieves, liars, counterfeiters, and dupes." A bystander agreed, telling the crowd that the Mormons had no more right to vote "than the niggers." The insults led to a brawl. The incident sparked a "war" that saw Mormon residents in nearby Daviess County continually attacked until they were driven from their homes. Smith vowed vengeance. "We are an injured people," he told the Saints. "From county to county we have been driven by unscrupulous mobs eager to seize the land we have cleared and improved with such love and toil. . . . If the people will let us alone, we will preach the gospel in peace. But if they come to molest us, we will establish our religion by the sword. We will trample down our enemies and make it one gore of blood from the Rocky Mountains to the Atlantic Ocean."[23]

The Saints responded to this call to arms by attacking towns in Daviess County. On October 18, 1838, Saints burned some fifty buildings in Gallatin, Millport, and elsewhere, plundering stores and livestock as they went. Smith's uncle was optimistic that "we have driven most of the enemy out of the Co." In actuality, the raid outraged Missourians and led them to retaliate by destroying Mormon homes and killing three Saints in a pitched battle. The state's recently elected governor, Lilburn W. Boggs, blamed the Mormons for the violence and ordered the state militia into the field with a mandate to kill: "The Mormons must be treated as enemies, and must be exterminated, or driven from the State if necessary for the public peace—their outrages are beyond all description."[24]

On October 30, three militia companies totaling some 240 soldiers attacked Haun's Mill, a Mormon settlement fifteen miles from Far West. The militia sprang out of the woods and began firing at the families of Saints working in the fields. Caught by surprise and outgunned, the Mormons tried to surrender, but the soldiers kept firing. Most of the Saints escaped into a nearby coppice. Eighteen Saints—fifteen men and three boys—retreated into a blacksmith shop built of logs, but the soldiers merely stuck their guns through the gaps in the log walls and fired, an attack one historian has likened to "plinking hogs in a pen." The death toll for the day totaled about seventeen, and Saints labeled the incident a massacre.[25]

In all, about forty Saints died in the 1838 fighting, with several others wounded. Twenty-five hundred troops had been dispatched to burn Far West to the ground, and Smith reluctantly concluded that the Saints faced annihilation if they continued armed resistance. On sunset on October 31, the prophet and four other Mormon leaders walked out of the city, with Smith telling his followers, "I shall offer myself up as a sacrifice to save your lives and save the Church." The militia commander, who was in no mood for negotiations, unilaterally imposed harsh surrender conditions. The Mormons had to reimburse the county's citizens for their losses. Individual Saints were to surrender their arms and face charges for their crimes. And the Mormons were to leave Missouri. On November 1, Far West formally surrendered. Facing swift frontier justice, Smith was convicted of treason and sentenced to die, though General Alexander Doniphan refused to carry out the order.[26]

Smith's conviction and the Saints' capitulation did not end the violence. The harassment was so bad that one Mormon reported, "The Brethren are hunted as wild game and shot down, severeal have been shot in site of the City." The continuing attacks further embittered the Mormons. "Those who were butchered at Haun's Mill crieth for vengeance," warned one Saint. "I from this day declare myself the Avenger of the blood of those innocent men."[27]

The Mormons spent the winter of 1839 preparing to leave Missouri, but a change in public opinion was beginning to occur. People who had earlier blamed the Saints for instigating the trouble began to feel sympathy for them after learning of the bloody attacks and especially of the killings at Haun's Mill. Smith walked out of jail in April 1839 while the sheriff literally looked the other way, and Illinois offered the Mormons a temporary refuge.

Smith remained optimistic that the latest new home would provide safety for the church, proclaiming, "Now we can enjoy peace, and can worship the God of heaven and earth without molestation." Illinois was not Missouri. It welcomed the Mormons, and Smith believed he had chosen an excellent site for the latest temple city—in Hancock County, along the Mississippi River. The site was remote and uninhabited and was not coveted by non-Mormons. The land was available because of its numerous physical shortcomings. It was a malarial swamp that Smith described as "so wet [and narrow] that it was with the utmost difficulty that a footman could get through." For Smith, this spit of land in the crook of the upper Mississippi represented a new beginning. He and his followers had survived the Missouri experience and had yet another chance to build a refuge for the Lord's chosen people. He pointedly compared this latest exodus to the children of Israel's escape from bondage in Egypt. The new city in Illinois would be called Nauvoo, a name "of Hebrew origin, [signifying] a beautiful situation, or place, carrying with it, also, the idea of rest; and is truly descriptive of this most delightful situation."[28]

Smith designated Nauvoo as the Mormons' international capital, and Mormon missionaries working abroad encouraged converts to come to the newest Zion. The response was immediate. The first shipload of migrants left England in 1840, and thousands more followed. Within five years, the city was home to fifteen thousand souls, and by 1844 it was the largest city in Illinois.[29]

Again, however, the Saints' success threatened their non-Mormon neighbors, and the people of Illinois turned against the Mormons and all that they were building in Nauvoo. Non-Mormons were alarmed by the city charter that Smith and his allies managed to get through the state legislature in late 1840, when the Mormons still enjoyed some public sympathy. The charter created a city-state with strong local rule and named Smith as "King, Priest, and Ruler over Israel on Earth." It also allowed Smith to create a five-thousand-member militia, the Nauvoo Legion—half the size of the entire U.S. Army. Critics charged that Smith had all the power of an emperor and was above the law. The prophet oversaw a growing church and served as mayor of the city and as chief magistrate of the municipal court.[30]

His actions as mayor only confirmed the fears of Smith's detractors. In May 1841, a posse from Missouri captured Smith, who was wanted for having escaped from jail. But Smith easily secured his release by turning to the Mormon-dominated city council, which issued a writ of habeas corpus. Critics became further alarmed when Smith delivered a speech in which he predicted that Boggs, who had issued the infamous order calling for the Mormons' extinction, would "die by violent hands within one year." On May 6, 1842, a gunman shot Boggs four times, although he survived. Suspicion immediately focused on Porter Rockwell, Smith's bodyguard, who was living in Independence with his in-laws as he awaited the birth of his fourth child.[31]

Gentiles thus believed that Smith was openly seeking to establish a "government of God" with himself as the unchallenged king. He also ran for president of the United States in 1844, a campaign that Smith's opponents saw as both crazy and dangerous. Smith faced internal opposition from church dissenters who agreed that Smith was turning into a tyrant. They especially disliked Smith's new doctrine of polygamy, and one dissenter, William Law, took Smith to court, accusing the Mormon leader of committing adultery. The growing internal dissension confirmed outsiders' suspicions that Mormonism posed a dire threat to public peace and safety and further angered Smith by causing the faith problems. On June 7, 1844, the dissenters published their charges against Smith and the church in a newspaper they founded, the *Nauvoo Expositor*. Smith derided the publication as a "greater nuisance than a dead carcass." At his instigation, the city council passed a libel ordinance, and Smith, acting in his capacity as mayor, ordered the destruction of the paper's printing press. A posse of one hundred men carried out his command.[32]

The destruction of the *Expositor* "confirmed a growing fear among non-Mormons that [Smith] was a megalomaniacal tyrant who posed a clear and present danger to the peace and stability of the region." Indeed, an editorial writer in neighboring Warsaw declared, "War and extermination is inevitable! CITIZENS ARISE, ONE AND ALL!" With tensions rising, a sword-wielding Smith, in full military regalia, declared martial law on June 18 and mobilized the Nauvoo Legion. Governor Ford did not want a repeat of the Missouri experience and ordered Smith to surrender and face charges for destroying the press. If Smith failed to comply, the governor explained, "I have great fears that your city will be destroyed, and your people many of them exterminated." He also personally vouched for Smith's safety. A skeptical Smith responded by fleeing with his brother in the dark of night on June 23. Rockwell rowed the two brothers across the Mississippi in a leaky rowboat, and the Smiths set out for either the Rocky Mountains or Washington, D.C. (sources vary on their destination). But as they awaited the arrival of horses, a messenger delivered a letter from the governor urging Joseph to return. The Smiths also learned that their fellow Saints were upset that their leader had abandoned the church. Though he still feared for his safety, Joseph Smith returned, surrendering on June 24. His twenty-five mile journey from Nauvoo to the jail in Carthage resembled Christ's journey to the cross, as jeering, hostile crowds lined the road, taunting, "We'll use him up and kill all the damn Mormons." In Carthage, armed citizens mobbed the streets, drinking alcohol and plotting their next steps. Ford tried to defuse the situation by ordering all local militias except the Carthage Greys to disband. Three days later, Smith was dead.[33]

A Movement at the Crossroads

With the prophet dead and the Saints facing eviction from their homes, the church's survival came into question. Hearing of Smith's demise, one Bostonian exclaimed, "So much for Mormonism!!!" He had reason to feel confident: Mormonism was the second-most-hated religious movement in Protestant-dominated America; only the Roman Catholic Church was more detested than Joseph Smith and his followers.[34]

Brigham Young knew that the Saints had to get out of Illinois and that they were facing yet another difficult migration, this time to an unknown destination westward across the broad, sere plains. During these dark days, however, the church also had several things going for it. Its remaining members possessed a steely resolve arising from their belief that the church's founder held the keys to religious knowledge and fulfillment. As outlandish as Smith's claims appeared to unbelievers, his theology evoked equally strong support among his followers because they approached his claims from a quite different perspective than did his critics. Talk of seer-stones, gold plates, angelic visits, ancient tribal wars, and temples tapped into a strain of Christianity, folklore, and mysticism that went back centuries and that remained popular in nineteenth-century America. As historian John L. Brooke has shown, early Mormon doctrines drew on a tradition of hermeticism, defined as the relationship between the visible and invisible worlds. "As a prophet, Smith claimed to be a vehicle of the continuing revelation of the 'Word,' opening a channel of divine power between the visible and invisible worlds," Brooke explains. "He laid claim to the authority of Enoch and Elijah, the biblical prophets who were carried bodily into heaven by divine power. This restoration was inaugurated with the miraculous writing of the *Book of Mormon*, translated by divine power from golden plates buried by the last survivor of an ancient people."[35]

Smith was an occult practitioner who, in Brooke's words, "presented himself as the Nephite, the prophet of the coming Kingdom, the vehicle for the restoration of the ancient mysteries." Understanding these hermetic talents is essential to understanding the popularity of Smith's movement. As Mormonism evolved in the years between the publication of the *Book of Mormon* in 1830 and Smith's assassination in 1844, he developed doctrines that offered believers the chance to become gods. As Brooke has observed, "The eventual success of Mormonism lay in the embedding of a shared charisma in the institutional fabric of the church. Joseph Smith would not maintain an absolute monopoly over spiritual power but rather doled it out in an evolving system of inclusive priesthoods, governed by an increasingly elaborate hierarchy." Beginning in April 1830, Smith served as the seer and revelator; in January 1831, he became president of the High Priesthood. In March 1833, he established the First Presidency, which included a president and two counselors. A Council of Twelve Apostles followed in February 1835, and a Quorum of Seventies in March 1835. All male members above the age of twelve belonged to the Aaronic Priesthood, the lowest order in the Mormon hierarchy. The next level up was the more powerful Priesthood of Melchizedek, or high priesthood, whose abilities included "'wonderful works' of exorcism, faith-healing, resistance to snakes, and handling snakes. . . . The Mormon high priests would in effect be *magi* [possessors of supernatural abilities], with powers extending up from the visible world on earth to the invisible world of the heavens."[36]

Smith did not stop with the inclusion of all males into the priesthood. In the early 1830s, he promised to reveal the secret workings of God's kingdom and the way to eternal life. In the cosmos constructed by the Mormon founder, Christianity's traditional heaven and hell were replaced by a heaven that corresponded to the stars, the moon, and the sun. People's behavior determined the world to which they would be assigned. The bottom rung, the telestial world, was reserved for "liars, and sorcerers, and adulterers, and whoremongers." Next came the terrestrial world, which would house non-Mormons who were better behaved than whoremongers but who had not grasped the "fullness of the Father." People who qualified for the terrestrial world would be granted salvation but not "divine exultation." That lofty status was reserved for Mormons on the top rung—those who entered the celestial kingdom and would thus rank as gods. "Smith's theology," Brooke observes, "promised a radical departure from traditional Protestant Christianity. The Mormon cosmos announced universal salvation for humanity and promised divinity to the Mormon faithful."[37]

The Mormon world was thus a hopeful world. In offering the prospect of divinity, Smith downplayed the central tenets of Christianity, rejecting the notion of original sin. Adam, as generations of children have learned in Sunday school, was the cause of man's downfall, and his original sin was passed on to all humans. But in Mormon theology, Adam was a hero, "the revered father of all," who mated with nature. This good Adam did not pass on his sins to humankind, and Jesus consequently played a smaller role in salvation. For Evangelicals and mainstream Christians, a belief in Jesus was paramount to earning eternal salvation. For Mormons, accepting Jesus as one's savior was important but earned believers only admittance into the terrestrial kingdom. Entering the celestial kingdom and earning godhood required "the faithful Mormon, inheriting an innocent condition from Adam, to remain sin free—and to obey the sacred ordinances of the church," Brooke notes. "This obedience to law—not the free gift of grace—would be the deciding factor in the soul's entry into the celestial kingdom." In the words of a Mormon proverb, "As man is now, so once was God; as God is now, man may become."[38]

The hopefulness of the Mormon faith was reflected in two other controversial Smith doctrines: baptism of the dead and plural marriage. Smith developed the baptism ritual based on a January 1836 revelation in which he saw his brother, Alvin, in the celestial kingdom with Adam and Abraham. The baptism was meant to soothe grieving survivors; people who had "died without a knowledge of the gospel," Smith decreed, could still enter the celestial kingdom if they were baptized after their demise.[39]

For Smith, polygamy (known to supporters as "celestial marriage") had several rationales. He believed that the practice was sanctioned in Genesis, which describes how Abraham, Isaac, and Jacob fathered numerous children with concubines. But he also saw plural marriage and its mandate to procreate as a way to strengthen the Mormon family and allow more members to gain access to the celestial kingdom. Taking on additional wives and raising more young Mormons would gain a patriarch a higher rank in the pantheon of gods and would assure the wives entry into the celestial kingdom. That polygamy proved to be so controversial only heightened its allure for some Saints. "Plural marriage," Brooke notes, "became a bond among a people set apart. It simply was illegal in the state of Illinois, so following the prophet meant risking arrest." The practice especially tightened the bonds among the leaders, who not only shared the risks but also reaped the rewards both in the afterlife and on earth. Brigham Young, for example, married three of Joseph Smith's wives after the prophet's assassination.[40]

Smith's theology of hope and the church's aggressive missionary efforts helped to attract an impressive following. In June 1830, two months after the church was founded, membership stood at twenty-seven. Ten years later, despite the setbacks in Ohio and Missouri, the church had thirty thousand members, and that figure reached eighty thousand by the end of 1860. Nauvoo, too, had prospered. In 1846, its population stood at eleven thousand, the temple was nearly completed, and the onetime swamp had taken on all the airs of a capital city. Young described Nauvoo as a "paradise" and noted that "many strangers are pouring in to view the Temple and the city. They express their astonishment and surprise to see the rapid progress of the Temple, and the beauty and grandeur of Mormon looks. Many brethren are coming from abroad, who seem highly delighted with the place and all its appendages."[41]

Adhering strongly to Smith's worldview, Mormons believed themselves to be members of the one true church. The church's formal name (Church of Jesus Christ of Latter-day Saints) was telling. Mormons viewed themselves as just that—latter-day saints, the modern heirs of ancient Israel. The criticism from internal dissenters such as James Strang and the intense persecution that devout members faced only reinforced this feeling of righteousness and strengthened their commitment to the church. Both verbal and physical attacks solidified the Saints' belief that they were the chosen ones, a confidence outsiders perceived as arrogance. At a time when antebellum America was

Joseph Smith and his brother, Hyrum, were killed at the Carthage jail on June 27, 1844. The assassination of the beloved prophet and church founder led to the massive Mormon exodus to Utah beginning in 1846. (Bettmann / CORBIS)

moving slowly but steadily toward ecumenicalism and greater cooperation among churches, the Saints proclaimed that they were right and that other faiths were wrong. Such an attitude made the Mormons easy targets, helping to feed the persecution that the church constantly faced.

Mormonism and all for which it stood attracted as many enemies as supporters. And some of the prophet's newer innovations, most notably polygamy, further heightened opponents' vitriol. Rumors that Mormon leaders had multiple wives scandalized nineteenth-century America. Smith's assassination only increased the pressure on the Saints. Following the bloody events at Carthage, opponents stepped up their assaults on Smith's followers: in January 1845, Nauvoo lost its city charter, and the following September, a mob of three hundred attacked outlying Mormon homes and farms, destroying forty-four buildings by Young's count. Many settlers retreated to Nauvoo, and the Council of Twelve publicly announced on September 22 that the Mormons would leave Illinois. The attacks, though, did not stop. That fall, opponents burned more than two hundred houses, shops, and farm buildings. On October 1, a committee of Saints led by Young reached an agreement with Governor Ford that echoed the agreement in Missouri: the Saints would leave Illinois by spring, "as soon as the grass is green and the water runs" following the winter thaws. The state would dispatch troops to protect Nauvoo, but the Mormons would get out and would assign trustees to dispose of any unsold property after the migrants had departed.[42]

The Exodus to Utah

Mormon leaders now had to decide where to go. A year earlier, when Smith was running for the U.S. presidency, church officials had pondered the desirability of establishing Mormon settlements in Texas, Oregon, or California. Stephen Douglas, the powerful senator from Illinois, helpfully suggested that the Mormons look to Oregon. Smith had had a revelation in 1842 "that the Saints would continue to suffer much affliction and would be driven to the Rocky Mountains"; he seemed to favor California when he sent out an exploration team in February 1844. Critics outside of Illinois, meanwhile, got wind of these plans and began worrying that the Mormons wanted to establish a huge western empire that, in the words of the New York Weekly Herald, could "rival the Arabians."[43]

But these plans remained amorphous, and when Young took over after the killings at the Carthage jail, he had no specific destination in mind. He knew that the church's new home would be someplace "over the mountains," and he suspected that it might well be the Great Basin region in the future territory of Utah. The Saints' needs were obvious. They required a large tract of land far from their enemies—as Young put it, to move "from a land of oppression and violence to some more congenial clime." In the winter of 1844–45, while mourning Smith's death, the Quorum of Twelve continued studying the options by reading newspaper stories, government reports, and travel accounts penned by fur trappers. Members of the quorum concluded that Texas and Vancouver Island were not suitable but still considered Oregon and California, despite their immense popularity with western-bound migrants. Another possibility was the Rocky Mountain region—specifically, the Great Salt Lake Valley and the Utah Valley. Both sites could hold more than sixteen thousand migrants but were empty of white settlers. The two valleys sat in a huge area the size of Texas known as the Great Basin, west of the Rocky Mountains, north of the Colorado River, east of the Sierra Nevada, and south of the Columbia River watershed. As a recent biographer of Young has noted, "The outstanding characteristics of the Great Basin were its isolation, aridity, and the scarcity of timber and game. Missouri Valley trading posts were twelve hundred miles away, transportation to and within the region was difficult, and rainfall varied from five to sixteen inches per year." The region, in short, was nearly perfect because of its isolation and difficult conditions, which would presumably discourage visitors and settlement by outsiders. The *Nauvoo Neighbor* certainly recognized the Great Basin's virtues and offered enthusiastic support. The Mormon newspaper printed excerpts from the journals of explorer John C. Frémont extolling the region, concluding that the Great Salt Lake was "one of the wonders of the world."[44]

As Young pondered the possibilities, he readied his followers for the difficult trek. The Saints, he preached at the end of a preparatory church conference in October 1845, were facing "a crisis of extraordinary and thrilling interests—the exodus of the nation of the only true Israel from these United States to a far distant region of the West." Deliverance was at hand, he continued, and he urged all "dear brethren" to "wake up, wake up . . . to the present glorious emergency in which the God of heaven has placed you to prove your faith by your works, preparatory to a rich endowment in the Temple of the Lord, and the obtaining of promises and deliverances, and glories for yourselves and your children and your dead." Young originally wanted the exodus to begin in April 1846, but events forced him to accelerate his timetable. With violence a constant threat, the Saints' leadership did not dismiss a warning from Governor Ford that federal troops in St. Louis planned to attack Mormon wagon trains and prevent their leaving for the West. In mid-January, Young decided that because of "the evil intended toward us," the migration would have to begin sooner than he had hoped.[45]

In contrast to their earlier migrations, the Mormons this time would be venturing into areas outside the control of the United States, lonely places dominated by potentially hostile Indians and without railroads or steamboats to assist in the journey. Mormon wagon trains would have to cross the Great Plains, then navigate steep Rocky Mountain passes. Distances were vast, and the weather and the difficulty of obtaining supplies posed challenges. In addition, the United States declared war on Mexico in May 1846, and the two nations were fighting over the Southwest precisely as the Mormons would be traveling west. The church estimated that a family of five adults would need "1 good strong wagon, well-covered. 3 good yokes of oxen between the ages of four and ten. Two or more cows," and more than a ton of supplies, including a thousand pounds of flour and enough goods to trade with the Indians. The Saints would have to construct more than two thousand wagons at a cost of about $120 apiece, a task carpenters began in the fall of 1845.[46]

The plan to move nearly sixteen thousand migrants underwent several changes and became mired in church politics. The first version envisioned sending a vanguard of a few hundred men—carpenters, farmers, millwrights, and other essential craftsmen—over the Rockies to the Great Basin (also known as the Bear River Valley) to prepare for the arrival of migrant camps by planting crops and building support structures. But the Council of Fifty, challenging the Council of Twelve and Brigham Young, developed a rival scheme that called for the establishment of a way station in Yellowstone, north of Fort Laramie. The Council of Fifty believed that the first plan was unrealistic because it rested on the premise that the vanguard could cross the mountains quickly, reaching the settlement area by June 1, 1847, in time to begin planting crops. The council proposed a longer and more leisurely migration that would take a northerly route to the Great Basin.[47]

Young viewed this plan as a slap in the face, arguing that the Yellowstone route was not only longer and slower but was also more dangerous because it would carry the migrants too far into Sioux country. The debate turned nasty. One member of the Council of Fifty, George Miller, attacked Young's plans and his leadership. An angry Young responded by warning "that Miller and [James] Emmett had a delusive spirit and any one that would follow them would go to hell." In January 1847, Young announced that God and Joseph Smith were on his side: he had a dream and a revelation that Smith and his mother appeared before Young and gave him advice about the best way to organize the migration. A subsequent revelation confirmed that the twelve apostles, not the Council of Fifty, were to control the migration. "For the first time since Joseph Smith," one historian recounted, "God had once again given direction . . . and had stated unequivocally who was in charge. . . . Not the Council of Fifty, not the High Council, nor any other group but the Twelve was in control."[48]

In reestablishing their authority, Young and the Council of Twelve came up with a third migration plan that settled the questions of who was in charge and of the overall strategy. The Saints would loosely follow the first plan—a vanguard would make a dash across the mountains so it could plant crops and begin building in the Mormons' new home. The church would organize the remaining migrants into Pioneer Companies and decide when each company would depart.[49]

The details of the migration—the exact route, the destination, and the timing—were far from settled, however, and were subject to change as events unfolded. The initial departure, for example, was pushed up to early February 1846 because of the ongoing persecution and because of wintry weather. On

February 4, the first party of Saints crossed the Mississippi. When the river froze later in the month, large wagon trains could cross more easily. Young remained in Illinois to attend to various matters before joining the exodus on February 15, accompanied by fifty members of his extended family (he had twelve wives at the time). They headed to the staging ground at Sugar Creek, nine miles into Iowa. By mid-May, more than ten thousand Mormons had crossed the Mississippi.[50]

For most, the departure from hostile and dangerous Illinois was a time of joy. "Some were singing, some were dancing, some were playing music, everyone seemed full of life and joy," recalled migrant George Whitaker. "We felt as though we had been released from bondage." Young actively encouraged this feeling of deliverance, reassuring the Saints that they were the rightful heirs of Israel. In an address he told the migrants that he was "constrained by the spirit to say to you, my brethren, in this camp of Pioneres [we] have come out of bondage to find a location for a Stake of Zion." The migrants also believed that in their new western home, they would finally achieve their longtime dream of constructing a true Zion. Thomas Bullock, who was thirty when he left Nauvoo, explained that the migrants wanted to devote "the remainder of our lives more to the honor and glory of God: that when our pilgrimage is ended, we may be crowned His, in the Celestial Kingdom of our God."[51]

At Sugar Creek, Brigham Young had more immediate and mundane concerns than the celestial kingdom. Although eastern Iowa, as the Inspirationists would soon learn, was growing rapidly, western Iowa remained sparsely populated, with few roads. Not until February 23, 1846, did the council arrive at a consensus about how to reach Nebraska. The Saints would move northwest along the Farmington road to Bonaparte, where they would cross the Des Moines River and head west to the Missouri. If all went well, the vanguard of Saints (also known as the Company of Twelve, the Camp of Israel, and the Pioneer Company), would reach the Missouri River by mid-April. They would then plant crops to supply food to the trailing migrants.[52]

But heavy rain and mud wreaked havoc with these plans. Because of record-breaking rains, the journey across Iowa to the Missouri took not six weeks but nearly four months. The Saints' wagons sunk in the mud, and crossing swollen, swift-moving streams became an ordeal. On some days, the rain fell so hard that the migrants could travel only a half mile, far less than the customary twelve to fifteen miles. For William Huntington, it was the cold and mud that stood out during this leg of the journey. He recalled camping one "miserable" night in April when "it was very cold with high wind and hard rain all night and no fire, mud knee deep around our tents, ground filled with and nearly covered with water."[53]

The delays caused Young and the council to reconsider the vanguard's route. To head northwest, as originally planned, would carry the migrants over more open—and emptier—land. To head southwest would take the migrants to more populated areas along the Missouri, where they could trade for badly needed supplies. Ultimately, however, the leaders decided to stick with the original northern route. The delays also meant that the vanguard would not cross the Rockies in 1846; the council decided in early August that the church would establish winter quarters in the Council Bluffs of Nebraska, along the western banks of the Missouri River.[54]

A huge temporary city was thus erected near Cutler's Park, wedged between two bluffs about two and a half miles west of the Missouri. By the end of December, nearly four thousand Saints were living there in six hundred log houses and hovels. The winter quarters encompassed nearly eight hundred acres and eventually featured a store, carding-machine house, and hostel; one visitor described the camp as "a regularly laid out town . . . extending along the river a mile or more." Another three thousand Saints camped on the Iowa side of the Missouri, while the remaining forty-five hundred sheltered across Iowa and as far east as St. Louis. The makeshift nature of the camps and the high concentrations of people led to malnutrition and disease, and by the end of 1846, some six hundred Saints had died.[55]

On April 14, 1847, Young and the Company of Twelve left the winter quarters with a party of 142 men, 3 women, and only 2 children. The company's seventy-two wagons covered about 15 miles that first day, halting "by a beautiful grove of timber." The following morning, the group "took up the line of march westward penetrating the unexplored regions of the far west. Singing the songs of Zion telling stories and anecdotes . . . around the Campfires at nights." The vanguard reached Grand Island, 214 miles from its starting point along the Missouri, by the end of April. The migrants felt an array of emotions as they left the lower Platte River Valley. Heber C. Kimball described the scenery as "beautiful and pleasing to the eye of the traveler, notwithstanding there is only the same kind of scenery from day to day, namely . . . the majestic Platte, with its muddy waters rolling over the universal beds of quicksands, the river frequently hid from view by the many handsome cotton groves, before and behind . . . a vast, level prairie, and on the right at distance the continued majestic bluffs."[56]

At the end of May, the Pioneer Company passed by Chimney Rock, which William Clayton likened to the "large factory chimneys in England, though

I could not see the form of its base." Others described "huge rocks that had been rolled out of their natural place by the wash of heavy rains or the convulsive throes of nature at the crucifixion of our Savior." A touch of nervousness accompanied the Saints as they admired the scenery; this was Sioux country. A band led by Chief Owashtecha approached the Mormon vanguard on May 24. Despite the Sioux's fierce reputation, the Mormons were impressed: "They were all dressed in their richest costumes," according to one migrant. "Some had fur caps and cloth coats. . . . [T]he rest were neatly dressed in skins ornamented with beads, feathers, paints, etc."[57]

The next leg of the migration carried the Pioneer Company from Fort Laramie, where the vanguard was resting, to Fort Bridger. The stopover at Fort Laramie ended a particularly lonely stretch of travel that saw the pioneers navigate six hundred miles of plains. With the Black Hills nearby, the fort commanded an imposing site on Laramie Fork, just above its confluence with the North Platte River. The post was owned by the American Fur Company and was home to about eighteen families. Its fifteen-inch-thick walls housed a blacksmith shop, a trading room, and sleeping quarters, and the fort allowed western migrants some much needed rest. The Saints welcomed the respite. According to Bullock's calculations, they had traveled 560 miles in seven weeks, and the journey had taken quite a toll: "My clothes are getting all worn out, my boot I lost the Sole of. . . . [B]oth my pantaloons have been ript from stem to stern. . . . This is the coldest, & most dusty journey I have ever traveled, I wash my hands & face some days twice, & three times, & yet I have been as dirty as a Sweep in two hours." When the Saints left the relative comfort of Fort Laramie, they had to reckon with other losses as well. Kimball reported that two horses had died in accidents and that the Pawnee had stolen another two at Gravel Creek. By Kimball's count, the company now had ninety-six horses and ninety oxen. At one point, Kimball reported, "Several of the horse teams gave out, and the horses are evidently failing daily, but our oxen are gaining. Mules stand the journey well."[58]

The North Platte River posed a major hurdle on this leg of the journey. An unusually snowy winter and an early, warm spring had enlarged the Platte from its usual sixty-yard width and six-foot depth to one hundred feet wide and fifteen feet deep. The Saints first tried emptying their wagons and ferrying them over individually, a time-consuming and laborious task. They then tried roping several wagons together and floating them across, but stiff winds and strong currents carried the wagons nearly three miles downstream. Finally, the Saints spent two days building a ferry big enough to transport fully loaded wagons and their teams across the river. The ferry featured two

To Utah, 1840s and 1850s: The first Mormon wagon train pulled out of Nauvoo in early February 1846; stopping points included the winter quarters and Fort Bridger. By 1852, nearly sixteen thousand Mormons organized into "pioneer companies" had made the trek to Salt Lake City.

twenty-four-foot-long canoes on which a platform floated and worked so well that the Mormons left behind a few brethren to operate a ferry service for any traveler trying to get across. The service proved quite lucrative, transporting 489 wagons and nearly two thousand people over a sixteen-day period and earning $593.05.[59]

The Saints soon came upon other rivers and streams, each of which presented challenges. Clayton described one such crossing that took the Mormon wagon train all day: "Some unloaded their goods on the bank, which were carried in the boat to the sand bar, the teams going down to the ferry to cross. After a few wagons had gone over it was perceived that they went over with less difficulty, and by doubling teams they soon took over the loaded wagons without much difficulty. I prepared to wade over the river . . . but Jackson Redding brought me Porter Rockwell's horse to ride over, and I mounted and proceeded. I found the current strong, indeed." Eight hours passed before the entire party crossed, but the train made it "without any loss or accident, which made the brethren feel thankful indeed."[60]

The Saints reached Fort Bridger on July 7, leaving them with only the last leg of their journey in front of them. But some Saints in the advance party still did not know the ultimate destination. In mid-June, a month before they reached Fort Bridger, Bullock reported to his wife, "We are now about 300 miles from Bridger, but where we go we know not." Leaders consulted with several western explorers, including Moses Harris, a mountain man who ran into the Mormons on June 27 near South Pass. He advised against settling in Salt Lake Valley because "the soil is sandy and barren." Another hunter and trader, Jim Bridger, strongly disagreed, proclaiming the Salt Lake Valley a good place to settle—it was well watered, abounded in game, had good soil, and was near mountains rich in gold, silver, and copper. Kimball nevertheless remained skeptical, considering Bridger's information "greatly exaggerated. He mingled his descriptions so much that it was scarce possible to form an idea of what he meant."[61]

Young and the Council of Twelve finally chose the valley because it met their most important criterion: isolation. Finding a lonely spot had always been their goal; in an August 9, 1846, letter to President James K. Polk, Mormon leaders had explained that the exodus would "end in a location west of the Rocky Mountains, and within the basin of the Great Salt Lake or Bear River Valley . . . believing that to be a point where a good living will require hard labor, and consequently will be coveted by no other people." In the end, the Salt Lake Valley won out over Bear River because it was more isolated. People had begun settling in the Utah Lake area, through which passed a well-traveled trail to Oregon and California.[62]

At Fort Bridger, the leadership mapped the route to the Salt Lake Valley as the brethren repaired equipment and rested. Lingering at Bridger was never a serious option. The homely pile of logs built by Jim Bridger in 1843 consisted merely of "two or three rudely constructed log cabins" and a "small enclosure for stock built of upright poles." With the winter cold drawing ever closer, Mormon officials remained eager to finish the migration. The final leg of the trip, about 115 miles, would carry the migrants over the "most mountainous course we have seen yet," on a route Frémont had first traveled in 1845. It involved taking the "Hastings Cutoff," a shortcut recommended by Lansford Hasting and endorsed by Bridger. The migrants would travel along the Oregon Trail before veering west and southwest over a salt desert to Pilot Peak and then to the valley at Salt Lake. The Mormons optimistically believed that they would need only ten days to reach their new home.[63]

But the steep mountain trails proved especially time-consuming. As one historian noted, "Climbing over the ridge dividing the waters of the Colorado from those of the Great Basin, they climbed 750 feet in two days, reaching an altitude of 7,700 feet on July 10—over 300 feet higher than South Pass." The ascent was challenging for fully loaded wagons pulled by balky oxen, "and the descents were more hazardous. . . . Usually, a dozen or more men held on tightly to ropes attached to the back of the wagon to ease the descent. Occasionally even a team of oxen were hitched to the back end of the wagon and held back in order to keep it from 'ending over.'"[64]

Bullock described the journey for those who would follow: "The mountains between Fort Bridger and the valley are very high, and the road winds through the valleys between them, some of which very narrow—in some places not more than ten yards wide, and the rocks are steep on either side, sometimes about a mile high. The elevation of the highest mountain ridge we have to cross over . . . is about 7,300 feet above sea level. From this ridge you will see the *Twin peaks*, which are covered with eternal snow. The slopes of these two mountains reach to the [Salt Lake] valley; and when you see them, you will shout out, 'I shall soon be home now.'"[65]

Many in the vanguard became sick with mountain fever, also called Rocky Mountain Fever. On July 3, Erastus Snow was the first to fall ill: "Its first appearance is like that of a severe cold, producing soreness in the flesh, and pains in the head and all parts of the body," he reported. Rejecting conventional treatments that called for inducing vomiting or bleeding, the Mormons prescribed mild herbs and the laying on of hands. Young became sick, and the company stopped for a time in the Bear River Valley while he suffered from a 105-degree fever and was "almost mad with pain" in his back and hands.[66]

While Young convalesced, Mormon leaders decided to send twenty-three wagons and forty-three brethren ahead without him. Led by Orson Pratt, these two divisions left camp on July 13 to mark the Hastings trail so that the remainder of the company could find it and cross the mountains at the approach to the Salt Lake Valley. Pratt's men reached East Canyon Creek on July 17, located the trail, and were at Big Mountain two days later. But Young's symptoms worsened, and many people began to fear that he would die. With his caretakers praying incessantly, Young at last began to improve, and he instructed Snow to join Pratt's divisions and instruct the exploring party to "halt at the first suitable spot after reaching the Lake Valley" and begin planting crops there, "regardless of our final location."[67]

Pratt's company descended Big Mountain into Mountain Dell Canyon and then moved into Emigration Canyon, a narrow ravine. The distance was only thirty-five miles, but the way remained difficult. In addition to steep descents, the trail featured thick groves of aspen, poplar, willow, and others. Boulders presented another serious obstacle, as did rattlesnakes and swarms of large crickets. On July 21, Snow met up with Pratt. The advance party had gotten its first look at "the 'Salt Lake,' together with a beautiful valley about twenty miles wide and thirty miles long," after crossing "a small creek twenty-one times in about five miles, and between mountains near a mile high, and after coming round a high knoll and making a sudden bend in the road." On July 22, "some 8 or ten of [Pratt's men] went into the valley to explore," recalled John Brown, finding "it covered with rich vegetation in the vicinity of the streams & on the low land green and beautiful."[68]

The Pioneer Company's safe arrival was a triumphant time. The party had traveled 1,073 miles over seventeen months. But the members of vanguard had little time to savor this achievement—they needed to plant crops and begin building a city for the thousands of migrants already on their way. In mid-June 1847, three large groups headed west from a staging area on the Elkhorn River, twenty-seven miles west of the winter quarters in Nebraska. This migration was dominated by families: for example, the three companies that departed on June 17 included 138 men, 114 women, and 214 children. The following day, the two companies that left totaled 408 people, among them 112 women and 206 children. In all, 1,486 migrants followed the Pioneer Company during the summer of 1847. These wagon trains arrived in the valley between September 19 and October 10.[69]

The advance companies gained valuable experience. The vanguard settled on the best routes, prepared accurate maps, and established way stations to help feed and resupply subsequent travelers. Recovered from his illness, Young returned to the winter quarters with a hundred men to help the Saints prepare for the next year's wagon trains. He arrived at the Nebraska encampment on October 31 and immediately issued a slew of orders regarding routes to be followed, clothing to be worn, and the places to procure supplies.[70]

But Young's biggest task was psychologically preparing the migrants for the ordeal ahead. He warned the Saints not to join the exodus to Salt Lake "unless you can obey the Word and Will of the Lord. I want all to live in all honesty, build up the temples and go and purify the people that they may build up the Kingdom on earth." Young thus presented the migration as a religious pilgrimage. According to Brown, Young told the camp residents that "he was in no hurry to Start for he did not intend to go any further while the camp was under the influence of the Spirit. . . . He said that he would rather go . . . to the mountains with six [good] men or even alone than to go with this whole camp with its present Spirit."[71]

Young lectured the waiting Saints on the attitude they would need to cross the plains. They needed to be committed to serving God. Shortly after the migrants left the winter quarters, he told them that if they were moving "for the riches, honors, glory, comfort, and enjoyment that they expect to receive in this world, they had better have stayed in the states or in their own country."

Young even offered safe passage back to winter quarters for all brethren who did not feel up to the task. But anyone who sought to continue "for the reward of immortality and eternal life beyond the veil [should] persevere and live so as to obtain it."[72]

Young also called for a reformation of behavior. He and his fellow leaders held prayer meetings throughout the migration, exhorting the Saints to "avoid all lightness and folly, and cultivate principles of industry and intelligence." These admonitions included strictures against card playing, checkers, dominoes, dancing, "loud laughing," and "profane language."[73]

Discipline, Young believed, was essential. The Mormons had just lost their founder, were facing attacks from enemies, were crossing the dangerous West, and were contending with dissension from disaffected coreligionists. Thus, Captain Luke Johnson recalled, Young began one prayer meeting by urging the migrants "to obey council [so that] every thing would go right; we will not be disturbed by the Indians if we would only obey council and do as you are told." But discipline also entailed maintaining the strictest religious behavior, and Young specifically warned against "corruptible nonsense and devilish principles," adding that Saints who did not reform their ways would "be cursed by the power of the Almighty God and dwindle away in unbelief. . . . [H]e then stated that he was not going another step with us until we humbled ourselves and [covenanted] to forsake those foolish principles that is a leading our minds to the devil." These threats proved powerful. When Young asked camp members "if we were willing to quit and turn our minds to being more . . . Prayerful and strive to serve our Heavenly Farther instead of the devil, nearly all the camp answered yes."[74]

Satisfied that the migrants were sufficiently committed, leaders divided them into companies consisting of fifty families and then further subdivided them into units of ten. The families were not grouped randomly but were instead assigned to companies based on their home wards (similar to parishes). The companies were led by the wards' bishops and presidents, who were designated as captains and were charged with maintaining discipline and overseeing myriad details from appointing guards and herders to deciding the order of march. Young, who had named himself lieutenant general, wanted military-style precision so that the Mormons would "be better able to defend ourselves in case of an attack from the Indians." Defense needs thus dictated that "every man . . . keep his loaded gun in his hand" and that "the wagons must keep together when traveling. . . . Every man to walk beside his own wagons and not leave it only by permission" of the captain. In practice these rules meant that a bugle sounded at five o'clock every morning to awaken the companies. After breakfast, the bugle sounded again, and the companies broke camp for the day's march, with armed teamsters walking alongside the wagons. In May 1847, Young wrote, "We usually travel single file, sometimes double, & when danger is apprehended, each company of 10 men or 5 wagons by platoons. We have a general & staff, Col & staff, capts of 10s and Artilery in the rear. Horsemen front, rear & Picket gaurd."[75]

The Mormons feared not just the Indians but also the Gentiles. With the 1838 war fresh in their minds, settlers particularly worried about running into migrants from Missouri. One migrant heading to California in 1846 was none other than Lilburn W. Boggs, the detested former governor of Missouri. The atmosphere was toxic when the Saints began leaving Illinois. They feared that the U.S. Army would intervene out of a mistaken belief that the Mormons planned to establish a western "empire." And they worried about clashing with the thousands of migrants—many from Missouri and Illinois—who were flocking west in the mid-1840s. Young vowed to fight back "if the Gentiles follow us to destroy us." For their part, the Gentiles feared the Mormons and their Nauvoo Legion, worrying that the Saints would be out for revenge following the assassination of their prophet. Amid rumors that the Mormons wanted to establish a western empire, unbelievers became suspicious when the Saints refused to say where they were going.[76]

Thus Young's military approach to the migration. On one occasion, some "Indians" snuck up on Kimball's company, but he and the other Saints present believed that the party in reality included Missourians attempting "to scare us back from this camp ground. We regard it as an old Missouri trick and an insult to the Camp. When we related the story to President Young he felt as we did, and should they attempt any more to play Indian tricks on us, it is very likely they will meet with Indian treatment." In several instances, the Mormon migrants encountered parties from Missouri, including participants from the 1838 war. One morning in early June 1847, for example, after holding a prayer meeting, the Mormon camp spotted a company of Missourians approaching who were "on their way to the west of the mountains," Kimball recalled. "Some of these four are recognized as taking part against us in the difficulties in Missouri, and the brethren judged from their appearance that they feared being known and trembled very much while our brethren were talking with them."[77]

The 2,368 migrants who journeyed in 1848 averaged twelve miles a day, and they needed 122 days to travel from winter quarters to Salt Lake City. Four years passed before all sixteen thousand Mormon refugees reached Salt Lake.

An average of 3,000 to 4,000 arrived a year. Thirty-five Saints lived in the region in 1857, 75,000 in 1869, and 125,000 in 1877, when Young died.[78]

The Mormon Exodus in Historical Perspective

The Mormon migration to Utah was unprecedented in its scope. The Saints' exodus dwarfed both earlier and later Protestant migrations within America. Also unprecedented was the degree to which persecution drove the Saints. Christian Metz may have encountered ridicule from a few outsiders, but the Inspirationist leader never faced a jeering mob intent on assassinating him. The Saints never doubted that they had to move to escape the violence of their many enemies.

But the Mormon and Inspirationist migrations also shared some characteristics. Both utopian movements felt a deep kinship with ancient Israel, seeing themselves as modern heirs to the sufferings and rigorous discipline of that ancient tribe. This identification with Israel ran much deeper with the Mormons, however. Revelations repeatedly reminded the Saints that they were the heirs of Israel. As early as 1831, the Lord told Joseph Smith to move to Ohio from New York with the words, "I will give you my law and there shall be endowed with power from on high . . . for I have a great work laid up in store, for Israel shall be served." Mormon theology reinforced the theme that the Saints were the chosen people whose movement represented the chance to restore ancient Israel. All male members served as "priests," a word that Protestant reformers detested and rejected. The Saints worshiped in "temples," another vile word in the Protestant lexicon. But Smith embraced such words and imagery, deliberately setting out to build his movement around Old Testament motifs that would help his followers realize the symbolism of Israel and the Exodus.[79]

Both the Mormons and the Inspirationists migrated to survive. Brigham Young and Christian Metz saw themselves as modern-day Moseses, leading their people out of the wilderness to safety and rebirth. The Mormons also shared the Inspirationists' reform spirit. Through migration, Young preached repeatedly in 1847 and 1848, the Saints could strengthen their faith.

This theme of migration as renewal is timeless. So is the need to acquire land to accomplish religious objectives. Putting distance between themselves and their enemies required the Saints to purchase land. Both themes link the Mormons with other religious groups across time and space. For all their uniqueness, the Mormons were part of something far larger.

Afterword

Religious migrations were more than colorful—they were an important part of American history. The wanderings of Protestants from the 1630s to the 1860s influenced the settlement of regions and the course of cultural development in both the thirteen colonies and the young United States. These internal migrations spanned three centuries and involved a fascinatingly large number of groups, but the striking thing was the continuities among the movements of Protestant pilgrims.

Understanding such continuities takes us back to the core question raised in the introduction: *what was it about Protestantism and America's dissenting culture that made Protestants so restless?* The preceding eight chapters suggest three main, and closely related, answers: migrants within the Protestant world were searching for salvation, Christian community, or reform—and sometimes for all three.

"Sinners" and the "reborn" alike sought salvation, consumed by thoughts of the afterlife and how to achieve everlasting happiness. As the experiences of Devereux Jarratt and others demonstrate, this search made people exceedingly restless. The effort to become reborn was a terrifying experience in many ways. Failure to achieve a new birth meant spending eternity in hell. Ministers as renowned as Jonathan Edwards and as obscure as Peter Cartwright loved to terrify their audiences with warnings that Lucifer's fires awaited those who did not turn to Jesus. Yet the fear of damnation could run still deeper. Calvinists believed that God preordained who was saved and who was not, and they worried incessantly about whether they had been chosen. Non-Calvinistic Evangelicals had their own set of worries. For them the challenge was how to achieve and maintain rebirth. "Backsliding" bedeviled Alfred Brunson and a host of others, producing endless anxiety and restlessness among these tormented souls. At the same time, nonevangelical groups sweated the question of how followers could achieve salvation. The Hutterites believed that finding salvation rested in building strong communities devoted to the Lord. The Mormons came up with the most elaborate theory involving a three-tiered cosmos in which mortals had the chance to become gods. Regardless of the group or its beliefs—evangelical or nonevangelical, utopian or nonutopian—seeking salvation introduced a palpable tension into the lives of Protestants, resulting in a longing that had many pilgrims moving about within America for answers.

The search for salvation produced something else: a deep need for Christian community among seekers. For James Finley, the Methodist itinerant in Ohio, the solitude of the forest no longer sufficed; Samuel McCobb and other Scotch-Irish Presbyterians on the frontier clustered together in strong church-based communities. Seekers craved Christian companionship because they needed the support of fellow believers in the quest to stay reborn or to practice their religion. Migration provided these individuals with an important means to a crucial end, enabling them to overcome their flaws and to lead lives of Christian rectitude.

Migrating to develop community was important as well. Methodists from Virginia established communities in a place far removed from the corrupting influence of slavery. Moravian parents wanted to raise their children in a wholesome Christian community and moved to backcountry North Carolina and painstakingly established settlements organized around the meetinghouse and the farm. Inspirationists created a tight communal settlement with some distance from the world. The Mormons demanded to live in communities of believers, free from the persecution of hostile outsiders and moved constantly to reach this goal.

The seekers' desire for community transcended time. In the seventeenth and eighteenth centuries, the desire to escape European conditions helped to spur religious migrations and the building of communities in the New World. The Puritans in particular felt the need to flee an England they perceived as hopelessly corrupt. By migrating to America, these religious reformers could erect purer communities of believers that would set an example for all to emulate—John Winthrop's City upon the Hill. Except for the Inspirationists, the nineteenth-century migration / communal impulse constituted a reaction not to developments in Europe but to the rampant individualism of the early national period. Religious utopians were especially uneasy with the greed, materialism, and selfishness associated with a market economy. Groups ranging from the Mormons to the Oneida Perfectionists exploited many Americans' unhappiness with individualism, instead stressing community and the need to sacrifice for a higher cause—for God.[1]

The third and final answer was closely related to the first two. These pilgrims also migrated in an effort to achieve some kind of reform. Reform, of course, goes to the heart of what it means to be a Protestant. Ever since Martin Luther tacked his Ninety-five Theses on a castle door in 1517, Protestants have grasped for alternatives to Catholicism; later, they began looking for alternatives to developments within Protestantism itself. Pietism, for instance, sought to spark a second Protestant Reformation. These alternatives have often entailed migrating. Hooker's Company moved to achieve reform. So did the Inspirationists. Devereux Jarratt moved to reform himself and eventually society. Virginia Methodists moved to reform a slave-tainted society. Even the Mormons, whose primary concern was escaping persecution, were interested in reform; migration would enable them to become better Saints and thereby increase their chances of entering the celestial kingdom. Only the migrations of Scotch-Irish Presbyterians within America lacked clear reform impulses, but their church, too, sought reform—the Scottish kirk detested the Church of England as fiercely as other Protestants detested Catholicism and especially Rome.

The dissenting tradition overlay all of these reform efforts. The desire to bring about change meant that reformers criticized and attacked the status quo, placing defenders of orthodoxy such as the Old Lights on the defensive and forcing them to explain their vision of Christianity. The eight case studies in this volume show the importance of dissent to the Protestant migratory milieu. Hartford's congregation feuded after Thomas Hooker's death, and the dissenters left. Determined dissenter Devereux Jarrett took on the Church of England in Virginia and moved about. Scotch-Irish Presbyterians split into Old and New Light factions, migrating repeatedly to live with like-minded believers. Internal strife among Pietistic Moravians in Broadbay, Maine, sent dissenters to backcountry North Carolina. Seventh Day Baptists in New Jersey argued among themselves before starting life anew someplace else. Regardless of the group or the specifics of the feuds, dissenters were often eager to move to rekindle their faith or start churches more to their liking. The presence of so much open land and so many frontiers made these wishes easily obtainable. The American Revolution gave a further boost to the dissenting tradition and to migration. As Gordon S. Wood observes, the revolution "accelerated the challenges to religious authority that had begun with the First Great Awakening. Just as the people were taking over their governments, so, it was said, they should take over their churches. . . . The people were their own theologians and had no need to rely on others to tell them what to believe."[2] Chapter 6 showed the multilayered and protean nature of the dissent, and how much of the conflict arose as a consequence of the inner workings and stresses of congregational life. Seventh Day Baptists in Shrewsbury, New Jersey, were clannish, devout, argumentative, and ultimately mobile.

Placing precise figures on the number of Protestant migrants in early America—or even coming up with loose estimates—is nearly impossible, but religion's role in migration and the settlement process was far more important than has been recognized. Moreover, the role of the religious impulse in the movements of some individuals has often been overlooked by general studies that treat these people as land-hungry farmers trying to get ahead. In *William Cooper's Town: Power and Persuasion on the Frontier of the Early American Republic*, for example, Alan Taylor argues that "population growth in the long-settled parts of New England set Yankees in motion northward and westward in search of the freehold land that grew increasingly expensive at home. By 1775 the typical southern New England farm of fifty acres was barely adequate to feed, house, and clothe a family." Thus, "to escape looming poverty, thousands of young Yankees sought their own substantial farms by emigrating" to the western New York frontier.[3] But such portrayals miss the underlying religious motivations discussed at length in chapters 2–5 of this volume. Because these studies fail to recognize Protestantism's complex contributions to internal migration, they tend to distort the process by which migrants founded and developed their settlements: secularly motivated migrants are lured to the frontier by the promise of cheap and plentiful land and live by themselves in places largely devoid of community. Historian Gregory H. Nobles has written, "Most people lived in dispersed, sparsely populated settlements. . . . [T]he institutions of public life on the southern frontier—the church and county court—were often weak, if they existed at all." Even more baldly, Gordon S. Wood has argued that because of massive migration and the accompanying large-scale selling of land, "any traditional sense of community became increasingly difficult to maintain. Each move made family and social ties more tenuous, the roots more shallow. [Migration] strained and broke apart households, churches, and neighborhoods."[4]

These portrayals, of course, offer a modern variation on the theme of migration as a threat: migration undermines community and leaves people living lives of virtual savagery in the wilderness. *Wandering Souls*, especially the book's middle section, demonstrates just how simplistic such portrayals are. Individuals (often with their families) migrated out of overlapping religious, economic, and social motivations; they wanted Christian community, moved for it, and worked hard to re-create it as fast as possible. Ohio's Philip Gatch and others—Methodist, Presbyterian, Moravian, Baptist—thought nothing of selling a tract and moving again so they could be closer to like-minded believers. As religious devotees gathered and began worshiping together, they established congregations and built meetinghouses, the seeds from which community life sprouted as people flocked from far and wide to hear God's word. Indeed, Gatch described in his memoir how "women would walk twenty and even thirty miles to attend" church services. Sundays became an important time to socialize and to escape the drudgery and loneliness of frontier life. The evangelical-minded also held camp meetings, which could attract throngs of people, while the arrival of an itinerant at a one-house clearing could draw settlers from the surrounding woods. In such ways did religiously inspired migrations quicken the pace of community development in Greene County, Ohio; Boothbay, Maine; and other places. Larger, church-led migrations had an even clearer effect on community. These churches sent carpenters and skilled craftsmen to erect entire villages that blossomed over time into cities that fueled regional growth: the Moravians' congregation town of Salem became Winston-Salem, North Carolina, the hub of modern Forsyth County.[5]

One historian who well understands the complexity of internal migration is Bernard Bailyn. Noting how massive internal migration was in early America, especially in the fifteen years before the American Revolution, he observes, "The greatest source of variety lay in the ethnic and cultural composition of the incoming groups. The population that spread inland from coastal nodes to form new communities was a composite of ethnic and religious groups . . . carrying with them different cultural baggage, different patterns of family organization and discipline, different ways of working and living together."[6]

The differences among groups *were* many, and the variations involved in mobility *were* complex. Yet Protestant migrations also shared a great deal. The various migrations fall into two broad categories: religiously minded people who moved to find some kind of spiritual and economic fulfillment; and churches or congregations that migrated en masse to escape persecution by outsiders, to establish a religious utopia, or to mitigate internal conflict.

Both migration types were important in the evolution of American society and the economy. One area in which migration had an important effect was the development of regions. Most notably, the Puritans' Great Migration to New England and the subsequent reshuffling of dissatisfied church members within the region placed a thoroughly Puritan stamp on New England's development over the next three centuries. Similarly, the Mormons turned a desert into a thriving colony that became the state of Utah and an important way station for California-bound migrants. Smaller religious migrations, even by individuals, also influenced regional development by hastening community formation.[7]

The migration of believers had another interesting and significant effect on society: it influenced acculturation among individuals. Migrants of diverse ethnic backgrounds came together to form communities of believers centered on the new birth or religious fellowship. The contact among German- and English-speakers at camp meetings, at Sunday services, at meetinghouses, and at prayer sessions led to extensive intermixing, including intermarriage. Religion's influence on acculturation was not uniform, however. Scotch-Irish Presbyterians, in particular sought precisely the opposite. But Presbyterianism also facilitated the formation of community among the Scotch-Irish and enabled them to preserve their identity as a distinct people, at least for a time. Thus migration served important cultural goals by bringing people together in places where they could build new communities and lives.[8]

One final thing. A Protestant migration could change the way that people viewed themselves and the world. Migrants from across the religious spectrum repeatedly described their journeys as tests, ordeals to be overcome. Migrants saw themselves as modern-day Israelites wandering in the wilderness that was North America. The Inspirationists perhaps put the feeling of sacrifice most baldly. Through a revelation, the Lord told members, "There is one more remedy against the decline, namely to change the place of abode so that there will be struggle and hardship—a separation. You will have to leave your property and go to a place where it is bare and scant."[9] The implications were clear. Members had become too comfortable in upstate New York. By challenging themselves with a cross-country journey to a new life on the frontier, pilgrims would regain their discipline and show their commitment to the Lord.

Thus, in believers' hands, migration became a blunt tool to achieve an important religious end. It became a way to set off a spark in themselves and society. In early America, the sparks were many, and the light was bright.

NORTH ARKANSAS COLLEGE LIBRARY
1515 Pioneer Drive
Harrison, AR 72601

Appendix

Tracking the number of migrants and religious adherents in early America is a perilous business. Churches had varying definitions of membership: the Moravians, for example, had different levels of membership, while the Anglicans counted parish residents who were not active members. Records were spottily kept or are not extant. Table A.1 shows membership numbers for three groups that kept fairly reliable records. Table A.2 approaches the question of church growth from a different angle, charting changes in the number of congregations.

Reliable figures for the total number of migrants within America also do not exist, although migration accounted for much of a region's population growth. Table A.3, therefore, shows population growth in three regions, offering an indicator of the level of migration in those areas. Table A.4 provides information on the size of various migration streams. Table A.5 shows how the average landholdings of three "classes"—large, middling, and small—varied by region and religious group. Puritan holdings were the smallest, and the Moravian *Landgemeinen* were the most "middling," while the Anglicans and Presbyterians fell between these two.

TABLE A.1. Church Membership in America

YEAR	METHODIST*	MORAVIAN**	MORMON
1765	—	166	—
1785	15,000	1,086	—
1800	64,000	—	—
1810	175,000	—	—
1830	475,000	1,565	27
1840	—	—	30,000
1860	1,400,000	1,935	80,000

Sources: Edwin Scott Gaustad and Philip L. Barlow, *New Historical Atlas of Religion in America* (Oxford, 2001); S. Scott Rohrer, *Hope's Promise: Religion and Acculturation in the Southern Backcountry* (Tuscaloosa, Ala., 2005); *Deseret News Church Almanac* (Salt Lake City, 1830, 1840, 1860).

  * Includes white and black members; for 1860, includes northern and southern branches.
 ** For Wachovia, N.C., only.

TABLE A.2. Number of American Congregations by Church

YEAR	ANGLICAN*	PURITAN	PRESBYTERIAN	METHODIST	BAPTIST**
1660	41	40	--	--	6
1700	100	200	20	--	15
1750	300	500	220	--	58
1780	400	720	495	50	500
1820	600	1,100	1,700	2,700	2,500
1860	2,100	2,200	6,400	20,000	21,000

Sources: Edwin Scott Gaustad and Philip L. Barlow, *New Historical Atlas of Religion in America* (Oxford, 2001); David Benedict, *A General History of the Baptist Denomination in America, and Other Parts of the World* (Boston, 1813); Robert G. Gardner, *Baptists of Early America: A Statistical History, 1639–1790* (Atlanta, 1983); Nathan O. Hatch, *The Democratization of American Christianity* (New Haven, Conn., 1989).
  * Renamed Episcopalian during the revolutionary period.
** Includes Seventh Day, Regular, Freewill, and Primitive Baptists.

TABLE A.3. Population Growth in Three Regions

New England in the Seventeenth and Early Eighteenth Centuries

YEAR	MASSACHUSETTS	CONNECTICUT	RHODE ISLAND
1660	19,600	7,955	1,474
1700	55,141	25,520	5,594
1720	88,858	57,737	11,137

*The South in the Eighteenth Century**

YEAR	VIRGINIA	NORTH CAROLINA	SOUTH CAROLINA
1720	61,158	18,270	5,048
1750	129,581	53,184	25,000
1780	317,422	179,133	83,000

The Midwest in the Early Nineteenth Century

YEAR	OHIO	INDIANA	ILLINOIS
1800	45,365	2,632	2,458
1810	230,760	24,520	12,282
1830	935,884	343,031	157,445

Sources: R. C. Simmons, *The American Colonies: From Settlement to Independence* (New York, 1976); U.S. Census.
  * White population only.

TABLE A.4. Four Migration Streams

Transatlantic: Europe to America

GROUP	NUMBER	YEARS
Puritan (to New England)	21,000	1630–42
Scotch-Irish (to America)	150,000	1717–76
German (to America)	111,000	1683–1775

Internal: Movements of Three Religious Groups in America

GROUP	NUMBER	YEARS
Moravian (to North Carolina *Landgemeinen*)	261	1755–75
Inspirationist (to Iowa)	1,100	1855–64
Mormon (to Utah)	16,000	1846–52

*Secular: Virginia, early national period**		*Secular: Westward, 1840–60*	
To Ohio	85,762	To Oregon	53,062
To Indiana	41,819	To California	200,335
To Illinois	24,697	To Utah**	42,862

Sources: Edwin Scott Gaustad and Philip L. Barlow, *New Historical Atlas of Religion in America* (Oxford, 2001); S. Scott Rohrer, *Hope's Promise: Religion and Acculturation in the Southern Backcountry* (Tuscaloosa, Ala., 2005); Marianne S. Wokeck, *Trade in Strangers: The Beginnings of Mass Migration to North America* (University Park, Pa., 1999); David Hackett Fischer and James C. Kelly, *Bound Away: Virginia and the Westward Movement* (Charlottesville, Va., 2000); John D. Unruh Jr., *The Plains Across: The Overland Emigrants and the Trans-Mississippi West, 1840–60* (Urbana, Ill., 1993).

* Figures represent the number of native Virginians living in these states in 1850, according to the U.S. Census; as an estimate of migration, the numbers are low because the figure includes only Virginians alive in 1850.

** Includes non-Mormons.

TABLE A.5. Average Landholdings by Settlement and "Class"

Size of Holding	HARTFORD, CONN., 1640S (N = 134)	NEW KENT COUNTY, VA., 1700 (N = 128)	AUGUSTA COUNTY, VA., 1740S* (N = 55)	WACHOVIA, N.C., 1780S** (N = 220)
Large	546 acres (12%)	10,000 acres (1%)	900 acres (22%)	1,000 acres (1%)
Middling	90 acres (36%)	300 acres (93%)	400 acres (71%)	217 acres (74%)
Small	20 acres (52%)	100 acres (6%)	200 acres (7%)	60 acres (25%)

Sources: *Original Distribution of the Lands in Hartford among the Settlers, 1639* (Hartford, Conn., 1912); New Kent County Land Patent Book, 1700, Library of Virginia, Richmond; Howard McKnight Wilson, *The Tinkling Spring: Headwater of Freedom* (Fishersville, Va., 1954); Stokes County Deed Books, Forsyth County Library, Winston-Salem, N.C.

* For the Presbyterian congregations of Tinkling Spring and Augusta Stone.

** For the Moravian Landgemeine settlements: Friedberg, Friedland, and Hope.

Notes

ABBREVIATIONS

LAC   Land Arbeiter Conferenz Minutes, MA-SP
LDS Archives   Archives of the Church of Jesus Christ of Latter-day Saints, Salt Lake
                     City, Utah
MA-NP   Moravian Archives–Northern Province, Bethlehem, Pa.
MA-SP   Moravian Archives–Southern Province, Winston-Salem, N.C.
MR   Adelaide Fries, Kenneth G. Hamilton, Douglas L. Rights, and Minnie J.
                     Smith, eds. *Records of the Moravians in North Carolina* (Raleigh, 1922–69)
Shrewsbury
Church Records   Records of the Shrewsbury, N.J., Seventh Day Baptist Church,
                     Seventh Day Baptist Historical Society, Janesville, Wis.

INTRODUCTION

1. William Least Heat-Moon, *Blue Highways: A Journey into America* (Boston, 1982), 252–62. The 1982 edition omits the hyphen in the author's name, but later editions as well as newer books by Heat-Moon use the hyphen so I use it here.

2. Whitney R. Cross, *The Burned-over District: The Social and Intellectual History of Enthusiastic Religion in Western New York, 1800–1850* (Ithaca, N.Y., 1950), 4, 54.

3. Heat-Moon, *Blue Highways*, 62; Richard Kluger, *Seizing Destiny: How America Grew from Sea to Shining Sea* (New York, 2007), xvii–xviii; Robert V. Remini, *Andrew Jackson and the Course of American Empire, 1767–1821* (New York, 1977), 54.

4. J. Hector St. John de Crèvecoeur, *Letters from an American Farmer*, edited by Albert E. Stone (New York, 1981), available online at <http://xroads.virginia.edu/~hyper/CREV/home.html>.

5. Conclusion is based on a broad reading of American religious history, including Edwin Scott Gaustad and Philip L. Barlow, *New Historical Atlas of Religion in America* (Oxford, 2001); Sydney E. Ahlstrom, *A Religious History of the American People* (New Haven, Conn., 1972); Harry S. Stout and D. G. Hart, eds., *New Directions in American Religious History* (Oxford, 1997); Winthrop S. Hudson and John Corrigan, *Religion in America: An Historical Account of the Development of American Religious Life*, 5th ed. (New York, 1992), 132;

Crèvecoeur, *Letters*. Other examples of contemporaries taking such a view include James Fenimore Cooper in *The Pioneers* (New York, 1884) and John Christopher Hartwick, a Lutheran clergyman and land developer, who believed that the dispersed settlement patterns of the frontier weakened American Christianity; Hartwick's views are discussed in Alan Taylor, *William Cooper's Town: Power and Persuasion on the Frontier of the Early American Republic* (New York, 1995), 40–44. For Puritan views of the wilderness, see William Hubbard, "A General History of New-England from the Discovery to 1680," *Collections of the Massachusetts Historical Society*, 2nd ser., 5 (1848): 139; Peter N. Carroll, *Puritanism and the Wilderness: The Intellectual Significance of the New England Frontier, 1629–1700* (New York, 1969), 65–66; John Canup, *Out of the Wilderness: The Emergence of an American Identity in Colonial New England* (Middletown, Conn., 1990).

6. The term "push-pull" was first used in 1926 in a study that tied emigration to economic cycles in the United States; see Harry Jerome, *Migration and Business Cycles* (New York, 1926). For two recent examples of historians employing the term, see Jan deVries, *European Urbanization, 1500–1800* (Cambridge, Mass., 1984), 214–15; Marianne S. Wokeck, *Trade in Strangers: The Beginnings of Mass Migration to North America* (University Park, Pa., 1999), xxv–xxvi. Wokeck notes that the theory remains popular with scholars charting migration trends in modern times. Historians of early America, however, have sought to better explain social and cultural motivations for migration. See Bernard Bailyn, *The Peopling of British North America: An Introduction* (New York, 1986), 12–15. Scholars of German migrations tend to stress the networking involved. In addition to Wokeck, *Trade in Strangers*, good treatments of German migrations to America include Aaron Spencer Fogleman, *Hopeful Journeys: German Immigration, Settlement, and Political Culture in Colonial America, 1717–1775* (Philadelphia, 1996); A. G. Roeber, *Palatines, Liberty, and Property: German Lutherans in Colonial British America* (Baltimore, 1993).

7. Social historians of early modern Europe have done the most impressive work on how family and social life influenced migration. Some of the best social history studies include David Warren Sabean, *Property, Production, and Family in Neckarhausen, 1700–1820* (Cambridge, Eng., 1990); deVries, *European Urbanization*; Keith Wrightson, *English Society, 1580–1680* (London, 1980); Keith Wrightson and David Levine, *Poverty and Piety in an English Village: Terling, 1525–1700* (New York, 1979); Peter Clark, *English Provincial Society from the Reformation to the Revolution: Religion, Politics, and Society in Kent, 1500–1640* (Sussex, 1977); Peter Clark and Paul Slack, *English Towns in Transition, 1500–1700* (London, 1976); Thomas Robisheaux, *Rural Society and the Search for Order in Early Modern Germany* (Cambridge, Eng., 1989). Russell R. Menard reviews the literature on migration in "Migration, Ethnicity, and the Rise of an Atlantic Economy: The Re-Peopling of British America, 1600–1790," in *A Century of European Migrations, 1830–1903*, edited by Rudolph J. Vecoli and Suzanne M. Sinke (Urbana, Ill., 1991), 58–77. See also Russell R. Menard, "Whatever Happened to Early American Population History?," *William and Mary Quarterly* 50 (Apr. 1993): 356–66.

8. This model is loosely based on the insights of Darrett B. Rutman and Anita H. Rutman. In their study of early American communities, they sought a conceptual framework that would allow them to account for the great variety in community formation while accommodating the similarities. They brought order to a chaotic process by taking a net-

work approach that placed the most important economic, social, and cultural forces on two planes and that linked the community under study to broader trends in American society. Their model, in other words, allows historians to account for similarities and differences. My model does the same, isolating the key factors within each migration pattern and explaining how these factors made a migration unique. See Darrett B. Rutman and Anita H. Rutman, *A Place in Time: Middlesex County, Virginia, 1650–1750* (New York, 1984), esp. 27–30. See also Darrett B. Rutman and Anita H. Rutman, *Small Worlds, Large Questions: Explorations in Early American Social History, 1600–1850* (Charlottesville, Va., 1994), esp. chap. 3.

9. For more on this later period and how America became Christianized, see Jon Butler, *Awash in a Sea of Faith: Christianizing the American People* (Cambridge, Mass., 1990).

10. Patricia U. Bonomi, "Religious Dissent and the Case for American Exceptionalism," in *Religion in a Revolutionary Age*, edited by Ronald Hoffman and Peter J. Albert (Charlottesville, Va., 1994), 45. For the classic treatment of American religion as democratizing, liberal, and market-oriented, see Nathan O. Hatch, *The Democratization of American Christianity* (New Haven, Conn., 1989). For more on the dissenting tradition, see Edwin S. Gaustad, *Dissent in American Religion* (Chicago, 2006).

11. Gordon S. Wood, "Religion and the American Revolution," in *New Directions*, edited by Stout and Hart, 175; Patricia U. Bonomi, *Under the Cope of Heaven: Religion, Society, and Politics in Colonial America* (New York, 1986), 3. Historians have long debated just how religious early Americans were. Many have argued that the colonists were indifferent to religion. I, of course, do not agree; a key premise of this book is that religion did matter to ordinary people and helped to define how they perceived themselves and how they lived. For more on this debate, see Patricia U. Bonomi and Peter R. Eisenstadt, "Church Adherence in the Eighteenth-Century British American Colonies," *William and Mary Quarterly* 39 (Apr. 1982): 245–86; Butler, *Awash*. For an interesting study that argues that early Americans developed identities based on religion rather than nationality, see Sally Schwartz, *"A Mixed Multitude": The Struggle for Toleration in Colonial Pennsylvania* (New York, 1987). And J. C. D. Clark, *The Language of Liberty, 1660–1832: Political Discourse and Social Dynamics in the Anglo-American World* (New York, 1994), does an expert job showing the ways that religion ordered ordinary peoples' lives. A recent forum in the *American Historical Review* also discusses the issue of religious identity; see "AHR Conversation: Religious Identities and Violence," *American Historical Review* 112 (Dec. 2007): 1433–81.

CHAPTER ONE

1. For a modern account of Hooker's life, see Frank Shuffelton, *Thomas Hooker, 1586–1647* (Princeton, 1977); for a contemporary view of Hooker, see Cotton Mather, *Magnalia Christi Americana; or, The Ecclesiastical History of New England from Its First Planting in the Year 1620 unto the Year of Our Lord, 1698* (New York, 1972), 3:57.

2. John Winthrop, *Winthrop's Journal, "History of New England," 1630–1649*, edited by James Kendall Hosmer (New York, 1908), Sept. 4, 1633, 1:105–6.

3. William Wood, *New Englands Prospect* (1634; reprint, New York, 1968), 39; Lucious R.

Paige, *History of Cambridge, Massachusetts* (Boston, 1877), 18; Shuffelton, *Thomas Hooker*, 164–65.

4. Edward Johnson, *Johnson's Wonder-Working Providence, 1628–1651*, edited by J. Franklin Jameson (New York, 1910), 90–91.

5. Arthur Gilman, ed., *The Cambridge of Eighteen Hundred and Ninety-six* (Cambridge, Mass., 1896), 3–4.

6. Thomas Dudley to Lady Bridget, Countess of Lincoln, Mar. 12, 1630/01, in Everett Emerson, ed., *Letters from New England: The Massachusetts Bay Colony, 1629–1630* (Amherst, Mass., 1976), 71–73; Winthrop, *Winthrop's Journal*, Dec. 6, 1630, Aug. 3, 1632, 54, 84–90; Shuffelton, *Thomas Hooker*, 163–64.

7. Winthrop, *Winthrop's Journal*, Aug. 3, 1632, 90; Shuffelton, *Thomas Hooker*, 198–205; John Winthrop to Sir Simonds D'Ewes, Sept. 26, 1633, in Emerson, *Letters*, 113.

8. Nathaniel B. Shurtleff, ed., *Records of the Governor and Company of the Massachusetts Bay in New England*, vol. 1, 1628–1641 (New York, 1853), 358; Winthrop, *Winthrop's Journal*, Nov. 3, 1635, 165; Shuffelton, *Thomas Hooker*, 198–99.

9. Shurtleff, *Records*, 119; Winthrop, *Winthrop's Journal*, May, June 1634, 124, 126, 128.

10. Winthrop, *Winthrop's Journal*, Sept. 4, 1634, 132–33.

11. Ibid., May 3, 1634, 124.

12. Ibid., Sept. 4, 1634, 133.

13. Ibid.

14. This discussion is based partly on Francis J. Bremer, *The Puritan Experiment* (New York, 1976); Alden T. Vaughan and Francis J. Bremer, eds., *Puritan New England: Essays on Religion, Society, and Culture* (New York, 1977); Perry Miller, *Errand into the Wilderness* (Cambridge, Mass., 1956); Edmund S. Morgan, *The Puritan Dilemma: The Story of John Winthrop* (Boston, 1958).

15. See the sources cited in the preceding note, esp. Bremer, *Puritan Experiment*, 9–17.

16. Shuffelton, *Thomas Hooker*, 121–31.

17. Edmund S. Morgan, *Puritan Dilemma*, xii, 31.

18. John Cotton to an unidentified clergyman, Dec. 3, 1634, in Emerson, *Letters*, 128; Shuffelton, *Thomas Hooker*, 131–35.

19. Thomas Hooker, *The Danger of a Desertion; or, A Farewell Sermon of Mr. Thomas Hooker* (London, 1641), 4, 5, 11; Perry Miller, *Errand*, 5–15; Johnson, *Johnson's Wonder-Working Providence*, 29.

20. R. C. Simmons, *The American Colonies: From Settlement to Independence* (New York, 1976), 28; Edmund S. Morgan, *Puritan Dilemma*, 47–52. For more on Winthrop and migration, see Francis J. Bremer, *John Winthrop: America's Forgotten Founding Father* (New York, 2003).

21. Shuffelton, *Thomas Hooker*, 135.

22. Ibid., 136–51.

23. Pietism is a relatively obscure but fascinating religious reform movement that has drawn much scholarly attention. Good starting points are F. Ernest Stoeffler, *German Pietism during the Eighteenth Century* (Leiden, 1973); W. R. Ward, *The Protestant Evangelical Awakening* (Cambridge, Eng., 1992), Stephen L. Longenecker, *Piety and Tolerance: Pennsylva-*

nia German Religion, 1700–1850 (Metuchen, N.J., 1994); Dale W. Brown, *Understanding Pietism* (Grand Rapids, Mich., 1978).

24. Shuffelton, *Thomas Hooker*, 157.

25. For an excellent discussion of Greater East Anglia during this period, see David Grayson Allen, *In English Ways: The Movement of Societies and the Transferal of English Local Law and Custom to Massachusetts Bay in the Seventeenth Century* (New York, 1982). See also Roger Thompson, *Mobility and Migration: East Anglian Founders of New England, 1629–1640* (Amherst, Mass., 1994); Virginia DeJohn Anderson, *New England's Generation: The Great Migration and the Formation of Society and Culture in the Seventeenth Century* (New York, 1991); Alison Games, *Migration and the Origins of the English Atlantic World* (Cambridge, Mass., 1999).

26. William Wood, *New Englands Prospect*, 10, 14–15.

27. Daniel Vickers, *Farmers and Fishermen: Two Centuries of Work in Essex County, Massachusetts, 1630–1850* (Chapel Hill, N.C., 1994), 14–20; Daniel Vickers, "Competency and Competition: Economic Culture in Early America," *William and Mary Quarterly* 47 (Jan. 1990): 3–29; Thomas Dudley to Lady Bridget, Mar. 12, 1630/01, in Emerson, *Letters*, 75. The interplay between Puritan religious values and the Protestant work ethic has received considerable attention. See, e.g., Stephen Innes, *Creating the Commonwealth: The Economic Culture of Puritan New England* (New York, 1995); Christine Leigh Heyrman, *Commerce and Culture: The Maritime Communities of Colonial Massachusetts* (New York, 1984); John Frederick Martin, *Profits in the Wilderness: Entrepreneurship and the Founding of New England Towns in the Seventeenth Century* (Chapel Hill, N.C., 1991); Richard L. Bushman, *From Puritan to Yankee: Character and the Social Order in Connecticut, 1690–1765* (New York, 1967).

28. Thompson, *Mobility and Migration*, 14–23; David Grayson Allen, *In English Ways*, 185–88, 292.

29. Thompson, *Mobility and Migration*, 23–27. For more on migration to the Chesapeake, see James Horn, "Servant Emigration to the Chesapeake in the Seventeenth Century," in *The Chesapeake in the Seventeenth Century*, edited by Thad W. Tate and David L. Ammerman (New York, 1979), 51–95; Russell R. Menard, "British Migration to the Chesapeake Colonies in the Seventeenth Century," in *Colonial Chesapeake Society*, edited by Lois Green Carr, Philip D. Morgan, and Jean B. Russo (Chapel Hill, N.C., 1988), 99–132; Bernard Bailyn, *Voyagers to the West: A Passage in the Peopling of America on the Eve of the Revolution* (New York, 1986).

30. Shuffelton, *Thomas Hooker*, 157.

31. Winthrop, *Winthrop's Journal*, Sept. 4, 1633, 105–6; Shuffelton, *Thomas Hooker*, 160–61.

32. Winthrop, *Winthrop's Journal*, Sept. 4, 1634, 132–33.

33. William Bradshaw, *English Puritanisme* (London, 1640), 25; Thomas Hooker, *A Survey of the Summe of Church-Discipline* (New York, 1972), 1:48–50; John Winthrop, "A Modell of Christian Charity, Written on Board the *Arbella*, on the Atlantic Ocean," *Collections of the Massachusetts Historical Society*, 3rd ser., 7 (1838): 44, 46.

34. William Hubbard, "A General History of New-England from the Discovery to 1680," *Collections of the Massachusetts Historical Society*, 2nd ser., 5 (1848): 139; Martin, *Profits*, 114–16,

Peter N. Carroll, *Puritanism and the Wilderness: The Intellectual Significance of the New England Frontier, 1629–1700* (New York, 1969), 65–66; John Canup, *Out of the Wilderness: The Emergence of an American Identity in Colonial New England* (Middletown, Conn., 1990), 10.

35. Thomas Hooker, *The Application of Redemption . . . the Ninth and Tenth Books*, 2nd ed. (London, 1659), 5; Thomas Hooker, "Thanksgiving Sermon," Oct. 4, 1638, in Andrew Thomas Denholm, "Thomas Hooker: Puritan Teacher, 1586–1647" (Ph.D. diss., Hartford Theological Seminary Foundation, 1961), 431; Carroll, *Puritanism*, 68.

36. Winthrop, *Winthrop's Journal*, Sept. 4, 1634, 133; Shurtleff, *Records*, Sept. 25, 1634.

37. Shurtleff, *Records*, May 6, June 6, 1635; Robert J. Taylor, *Colonial Connecticut: A History* (Millwood, N.Y., 1979), 6; Johnson, *Johnson's Wonder-Working Providence*, 96; David Grayson Allen, *In English Ways*, 119. See also Perry Miller, *Errand*, 24.

38. Winthrop, *Winthrop's Journal*, May 31, 1636, 180–81; Gilman, *Cambridge*, 6. The description of the trail is largely from William DeLoss Love, *The Colonial History of Hartford* (Hartford, Conn., 1935), 34–46.

39. The demographic portrait of Hartford migrants is compiled from genealogical information in J. Hammond Trumbull, ed., *The Memorial History of Hartford, Connecticut, 1633–1884* (Boston, 1886), vol. 1, sec. 2, "The Original Proprietors."

40. Israel Stoughton to John Stoughton, in Emerson, *Letters*, 151; Trumbull, *Memorial History*, vol. 1, sec. 2, 243, 271.

41. Winthrop, *Winthrop's Journal*, Nov. 3, 1635, 165; Trumbull, *Memorial History*, vol. 1, sec. 2, 255; "John Pratt's Answer to the Court," in Shurtleff, *Records*, 358.

42. Evan Hill, *The Connecticut River* (Middletown, Conn., 1972), 96; see also 15–20. Puritans used the term "Great River" in land deeds, wills, and other Hartford town records.

43. This analysis is based on land records in *Original Distribution of the Lands in Hartford among the Settlers, 1639* (Hartford, Conn., 1912) and on maps of early Hartford printed in Love, *Colonial History*.

44. Bushman, *From Puritan to Yankee*, 54–56.

45. *Hartford Town Votes, 1635–1716* (Hartford, Conn., 1897), Aug. 16, Jan. 7, 14, 1639.

46. Landholding averages are derived from an examination of *Original Distribution*. This volume contains later land divisions as well.

47. See, e.g., John J. McCusker and Russell R. Menard, *The Economy of British America, 1607–1789* (Chapel Hill, N.C., 1991); Robert D. Mitchell, *Commercialism and Frontier: Perspectives on the Early Shenandoah Valley* (Charlottesville, Va., 1977); Richard R. Beeman, *The Evolution of the Southern Backcountry: A Case Study of Lunenburg County, Virginia, 1746–1832* (Philadelphia, 1984).

48. Pratt's landholdings are from *Original Distribution*, and his estate's value is from his will, reprinted in Charles William Manwaring, ed., *A Digest of the Early Connecticut Probate Records*, vol. 1, *Hartford District, 1635–1700* (Hartford, Conn., 1904), 144.

49. *The Regestere Booke of the Lands and Houses in "New Towne" and the "Town of Cambridge"* (Cambridge, Mass., 1896) shows that the holdings were small and scattered. Although the acreage owned in Hartford may have been somewhat larger than in Newtown, the basic land system did not change.

50. *Historical Catalogue of the First Church in Hartford, 1633–1885* (Hartford, Conn., 1885), 19, XVI. The covenant quoted is not from the original covenant but is from the covenant written in February 1670 at the founding of Hartford's Second Church. Congregational records from the earliest years and the original covenant are not extant. Historians agree, however, that the 1670 covenant was extremely close to the original. They base that conclusion on the fact that the second church was founded on the principles of the original church and that dissenters who left the first church in a dispute over the "halfway" covenant wanted to return to the original vision espoused by Hooker and the founders of the first church. See *Historical Catalogue*, X, for details. See also Paul R. Lucas, *Valley of Discord: Church and Society along the Connecticut River, 1636–1725* (Hanover, N.H., 1976), 69.

51. J. Hammond Trumbull, ed., *The Public Records of the Colony of Connecticut* (Hartford, 1850), 1:20–21; *Hartford Town Votes*, Feb. 2, 1659; see also Nov. 20, 1660.

52. For more on Hooker's role in the Hutchinson affair, see Shuffelton, *Thomas Hooker*, 238–52.

53. For more on this war, see Alfred A. Cave, *The Pequot War* (Amherst, Mass., 1996); Alfred A. Cave, "Who Killed John Stone?: A Note on the Origins of the Pequot War," *William and Mary Quarterly* 49 (July 1992): 509–21.

54. William Hammond to Sir Simonds D'Ewes, Sept. 26, 1633, in Emerson, *Letters*, 110. Hooker owned 135 acres in Hartford, and the town awarded him a 240-acre tract outside the village, *Original Distribution*, 299. Hooker's will is reprinted in Manwaring, *Early Connecticut Probate Records*, 1:16.

55. The traditional view, in Perry Miller's words, was that the Newtown migration represented a "'democratic' secession from 'theocratic' Massachusetts." For an excellent overview of this argument, see Perry Miller, *Errand*, 16.

56. Hubbard, "General History," 173; John Winthrop to Sir Simonds D'Ewes, July 20, 1635, in Emerson, *Letters*, 154; Perry Miller, *Errand*, 17.

57. For a concise and clear summary of the five conversion stages, see Bremer, *Puritan Experiment*, 22–23. For more on Hooker's views of the conversion process and salvation, see Hooker, *Application of Redemption*; *Soules Preparation for Christ; or, A Treatise of Contrition* (London, 1638). For Hooker's struggles with this question, see also Shuffelton, *Thomas Hooker*, esp. 21–26.

58. Thomas Hooker, *Survey*, 1:14, 20–22; Shuffelton, *Thomas Hooker*, 170–72.

59. Some studies on internal Puritan migrations include Douglas Lamar Jones, *Village and Seaport: Migration and Society in Eighteenth-Century Massachusetts* (Hanover, N.H., 1981); Linda Auwers Bissell, "From One Generation to Another: Mobility in Seventeenth-Century Windsor, Connecticut," *William and Mary Quarterly* 41 (Jan. 1974): 74–110; John J. Waters, "Family, Inheritance, and Migration in Colonial New England: The Evidence from Guilford, Connecticut," *William and Mary Quarterly* 49 (Jan. 1982): 64–86; Darrett B. Rutman, "People in Process: The New Hampshire Towns of the Eighteenth Century," *Journal of Urban History* 1 (May 1975): 268–92.

60. Virginia DeJohn Anderson, *New England's Generation*, 114.

61. Trumbull, *Memorial History*, vol. 1, sec. 2; Jackson Turner Main, *Society and Economy*

in *Colonial Connecticut* (Princeton, 1985), 7; Games, *Migration*, 164. The founding of New Haven was an exception: its founders came directly from England. See Bruce C. Daniels, *The Connecticut Town: Growth and Development, 1635–1790* (Middletown, Conn., 1979), 11, 13. Main notes that 28 percent of the early migrants in Hartford left the colony, and 16 percent moved to other towns.

62. Bushman, *From Puritan to Yankee*, 54–57. The idea of a Puritan "declension"—that the piety and communal values of the founders gave way under the economic development of the eighteenth century—has come under withering and effective attack. I am not suggesting that Hartford underwent a declension, but I do find Bushman's identification of the outlivers problem germane to understanding internal migration and mobility. A village's population inevitably became spread out in the seventeenth century, and many families scattered. For more on the debate over a Puritan declension and towns' evolution, see Stephen Innes, *Labor in a New Land: Economy and Society in Seventeenth-Century Springfield* (Princeton, 1983), and Heyrman, *Commerce and Culture*, both of which critique older studies such as Bushman's *From Puritan to Yankee*; Philip J. Greven Jr., *Four Generations: Population, Land, and Family in Colonial Andover, Massachusetts* (Ithaca, N.Y., 1970); Kenneth A. Lockridge, *A New England Town: The First Hundred Years* (New York, 1970).

63. Bushman, *From Puritan to Yankee*, 73–83; Lord family activities were reconstructed from the will of Thomas Jr., Hartford land records, and Trumbull, *Memorial History*, vol. 1, sec. 2.

64. For an interesting look at one town's inheritance practices, see Philip J. Greven Jr., "Family Structure in Seventeenth-Century Andover, Massachusetts," *William and Mary Quarterly* 23 (Apr. 1966): 234–56, which argues that fathers used land bequests to control their children. Greven portrays Andover as a relatively static place with little mobility; Hartford's situation differed substantially, with relatively high mobility. Extant wills do not indicate that fathers were as controlling as in Andover.

65. Manwaring, *Early Connecticut Probate Records*, 1:40–41.

66. For a look at inheritance practices among the English in the Chesapeake, see Lois Green Carr, "Inheritance in the Colonial Chesapeake," in *Women in the Age of the American Revolution*, edited by Ronald Hoffman and Peter J. Albert (Charlottesville, 1989), 155–97. For a comparison to German speakers, see Daniel Snydacker, "Kinship and Community in Rural Pennsylvania, 1749–1820," *Journal of Interdisciplinary History* 13 (Summer 1982): 41–61; Kathleen Neils Conzen, "Peasant Pioneers: Generational Succession among German Farmers in Frontier Minnesota," in *The Countryside in the Age of Capitalist Transformation: Essays in the Social History of Rural America*, edited by Steven Hahn and Jonathan Prude (Chapel Hill, N.C., 1985), 259–92; Lutz K. Berkner, "Inheritance, Land Tenure, and Peasant Family Structure: A German Regional Comparison," in *Family and Inheritance: Rural Society in Western Europe, 1200–1800*, edited by Jack Goody, Joan Thirsk, and E. P. Thompson (Cambridge, Eng., 1976), 71–95, esp. 82.

67. Martin, *Profits*; Gloria L. Main and Jackson Turner Main, "The Red Queen in New England?," *William and Mary Quarterly* 66 (Jan. 1999): 121–47; Bissell, "Mobility," 93–94; Waters, "Family, Inheritance, and Migration," 65.

68. Bissell, "Mobility," 86–94.

1. Devereux Jarratt, *The Autobiography of the Reverend Devereux Jarratt, Rector of Bath Parish, Dinwiddie County, Virginia, Written by Himself, in a Series of Letters* . . . (Baltimore, 1806); the first letter, which covers his upbringing and early career, is reprinted in *William and Mary Quarterly* 9 (July 1952): 346–93; quotations are on 367.

2. Frank Shuffelton, *Thomas Hooker, 1586–1647* (Princeton, 1977), 7; Jarratt, *Autobiography*, 362.

3. Shuffelton, *Thomas Hooker*, 7; Jarratt, *Autobiography*, 362.

4. Jarratt, *Autobiography*, 363.

5. Ibid., 363–64.

6. Ibid., 366–67.

7. Good starting points for students of the Chesapeake include Thad W. Tate and David L. Ammerman, eds., *The Chesapeake in the Seventeenth Century: Essays on Anglo-American Society and Politics* (New York, 1979); Rhys Isaac, *The Transformation of Virginia, 1740–1790* (Chapel Hill, N.C., 1982); Allan Kulikoff, *Tobacco and Slaves: The Development of Southern Cultures in the Chesapeake, 1680–1800* (Chapel Hill, N.C., 1986); Lois Green Carr, Russell R. Menard, and Lorena S. Walsh, *Robert Cole's World: Agriculture and Society in Early Maryland* (Chapel Hill, N.C., 1991).

8. Dumas Malone, *Jefferson the Virginian* (Boston, 1948), 1:18–19, 40; Jarratt, *Autobiography*, 367–68.

9. Jarratt, *Autobiography*, 368–69.

10. Ibid., 369–70.

11. Ibid., 370–71.

12. Ibid.

13. Ibid., 371.

14. Ibid., 371–72.

15. Ibid., 372–74.

16. Ibid., 374.

17. Ibid.

18. Ibid., 375–76.

19. "Mr. Nicholas Moreau, to the Right Honorable the Lord Bishop of Lichfield and Coventry, His Majesty's High Almoner," Apr. 12, 1697, in *The Vestry Book and Register of St. Peter's Parish, New Kent and James City Counties, Virginia, 1706–1786*, edited by C. G. Chamberlayne (Richmond, Va., 1989), 620.

20. Thomas Jefferson, *Notes on the State of Virginia*, in *Thomas Jefferson, Writings*, edited by Merrill D. Peterson (New York, 1984), 34; Jarratt, *Autobiography*, 364.

21. *Hening's Statutes at Large*, vol. 1, 1619–60 (New York, 1823), 122–24; Perry Miller, "The Religious Impulse in the Founding of Virginia: Religion and Society in the Early Literature," *William and Mary Quarterly* 5 (Oct. 1948): 492–522.

22. *Hening's Statutes*, 157.

23. Ibid., 156.

24. Perry Miller, "Religious Impulse," 493; Thomas Lord De la Ware, Sir Thomas Smith,

Sir Walter Cope, and Master Waterson, *A True and Sincere Declaration of the Purpose and Ends of the Plantation Begun in Virginia* . . . (London, 1610), in Warren M. Billings, *The Old Dominion in the Seventeenth Century: A Documentary History of Virginia, 1606–1689* (Chapel Hill, N.C., 1975), 14.

25. W. M. Jacob, *Lay People and Religion in the Eighteenth Century* (Cambridge, Eng., 1996), 6. See also John K. Nelson, *A Blessed Company: Parishes, Parsons, and Parishioners in Anglican Virginia, 1690–1776* (Chapel Hill, N.C., 2001); William H. Seiler, "The Anglican Parish in Virginia," in *Seventeenth-Century America: Essays in Colonial History*, edited by James Morton Smith (Chapel Hill, N.C., 1959), 119–42; Jan Lewis, *The Pursuit of Happiness: Family and Values in Jefferson's Virginia* (Cambridge, Eng., 1983), 40–44, which has a nice summary of the parish's importance to prerevolutionary community in Virginia.

26. Shuffelton, *Thomas Hooker*, 6–7; Dell Upton, *Holy Things and Profane: Anglican Parish Churches in Colonial Virginia* (New Haven, Conn., 1997), 47–56.

27. *Vestry Book and Register*, 503.

28. Rhys Isaac, *Landon Carter's Uneasy Kingdom: Revolution and Rebellion on a Virginia Plantation* (Oxford, 2004), 92–84; Perry Miller, "Religious Impulse," 498–99.

29. Jarratt, *Autobiography*, 373.

30. Ibid., 376.

31. Ibid., 361, 364; Helen Bryan, *Martha Washington: First Lady of Liberty* (New York, 2002), 35–36.

32. Robert Beverley, *The History and Present State of Virginia*, edited by Louis B. Wright (Chapel Hill, N.C., 1947), 253; *Vestry Book and Register*; Virginia Land Patent Books, 1623–1774, available online at <http://ajax.lva.lib.va>. For background on New Kent, see Malcolm H. Harris, *Old New Kent County: Some Account of the Planters, Plantations, and Places in New Kent County,* (n.p., 1977), vol. 1.

33. Beverley, *History*, 253.

34. Harris, *Old New Kent County*, 95–96. Reference to the holy and profane is from the title of Upton, *Holy Things*.

35. For some references to the building of the church, see *Vestry Book and Register*, 75, 199. See also Upton, *Holy Things*, 203–4.

36. *Vestry Book and Register*, 36.

37. Indenture of Apr. 27, 1738, in ibid., 505.

38. Ibid., 69.

39. Ibid., 77, 79; "An Act for Dividing New Kent Countie," in *Vestry Book and Register*, 617. For more on the Church of England's ability to expand the parish system to keep pace with population growth, see Nelson, *Blessed Company*.

40. For this discussion of Anglicanism, I draw mainly on Nelson, *Blessed Company*; Jacob, *Lay People*; Upton, *Holy Things*; George MacLaren Brydon, *Virginia's Mother Church and the Political Conditions under Which It Grew* (Richmond, Va., 1947).

41. "Mr. Lang to the Bishop of London," Feb. 7, 1725/26, extract in *Vestry Book and Register*, 632; 1724 list of "Queries to Be Answered," in *Vestry Book and Register*, 630–31; *The Parish Register of Saint Peter's, New Kent County, Va., from 1680 to 1787* (Baltimore, 1966). The parish register was too spottily kept to give an accurate reading on how many in the total popu-

lation were baptized as Anglicans. For more on church attendance in early America, see Patricia U. Bonomi and Peter R. Eisenstadt, "Church Adherence in the Eighteenth-Century British American Colonies," *William and Mary Quarterly* 39 (Apr. 1982): 245–86.

42. *Vestry Book and Register*, appendix C, 691.

43. Ibid., 104, 240–41.

44. J. Hammond Trumbull, ed., *The Public Records of the Colony of Connecticut* (Hartford, 1850), 1:20–21. For more on the union of church and state, see Upton, *Holy Things*, 55–56; Isaac, *Landon Carter's Uneasy Kingdom*, 173; Gordon S. Wood, *The Radicalism of the American Revolution* (New York, 1991), 17–19.

45. Upton, *Holy Things*, 55, 97–98.

46. Ibid., 164; Gordon S. Wood, *Radicalism*, 18–20.

47. Upton, *Holy Things*, 175–83.

48. For more on these dissenters, see James Horn, *Adapting to a New World: English Society in the Seventeenth-Century Chesapeake* (Chapel Hill, N.C., 1994), 386–87, 389–90; Isaac, *Transformation*, 260–64, 299–310; Kevin Butterfield, "Puritans and Religious Strife in the Early Chesapeake," *Virginia Magazine of History and Biography* 109, no. 1 (2001): 5–36. For developments in western Virginia, see chap. 3 in this volume; Warren R. Hofstra, *The Planting of New Virginia: Settlement and Landscape in the Shenandoah Valley* (Baltimore, 2004).

49. Horn, *Adapting*, 136–41; James Horn, "Servant Emigration to the Chesapeake in the Seventeenth Century," in *Chesapeake in the Seventeenth Century*, edited by Tate and Ammerman, 51–95; Kulikoff, *Tobacco and Slaves*, 48–49, 59–60. See also David Hackett Fischer and James C. Kelly, *Bound Away: Virginia and the Westward Movement* (Charlottesville, Va., 2000). Because of major gaps in the historical record, there are no comprehensive studies of internal mobility in Chesapeake Virginia.

50. Kulikoff, *Tobacco and Slaves*, 92–99; Lorena S. Walsh, "Staying Put or Getting Out: Findings for Charles County, Maryland, 1650–1720," *William and Mary Quarterly* 44 (Jan. 1987): 89–103.

51. Kulikoff, *Tobacco and Slaves*, 47; Richard R. Beeman, *The Evolution of the Southern Backcountry: A Case Study of Lunenburg County, Virginia, 1746–1832* (Philadelphia, 1984), 69–71; Horn, *Adapting*, 140–46.

52. For this discussion, I draw mainly on Horn, *Adapting*; Russell R. Menard, "British Migration to the Chesapeake Colonies in the Seventeenth Century," in *Colonial Chesapeake Society*, edited by Lois Green Carr, Philip D. Morgan, and Jean B. Russo (Chapel Hill, N.C., 1988), 99–132; Bernard Bailyn, *Voyagers to the West: A Passage in the Peopling of America on the Eve of the Revolution* (New York, 1986).

53. Patricia Caldwell, *The Puritan Conversion Narrative: The Beginning of American Expression* (Cambridge, Eng., 1983), 31, 35, 120.

54. Ibid., 31, 35, 119, 123, 127.

55. Thomas Hooker, *A Survey of the Summe of Church-Discipline* (New York, 1972), 1:13; Jarratt, *Autobiography*, 83, 84.

56. Beeman, *Evolution*, 68, 116–18; Richard R. Beeman, "Social Change and Cultural Conflict in Virginia: Lunenburg County, 1746 to 1774," *William and Mary Quarterly* 35 (July 1978): 455–76.

57. Walsh, "Staying Put or Getting Out," 98; Darrett B. Rutman and Anita H. Rutman, *A Place in Time: Middlesex County, Virginia, 1650–1750* (New York, 1984), 236–37. See also James R. Perry, *The Formation of a Society on Virginia's Eastern Shore, 1615–1655* (Chapel Hill, N.C., 1990).

58. Jarratt, *Autobiography*, 373.

59. Ibid., 372–78.

60. For more on the new birth, see S. Scott Rohrer, *Hope's Promise: Religion and Acculturation in the Southern Backcountry* (Tuscaloosa, Ala., 2005), chap. 2; John B. Boles, *The Great Revival: Beginnings of the Bible Belt*, 2nd ed. (Lexington, Ky., 1996); Mark A. Noll, *The Rise of Evangelicalism: The Age of Edwards, Whitefield, and the Wesleys* (Downers Grove, Ill., 2003).

61. Jarratt, *Autobiography*, 378.

62. Ibid., 378–83.

63. Ibid., Letter II, 83–87, 99. Although Jarratt aroused great hostility, his statement that he was alone in trying to spark a great awakening was an exaggeration. Virginia experienced a great awakening beginning in the 1740s. See Isaac, *Transformation*; Rhys Isaac, "Religion and Authority: Problems of the Anglican Establishment in Virginia in the Era of Great Awakening and the Parsons' Cause," *William and Mary Quarterly* 30 (Jan. 1973): 3–36.

64. Jarratt, *Autobiography*, Letter II, 91, 94, 97. For an excellent discussion of itinerancy and its threat to the territorial church, see Timothy D. Hall, *Contested Boundaries: Itinerancy and the Reshaping of the Colonial American Religious World* (Durham, N.C., 1994).

65. For Jarratt's views of the Baptists and Methodists, see Jarratt, *Autobiography*, 105, 107.

CHAPTER THREE

1. Graeme Kirkham, "Ulster Emigration to North America, 1680–1720," in *Ulster and North America: Transatlantic Perspectives on the Scotch-Irish*, edited by H. Tyler Blethen and Curtis W. Wood Jr. (Tuscaloosa, Ala., 1997), 95; Patrick Griffin, *The People with No Name: Ireland's Ulster Scots, America's Scots Irish, and the Creation of a British Atlantic World, 1689–1764* (Princeton, 2001), 2, 103. For the hostility encountered by the Scotch-Irish in New England, see Ralph Stuart Wallace, "The Scotch-Irish of Provincial New Hampshire" (Ph.D. diss., University of New Hampshire, 1984).

2. Some good general treatments of the Scots and Scotch-Irish include Ned C. Landsman, *Scotland and Its First American Colony, 1683–1765* (Princeton, 1985); Jenny Wormald, ed., *Scotland: A History* (Oxford, 2005); James G. Leyburn, *The Scotch-Irish: A Social History* (Chapel Hill, N.C., 1962).

3. Harry S. Stout, "Ethnicity: The Vital Center of Religion in America," *Ethnicity* 2 (June 1975): 207. Other key works on ethnicity and religion include Jonathan D. Sarna, "From Immigrants to Ethnics: Toward a New Theory of 'Ethnicization,'" *Ethnicity* 5 (1978): 370–78; Harold J. Abramson, "Religion," in *Harvard Encyclopedia of American Ethnic Groups*, edited by Stephan Thernstrom (Cambridge, Mass., 1980), 869–76.

4. Several depositions of early settlers are reprinted in Francis Byron, *History of Boothbay, Southport, and Boothbay Harbor, Maine* (Somersworth, Mass., 1984), 116–22. See also "Samuel

McCobb, 1729–1772," in *Irish Immigrants in the Land of Canaan: Letters and Memoirs from Colonial and Revolutionary America*, edited by Kerby A. Miller, Arnold Schrier, Bruce D. Boling, and David N. Doyle (Oxford, 2003), 128–34.

5. For a good overview of the Maine frontier in a later period, see Alan Taylor, *Liberty Men and Great Proprietors: The Revolutionary Settlement on the Maine Frontier, 1760–1820* (Chapel Hill, N.C., 1990).

6. "Samuel McCobb," 129–30; Alan Taylor, *Liberty Men*, 11, 32; Wallace, "Scotch-Irish," chap. 4; Byron, *History*, 109–16.

7. "Samuel McCobb, 1729–1772," 131.

8. Ibid., 131–33.

9. Wallace, "Scotch-Irish," chaps. 3, 4; Leyburn, *Scotch-Irish*, 236–41.

10. Leyburn, *Scotch-Irish*, 236–41; Charles Nutt, *History of Worcester and Its People* (New York, 1919), 1:27–29.

11. Wallace, "Scotch-Irish," 117–19; C. O. Parmenter, *History of Pelham, Mass., from 1738 to 1898* (Amherst, Mass., 1898), 8–16.

12. Leyburn, *Scotch-Irish*, 238–39.

13. Ibid.

14. Ibid.

15. Ibid.

16. Elizabeth Freeman Reed, ed., "The Sessional Records of Booth Bay," *Journal of the Presbyterian Historical Society* 16 (Mar. 1935): 214.

17. Quoted in Francis Byron Greene, *History of Boothbay, Southport, and Boothbay Harbor, Maine* (Somersworth, N.H., 1984), 133.

18. Reed, "Sessional Records," 210.

19. Ibid., 215–16.

20. Ibid.

21. Greene, *History of Boothbay*, 136–37.

22. Reed, "Sessional Records," 214–15.

23. Ibid., 216–24.

24. Ibid., 224–30.

25. Ibid., 232–33.

26. Leyburn, *Scotch-Irish*, 51–52. See also Duncan B. Forrester, "The Reformed Tradition in Scotland," in *The Oxford History of Christian Worship*, edited by Geoffrey Wainwright and Karen B. Westerfield Tucker (Oxford, 2006), 473–83; Edwin Scott Gaustad and Philip L. Barlow, *New Historical Atlas of Religion in America* (Oxford, 2001), 38–41.

27. Leyburn, *Scotch-Irish*, 53–56.

28. David Hackett Fischer, *Albion's Seed: Four British Folkways in America* (Oxford, 1989), 623–24.

29. Landsman, *Scotland*, 51–55.

30. Leyburn, *Scotch-Irish*, 128–32. See also Griffin, *People*, 9, 11–13; S. J. Connolly, "Ulster Presbyterians: Religion, Culture, and Politics, 1660–1850," in *Ulster and North America*, edited by Blethen and Wood, 24–40.

31. Griffin, *People*, 19; Leyburn, *Scotch-Irish*, 125–26.

32. Forrester, "Reformed Tradition," 478; Leigh Eric Schmidt, *Holy Fairs: Scotland and the Making of American Revivalism*, 2nd ed. (Grand Rapids, Mich., 2001), 14. See also Marilyn J. Westerkamp, *Triumph of the Laity: Scots-Irish Piety and the Great Awakening, 1625–1760* (New York, 1988).

33. Schmidt, *Holy Fairs*, 21–23.

34. Ibid., 49, 53.

35. Reed, "Sessional Records," 232.

36. Ibid., 238–39.

37. Ibid., 244–45.

38. Ibid., 249. The revival was so successful in Boothbay that Murray decided to visit neighboring towns on "the Gospel errand." During a two-week period, the pastor preached every day (250–51).

39. The best work on Augusta is Nathaniel Turk McCleskey, "Across the First Divide: Frontiers of Settlement and Culture in Augusta County, Virginia, 1738–1770" (Ph.D. diss., College of William and Mary, 1990).

40. "The Autobiography of John Craig," excerpts reprinted in Howard McKnight Wilson, *The Tinkling Spring, Headwater of Freedom* (Fishersville, Va., 1954), 123–34. The full text is available at the Union Theological Seminary in Richmond, Va.; the Presbyterian Historical Society in Philadelphia has part of the autobiography on microfilm.

41. Ibid., 126

42. Ibid., 127.

43. Ibid., 129.

44. Ibid., 130–31.

45. Ibid., 130.

46. Schmidt, *Holy Fairs*, 56; Landsman, *Scotland*, 181–83, 231. For a counter view, see Kenneth W. Keller, "What Is Distinctive about the Scotch-Irish?," in *Appalachian Frontiers: Settlement, Society, and Development in the Pre-Industrial Era*, edited by Robert D. Mitchell (Lexington, Ky., 1991), 69–86, esp. 81.

47. Landsman, *Scotland*, 186–87.

48. Timothy D. Hall, *Contested Boundaries: Itinerancy and the Reshaping of the Colonial American Religious World* (Durham, N.C., 1994), 34; Landsman, *Scotland*, 227–39. Some historians disagree with this view. Mitchell argues that the Great Awakening and later revivals "helped to break down the ethnic homogeneity of some immigrant groups"; he cites the Scotch-Irish in particular as so "altered by religious change . . . that it is difficult to discuss them realistically as a group after the Revolution" (*Commercialism and Frontier: Perspectives on the Early Shenandoah Valley* [Charlottesville, Va., 1977], 105–6). What happens to Scottish and Scotch-Irish Presbyterian identity, especially after the American Revolution, is an interesting question that is beyond the scope of this chapter. In the antebellum period, these Scots eventually became "American." For distinct religious groups such as the Moravians, Mennonites, or Scotch-Irish Presbyterians, assimilation was a three-step process: interaction in the meetinghouse among (in this case) Presbyterians of different ethnicities began to change both sides on a cultural level, with each side taking on the social traits of the other. While this acculturation was occurring in the religious sphere,

Scottish Presbyterians were interacting with outside "American" influences, producing further change. The two stages of acculturation produced a third stage, with Scots and Scotch-Irish Presbyterians achieving a hybrid identity as Scottish-American Presbyterians. For details on this model, see S. Scott Rohrer, *Hope's Promise: Religion and Acculturation in the Southern Backcountry* (Tuscaloosa, Ala., 2005), xxv–xxvii. See also Landsman, *Scotland*, chap. 9; H. Tyler Blethen and Curtis W. Wood Jr., "Scotch-Irish Frontier Society in Southwestern North Carolina, 1780–1840," in *Ulster and North America*, edited by Blethen and Wood, 213–26; Stephen L. Longenecker, *Shenandoah Religion: Outsiders and the Mainstream, 1716–1865* (Waco, Tex., 2002).

49. Rev. Samuel Blair to Rev. Thomas Prince, Aug. 6, 1744, in *Irish Immigrants*, edited by Kerby A. Miller et al., 401. Key documents are in Richard L. Bushman, ed., *The Great Awakening: Documents on the Revival of Religion, 1740–1745* (Chapel Hill, N.C., 1969), including Gilbert Tennent, "The Danger of an Unconverted Ministry, 1740," 87; "A Plea for Moderation, Solomon Williams, a Letter, 1744," 94; and "The Synod of Philadelphia Divides: Records of the Presbyterian Church," 97.

50. George William Pilcher, *Samuel Davies: Apostle of Dissent in Colonial Virginia* (Knoxville, Tenn., 1971), 65–66, 75.

51. Records of Donegal Presbytery, vol. 1a, 1732–35, Sept. 4, 1735, Presbyterian Historical Society, Philadelphia; see also Howard McKnight Wilson, *The Lexington Presbytery Heritage* (Verona, Va., 1971), 38–43.

52. Howard McKnight Wilson, *Lexington Presbyterian Heritage*, 42–43; Pilcher, *Samuel Davies*, 62; William M. E. Rachal, ed., "Early Minutes of Hanover Presbytery," Mar. 18, 1755, Apr. 2, 1761, *Virginia Magazine of History and Biography* 63 (Apr. 1955): 53–75; Rev. Samuel Blair to Rev. Thomas Prince, Aug. 6, 1744, in *Irish Immigrants*, edited by Kerby A. Miller et al., 407.

53. Records of Donegal Presbytery, vol. 1a, June 7, 1734, May 17, 1736.

54. Robert Witherspoon Memoir, 1734–1780, in *Irish Immigrants*, edited by Kerby A. Miller et al., 137–41.

55. Howard McKnight Wilson, *Tinkling Spring*, 417–19, 69–70. See also McCleskey, "Across the First Divide," chap. 2.

56. Rev. Samuel Blair to Rev. Thomas Prince, in *Irish Immigrants*, edited by Kerby A. Miller et al., 404; James Magraw to John Magraw, May 21, 1733, in *Irish Immigrants*, edited by Kerby A. Miller et al., 144–45; Howard McKnight Wilson, *Lexington Presbyterian Heritage*, 15–17.

57. Warren R. Hofstra, *The Planting of New Virginia: Settlement and Landscape in the Shenandoah Valley* (Baltimore, 2004), 22; Howard McKnight Wilson, *Tinkling Spring*, 417–19.

58. Howard McKnight Wilson, *Tinkling Spring*, 76–79, 85–86, 99, 169; deposition of Mary Elizabeth McDowell, Nov. 10, 1806, in *Irish Immigrants*, edited by Kerby A. Miller et al., 153–54; Warren R. Hofstra, "Land, Ethnicity, and Community at the Opequon Settlement, Virginia, 1730–1800," in *Ulster and North America*, edited by Blethen and Wood, 168, 174. For an example of how migration worked in Canada, see Catharine Anne Wilson, "The Scotch-Irish and Immigrant Culture on Amherst Island, Ontario," in *Ulster and North America*, edited by Blethen and Wood, 134–45.

59. George William Pilcher, ed., *The Reverend Samuel Davies Abroad: The Diary of a Journey to England and Scotland* (Chicago, 1967), 88; Landsman, *Scotland*, 17–18.

60. Landsman, *Scotland*, 17–20. See also Leyburn, *Scotch-Irish*, chaps. 1, 2.

61. Landsman, *Scotland*, 21.

62. Ibid., 47; Leyburn, *Scotch-Irish*, 84–88; Connolly, "Ulster Presbyterians," 24.

63. Ibid. See also Kirkham, "Ulster Emigration"; Marianne S. Wokeck, *Trade in Strangers: The Beginnings of Mass Migration to North America* (University Park, Pa., 1999), chap. 5.

64. Eric Richards, "Scotland and the Uses of the Atlantic Empire," in *Strangers within the Realm: Cultural Margins of the First British Empire*, edited by Bernard Bailyn and Philip D. Morgan (Chapel Hill, N.C., 1991), 69.

65. Wokeck, *Trade in Strangers*, 169–77, 186. See also Nicholas Canny, "The Marginal Kingdom: Ireland as a Problem in the First British Empire," in *Strangers within the Realm*, edited by Bailyn and Morgan, 35–66.

66. Kirkham, "Ulster Emigration," 77; Griffin, *People*, 90.

67. Trevor Parkhill, "Philadelphia Here I Come: A Study of the Letters of Ulster Immigrants in Pennsylvania, 1750–1875," in *Ulster and North America*, edited by Blethen and Wood, 123; Henry Johnston to Moses Johnston, Apr. 28, 1773, in *Irish Immigrants*, edited by Kerby A. Miller et al., 32; Griffin, *People*, 66. See also Wayland F. Dunaway, *The Scotch-Irish of Colonial Pennsylvania* (Baltimore, 1979).

68. William Henry Foote, *Sketches of Virginia, Historical and Bibliographical*, 2nd ser. (Philadelphia, 1855), 2:117; Howard McKnight Wilson, *Tinkling Spring*, 170–73; Gaustad and Barlow, *New Historical Atlas*, 38–40. For a look at this period, see Russel L. Gerlach, "Scotch-Irish Landscapes in the Ozarks," in *Ulster and North America*, edited by Blethen and Wood, 146–66.

69. For more on religion's impact on ethnicity and acculturation, see Rohrer, *Hope's Promise*.

CHAPTER FOUR

1. The movements of the Frey family are derived from the *Lebenslaufs*, or life stories, of sons Christian and Valentine, as well as from the death notice of Peter in the first church register of Friedberg, MA-SP. See also *Kirchen Buch* for Heidelberg, MA-NP.

2. See sources cited in n. 1, as well as biographical cards on the Frey family at the research library at the Museum of Early Southern Decorative Arts, Old Salem, Winston-Salem, N.C.; landholding records, MA-SP.

3. *Lebenslaufs* of Christian and Valentine Frey.

4. Thomas Jefferson to John Jay, Aug. 23, 1785, in *Thomas Jefferson: Writings*, edited by Merrill D. Peterson (New York, 1984), 818.

5. Deeds, Apr. 29, 1765, Berks County Courthouse, Berks County, Pa.

6. For an excellent account of the *Ortsgemeinen* and the founding of Wachovia, see Daniel B. Thorp, *The Moravian Community in Colonial North Carolina: Pluralism on the Southern Frontier* (Knoxville, Tenn., 1989). See also Elisabeth W. Sommer, *Serving Two Masters: Moravian Brethren in Germany and North Carolina, 1727–1801* (Lexington, Ky., 2000). The best

study of Bethlehem, Pennsylvania, is Beverly Prior Smaby, *The Transformation of Moravian Bethlehem: From Communal Mission to Family Economy* (Philadelphia, 1988).

7. For an in-depth study of the *Landgemeinen* and the Society movement, see S. Scott Rohrer, *Hope's Promise: Religion and Acculturation in the Southern Backcountry* (Tuscaloosa, Ala., 2005).

8. For a good treatment of Lutheran Pietism, see A. G. Roeber, *Palatines, Liberty, and Property: German Lutherans in Colonial British America* (Baltimore, 1993). For more on the Pietist movement and its theological underpinnings, see F. Ernest Stoeffler, *German Pietism during the Eighteenth Century* (Leiden, 1973); F. Ernest Stoeffler, *The Rise of Evangelical Pietism* (Leiden, 1965); Stephen L. Longenecker, *Piety and Tolerance: Pennsylvania German Religion, 1700–1850* (Metuchen, N.J., 1994); Dale Brown, *Understanding Pietism* (Grand Rapids, Mich., 1978). Recent works on Pietism include Paul P. Kuenning, *The Rise and Fall of American Lutheran Pietism* (Macon, Ga., 1988); Johannes Wallmann, *Der Pietismus* (Gottingen, 1990).

9. Rohrer, *Hope's Promise*, xxi. For a good overview of Moravian beliefs, see Stoeffler, *German Pietism*, chap. 4; W. R. Ward, *The Protestant Evangelical Awakening* (Cambridge, Eng., 1992), chap. 4.

10. "Diary of L. C. Bachhof," Jan. 7–27, 1770, translated by Donald J. Lineback, MA-SP.

11. MR, 2:616.

12. LAC, Sept. 15, 1780; Thorp, *Moravian Community*, 71–72.

13. Hope Brotherly Agreement, MA-SP; Rohrer, *Hope's Promise*, 44–45.

14. Stokes County Deed Books, Forsyth County Library, Winston-Salem, N.C. For more on landholding practices, see Rohrer, *Hope's Promise*, chap. 3. For good treatments of Quaker families and their land use, see Barry J. Levy, "'Tender Plants': Quaker Farmers and Children in the Delaware Valley, 1681–1735," in *Colonial America: Essays in Politics and Social Development*, edited by Stanley N. Katz and John M. Murrin, 3rd ed. (New York, 1983), 177–203; Barry J. Levy, *Quakers and the American Family: British Settlement in the Delaware Valley* (Oxford, 1988).

15. Stokes County Deed Books, 3:328, 5:7, 253, 615, 616; Stokes County Will Books, Forsyth County Library, Winston-Salem, N.C., 3:42, 2:80. Jacob Hauser later bought Timothy's share and sold it to his oldest brother, Abraham Jr. (Stokes County Deed Books, 5:730, 6:228). For other examples of childless couples forgoing the land market, see deed indexes for Lorenz Sides, Philip Lagenauer, and David Rominger.

16. Kathleen Neils Conzen, "Peasant Pioneers: Generational Succession among German Farmers in Frontier Minnesota," in *The Countryside in the Age of Capitalist Transformation: Essays in the Social History of Rural America*, edited by Steven Hahn and Jonathan Prude (Chapel Hill, N.C., 1985), 259–92, esp. 266; Roeber, *Palatines, Liberty, and Property*, 50–53, 109–10, 149–57.

17. This conclusion is based on an examination of 215 wills for Wachovia's inhabitants found at the Forsyth County Library, Winston-Salem, N.C., and MA-SP.

18. Stokes County Will Books, 1:104; wills of Lazarus Hege and Peter Fry Jr., C141A, MA-SP.

19. For more on these plans and the leadership's decision to abandon them, see Daniel B.

Thorp, "Assimilation in North Carolina's Moravian Community," *Journal of Southern History* 52 (Feb. 1986): 19–42.

20. Resolutions of the 1775 Synod, MA-SP; LAC, Oct. 1780, Francis Cumnock translation. For an example of a church leader admonishing members to put Jesus first, see Bishop Augustus Spangenberg to Bethania's residents, Oct. 11, 1759, H272:6:2:a, MA-SP.

21. LAC, Nov. 1780.

22. LAC, Sept. 15, 1780, Cumnock translation.

23. "Friedland Diary," Feb. 10, 1799; LAC, Sept. 15, 1780, Oct. 1780, Mar. 3, 1799, Cumnock translation. On the importance of family, see Resolutions of the 1775 Synod; LAC, Oct. 1780.

24. Jon F. Sensbach, *A Separate Canaan: The Making of an Afro-Moravian World in North Carolina, 1763–1840* (Chapel Hill, N.C., 1998), 415–38, has an excellent discussion of godparenthood as well as a good comparison of the differences and similarities between white and black godparenthood. See also John Bossy, "Blood and Baptism: Kinship, Community, and Christianity in Western Europe from the Fourteenth to the Seventeenth Centuries," in *Sanctity and Secularity: The Church and the World*, edited by Derek Baker (Oxford, 1973), 129–43; David Warren Sabean, "Aspects of Kinship Behavior and Property in Rural Western Europe before 1800," in *Family and Inheritance: Rural Society in Western Europe, 1200–1800*, edited by Jack Goody, Joan Thirsk, and E. P. Thompson (Cambridge, Eng., 1976), 96–111.

25. Friedberg Register A, 1774–92, nos. 6, 42, MA-SP. Family relationships are derived from biographical cards at the Museum of Early Southern Decorative Arts Research Library.

26. See, e.g., no. 3 in Register 1 for Eva Rothrock, MA-SP.

27. Conclusion is based on an examination of maps and congregational records.

28. MR 4:1839; "Diary of L. C. Bachhof," Aug. 1, 1773.

29. *Heidelberg Bericht*, May 10, 1765, MA-NP; "Diary of L. C. Bachhof," Sept. 10, 1770, Oct. 14, 15, 19, 1770; Roeber, *Palatines, Liberty, and Property*, 113–17. See also Aaron Spencer Fogleman, *Hopeful Journeys: German Immigration, Settlement, and Political Culture in Colonial America, 1717–1775* (Philadelphia, 1996), chap. 3.

30. These five farms belonged to the Tesches, Hausers, Eberts, Hahns, and Hohners. See "Friedberg Diary," May 10, 1780, MR 4:1649.

31. MR 1:294, 4:1649; 1804 map of Wachovia by Frederick Meinung, Museum of Early Southern Decorative Arts Research Library.

32. "Diary of L. C. Bachhof," Sept. 10, Oct. 14, 15, 19, 1770.

33. Ibid., Mar. 22, 1770.

34. Taylor J. Hamilton and Kenneth G. Hamilton, *History of the Moravian Church: The Renewed Unitas Fratrum, 1722–1958* (Bethlehem, Pa., 1967), 132–34; Dietmar Rothermund, *The Layman's Progress: Religious and Political Experience in Colonial Pennsylvania, 1740–1770* (Philadelphia, 1961), 31.

35. *Historiche Nachricht von dem Anfang u. Fortgang der Evangelischen Bruder Gemeinlein in Heidelberg Township, Berks County, in der Provinz Pensilvania*, MA-NP; *Kirchen Buch* for Heidelberg, MA-NP.

36. Ronald Hoffman, in collaboration with Sally D. Mason, *Princes of Ireland, Planters of Maryland: A Carroll Saga, 1500–1782* (Chapel Hill, N.C., 2000), 100–118.

37. Elizabeth Augusta Kessel, "Germans on the Maryland Frontier: A Social History of Frederick County, Maryland, 1730–1800," 2 vols. (Ph.D. diss., Rice University, 1981), 3; Mary Clement Jeske, "Autonomy and Opportunity: Carrollton Manor Tenants, 1734–1790" (Ph.D. diss., University of Maryland, 1999), 120–21, 167–69; *Lebenslauf* of Mary Padgett, MA-SP. (Other primary sources spell this name Padget, and I use that spelling in the text.)

38. "An Account of the Beginning to Preach the Gospel on Esq. Carroll's Manor," Carroll's Manor Box, MA-NP; Hoffman with Mason, *Princes of Ireland*, 344.

39. Taken from an "Observation," Ci Manor Acc, MA-NP, that was part of "An Account of the Beginning to Preach the Gospel"; Joseph Powell to Nathanael Seidel, [1770], MyA: Maryland: II, MA-NP.

40. *Lebenslauf* of William Barton Peddycoard, MA-SP.

41. "Joseph Powell's Diary of Carroll's Manor," July 27, Aug. 20, Sept. 7, 1766, MyA: Maryland, folder VI, MA-NP; Jeske, "Carrollton Manor Tenants," 121.

42. "Joseph Powell's Diary," Jan. 18, 1767, Mar. 4, 1768; memoirs of Sophia Elisabeth Peddycoart and William Barton Peddycoard, MA-SP. (The primary sources have varying spellings of this family's name.)

43. "Joseph Powell's Diary," Nov. 2, Aug. 7, 11, 12, 1766; "The Work of Our Church on Carroll's Manor," 302, MA-NP.

44. "Joseph Powell's Diary," Sept. 5–Dec. 3, 1768, May 19, 1772; Joseph Powell to Nathanael Seidel, Jan. 18, 1769, MyA V, MA-NP.

45. "Joseph Powell's Diary," Sept. 5–Dec. 3, 1768, May 19, 1772; Joseph Powell to Nathanael Seidel, Jan. 18, 1769, MyA V, MA-NP.

46. "Joseph Powell's Diary," July 10, 1768, Nov. 15, 1770, July 27, 1766, Jan. 27, 1767.

47. Joseph Powell to Nathanael Seidel, May 7, 1772, MA-NP.

48. For Smith's lease-purchase indenture with Marshall, see Notebook D, MA-SP; Jeske, "Carrollton Manor Tenants," 21, 23, 57.

49. *Lebenslauf* of John Jacob Peddycoart, MA-SP.

50. Congregational address to Bethlehem, Aug. 26, 1772, MA-NP.

51. *MR* 4:1895; figures on arriving families are from the 1774 and 1775 Wachovia Memorabilias. For another example of a family moving reluctantly to join other kin, see the Chittys, Hope Church Book, Register A, Burials at Hope, MA-SP.

52. *Lebenslauf* of George Hahn, MA-SP; *Historicher Bericht vom Anfange und fortgange des Bruder = Establishments in der Wachau*, MA-NP; *Kurzen Historiche Nachricht von dem Hauflein in Broadbay vom Anfang an bis jezt*, MA-NP.

53. Correspondence of George Soelle, box NeA IV, MA-NP; *Kurzen Historiche*.

54. *Kurzen Historiche*.

55. *MR* 2:611, 610; *Kurzen Historiche*; *Lebenslauf* of Catharine Rominger Lanius, MA-SP.

56. *MR* 1:383, 393, 2:616; for a description of the village, see *MR* 1:436.

57. *MR* 2:611, 610; *Kurzen Historiche*; *Lebenslauf* of Catharine Rominger Lanius, MA-SP.

58. *Lebenslauf* of Matthias Wesner, MA-SP.

59. "Diary of a Journey of Moravians from Bethlehem, Pa., to Bethabara, N.C., 1753," in *Travels in the American Colonies*, edited by Newton D. Mereness (New York, 1961), 328.

60. Migration figures are derived from diaries, memorabilias, and historical accounts for individual congregations in MA-NP and MA-SP. The totals for Friedberg are understated.

61. *MR* 1:303; *Extract aus den Diariis der Stadt und Land-Gemeinen*, May 10, 1765, MA-NP; Fogleman, *Hopeful Journeys,* 123.

62. Mobility rates are derived from an examination of extant memoirs of founding members of North Carolina *Landgemeinen*, MA-SP. These mobility rates could not be cross-checked with Pennsylvania's *Landgemeine* settlers because of gaps in the church's Northern Province records and the fluidity of the Society movement. Burial records for the Pennsylvania *Landgemeinen*, unlike those for the *Ortsgemeinen*, did not indicate the number of times people moved.

63. Advertisement, Mar. 1763, MA-NP.

64. James T. Lemon, *The Best Poor Man's Country: A Geographical Study of Early South-eastern Pennsylvania* (New York, 1972), xv; Jack P. Greene, "Independence, Improvement, and Authority: Toward a Framework for Understanding the Histories of the Southern Backcountry during the Era of the American Revolution," in *An Uncivil War: The Southern Backcountry during the American Revolution*, edited by Ronald Hoffman, Thad W. Tate, and Peter J. Albert (Charlottesville, Va., 1985), 12–14. See also Gregory H. Nobles, "Breaking into the Backcountry: New Approaches to the Early American Frontier, 1750–1800," *William and Mary Quarterly* 46 (Oct. 1989): 648; Patrick Griffin, *The People with No Name: Ireland's Ulster Scots, America's Scots Irish, and the Creation of a British Atlantic World, 1689–1764* (Princeton, 2001).

65. Susanne Mostelle Rolland, "From the Rhine to the Catawba: A Study of Eighteenth Century Germanic Migration and Adaptation" (Ph.D. diss., Emory University, 1991), 267–81. See also Fogleman, *Hopeful Journeys*, esp. 93–99, which describes the movements of Lutherans and Reformed settlers in "Greater Pennsylvania." For a look at the Amish in a later period, see Steven D. Reschly, *The Amish on the Iowa Prairie, 1840 to 1910* (Baltimore, 2000).

66. Richard K. MacMaster, *Land, Piety, Peoplehood: The Establishment of Mennonite Communities in America, 1683–1790* (Scottsdale, Pa., 1985), 111–14; Levy, "'Tender Plants,'" 177–92.

CHAPTER FIVE

1. Philip Gatch to his brother, Feb. 11, 1802, in William Warren Sweet, *Religion on the American Frontier, 1783–1840* (Chicago, 1946), 152–55.

2. John McLean, ed., *Sketch of Rev. Philip Gatch* (Cincinnati, 1854), 152; Frederick Bonner to Brother Drumgole, July 19, 1807, James H. Keys to his brother, Oct. 22, 1805, John Sale to his brother, Feb. 20, 1807, Philip Gatch to his brother, Feb. 11, 1802, in Sweet, *Religion*, 170, 158, 160, 152–54. The precise number of migrants is unknown; for more on their motivations, see John Wigger, "Ohio Gospel: Methodism in Early Ohio," in *The Center of a Great Empire: The Ohio Country in the Early Republic*, edited by Andrew R. L. Cayton and Stuart D. Hobbs (Athens, Ohio, 2005), 62–80.

3. *Historical Statistics of the United States, Colonial Times to 1957* (Washington, 1960), 13.

Good studies on the early national period are numerous; those on which I drew include Robert H. Wiebe, *The Opening of American Society: From the Adoption of the Constitution to the Eve of Disunion* (New York, 1984); Joyce Appleby, *Inheriting the Revolution: The First Generation of Americans* (Cambridge, Mass., 2000); Robert W. Tucker and David C. Hendrickson, *Empire of Liberty: The Statecraft of Thomas Jefferson* (Oxford, 1990).

4. McLean, *Sketch*, 88–92.

5. Ibid., 92. For more on Gatch during this period, see Elizabeth Connor, *Methodist Trail Blazer: Philip Gatch, 1751–1834: His Life in Maryland, Virginia, and Ohio* (Cincinnati, 1970), 143–66.

6. McLean, *Sketch*, 92–93 (which says incorrectly that Gatch freed his slaves in 1780). See also Connor, *Methodist Trail Blazer*, 150.

7. Connor, *Methodist Trail Blazer*, 151–52. See also Donald G. Mathews, *Slavery and Methodism: A Chapter in American Morality, 1780–1845* (Princeton, 1965).

8. Richard S. Dunn, "Black Society in the Chesapeake, 1776–1810," in *Slavery and Freedom in the Age of the American Revolution*, edited by Ira Berlin and Ronald Hoffman (Urbana, Ill., 1986), 49–50; Dee E. Andrews, *The Methodists and Revolutionary America, 1760–1800: The Shaping of an Evangelical Culture* (Princeton, 2000), 124–25; Christine Leigh Heyrman, *Southern Cross: The Beginnings of the Bible Belt* (New York, 1997), 138–39; Connor, *Methodist Trail Blazer*, 152–53.

9. McLean, *Sketch*, 93–95; 1790 Census for Virginia; Connor, *Methodist Trail Blazer*, 160; Andrews, *Methodists and Revolutionary America*, 126.

10. Alexis de Tocqueville, *Democracy in America* (New York, 1980), 1:362.

11. James Smith, "Tours into Kentucky and the Northwest Territory," *Ohio Architecture and Historical Society Publications* 16 (1907): 380; McLean, *Sketch*, 95–99; Connor, *Methodist Trail Blazer*, 167–76.

12. McLean, *Sketch*, 95; James Smith, "Tours."

13. James B. Finley, *Autobiography of Rev. James B. Finley; or, Pioneer Life in the West*, edited by W. P. Strickland (Cincinnati, 1854), 161–63.

14. Ibid., 161–62.

15. Ibid., 164–65.

16. Ibid., 105–6.

17. Ibid., 112–18.

18. Ibid., 114–15.

19. Ibid., 149–50, 164–66.

20. Ibid., 167–68.

21. Ibid., 169–70.

22. Ibid., 171.

23. Ibid., 172–73.

24. Ibid., 174.

25. Ibid., 175–78.

26. Ibid., 181–83.

27. McLean, *Sketch*, 96–99; Connor, *Methodist Trail Blazer*, 178–79. Connor, *Methodist Trail Blazer*, 81, estimates that the journey was some 600 miles, while Sweet, *Religion*, 150,

postulates that the distance was 325 miles; both, I believe, are incorrect, since Gatch followed well-established routes most of the way.

28. Elias Pym Fordham, *Personal Narrative of Travels in Virginia, Maryland, Pennsylvania, Ohio, Indiana, Kentucky, and of a Residence in the Illinois Territory, 1817–1818,* edited by Frederic Austin Ogg (Cleveland, 1906), 256–57; François André Michaux, *Travels West of Alleghany Mountains* (Cleveland, 1904), 166; Bayrd Still, "The Westward Migration of a Planter Pioneer in 1796," *William and Mary Quarterly* 21 (Oct. 1941): 325.

29. McLean, *Sketch,* 96–99; Michaux, *Travels,* 164–65; Fordham, *Personal Narrative,* 79.

30. McLean, *Sketch,* 96–99; Connor, *Methodist Trail Blazer,* 181–83.

31. McLean, *Sketch,* 99.

32. Philip Gatch to his brother, Feb. 11, 1802, Frederick Bonner to Brother Drumgole, July 19, 1807, in Sweet, *Religion,* 154, 171.

33. John Sale to his brother, Feb. 20, 1807, Peter Pelham to his brother, June 20, 1807, Frederick Bonner to his brother, July 19, 1807, in Sweet, *Religion,* 160, 163–67, 170–71.

34. Frederick Bonner to Brother Drumgole, July 19, 1807, Bennett Maxey to his brother, July 27, 1807, in Sweet, *Religion,* 171, 175.

35. The five families were the Bonners, Sales, Butlers, Davises, and Heathes. See Sweet, *Religion,* 151, 164, 179. The first-person account of Frederick Bonner Jr. is in George F. Robinson, *History of Greene County, Ohio* (Chicago, 1902), 153–55.

36. Bennett Maxey to his brother, July 27, 1807, in Sweet, *Religion,* 175.

37. Ibid.; Gatch to his brother, Feb. 11, 1802, in Sweet, *Religion,* 154; Peter Pelham to his brother, July 27, 1807, in Sweet, *Religion,* 172–73.

38. McLean, *Sketch,* 127; Connor, *Methodist Trail Blazer,* 186–88.

39. Edward Dromgoole Jr. to his parents, June 24, 1807, Peter Pelham to his brother, July 27, 1807, in Sweet, *Religion,* 169–70, 172.

40. McLean, *Sketch,* 102–3.

41. Ibid.; Francis Asbury, *Journal of the Rev. Francis Asbury, Bishop of the Methodist Episcopal Church, from August 7, 1771, to December 7, 1815* (New York, 1821), 1:178, 248.

42. For this discussion, I draw mainly on Andrews, *Methodists and Revolutionary America;* David Hempton, *Methodism: Empire of the Spirit* (New Haven, Conn., 2005); Nathan O. Hatch and John H. Wigger, eds., *Methodism and the Shaping of an American Culture* (Nashville, Tenn., 2001); Cynthia Lynn Lyerly, *Methodism and the Southern Mind, 1770–1810* (Oxford, 1998).

43. Andrews, *Methodists and Revolutionary America,* 22–23.

44. Ibid., 26.

45. Finley, *Autobiography,* 178–79; McLean, *Sketch,* 138–39.

46. McLean, *Sketch,* 101–2, 138–39; Finley, *Autobiography,* 191, 200–201. For an example of frontier sermons, see Benjamin Lakin in Sweet, *Religion,* 721–24.

47. James Shaw, *Twelve Years in America* (London, 1867), 172; Asbury, *Journal,* 249. For more on revivals, see John B. Boles, *The Great Revival: Beginnings of the Bible Belt,* 2nd ed. (Lexington, Ky., 1996); Mark A. Noll, *The Rise of Evangelicalism: The Age of Edwards, Whitefield, and the Wesleys* (Downers Grove, Ill., 2003).

48. Peter Cartwright, *Autobiography of Peter Cartwright, the Backwoods Preacher,* edited by

W. P. Strickland (Cincinnati, 1859), 45; for more on Cane Ridge, see Boles, *Great Revival*, esp. 63–65; Paul K. Conkin, *Cane Ridge: America's Pentecost* (Madison, Wis., 1990).

49. Cartwright, *Autobiography*, 44, 86.

50. Asbury, *Journal*, 109; McLean, *Sketch*, 100–102; Finley, *Autobiography*, 200–202; the Reverend H. Smith quoted in James B. Finley, *Sketches of Western Methodism* (New York, 1969), 194–95. For a nice summary of Methodist itinerancy, see John H. Wigger, "Fighting Bees: Methodist Itinerants and the Dynamics of Methodist Growth, 1770–1820," in *Methodism*, edited by Hatch and Wigger, 88–91. For a broader look at itinerancy, see Timothy D. Hall, *Contested Boundaries: Itinerancy and the Reshaping of the Colonial American Religious World* (Durham, N.C., 1994).

51. *Minutes of the Methodist Conferences, Annually Held in America, from 1773 to 1813* (New York, 1813), 243; Edwin Scott Gaustad and Philip L. Barlow, *New Historical Atlas of Religion in America* (Oxford, 2001), 221.

52. *Minutes of the Methodist Conferences*, 243, 290, 343, 480; Sweet, *Religion*, 51–63.

53. Wigger, "Fighting Bees," 91.

54. Appleby, *Inheriting*, 7.

55. Ibid., 6.

56. Tocqueville, *Democracy in America*, 361–62; Asbury, *Journal*, 296. For the importance of Ohio to U.S. history, see Andrew R. L. Cayton, "The Significance of Ohio in the Early Republic," in *Center*, edited by Cayton and Hobbs, 1–10; Andrew R. L. Cayton, *The Frontier Republic: Ideology and Politics in the Ohio Country, 1780–1825* (Kent, Ohio, 1986).

57. R. Douglas Hurt, *The Ohio Frontier: Crucible of the Old Northwest, 1720–1830* (Bloomington, Ind., 1996), 95.

58. Ibid., 144. For additional background, see Thomas D. Clark, *Frontier America: The Story of the Westward Movement* (New York, 1959), esp. 143–44, 147.

59. Hurt, *Ohio Frontier*, chaps. 4, 5.

60. Alan Taylor, *Liberty Men and Great Proprietors: The Revolutionary Settlement on the Maine Frontier, 1760–1820* (Chapel Hill, N.C., 1990), 239; *Historical Statistics*, 13; Hubert G. H. Wilhelm, *The Origin and Distribution of Settlement Groups: Ohio, 1850* (n.p., 1982), 25, 56.

61. Alfred Brunson, *A Western Pioneer* (New York, 1975), 12–19.

62. Ibid., 27–30.

63. Ibid., 14–18, 27–32.

64. Ibid., 33–37.

65. Ibid., 40–41.

66. Ibid., 43–45.

67. Ibid., 45.

68. Ibid., 45–46, 97–99.

69. Ibid., 167.

70. Ibid., 100–101.

71. Ibid., 167–69.

72. Ibid., 169, 174–80.

73. Cartwright, *Autobiography*, 81.

74. Finley, *Autobiography*, 194–96.

1. The migrants' departure is reconstructed from Shrewsbury Church Records, Sept. 6, 1789; Corliss Fitz Randolph, *A History of Seventh Day Baptists in West Virginia, including the Woodbridgetown and Salemville Churches in Pennsylvania and the Shrewsbury Church in New Jersey* (Plainfield, N.J., 1905), 29–30; Don A. Sanford, *A Free People in Search of a Free Land* (Janesville, Wis., 1987), 34–38. For more on the Seventh Day Baptist movement, see Don A. Sanford, *A Choosing People: The History of Seventh Day Baptists* (Nashville, Tenn., 1992).

2. Morgan Edwards, "Materials towards a History of the Baptists in New Jersey" (Philadelphia 1792), 3:142; Randolph, *History*, 1–7.

3. Randolph, *History*, 1–2; Sanford, *Free People*, 7, 13–14; Don A. Sanford, *Conscience Taken Captive: A Short History of Seventh Day Baptists* (Janesville, Wis., 1991), 10.

4. Randolph, *History*, 1–2; Sanford, *Free People*, 7, 13–14.

5. Randolph, *History*, 1–2; Sanford, *Free People*, 7, 13–14.

6. Randolph, *History*, 1–2; Sanford, *Free People*, 7, 13–14.

7. Shrewsbury Church Records, first entry, [1745]; John E. Pomfret, *The Province of East Jersey, 1609–1702: The Rebellious Proprietary* (Princeton, 1962), 34; Dennis P. Ryan, "Six Towns: Continuity and Change in Revolutionary New Jersey, 1770–1792" (Ph.D. diss., New York University, 1974), 16–18; Sanford, *Conscience*, 12.

8. Ryan, "Six Towns," 20; Richard P. McCormick, *New Jersey from Colony to State, 1609–1789* (Newark, N.J., 1981), 25, 43. See also Peter O. Wacker, *Land and People, a Cultural Geography of Preindustrial New Jersey: Origins and Settlement Patterns* (New Brunswick, N.J., 1975).

9. Wacker, *Land and People*, 16, 52, 157, 250; Randolph, *History*, 9–10; Ryan, "Six Towns," 280.

10. Shrewsbury Church Records, Dec. 25, 1773, Jan. 2, 16, 22, 1774.

11. William H. Brackney, *Baptists in North America* (Malden, Mass., 2006), 273; see also William H. Brackney, *The Baptists* (Westport, Conn., 1988); John B. Boles, *The Great Revival: Beginnings of the Bible Belt*, 2nd ed. (Lexington, Ky., 1996); Bill J. Leonard, *Baptist Ways: A History* (Valley Forge, Pa., 2003); Robert G. Torbet, *A History of the Baptists* (Valley Forge, Pa., 1963). On the Anabaptists, see Cornelius J. Dyck, ed., *An Introduction to Mennonite History: A Popular History of the Anabaptists and the Mennonites* (Scottdale, Pa., 1981); Richard K. MacMaster, *Land, Piety, Peoplehood: The Establishment of Mennonite Communities in America, 1683–1790* (Scottdale, Pa., 1985).

12. Brackney, *Baptists in North America*, 1–3, 8–10; Boles, *Great Revival*, 3–4.

13. Shrewsbury Church Records, June 19, 1774.

14. Ibid., Dec. 25, 1774.

15. Ibid., Feb. 12, 27, 1775; Edwards, "Materials," 3:143.

16. John Ferling, *Almost a Miracle: The American Victory in the War of Independence* (Oxford, 2007), 156–86. See also Arthur S. Lefkowitz, *The Long Retreat: The Calamitous American Defense of New Jersey, 1776* (New Brunswick, N.J., 1999); David Hackett Fischer, *Washington's Crossing* (Oxford, 2004).

17. David J. Fowler, "'These Were Troublesome Times Indeed': Social and Economic Conditions in Revolutionary New Jersey," in *New Jersey in the American Revolution*, edited by Barbara J. Mitnick (New Brunswick, N.J., 2005), 15–30; Larry R. Gerlach, *Prologue to Inde-*

pendence: New Jersey in the Coming of the American Revolution (New Brunswick, 1976), 20–22; Ryan, "Six Towns," 118–22, 166.

18. William Livingston to Samuel Tucker, July 26, 1776, William Livingston to Henry Laurens, Aug. 22, 1778, in *The Papers of William Livingston*, edited by Carl E. Prince (Trenton, N.J., 1979), 1:107, 423.

19. Ryan, "Six Towns," 161; Patricia U. Bonomi, "Religious Dissent and the Case for American Exceptionalism," in *Religion in a Revolutionary Age*, edited by Ronald Hoffman and Peter J. Albert (Charlottesville, Va., 1994), 48; Jacob Green, *Observations, on the Reconciliation of Great-Britain, and the Colonies . . . by a Friend of American Liberty* (Philadelphia, 1776), 13, 22; S. Scott Rohrer, *Jacob Green's Revolution: Inside a Presbyterian-Whig Stronghold, 1760–1790* (forthcoming).

20. Shrewsbury Church Records, Jan. 2, 30, Dec. 25, 1774, May 5, Dec. 3, 1775, Sept. 8, 1776.

21. Ibid., May 5, July 30, Sept. 24, Dec. 3, 1775.

22. Ibid., Sept. 8, 1776.

23. Ryan, "Six Towns," 186.

24. Quoted in Sanford, *Free People*, 26.

25. Ibid., 182–90; see also Donald Wallace White, *A Village at War: Chatham, New Jersey, and the American Revolution* (Madison, N.J., 1979).

26. William Livingston to Isaac Smith, Nov. 21, 1776, "Proclamation by His Excellency William Livingston, Esquire," in *Papers*, edited by Prince, 1:182–83, 2:454.

27. William Livingston to George Washington, Jan. 12, Dec. 12, 1778, in ibid., 2:175–76, 505; Mark Edward Lender, "The 'Cockpit' Reconsidered: Revolutionary New Jersey in a Military Theater," in *New Jersey*, edited by Mitnick, 45–60.

28. Randolph, *History*, 27.

29. Shrewsbury Church Records, Jan. June 13, July 11, 1778; Randolph, *History*, 28–29; Ryan, "Six Towns," 190–92.

30. J. F. D Smyth, *A Tour in the United States of America* (Dublin, 1784), 250; Dennis P. Ryan, "Landholding, Opportunity, and Mobility in Revolutionary New Jersey," *William and Mary Quarterly* 36 (Oct. 1979): 575, 584; Ryan "Six Towns," 269, 270; McCormick, *New Jersey*, 161–63.

31. 1785 tax ratables for Shrewsbury, Reel 15, Book 1166, New Jersey State Archives, Trenton; Shrewsbury Church Records, Aug. 8, 1789; Ryan, "Landholding, Opportunity, and Mobility," 588.

32. 1786 tax ratables for Shrewsbury, Reel 15, Book 1167, New Jersey State Archives; Shrewsbury Church Records, June 9, 1782. Membership figures are derived from the minutes for 1781–89.

33. Shrewsbury Church Records, July 13, 1783.

34. Ibid., Jan. 2, 1774, Feb. 12, 1775.

35. Ibid., Jan. 30, June 19, Sept. 20, 1774, Feb. 12, Oct. 29, 1775, Jan. 12, 1777, June 8, July 13, Aug. 30, 1783, Aug. 8, 1784.

36. Frank Shuffelton, *Thomas Hooker, 1586–1647* (Princeton, 1977), 279; for more on Hooker's final years, see 264–81.

37. Cotton Mather, *Magnalia Christi Americana; or, The Ecclesiastical History of New*

England from Its First Planting in the Year 1620 unto the Year of Our Lord, 1698 (New York, 1972), 1:349.

38. Ibid.

39. Ibid., 3:58, 116–17. The best analysis of the turmoil in the Hartford congregation and its larger meaning is Paul R. Lucas, *Valley of Discord: Church and Society along the Connecticut River, 1636–1725* (Hanover, N.H., 1976). This discussion relies heavily on his study.

40. Thomas Hooker, *A Survey of the Summe of Church-Discipline* (New York, 1972), 1:13, 2:19–20.

41. Ibid.; Shuffelton, *Thomas Hooker*, 222.

42. Lucas, *Valley of Discord*, 31–33.

43. "1657, Mr. Stone's Letter from the Bay, and Propositions," in *Historical Catalogue of the First Church in Hartford, 1633–1885* (Hartford, Conn., 1885), 75–76; Lucas, *Valley of Discord*, 35–36.

44. Sylvester Judd, *History of Hadley* (Springfield, Mass., 1905), 4–5; Lucas, *Valley of Discord*, 36.

45. "From Ministers in Massachusetts to Capt. John Cullick and Elder William Goodwin," June 6, 1656, *Collections of the Connecticut Historical Society* 2 (1860): 59.

46. "Mr. Stone's Charges against the Withdrawers," *Collections of the Connecticut Historical Society* 2 (1860): 104; Judd, *History*, 7–8.

47. Judd, *History*, 10–15.

48. Ibid., 12.

49. Ibid., 11, 15.

50. Ibid., 14–15; Stephen Innes, *Labor in a New Land: Economy and Society in Seventeenth-Century Springfield* (Princeton, 1983), 25–27; John Frederick Martin, *Profits in the Wilderness: Entrepreneurship and the Founding of New England Towns in the Seventeenth Century* (Chapel Hill, N.C., 1991), 43–44.

51. *Original Distribution of the Lands in Hartford among the Settlers, 1639* (Hartford, Conn., 1912); Samuel Maverick, *A Briefe Discription of New England and the Severall Townes Therein Together with the Present Government There* (Boston, 1885), 23; May 1, 1637, June 2, 1638, in *The Memorial History of Hartford, Connecticut, 1633–1884*, edited by Hammond Trumbull (Boston, 1886), vol. 1.

52. Rhys Isaac, *The Transformation of Virginia, 1740–1790* (Chapel Hill, N.C., 1982); Thomas Jefferson, *Notes on the State of Virginia*, in *Thomas Jefferson: Writings*, edited by Merrill D. Peterson (New York, 1984), 284; Sanford, *Free People*, 30.

53. Gregory Evans Dowd, *A Spirited Resistance: The North American Indian Struggle for Unity, 1745–1815* (Baltimore, 1992), 47.

54. Shrewsbury Church Records, Aug. 8, Sept. 6, 1789; Sanford, *Free People*, 33–34; Randolph, *History*, 29–30.

55. Sanford, *Free People*, 34; Randolph, *History*, 30–31, 56–59; Davis, *History*, 51. For background on Harrison County, see Henry Haymond, *History of Harrison County, West Virginia* (Morgantown, W.Va., 1910); Dorothy Davis, *History of Harrison County, West Virginia* (Clarksburg, W.Va., 1970).

56. Randolph, *History*, 29–31, 47–62.

57. Sanford, *Free People*, 100.

58. Ibid.

59. Nathan O. Hatch, *The Democratization of American Christianity* (New Haven, Conn., 1989), 6. William G. McLoughlin also argues that the Baptists and their growing popularity were tied to the rise of Jeffersonian and Jacksonian democracy (*New England Dissent, 1630–1833: The Baptists and the Separation of Church and State* [Cambridge, Mass., 1971], 1:xx).

CHAPTER SEVEN

1. Gottlieb Scheuner, *1817–1850 Inspirations—Historie; or, Historical Account of the New Awakening, Assembly, and Establishment of the Community of True Inspiration in Germany through the Year 1850, Including the Emigration to America* (Amana, Iowa, 1891), translated by Janet W. Zuber, 3:185; Christian Metz's diary of the sea voyage is reprinted in the appendix, 285.

2. Ibid., 191. For more on this period, see Frank J. Lankes, *The Ebenezer Society* (West Seneca, N.Y., 1949); Johann Gary Andelson, "Communalism and Change in the Amana Society, 1855–1932," 2 vols. (Ph.D. diss., University of Michigan, 1974).

3. Scheuner, *1817–1850 Inspirations*, 192; see also F. Alan DuVal, *Christian Metz: German-American Religious Leader and Pioneer*, edited by Peter Hoehnle (Iowa City, 2005), 46–55.

4. Scheuner, *1817–1850 Inspirations*, 193–94.

5. Ibid., 198–200; DuVal, *Christian Metz*, 48–53.

6. For a detailed account of the Inspirationists' troubles with the Indians, see Lankes, *Ebenezer Society*, 36–57.

7. DuVal, *Christian Metz*, 60–61.

8. Scheuner, *1817–1850 Inspirations*, 205–12; Lankes, *Ebenezer Society*, 59.

9. Scheuner, *1817–1850 Inspirations*, 209; DuVal, *Christian Metz*, 60–62.

10. Lankes, *Ebenezer Society*, 72.

11. Scheuner, *1817–1850 Inspirations*, 242; Lankes, *Ebenezer Society*, 82–83.

12. Lankes, *Ebenezer Society*, 98–99; Andelson, "Communalism," 49; Charles Nordhoff, *The Communalistic Societies of the United States: From Personal Visit and Observation* (New York, 1966), 29–30.

13. DuVal, *Christian Metz*, 81.

14. Andelson, "Communalism," 63; DuVal, *Christian Metz*, 81–82.

15. Historians of the movement agree that few members left during the Ebenezer years but they have been unable to determine precise figures. See Andelson, "Communalism," 62.

16. Diane L. Barthel, *Amana: From Pietist Sect to American Community* (Lincoln, Neb., 1984), 6.

17. For background on the Inspirationists' religious beliefs, see Andelson, "Communalism"; DuVal, *Christian Metz*; Barthel, *Amana*. For a good introduction to utopian groups in America, including the Inspirationists, see Donald E. Pitzer, ed., *America's Communal Utopias* (Chapel Hill, N.C., 1997).

18. Andelson, "Communalism," 15–21; Barthel, *Amana*, 6–7.

19. Andelson, "Communalism," 17–20.

20. Ibid., 25, 31–34; Barthel, *Amana*, 8–11.

21. DuVal, *Christian Metz*, 16–24, 27; Andelson, "Communalism," 35–37.

22. DuVal, *Christian Metz*, 25.

23. Ibid., 27.

24. Ibid., 26, quoted in Barthel, *Amana*, 13.

25. Barthel, *Amana*, 7.

26. Scheuner, *1817–1850 Inspirations*, 201–2.

27. Ibid., 236.

28. Ibid., 207; DuVal, *Christian Metz*, 53–55.

29. Scheuner, *1817–1850 Inspirations*, 213, 230; DuVal, *Christian Metz*, 53–55, 70–71.

30. Gertrude E. Huntington, "Living in the Ark: Four Centuries of Hutterite Faith and Community," and Lawrence Foster, "Free Love and Community: John Humphrey Noyes and the Oneida Perfectionists," both in *America's Communal Utopias*, edited by Pitzer, 319–51, 252–78.

31. Scheuner, *1817–1850 Inspirations*, 230; Andelson, "Communalism," 50–51.

32. Scheuner, *1817–1850 Inspirations*, 257–58, 262–63; Andelson, "Communalism," 61.

33. Ibid., 265, 268, 274–75.

34. Ibid.; Andelson, "Communalism," 57–61.

35. Andelson, "Communalism," 63; DuVal, *Christian Metz*, 81.

36. DuVal, *Christian Metz*, 81–85; Andelson, "Communalism," 63.

37. Edmund Patten, *A Glimpse at the United States and the Northern States of America, with the Canadas, Comprising Their Rivers, Lakes, and Falls during the Autumn of 1852* (London, 1853), 69–71; DuVal, *Christian Metz*, 85; William Least Heat-Moon, *River-Horse: Across America by Boat* (New York, 1999), 68.

38. DuVal, *Christian Metz*, 85.

39. Ibid., 86.

40. The literature on the coming of the Civil War and the crisis in Kansas is vast. Starting points include David M. Potter, *The Impending Crisis, 1848–1861* (New York, 1976), and William W. Freehling, *The Road to Disunion: Secessionists at Bay, 1776–1854* (Oxford, 1990).

41. DuVal, *Christian Metz*, 87–89.

42. Ibid., 90.

43. John D. Unruh Jr., *The Plains Across: The Overland Emigrants and the Trans-Mississippi West, 1840–60* (Urbana, Ill., 1993), 120. For a good introduction to western history and its development, see Clyde A. Milner II, Carol A. O'Connor, and Martha A. Sandweiss, eds., *The Oxford History of the American West* (Oxford, 1994); Ray Allen and Martin Ridge, *Westward Expansion: A History of the American Frontier* (Albuquerque, N.M., 2001). For a nice essay on Iowa and its history, see Dorothy Schwieder, "Iowa: The Middle Land," in *Iowa History Reader*, edited by Marvin Bergman (Ames, Iowa, 1996), 1–18. See also James C. Dinwiddie, *History of Iowa County, Iowa, and Its People* (Chicago, 1915), vol. 1.

44. Leland L. Sage, *A History of Iowa* (Ames, Iowa, 1974), 7–10, 69–70; Andelson, "Communalism," 71.

45. Barthel, *Amana*, 33–35; Andelson, "Communalism," 66–68; DuVal, *Christian Metz*, 92.

46. Andelson, "Communalism," 70; DuVal, *Christian Metz*, 9.

47. Du Val, *Christian Metz*, 94–95. See also Lankes, *Ebenezer Society*, 124–26.

48. Andelson, "Communalism," 70–74, 444–49.

49. Ibid., 70–74.

50. Ibid., 75.

51. Ibid., 68; Du Val, *Christian Metz*, 92.

52. S. Scott Rohrer, "Searching for Land and God: The Pietist Migration to North Carolina in the Late Colonial Period," *North Carolina Historical Review* 79 (Oct. 2002): 430. See also Aaron Spencer Fogleman, *Hopeful Journeys: German Immigration, Settlement, and Political Culture in Colonial America, 1717–1775* (Philadelphia, 1996), chap. 4; Daniel B. Thorp, *The Moravian Community in Colonial North Carolina: Pluralism on the Southern Frontier* (Knoxville, Tenn., 1989), chap. 1.

53. Fogleman, *Hopeful Journeys*, 122.

54. Ibid., 114–15.

55. Huntington, "Living in the Ark," 335.

56. Priscilla J. Brewer, "The Shakers of Mother Ann Lee," in *America's Communal Utopias*, edited by Pitzer, 37–56.

CHAPTER EIGHT

1. "Joseph Smith's Martyrdom, June 27, 1844," in *A Documentary History of Religion in America*, edited by Edwin S. Gaustad and Mark A. Noll (Grand Rapids, Mich., 2003), 346; Richard L. Bushman, *Joseph Smith: Rough Stone Rolling* (New York, 2005), 545–50; Jon Krakauer, *Under the Banner of Heaven: A Story of Violent Faith* (New York, 2003), 131–35.

2. Leonard J. Arrington, *Brigham Young: American Moses* (Urbana, Ill., 1986), 111–16; Krakauer, *Under the Banner*, 193–200.

3. Arrington, *Brigham Young*, 125; Krakauer, *Under the Banner*, 198–200.

4. The best treatments of the Mormon migration include Richard E. Bennett, *We'll Find the Place: The Mormon Exodus, 1846–1848* (Salt Lake City, 1997); Richard E. Bennett, *Mormons at the Mississippi: Winter Quarters, 1846–1852* (Norman, Okla., 1987); Lewis Clark Christian, "A Study of the Mormon Westward Migration between February 1846 and July 1847 with Emphasis on and Evaluation of the Factors That Led to the Mormons' Choice of Salt Lake Valley as the Site of Their Initial Colony" (Ph.D. diss., Brigham Young University, 1976). See also Bernard DeVoto, *Year of Decision, 1846* (Boston, 1943).

5. Thomas Bullock, "Travel Account of the Mormon Journey from Council Bluffs to California," in *Prophet of the Jubilee*, translated and edited by Ronald D. Dennis (1997), 92–94, available online at <http://www.lds.org/churchhistory/library/pioneerdetails/ 0,15791,4018-1-352,00.html>.

6. The Mormon Church remains controversial to this day, and these controversies are reflected in the historical literature. Early Mormon historians went to great lengths to defend the faith, while scholars in the 1960s began constructing a new historiography that was far more critical of the church. More recent work has attempted to take a middle ground, but the debate remains quite heated. For an excellent overview, see Jan Shipps, "Richard Lyman Bushman, the Story of Joseph Smith and Mormonism, and the New

Mormon History," *Journal of American History* 94 (Sept. 2007): 498–516. Richard L. Bushman responded in "What's New in Mormon History: A Response to Jan Shipps," *Journal of American History* 94 (Sept. 2007): 517–21.

7. John L. Brooke, *The Refiner's Fire: The Making of Mormon Cosmology, 1644–1844* (Cambridge, Eng., 1994), 149–50; Bushman, *Joseph Smith*, 8–29; Krakauer, *Under the Banner*, 54–56.

8. Bushman, *Joseph Smith*, 43–44; Brooke, *Refiner's Fire*, 152–53. For an excellent but more critical exploration of Joseph Smith's life, see Fawn McKay Brodie, *No Man Knows My History: The Life of Joseph Smith, the Mormon Prophet* (New York, 1945). See also Dan Vogel, *Joseph Smith: The Making of a Prophet* (Salt Lake City, 2004); Jan Shipps, *Mormonism: The Story of a New Religious Tradition* (Urbana, 1985).

9. Bushman, *Joseph Smith*, 44–45.

10. Ibid., 45.

11. Brooke, *Refiner's Fire*, 156; Bushman, *Joseph Smith*, 72.

12. The best treatments of the *Book of Mormon* are Bushman, *Joseph Smith*, chap. 20; Terry L. Givens, *By the Hand of Mormon: The American Scripture That Launched a New World Religion* (Oxford, 2002). See also Brent Lee Metcalfe, ed., *New Approaches to the Book of Mormon: Explorations in Critical Methodology* (Salt Lake City, 1993).

13. Bushman, *Joseph Smith*, 84–87; Krakauer, *Under the Banner*, 68–69; Brooke, *Refiner's Fire*, 156.

14. Brooke, *Refiner's Fire*, 156; Bushman, *Joseph Smith*, 76.

15. Bushman, *Joseph Smith*, 80–83, 124–27.

16. Ibid., 124–25, 144–45.

17. Ibid., 165.

18. Ibid., 164–67, 219–21.

19. Krakauer, *Under the Banner*, 98; Bushman, *Joseph Smith*, 224.

20. Bushman, *Joseph Smith*, 225.

21. Ibid., 227–30.

22. Ibid., 342–46.

23. Krakauer, *Under the Banner*, 101–2.

24. Ibid., 103; Bushman, *Joseph Smith*, 365.

25. Krakauer, *Under the Banner*, 103–4; Bushman, *Joseph Smith*, 361–66.

26. Bushman, *Joseph Smith*, 366–67; Krakauer, *Under the Banner*, 104–5.

27. Bushman, *Joseph Smith*, 372.

28. Krakauer, *Under the Banner*, 107–8; Bushman, *Joseph Smith*, 403.

29. Bushman, *Joseph Smith*, 403–10; Krakauer, *Under the Banner*, 107–8.

30. Bushman, *Joseph Smith*, 411–12; Krakauer, *Under the Banner*, 108.

31. Krakauer, *Under the Banner*, 109–10; Bushman, *Joseph Smith*, 468–69. Rockwell, who was spotted sneaking out of town, was later arrested, tried in the shooting, and acquitted.

32. Bushman, *Joseph Smith*, 537–41.

33. *Warsaw Signal*, June 12, 1844; Vilate Kimball to Heber C. Kimball, June 9, 1844, with

June 24, 1844, addendum, in Kimball, "Martyrdom Letters," 235, LDS Archives; Bushman, *Joseph Smith*, 546; Krakauer, *Under the Banner*, 130–32.

34. Thomas Edmonds Journal, July 11, 13, 1844, William Huntington Library, San Marino, Calif.; Bennett, *We'll Find the Place*, 1.

35. Brooke, *Refiner's Fire*, 3. See also D. Michael Quinn, *Early Mormonism and the Magic World View* (Salt Lake City, 1987). Another school of thought argues that Mormonism became popular because it was a "democratic" movement that reflected American values. See, e.g., Nathan O. Hatch, *The Democratization of American Christianity* (New Haven, Conn., 1989).

36. Brooke, *Refiner's Fire*, 181, 191–94.

37. Ibid., 199–200.

38. Ibid., 202–4; Thomas F. O'Dea, *The Mormons* (Chicago, 1957), 128.

39. *The Doctrines and Covenants of the Church of Jesus Christ of Latter-day Saints, Containing Revelation Given to Joseph Smith* . . . (Salt Lake City, 1985), 137:1–10, 110:15; Brooke, *Refiner's Fire*, 242–43.

40. Brooke, *Refiner's Fire*, 216–18, 265–66.

41. Membership figures are based on the estimates of the Mormon conference; see the biennial *Deseret News Church Almanac* for relevant years. See also B. H. Roberts, ed., *History of the Church of Jesus Christ of Latter-day Saints*, Period II (Salt Lake City, 1932), 7:431; Arrington, *Brigham Young*, 120.

42. Arrington, *Brigham Young*, 125.

43. Joseph Smith, *History of the Church of Jesus Christ of Latter-day Saints*, edited by B. H. Roberts (Salt Lake City, 1950), 5:85; *New York Weekly Herald*, July 3, 1841; Christian, "Study," 26–31; Bushman, *Joseph Smith*, 517–18.

44. Brigham Young to the Saints at Mt. Pisgah and Garden Grove, Iowa Territory, Jan. 25, 1847, Young to Orson Hyde, Apr. 2, 1846, both in Brigham Young Papers, Library-Archives of the Historical Department, LDS Archives; Bennett, *We'll Find the Place*, 9–10; *Nauvoo Neighbor*, Sept. 17, 1845; Arrington, *Brigham Young*, 123–24, 167. Christian maintains that the Mormon leadership wanted to establish numerous colonies in the West, including in Oregon and California, with the Salt Lake Valley serving as the headquarters. He also asserts that the Great Basin was an early favorite of Young's, an assertion with which Arrington and Bennett agree ("Study," esp. 35–36, 182–84, 199).

45. "Exodus Announced, October 8, 1845," in *Documentary History*, edited by Gaustad and Noll, 348–49; Arrington, *Brigham Young*, 126–27.

46. "Requirements for the Journey," in *Documentary History*, edited by Gaustad and Noll, 349–50; Bennett, *We'll Find the Place*, 51.

47. Bennett, *Mormons*, 148–52.

48. Hosea Stout Diary, Oct. 29, 1846, in *On the Mormon Frontier: The Diary of Hosea Stout, 1844–1861*, edited by Juanita Brooks (Salt Lake City, 1964), 1:208; Bennett, *Mormons*, 154, 156–57. Miller and Emmett remained opposed to Young's plans and leadership, and they left the church in July 1847.

49. Bennett, *Mormons*, 159–60.

50. Arrington, *Brigham Young*, 127.

51. "Life of George Whitaker: A Utah Pioneer," Mar. 1846, Utah State Historical Society, Salt Lake City; Bennett, *We'll Find the Place*, 32; Brigham Young to Camp of Israel's Pioneers, Platte River, May 28, 1847, Thomas Bullock, "Correspondence, 1836–1857," available online at <http://www.lds.org/churchhistory/library/pioneerdetails/0,15791,4018-1 -352,00.html>.

52. Bennett, *Mormons*, 26–30.

53. Journal of William Huntington, Apr. 9, 1846, LDS Archives; Bennett, *We'll Find the Place*, 35; Bennett, *Mormons*, 37.

54. Stout, *On the Mormon Frontier*, 1:158; Bennett, *We'll Find the Place*, 37; Bennett, *Mormons*, 37–39.

55. Bennett, *We'll Find the Place*, 44–45, 56–58; Bennett, *Mormons*, 46–74.

56. Lewis Barney Autobiography and Diary, 1878–83, reel 5, item 5, 32–38, LDS Archives, available online at <http://www.lds.org/churchhistory/library/pioneerdetails/0,15791,4018 -1-344,00.html>; Heber C. Kimball Journal, 1837–66, available online at <http://www.lds .org/churchhistory/library/pioneerdetails/0,15791,4018-1-352,00.html>.

57. William Clayton Diary, May 22, 1847, available online at <http://www.lds.org/church history/library/pioneerdetails/0,15791,4018-1-417,00.html>; Appleton Milo Harmon, *Appleton Milo Harmon Goes West*, edited by Maybelle Harmon Anderson (Berkeley, Calif., 1946), 22; Horace K. Whitney Journal, May 25, 1847, available online at <http://www.lds .org/churchhistory/library/pioneerdetails/0,15791,4018-1-417,00.html>; Bennett, *We'll Find the Place*, 148–54.

58. Bullock, "Correspondence," May 14, 1847; Kimball Journal; Bennett, *We'll Find the Place*, 172; Arrington, *Brigham Young*, 137–38.

59. Bennett, *We'll Find the Place*, 182–84, 199; Dale L. Morgan, "The Mormon Ferry on the North Platte," *Annals of Wyoming* 21 (July–Oct. 1949): 111–68.

60. Clayton Diary.

61. Thomas Bullock to his wife, June 9, 1847, available online at <http://www.lds .org/churchhistory/library/pioneerdetails/0,15791,4018-1-417,00.html>; Kimball Journal, in Christian, "Study," 308–9.

62. Brigham Young to James K. Polk, Aug. 9, 1846, Brigham Young Letterbooks, LDS Archives; Christian, "Study," 83–84, 205. Christian stresses that even at this late date, the settlement site remained tentative; Salt Lake Valley would become the permanent home only if it proved suitable after the vanguard arrived and began building.

63. Clayton Diary, July 10, 1847, 289; Bennett, *We'll Find the Place*, 204–8; Arrington, *Brigham Young*, 142.

64. Bennett, *We'll Find the Place*, 208–9.

65. Bullock, "Travel Account."

66. Erastus Snow Journal, July 3, 1847, available online at <http://www.lds.org/church history/library/pioneerdetails/0,15791,4018-1-417,00.html>; Bennett, *We'll Find the Place*, 211–13.

67. Snow Journal, July 19, 1847, 275; Bennett, *We'll Find the Place*, 213–14; Arrington, *Brigham Young*, 143.

68. Bullock, "Travel Account"; John Brown Reminiscences and Journals, vol. 1, available

online at <http://www.lds.org/churchhistory/library/pioneerdetails/0,15791,4018-1-417,00
.html>; Bennett, *We'll Find the Place*, 215–16; Arrington, *Brigham Young*, 143–45.

69. I have compiled these figures from the LDS Church Web site, <http://www.lds
.org/churchhistory/library/pioneerdetails/0,15791,4017-1-1,00.html>.

70. Roberts, *History*, 7:616–17; Arrington, *Brigham Young*, 151–52.

71. John Brown Reminiscences and Journals; Willard Richards Journal, Jan. 18, 1847,
available online at <http://www.lds.org/churchhistory/library/pioneerdetails/0,15791,4018
-1-360,00.html>; Bennett, *We'll Find the Place*, 78–79.

72. *Millennial Star*, Mar. 15, 1848, 81–88; *Mormon Chronicle*, June 18, 1848, 41–42; Arrington,
Brigham Young, 156–59.

73. Kimball Journal.

74. "Pioneer Journal of 1847," and "Luke S. Johnson Captain of Ten," both available online
at <http://www.lds.org/churchhistory/library/pioneerdetails/0,15791,4018-1-360,00.html>.

75. Kimball Journal; Brigham Young to John Smith, May 4, 1847, available online at
<http://www.lds.org/churchhistory/library/pioneerdetails/0,15791,4018-1-417,00.html>.

76. Bennett, *Mormons*, 20–21.

77. Kimball Journal.

78. Migration figures compiled from LDS Church Web site; Stout, *On the Mormon Frontier*, 1:327; Arrington, *Brigham Young*, 166, 172.

79. Shipps, *Mormonism*, 81–83.

AFTERWORD

1. The theme that utopians were unhappy with a selfish, materialistic market economy
dominates the essays in Donald E. Pitzer, ed., *America's Communal Utopias* (Chapel Hill,
N.C., 1997); see esp. foreword, xi. Another school of thought maintains that religious
groups such as the Methodists and Mormons thrived in the early national period because
of their egalitarian, democratic impulses. The leading practitioner of this view is Nathan O.
Hatch, *The Democratization of American Christianity* (New Haven, Conn., 1989).

2. Gordon S. Wood, *The Radicalism of the American Revolution* (New York, 1991), 332.

3. Alan Taylor, *William Cooper's Town: Power and Persuasion on the Frontier of the Early
American Republic* (New York, 1995), 89–90. Many social historians, of course, recognize that
social factors influenced migration. See, e.g., the historiographical essay by Gregory H.
Nobles, "Breaking into the Backcountry: New Approaches to the Early American Frontier," *William and Mary Quarterly* 46 (Oct. 1989): 641–70. This article notes, "Recent scholar-
ship suggests that most migrants did not come as rootless individuals but as members of
well-defined ethnic, religious, or kinship groups," with many migrants ending up living in
religious or ethnic enclaves (648). But with the exception of the migrations of persecuted
sectarian groups, most studies cannot explain the role of religion in migration and how
migrants came to live in religious enclaves; they instead portray migration as working independently of Protestantism. Since the 1970s, social historians' attempts to explain settlers'
behavior have fallen into three broad camps, all of which stress nonreligious factors in migration. James T. Lemon believes that early Americans were "liberals" who moved about

for individualistic reasons (*The Best Poor Man's Country: A Geographical Study of Early South-eastern Pennsylvania* [Baltimore, 1972], xv). James A. Henretta takes Lemon to task, arguing that settlers were more traditional and that family and testate considerations thus underlay migration ("Families and Farms: Mentalité in Pre-Industrial America," *William and Mary Quarterly* 35 [Jan. 1978]: 3–32; see also Allan Kulikoff, *Tobacco and Slaves: The Development of Southern Cultures in the Chesapeake, 1680–1800* [Chapel Hill, N.C., 1986], 158; Richard L. Bushman, "Markets and Composite Farms in Early America," *William and Mary Quarterly* 55 [July 1998]: 351–74). Finally, Jack P. Greene sees a democratic impulse at work: individuals migrated because they wanted to transform the "new societies into *improved* societies that could both guarantee the independence or, for the fortunate few, affluence they expected to achieve and enable them to enjoy the fruits of that independence or affluence to the fullest possible extent" ("Independence, Improvement, and Authority: Toward a Frame-work for Understanding the Histories of the Southern Backcountry during the Era of the American Revolution," in *An Uncivil War: The Southern Backcountry during the American Revolution*, edited by Ronald Hoffman, Thad W. Tate, and Peter J. Albert [Charlottesville, Va., 1985], 12, 15).

4. Nobles, "Breaking into the Backcountry," 649; Gordon S. Wood, *Radicalism*, 128–29. This view is deeply entrenched in the literature. See also Richard R. Beeman, *The Evolution of the Southern Backcountry: A Case Study of Lunenburg County, Virginia, 1746–1832* (Philadel-phia, 1984). Beeman observes that settlers' "astonishing mobility . . . nearly eliminated the hope of creating a stable and all-encompassing locally based community life" (8–9).

5. John McLean, ed., *Sketch of Rev. Philip Gatch* (Cincinnati, 1854), 108. For the transfor-mation of Salem, see Michael Shirley, *From Congregation Town to Industrial City: Cultural and Social Change in a Southern Community* (New York, 1994). For a recent treatment of religion's importance to community formation on the frontier, see Peter N. Moore, *World of Toil and Strife: Community Transformation in Backcountry South Carolina, 1750–1805* (Columbia, S.C., 2007).

6. Bernard Bailyn, *The Peopling of British North America: An Introduction* (New York, 1986), 59. See also Bernard Bailyn, *Voyagers to the West: A Passage in the Peopling of America on the Eve of the Revolution* (New York, 1986), 8–12.

7. In a great irony, the Mormons never achieved the isolation they desired. Their success in building a new home attracted outsiders in droves. For a nice summary of the Saints' early years in Utah, see the chapter on the Mormons in John D. Unruh Jr., *The Plains Across: The Overland Emigrants and the Trans-Mississippi West, 1840–60* (Urbana, Ill., 1993).

8. For a detailed examination of religion's influence on acculturation, see S. Scott Rohrer, *Hope's Promise: Religion and Acculturation in the Southern Backcountry* (Tuscaloosa, Ala., 2005). For a contrarian view that argues that religion divided people, see Aaron Spen-cer Fogleman, *Jesus Is Female: Moravians and the Challenge of Radical Religion in Early America* (Philadelphia, 2007).

9. Johann Gary Andelson, "Communalism and Change in the Amana Society, 1855–1932," 2 vols. (Ph.D. diss., University of Michigan, 1974), 63.

Topical Bibliography

Wandering Souls is not meant to be the final word on a challenging topic. Much work needs to be done on the influence of religion on internal migration in early America. The most and best migration studies examine two giants of American Protestantism, the Puritans and the Mormons. Both groups have been studied extensively; both have outstanding archival material that allows historians to examine each movement in great detail. Among the smaller groups, many fine studies have been done on the Moravians, also because of the strength of this movement's sources: the Moravians were outstanding record keepers. The three big Protestant churches—Presbyterian, Methodist, and Baptist—have received a great deal of attention, especially for their influence on American society in the early national period, but we know surprisingly little about how faith influenced the wanderlust of their members.

This bibliography lists the key secondary works for the groups highlighted in the eight case studies, along with a brief summary of the strengths and weaknesses of the religious migration literature. For students of religious migration and American Christianity, the best starting point is Edwin Scott Gaustad and Philip L. Barlow, *New Historical Atlas of Religion in America* (New York: Oxford University Press, 2001). It gives concise summaries of the various Protestant groups, describes how each group spread geographically, and charts denominational growth over four centuries.

ANGLICANS

The literature on the economic and social development of the Chesapeake and early Virginia is large and impressive, but the Anglican establishment has received far less attention for the simple reason that historians assume that the Anglican church had no influence on migration.

Beeman, Richard R. *The Evolution of the Southern Backcountry: A Case Study of Lunenburg County, Virginia, 1746–1832*. Philadelphia: University of Pennsylvania Press, 1984.
———. "Social Change and Cultural Conflict in Virginia: Lunenburg County, 1746 to 1774." *William and Mary Quarterly* 35 (July 1978): 455–76.
Billings, Warren M. *The Old Dominion in the Seventeenth Century: A Documentary History of Virginia, 1606–1689*. Chapel Hill: University of North Carolina Press, 1975.

Bolton, S. Charles. *Southern Anglicanism: The Church of England in Colonial South Carolina.* Westport, Conn.: Greenwood, 1982.

Brydon, George MacLaren. *Virginia's Mother Church and the Political Conditions under Which It Grew.* Richmond: Virginia Historical Society, 1947.

Butterfield, Kevin. "Puritans and Religious Strife in the Early Chesapeake." *Virginia Magazine of History and Biography* 109, no. 1 (2001): 5–36.

Carr, Lois Green, Russell R. Menard, and Lorena S. Walsh. *Robert Cole's World: Agriculture and Society in Early Maryland.* Chapel Hill: University of North Carolina Press, 1991.

Fischer, David Hackett, and James C. Kelly. *Bound Away: Virginia and the Westward Movement.* Charlottesville: University Press of Virginia, 2000.

Hofstra, Warren R. *The Planting of New Virginia: Settlement and Landscape in the Shenandoah Valley.* Baltimore: Johns Hopkins University Press, 2004.

Horn, James. *Adapting to a New World: English Society in the Seventeenth-Century Chesapeake.* Chapel Hill: University of North Carolina Press, 1994.

Isaac, Rhys. *Landon Carter's Uneasy Kingdom: Revolution and Rebellion on a Virginia Plantation.* Oxford: Oxford University Press, 2004.

———. "Religion and Authority: Problems of the Anglican Establishment in Virginia in the Era of Great Awakening and the Parsons' Cause." *William and Mary Quarterly* 30 (January 1973): 3–36.

———. *The Transformation of Virginia, 1740–1790.* Chapel Hill: University of North Carolina Press, 1982.

Jacob, W. M. *Lay People and Religion in the Eighteenth Century.* Cambridge: Cambridge University Press, 1996.

Kulikoff, Allan. *Tobacco and Slaves: The Development of Southern Cultures in the Chesapeake, 1680–1800.* Chapel Hill: University of North Carolina Press, 1986.

Lewis, Jan. *The Pursuit of Happiness: Family and Values in Jefferson's Virginia.* Cambridge: Cambridge University Press, 1983.

Menard, Russell R. "British Migration to the Chesapeake Colonies in the Seventeenth Century." In *Colonial Chesapeake Society*, edited by Lois Green Carr, Philip D. Morgan, and Jean B. Russo. Chapel Hill: University of North Carolina Press, 1988.

Miller, Perry. "The Religious Impulse in the Founding of Virginia: Religion and Society in the Early Literature." *William and Mary Quarterly* 5 (October 1948): 492–522.

Nelson, John K. *A Blessed Company: Parishes, Parsons, and Parishioners in Anglican Virginia, 1690–1776.* Chapel Hill: University of North Carolina Press, 2001.

Perry, James R. *The Formation of a Society on Virginia's Eastern Shore, 1615–1655.* Chapel Hill: University of North Carolina Press, 1990.

Rutman, Darrett B., and Anita H. Rutman. *A Place in Time: Middlesex County, Virginia, 1650–1750.* New York: Norton, 1984.

Seiler, William H. "The Anglican Parish in Virginia." In *Seventeenth-Century America: Essays in Colonial History*, edited by James Morton Smith. Chapel Hill: University of North Carolina Press, 1959.

Tate, Thad W., and David L. Ammerman, eds. *The Chesapeake in the Seventeenth Century: Essays on Anglo-American Society and Politics.* New York: Norton, 1979.

Upton, Dell. *Holy Things and Profane: Anglican Parish Churches in Colonial Virginia*. New Haven: Yale University Press, 1997.

Walsh, Lorena S. "Staying Put or Getting Out: Findings for Charles County, Maryland, 1650–1720." *William and Mary Quarterly* 44 (January 1987): 89–103.

BAPTISTS

The Baptists are a complex and fascinating religious movement with a bewildering number of branches. For students, the works of William H. Brackney and John B. Boles serve as good introductions; the study of New England dissent by William G. McLoughlin remains a classic. But migration studies—both transatlantic and internal—are sorely needed.

Baker, Robert A. *Relations between Northern and Southern Baptists*. Fort Worth, Tex.: Seminary, 1948.

Baxter, Norman A. *History of the Freewill Baptists: A Study in New England Separatism*. Rochester, N.Y.: American Baptist Historical Society, 1957.

Boles, John B. *The Great Revival: Beginnings of the Bible Belt*. 2nd ed. Lexington: University Press of Kentucky, 1996.

Brackney, William H. *The Baptists*. New York: Greenwood, 1988.

———. *Baptists in North America*. Malden, Mass.: Blackwell, 2006.

Edwards, Morgan. *Materials towards a History of the Baptists in Jersey*. Vols. 2, 3. Philadelphia: Dobson, 1792.

Gardner, Robert G. *Baptists of Early America: A Statistical History, 1639–1790*. Atlanta: Georgia Baptist Historical Society, 1983.

Latch, Ollie. *History of the General Baptists*. Poplar Bluff, Mo.: General Baptist, 1972.

Leonard, Bill J. *Baptist Ways: A History*. Valley Forge, Pa.: Judson, 2003.

Lindman, Janet Moore. *Bodies of Belief: Baptist Community in Early America*. Philadelphia: University of Pennsylvania Press, 2008.

McLoughlin, William G. *New England Dissent, 1630–1833: The Baptists and the Separation of Church and State*. Vol. 1. Cambridge: Harvard University Press, 1971.

Maring, Norman H. *Baptists in New Jersey: A Study in Transition*. Valley Forge, Pa.: Judson, 1964.

Mills, Randy. *Christ Tasted Death for Every Man: The Story of America's Frontier General Baptists*. Poplar Bluff, Mo.: Stinson, 2000.

Posey, Walter B. *The Baptist Church in the Lower Mississippi Valley, 1776–1845*. Lexington: University Press of Kentucky, 1957.

Randolph, Corliss Fitz. *A History of Seventh Day Baptists in West Virginia, Including the Woodbridgetown and Salemville Churches in Pennsylvania and the Shrewsbury Church in New Jersey*. Plainfield, N.J.: American Sabbath Tract Society, 1905.

Rogers, Albert N. *Seventh Day Baptists in Europe and America*. 3 vols. Plainfield, N.J.: Seventh Day Baptist, 1972.

Ryland, Garnett. *The Baptists of Virginia, 1699–1926*. Richmond, Va.: Baptist Board of Missions and Education, 1955.

Sanford, Don A. *A Choosing People: The History of Seventh Day Baptists*. Nashville, Tenn.: Broadman, 1992.

———. *Conscience Taken Captive: A Short History of Seventh Day Baptists*. Janesville, Wis.: Seventh Day Baptist Historical Society, 1991.

———. *A Free People in Search of a Free Land*. Janesville, Wis.: Seventh Day Baptist Historical Society, 1987.

Sweet, Warren W. *Religion on the American Frontier: The Baptists*. New York: Holt, 1931.

Torbet, Robert G. *A History of the Baptists*. Valley Forge, Pa.: Judson, 1963.

Torbet, Robert G., and Samuel S. Hill Jr. *Baptists North and South*. Valley Forge, Pa.: Judson, 1964.

Underwood, A. C. *History of the English Baptists*. London: Carey Kingsgate, 1947.

White, B. R. *The English Separatists*. Oxford: Clarendon, 1971.

METHODISTS

In recent years, the Methodists have been receiving a great deal of attention from talented historians. In particular, Dee E. Andrews and John H. Wigger are most interested in explaining the explosive growth of Methodism and its impact on a democraticizing America. As with the Baptists, however, Methodist migration has been barely explored. The migrations of the Virginia Methodists to the Ohio Country are especially deserving of full-scale study.

Andrews, Dee E. *The Methodists and Revolutionary America, 1760–1800: The Shaping of an Evangelical Culture*. Princeton: Princeton University Press, 2000.

Clark, Elmer T. *Methodism in Western North Carolina*. Nashville, Tenn.: Western North Carolina Conference, Methodist Church, 1966.

Conkin, Paul K. *Cane Ridge: America's Pentecost*. Madison: University of Wisconsin Press, 1990.

Connor, Elizabeth. *Methodist Trail Blazer: Philip Gatch, 1751–1834: His Life in Maryland, Virginia, and Ohio*. Cincinnati: Creative, 1970.

Cowan, Raymond P. "The Arminian Alternative: The Rise of the Methodist Episcopal Church, 1765–1850." Ph.D. diss., Georgia State University, 1991.

Hall, Timothy D. *Contested Boundaries: Itinerancy and the Reshaping of the Colonial American Religious World*. Durham: Duke University Press, 1994.

Hatch, Nathan O., and John H. Wigger, eds. *Methodism and the Shaping of an American Culture*. Nashville, Tenn.: Kingswood, 2001.

Hempton, David. *Methodism: Empire of the Spirit*. New Haven: Yale University Press, 2005.

Heyrman, Christine Leigh. *Southern Cross: The Beginnings of the Bible Belt*. New York: Knopf, 1997.

Long, Ronald W. "Religious Revivalism in the Carolinas and Georgia, 1740–1805." Ph.D. diss., University of Georgia, 1968.

Lupold, Dorothy M. "Methodism in Virginia from 1772–1784." Master's thesis, University of Virginia, 1949.

Lyerly, Cynthia Lynn. *Methodism and the Southern Mind, 1770–1810*. Oxford: Oxford University Press, 1998.

Mathews, Donald G. *Religion in the Old South*. Chicago: University of Chicago Press, 1977.

———. *Slavery and Methodism: A Chapter in American Morality, 1780–1845*. Princeton: Princeton University Press, 1965.

May, James William. "From Revival Movement to Denomination: A Re-Examination of the Beginnings of American Methodism (1765–1808)." Ph.D. diss., Columbia University, 1962.

Miyakawa, T. Scott. *Protestants and Pioneers: Individualism and Conformity on the American Frontier*. Chicago: University of Chicago Press, 1964.

Noll, Mark A. *The Rise of Evangelicalism: The Age of Edwards, Whitefield, and the Wesleys*. Downers Grove, Ill.: InterVarsity, 2003.

Richey, Russell E. *Early American Methodism*. Bloomington: Indiana University Press, 1991.

Sweet, William Warren. *Methodism in American History*. Nashville, Tenn.: Abingdon, 1954.

———. *Religion on the American Frontier, 1783–1840: The Methodists*. Vol. 4. New York: Cooper Square, 1964.

Tuttle, Robert G. *John Wesley: His Life and Theology*. Grand Rapids, Mich.: Zondervan, 1978.

Wearmouth, Robert F. *Methodism and the Common People of the Eighteenth Century*. London: Epworth, 1945.

Wigger, John H. "Fighting Bees: Methodist Itinerants and the Dynamics of Methodist Growth, 1770–1820." In *Methodism and the Shaping of an American Culture*, edited by Nathan O. Hatch and John H. Wigger. Nashville, Tenn.: Kingswood, 2001.

———. "Ohio Gospel: Methodism in Early Ohio." In *The Center of a Great Empire: The Ohio Country in the Early Republic*, edited by Andrew R. L. Cayton and Stuart D. Hobbs. Athens: Ohio University Press, 2005.

———. *Taking Heaven by Storm: Methodism and the Rise of Popular Christianity in America*. New York: Oxford University Press, 1998.

MORMONS

Mormon archival material is legendary for its extensiveness, and much of it is now available online. Yet this group remains a scorching-hot topic because of the church's controversial doctrines and the persecution that Mormon believers faced. Jon Krakauer's book, a nonacademic work written for a broader audience, came under withering fire from the Mormon Church, for example. Early Mormon historians went to great lengths to defend the faith, while scholars in the 1960s began constructing a new historiography that was far more critical of the church. More recent work has attempted to take a middle ground, but the debate remains quite heated, with migration studies often falling into the various camps as either defenders or critics of Joseph Smith's church.

Allen, James B., and Glen M. Leonard. *The Story of the Latter-day Saints*. Salt Lake City: Deseret, 1992.

Arrington, Leonard J. *Brigham Young: American Moses*. Urbana: University of Illinois Press, 1986.

———. *Great Basin Kingdom: An Economic History of the Latter-day Saints, 1830–1900*. Cambridge: Harvard University Press, 1974.

Arrington, Leonard J., and Davis Bitton. *The Mormon Experience: A History of the Latter-day Saints*. New York: Vintage, 1980.

Bennett, Richard E. "Finalizing Plans for the Trek West: Deliberations at Winter Quarters, 1846–1847." *BYU Studies* 24 (Summer 1984): 301–20.

———. *Mormons at the Mississippi: Winter Quarters, 1846–1852*. Norman: University of Oklahoma Press, 1987.

———. *We'll Find the Place: The Mormon Exodus, 1846–1848*. Salt Lake City: Deseret, 1997.

Black, Susan Easton, and William G. Hartley, eds. *The Iowa Mormon Trail: Legacy of Faith and Courage*. Orem, Utah: Helix, 1997.

Brodie, Fawn McKay. *No Man Knows My History: The Life of Joseph Smith, the Mormon Prophet*. New York: Knopf, 1945.

Brooke, John L. *The Refiner's Fire: The Making of Mormon Cosmology, 1644–1844*. Cambridge: Cambridge University Press, 1994.

Bushman, Richard Lyman. *Joseph Smith: Rough Stone Rolling*. New York: Knopf, 2005.

———. "What's New in Mormon History: A Response to Jan Shipps." *Journal of American History* 94 (September 2007): 517–21.

Campbell, Eugene F. *Establishing Zion: The Mormon Church in the American West, 1847–1869*. Salt Lake City: Signature, 1988.

Christian, Lewis Clark. "A Study of the Mormon Westward Migration between February 1846 and July 1847 with Emphasis on and Evaluation of the Factors That Led to the Mormons' Choice of Salt Lake Valley as the Site of Their Initial Colony." Ph.D. diss., Brigham Young University, 1976.

DeVoto, Bernard. *Year of Decision, 1846*. Boston: Little, Brown, 1943.

Flanders, Robert Bruce. *Nauvoo: Kingdom on the Mississippi*. Urbana: University of Illinois Press, 1965.

Givens, Terry L. *By the Hand of Mormon: The American Scripture That Launched a New World Religion*. Oxford: Oxford University Press, 2002.

Gowans, Fred R. "Fort Bridger and the Mormons." *Utah Historical Quarterly* 42 (Winter 1974): 49–67.

Hansen, Klaus J. *Quest for Empire: The Political Kingdom of God and the Council of Fifty in Mormon History*. East Lansing: Michigan State University Press, 1967.

Hartley, William G. *My Best for the Kingdom: History and Autobiography of John Lowe Butler, a Mormon Frontiersman*. Salt Lake City: Aspen, 1993.

Jackson, Richard H., ed. *The Mormon Role in the Settlement of the West*. Provo, Utah: Brigham Young University Press, 1978.

Kimball, Stanley B. *Heber C. Kimball: Mormon Patriarch and Pioneer*. Urbana: University of Illinois Press, 1981.

Krakauer, Jon. *Under the Banner of Heaven: A Story of Violent Faith*. New York: Anchor, 2003.

Launius, Roger D. *Zion's Camp: Expeditions to Missouri, 1834*. Independence, Mo.: Herald, 1984.

Launius, Roger D., and Linda Thatcher, eds. *Differing Visions: Dissenters in Mormon History*. Urbana: University of Illinois Press, 1994.

McGavin, E. Cecil. *The Mormon Pioneers*. Salt Lake City: Stevens and Wallis, 1947.

Metcalfe, Brent Lee, ed. *New Approaches to the Book of Mormon: Explorations in Critical Methodology*. Salt Lake City: Signature, 1993.

Morgan, Dale L. "The Mormon Ferry on the North Platte." *Annals of Wyoming* 21, nos. 2, 3 (1949): 111–33.

Mortensen, A. R. "Mormons, Nebraska, and the Way West." *Nebraska History* 46, no. 4 (1965): 259–71.

Nibley, Preston. *Exodus to Greatness: The Story of the Mormon Migration*. Salt Lake City: Deseret News Press, 1947.

O'Dea, Thomas F. *The Mormons*. Chicago: University of Chicago Press, 1957.

Roberts, B. H., ed. *History of the Church of Jesus Christ of Latter-day Saints*. Period II, vol. 7. Salt Lake City: Deseret, 1932.

Ricks, Joel Edward. *Forms and Methods of Early Mormon Settlement in Utah and the Surrounding Region, 1847 to 1877*. Logan: Utah State University Press, 1964.

Schindler, Harold. *Orrin Porter Rockwell: Man of God, Son of Thunder*. Salt Lake City: University of Utah Press, 1983.

Shipps, Jan. *Mormonism: The Story of a New Religious Tradition*. Urbana: University of Illinois Press, 1985.

———. "Richard Lyman Bushman, the Story of Joseph Smith and Mormonism, and the New Mormon History." *Journal of American History* 94 (September 2007): 498–516.

Stegner, Wallace. *The Gathering of Zion: The Story of the Mormon Trail*. Salt Lake City: Westwater, 1964.

Taylor, P. A. M. "The Mormon Crossing of the United States, 1840–1870." *Utah Historical Quarterly* 25 (1957): 319–37.

Vogel, Dan. *Joseph Smith: The Making of a Prophet*. Salt Lake City: Signature, 2004.

PIETISTS (MORAVIANS AND INSPIRATIONISTS)

Solid studies abound here, especially for the Moravians. Historians have dissected both the migrations and the theological underpinnings of Pietism. The Inspirationists have received less attention than the larger and more influential Moravians, but the work that has been done has been quite solid.

Andelson, Johann Gary. "Communalism and Change in the Amana Society, 1855–1932." 2 vols. Ph.D. diss., University of Michigan, 1974.

Atwood, Craig D. *Community of the Cross: Moravian Piety in Colonial Bethlehem*. University Park: Pennsylvania State University Press, 2004.

Barthel, Diane L. *Amana: From Pietist Sect to American Community*. Lincoln: University of Nebraska Press, 1984.

Brown, Dale W. *Understanding Pietism*. Grand Rapids, Mich.: Eerdmans, 1978.

DuVal, F. Alan. *Christian Metz: German-American Religious Leader and Pioneer*. Edited by Peter Hoehnle. Iowa City: Penfield, 2005.

Engel, Katherine Carté. *Religion and Profit: Moravians in Early America*. Philadelphia: University of Pennsylvania Press, 2008.

Gillespie, Michele, and Robert Beachy, eds. *Pious Pursuits: German Moravians in the Atlantic World*. New York: Berghahn, 2007.

Gollin, Gillian Lindt. *Moravians in Two Worlds: A Study of Changing Communities*. New York: Columbia University Press, 1967.

Hamilton, Taylor J., and Kenneth G. Hamilton. *History of the Moravian Church: The Renewed Unitas Fratrum, 1722–1958*. Bethlehem, Pa.: Interprovincial Christian Board of Education, Moravian Church in America, 1967.

Kuenning, Paul P. *The Rise and Fall of American Lutheran Pietism*. Macon, Ga.: Mercer University Press, 1988.

Lankes, Frank J. *The Ebenezer Society*. West Seneca, N.Y.: West Seneca Historical Society, 1949.

Longenecker, Stephen L. *Piety and Tolerance: Pennsylvania German Religion, 1700–1850*. Metuchen, N.J.: Scarecrow, 1994.

Pitzer, Donald E., ed. *America's Communal Utopias*. Chapel Hill: University of North Carolina Press, 1997.

Roeber, A. G. *Palatines, Liberty, and Property: German Lutherans in Colonial British America*. Baltimore: Johns Hopkins University Press, 1993.

Rohrer, S. Scott. *Hope's Promise: Religion and Acculturation in the Southern Backcountry*. Tuscaloosa: University of Alabama Press, 2005.

———. "Searching for Land and God: The Pietist Migration to North Carolina in the Late Colonial Period." *North Carolina Historical Review* 79 (October 2002): 409–39.

Rolland, Susanne Mostelle. "From the Rhine to the Catawba: A Study of Eighteenth Century Germanic Migration and Adaptation." Ph.D. diss., Emory University, 1991.

Rothermund, Dietmar. *The Layman's Progress: Religious and Political Experience in Colonial Pennsylvania, 1740–1770*. Philadelphia: University of Pennsylvania Press, 1961.

Shirley, Michael. *From Congregation Town to Industrial City: Cultural and Social Change in a Southern Community*. New York: New York University Press, 1994.

Smaby, Beverly Prior. *The Transformation of Moravian Bethlehem: From Communal Mission to Family Economy*. Philadelphia: University of Pennsylvania Press, 1988.

Sommer, Elisabeth W. *Serving Two Masters: Moravian Brethren in Germany and North Carolina, 1727–1801*. Lexington: University Press of Kentucky, 2000.

Stoeffler, F. Ernest, ed. *Continental Pietism and Early American Christianity*. Grand Rapids, Mich.: Eerdmans, 1976.

———. *German Pietism during the Eighteenth Century*. Leiden: Brill, 1973.

———. *The Rise of Evangelical Pietism*. Leiden: Brill, 1965.

Thorp, Daniel B. *The Moravian Community in Colonial North Carolina: Pluralism on the Southern Frontier*. Knoxville: University of Tennessee Press, 1989.

Surratt, Jerry Lee. "From Theocracy to Voluntary Church and Secularized Community:

A Study of the Moravians in Salem, North Carolina, 1772–1860." Ph.D. diss., Emory University, 1968.

Ward, W. R. *The Protestant Evangelical Awakening*. Cambridge: Cambridge University Press, 1992.

PRESBYTERIANS

Studies are strongest for the transatlantic migrations of Scotch-Irish Presbyterians. We have much to learn about the internal movements of Presbyterians—both for non-Scottish and Scotch-Irish—in the British colonies, especially out of New England to the middle colonies and from Pennsylvania to the southern backcountry.

Adams, William Forbes. *Ireland and Irish Emigration to the New World from 1815 to the Famine*. New Haven: Yale University Press, 1932.

Blethen, H. Tyler, and Curtis W. Wood Jr. *From Ulster to Carolina: The Migration of the Scotch-Irish to Southwestern North Carolina*. Cullowhee, N.C.: Western Carolina University Press, 1986.

———, eds. *Ulster and North America: Transatlantic Perspectives on the Scotch-Irish*. Tuscaloosa: University of Alabama Press, 1997.

Bolton, C. K. *Scotch Irish Pioneers in Ulster and America*. Boston: Bacon and Brown, 1910.

Canny, Nicholas. *Kingdom and Colony: Ireland in the Atlantic World, 1560–1800*. Baltimore: Johns Hopkins University Press, 1988.

Dickson, R. J. *Ulster Emigration to Colonial America, 1718–1775*. Belfast: Ulster Historical Association, 1988.

Fitzpatrick, Rory. *God's Frontiersmen: The Scots-Irish Epic*. London: Weidenfeld and Nicolson, 1989.

Griffin, Patrick. *The People with No Name: Ireland's Ulster Scots, America's Scots Irish, and the Creation of a British Atlantic World, 1689–1764*. Princeton: Princeton University Press, 2001.

Gree, E. R. R. "Queensborough Township: Scotch-Irish Emigration and the Expansion of Georgia, 1763–1776." *William and Mary Quarterly* 17 (April 1960): 183–99.

Hanna, C. A. *The Scotch-Irish*. 2 vols. New York: Putnam, 1902.

Hofstra, Warren R. "Land, Ethnicity, and Community at the Opequon Settlement, Virginia, 1730–1800." In *Ulster and North America: Transatlantic Perspectives on the Scotch-Irish*, edited by H. Tyler Blethen and Curtis W. Wood Jr. Tuscaloosa: University of Alabama Press, 1997.

———. *The Planting of New Virginia: Settlement and Landscape in the Shenandoah Valley*. Baltimore: Johns Hopkins University Press, 2004.

Keller, Kenneth W. "What Is Distinctive about the Scotch-Irish." In *Appalachian Frontiers: Settlement, Society, and Development in the Pre-Industrial Era*, edited by Robert D. Mitchell. Lexington: University Press of Kentucky, 1991.

Klett, G. S. *Presbyterians in Colonial Pennsylvania*. Philadelphia: University of Pennsylvania Press, 1937.

Jones, Maldwyn. "The Scotch-Irish in British North America." In *Strangers within the Realm: Cultural Margins of the First British Empire*, edited by Bernard Bailyn and Phillip Morgan. Chapel Hill: University of North Carolina Press, 1991.

Kirkham, Graeme. "Ulster Emigration to North America, 1680–1720." In *Ulster and North America: Transatlantic Perspectives on the Scotch-Irish*, edited by H. Tyler Blethen and Curtis W. Wood Jr. Tuscaloosa: University of Alabama Press, 1997.

Landsman, Ned C. *Scotland and Its First American Colony, 1683–1765*. Princeton: Princeton University Press, 1985.

———. "Border Cultures, the Backcountry, and 'North British' Emigration to America." *William and Mary Quarterly* 48 (April 1991): 253–59.

Leyburn, James G. *The Scotch-Irish: A Social History*. Chapel Hill: University of North Carolina Press, 1962.

MacMaster, Richard. *Donegal Presbyterians: A Scots-Irish Congregation in Pennsylvania*. Morgantown, Pa.: Masthof, 1995.

Miller, Kerby A. *Emigrants and Exiles: Ireland and the Irish Exodus to North America*. New York: Oxford University Press, 1985.

Miller, Kerby A., Arnold Schrier, Bruce D. Boling, and David N. Doyle, eds. *Irish Immigrants in the Land of Canaan: Letters and Memoirs from Colonial and Revolutionary America*. Oxford: Oxford University Press, 2003.

Mitchell, Robert D. *Commercialism and Frontier: Perspectives on the Early Shenandoah Valley*. Charlottesville: University Press of Virginia, 1977.

Parkhill, Trevor. "Philadelphia Here I Come: A Study of the Letters of Ulster Immigrants in Pennsylvania, 1750–1875." In *Ulster and North America: Transatlantic Perspectives on the Scotch-Irish*, edited by H. Tyler Blethen and Curtis W. Wood Jr. Tuscaloosa: University of Alabama Press, 1997.

Perceval-Maxwell, M. *The Scottish Migration to Ulster in the Reign of James I*. Belfast: Ulster Historical Foundation, 1990.

Pilcher, George William, ed. *The Reverend Samuel Davies Abroad: The Diary of a Journey to England and Scotland*. Urbana: University of Illinois Press, 1967.

———. *Samuel Davies: Apostle of Dissent in Colonial Virginia*. Knoxville: University of Tennessee Press, 1971.

Schmidt, Leigh Eric. *Holy Fairs: Scotland and the Making of American Revivalism*. 2nd ed. Grand Rapids, Mich.: Eerdmans, 2001.

Taylor, Alan. *Liberty Men and Great Proprietors: The Revolutionary Settlement on the Maine Frontier, 1760–1820*. Chapel Hill: University of North Carolina Press, 1990.

Trinterud, Leonard J. *The Forming of an American Tradition: A Re-Examination of Colonial Presbyterianism*. Philadelphia: Westminster, 1949.

Wallace, Ralph Stuart. "The Scotch-Irish of Provincial New Hampshire." Ph.D. diss., University of New Hampshire, 1984.

Westerkamp, Marilyn J. *Triumph of the Laity: Scots-Irish Piety and the Great Awakening, 1625–1760*. New York: Oxford University Press, 1988.

Wilson, Catharine Anne. "The Scotch-Irish and Immigrant Culture on Amherst Island, Ontario." In *Ulster and North America: Transatlantic Perspectives on the Scotch-Irish*, edited by H. Tyler Blethen and Curtis W. Wood Jr. Tuscaloosa: University of Alabama Press, 1997.

Wormald, Jenny, ed. *Scotland: A History*. Oxford: Oxford University Press, 2005.

PURITANS

The Puritans represent the mother lode of American Protestantism: no other early American group has received as much attention from historians. Studies of the Puritans' transatlantic migrations are outstanding, and those on mobility within America are nearly as compelling. All of this attention has led to a healthy debate over the dynamics of New England migration. Some historians see little mobility among the Puritan faithful, while others see a great deal of mobility. Few studies, though, have compared Puritan mobility to the mobility rates of other religious groups in early America.

Allen, David Grayson. *In English Ways: The Movement of Societies and the Transferal of English Local Law and Custom to Massachusetts Bay in the Seventeenth Century*. New York: Norton, 1982.

Anderson, Virginia DeJohn. *New England's Generation: The Great Migration and the Formation of Society and Culture in the Seventeenth Century*. New York: Cambridge University Press, 1991.

Bissell, Linda Auwers. "From One Generation to Another: Mobility in Seventeenth-Century Windsor, Connecticut." *William and Mary Quarterly* 41 (January 1974): 74–110.

Bremer, Francis J. *The Puritan Experiment: New England Society from Bradford to Edwards*. New York: St. Martin's, 1976.

Bremer, Francis J., and Alden T. Vaughan, eds. *Puritan New England: Essays on Religion, Society, and Culture*. New York: St. Martin's, 1977.

Bushman, Richard L. *From Puritan to Yankee: Character and the Social Order in Connecticut, 1690–1765*. Cambridge: Harvard University Press, 1967.

Caldwell, Patricia. *The Puritan Conversion Narrative: The Beginning of American Expression*. Cambridge: Cambridge University Press, 1983.

Canup, John. *Out of the Wilderness: The Emergence of an American Identity in Colonial New England*. Middletown, Conn.: Wesleyan University Press, 1990.

Carroll, Peter N. *Puritanism and the Wilderness: The Intellectual Significance of the New England Frontier, 1629–1700*. New York: Columbia University Press, 1969.

Daniels, Bruce C. *The Connecticut Town: Growth and Development, 1635–1790*. Middletown, Conn.: Wesleyan University Press, 1979.

Games, Alison. *Migration and the Origins of the English Atlantic World*. Cambridge: Harvard University Press, 1999.

Gaustad, Edwin S. *Liberty of Conscience: Roger Williams in America*. Grand Rapids, Mich.: Eerdmans, 1991.

Greven, Philip J., Jr. "Family Structure in Seventeenth-Century Andover, Massachusetts." *William and Mary Quarterly* 23 (April 1966): 234–56.

———. *Four Generations: Population, Land, and Family in Colonial Andover, Massachusetts.* Ithaca: Cornell University Press, 1970.

Hall, Timothy L. *Separating Church and State: Roger Williams and Religious Liberty.* Urbana: University of Illinois Press, 1998.

———. *Religion in America.* New York: Facts on File, 2007.

Heyrman, Christine Leigh. *Commerce and Culture: The Maritime Communities of Colonial Massachusetts.* New York: Norton, 1984.

Innes, Stephen. *Creating the Commonwealth: The Economic Culture of Puritan New England.* New York: Norton, 1995.

———. *Labor in a New Land: Economy and Society in Seventeenth-Century Springfield.* Princeton: Princeton University Press, 1983.

Jones, Douglas Lamar. *Village and Seaport: Migration and Society in Eighteenth-Century Massachusetts.* Hanover, N.H.: University Press of New England for Tufts University, 1981.

Lucas, Paul R. *Valley of Discord: Church and Society along the Connecticut River, 1636–1725.* Hanover, N.H.: University Press of New England, 1976.

Main, Gloria L., and Jackson Turner Main. "The Red Queen in New England?" *William and Mary Quarterly* 66 (January 1999): 121–47.

Martin, John Frederick. *Profits in the Wilderness: Entrepreneurship and the Founding of New England Towns in the Seventeenth Century.* Chapel Hill: University of North Carolina Press, 1991.

Miller, Perry. *Errand into the Wilderness.* Cambridge: Belknap Press of Harvard University Press, 1956.

Morgan, Edmund S. *The Puritan Dilemma: The Story of John Winthrop.* Boston: Little Brown, 1958.

Rosenmeier, Jesper. "The Teacher and the Witness: John Cotton and Roger Williams." *William and Mary Quarterly* 25 (July 1968): 408–31.

Rutman, Darrett B. "People in Process: The New Hampshire Towns of the Eighteenth Century." *Journal of Urban History* 1 (May 1975): 268–92.

Shuffelton, Frank. *Thomas Hooker, 1586–1647.* Princeton: Princeton University Press, 1977.

Stoever, William K. B. *"A Faire and Easie Way to Heaven": Covenant Theology and Antinomianism in Early Massachusetts.* Middletown, Conn.: Wesleyan University Press, 1978.

Thompson, Roger. *Mobility and Migration: East Anglian Founders of New England, 1629–1640.* Amherst: University of Massachusetts Press, 1994.

Vickers, Daniel. "Competency and Competition: Economic Culture in Early America." *William and Mary Quarterly* 47 (January 1990): 3–29.

———. *Farmers and Fishermen: Two Centuries of Work in Essex County, Massachusetts, 1630–1850.* Chapel Hill: University of North Carolina Press, 1994.

Waters, John J. "Family, Inheritance, and Migration in Colonial New England: The Evidence from Guilford, Connecticut." *William and Mary Quarterly* 49 (January 1982): 64–86.

Acknowledgments

I began thinking about writing this book in the mid-1980s, when I was a young master's degree student in history at the University of Virginia. Undertaking a study of internal migration in early America seemed too daunting at the time, and I filed the idea away in the recesses of my mind. A decade later, when I decided to pursue a doctorate in American history, my research interests had evolved from the study of social history to the study of religion's influence on the cultural development of the United States.

The idea of writing a book on migration thus began to resurface, with one obvious change: I would examine religion's role in the wanderings of the American people. I owe a number of people my gratitude for helping to turn this rather vague idea into a reality. Aaron Spencer Fogleman encouraged me at an early stage in the project and persuaded me to write a more ambitious book that would include the seventeenth and nineteenth centuries. Numerous specialists in my field, all of whom were anonymous reviewers, read the manuscript at various stages. Their critiques were, without exception, rigorous and insightful and did much to improve the final product. I especially thank the reviewers at the University of North Carolina Press for their excellent help. In particular, the introduction and afterword benefited from their expertise. I also thank Charles Grench, assistant director and senior editor at the press, for all of his help, guidance, and support during the past several years.

I conducted the bulk of the research at the Library of Congress, and I thank the staff there for its assistance. I also thank Nicholas J. Kersten, librarian-historian at the Seventh Day Baptist Historical Society, who mailed me the vital records I needed to write chapter 6, and Jennifer Bean Bower of Old Salem, who assisted in the search for illustrations. I also received assistance from the staff at several other archives, including the Massachusetts Historical Society in Boston and the Presbyterian Historical Society in Philadelphia.

I also owe a big thanks to my colleagues at *National Journal*, the magazine where I work in Washington, D.C., as copy desk chief. Ryan Morris, a talented graphics editor, took time out of his incredibly hectic schedule to do the maps that appear in this book. Lauren Sandkuhler, our photo coordinator, helped me track down illustrations. And my colleagues on the copy desk graciously tolerate a chief who spends too much of his spare time working on history books light-years removed from the rough-and-tumble world of contemporary Washington politics.

Most of all, I owe thanks to my family: my wife, Anne, who shares my love of language and books (but not the New York Mets), and my son, Josh, a promising fiction writer at work on his first novel. This book is dedicated to my parents. It was they who introduced me to migration at an early age; in my first ten years on this earth, I lived in five houses in three towns in two states. My parents exemplified the best of the American spirit: they were kind, devout, hardworking, talented, generous, and wanderers to the core.

Index

Luther, Martin, 63, 246

Lutherans, 6, 7, 13, 76, 111, 119, 121, 130, 133

Mad River circuit. *See* Miami circuit

Magraw, James, 100

Maine, 7, 42, 75, 78, 81, 82, 111, 122

Manifest Destiny, 208

Marfield, Eng., 15, 48, 57–58

Markland, Matthew, 124

Marshall, Frederick, 113, 120

Martin, John Frederick, 42

Mary I (queen of England), 21

Maryland, 7, 67, 108, 111, 121, 130, 133, 134, 189

Massachusetts Bay Colony, 5, 6, 10, 15, 17, 37, 42, 78, 80, 81, 171, 183, 187

Masters, Noodley, 124

Mather, Cotton, 183, 184

Maxey, Bennett, 149, 150

Maxson family, 171, 174, 182, 192; Simeon, 176–77, 178, 182, 191

Maynard, John, 35

McCobb, Samuel, 80, 92, 245

McCormick, Francis, 150

McGregor, James, 104

Mennonites, 6, 134

Merrimack River, 19

Methodists, 4, 6, 7, 11, 12, 74, 135, 245, 246; and reform causes, 136; as itinerants, 136, 154–55, 156, 161, 162–63; mobility, 137, 150, 156, 161–63; growth, 137, 155–56; anti-slavery views, 139–42; migration to Ohio, 148–51; missionary movement of, 151–56; founding of, 152–53; sermons, 153

Metz, Christian, 194, 196, 199, 203, 204, 212, 213, 214, 243; as *der Werkzeuge*, 194, 201–2; views of South, 207

Mexican War (1846–47), 232

Miami circuit (Ohio), 155–56

Middlesex County, Va., 71

Middletown, Conn., 40

Middletown, N.J., 167, 171, 174, 178, 190

Midwest, 7, 197, 205

Migrations: short distance, 6; general patterns of, 7; theories of, 7–8; general model of, 8–10, 214; transatlantic, to New England, 26–27; demographics of, 27;

transatlantic, to Virginia, 68; influence on communities, 243, 247–48; influence on reform, 245–46; influence on regions, 248; influence on acculturation, 249. *See also* Anglicans; Inspirationists; Methodists; Moravians; Mormons; Scotch-Irish Presbyterians; Puritans

Miller, George, 233

Miller, Jacob, 116

Miller, Perry, 38, 56, 57, 58

Mississippi River, 210, 224, 234

Missouri, 207, 217, 221, 224, 231, 242

Missouri River, 221, 234, 235

Missouri Valley, 232

Mobility. *See* Migrations

Monmouth, N.J., 171, 174, 175, 178, 181, 190

Monocacy, Md., 131

Monongalia County, W.Va., 190

Monroe, Mich., 206

Moon, Jacob, 49, 50, 51, 52, 53, 54, 58, 59

Moravians, 6, 7, 11, 13, 106, 161, 199, 202, 246; views of land, 108–9; settlements, 110–11; and role of new birth, 111; *Landgemeinen*, 111, 112–14; and Diaspora (Society) movement, 111, 121–26, 128–29; meetinghouses, 113–14, 120; Brotherly Agreements, 114; family life, 114–20; inheritance practices, 115–16; landholdings, 115–16, 126; and lease-purchase agreements, 117, 126–27, 132; baptismal sponsorships, 118–19; networking, 119–20; migration to Wachovia, 120–33, 62; and slavery, 122; mobility, 132; internal networking, 213; sea congregations, 213; migration to *Ortsgemeinen*, 213–14. *See also* Pietists

Moreau, Nicholas, 55

Morgantown, W.Va., 189

Mormons, 6, 10, 11, 195, 245, 246, 248; and assassination of Joseph Smith, 215; Quorum of the Twelve, 216; migration to Utah, 216–17, 231–43; and celestial kingdom, 217; persecution faced by, 217, 220–26, 230–31; and polygamy, 225, 228–29, 230; doctrines and church offices, 227–30; baptism of dead, 228; membership growth, 229; Pioneer Companies, 233, 234, 240–43; winter

quarters, 235, 241, 242; comparisons with Inspirationists, 243
Moroni (angel), 218, 219, 220
Mossom, David, 60
Mount Wollaston, Mass., 17, 19
Murray, John, 84–86, 90–92, 94
Muscatine, Iowa, 210
Mysticism, 227

National Covenant of 1638, 88
Nauvoo, Ill., 215, 217, 224–26, 229, 230, 231
Nauvoo Expositor, 226
Nauvoo Legion, 225
Nauvoo Neighbor, 232
Navigation Act (1660), 103
Nephi, 219
Nephites, 219
Neshaminy, Pa., 96
Netherlands, 6, 15, 22, 172, 184
Neuwied, Prussia, 199
Newark, N.J., 170
New birth, 10, 11, 53, 68–74, 97, 107–8, 144–46, 153, 162, 244
New Brunswick, N.J., 95
New Castle, Del., 93, 105
New England, 3, 5, 6, 7, 10, 15, 27, 115, 159, 170, 189, 247; promotional literature, 25; mobility rates and patterns in, 40–43
New England Emigrant Aid Society, 207
New Hampshire, 6, 42, 80, 171
New Haven, Conn., 170
New Haven colony, 158
New Jersey, 6, 42, 95, 155, 174, 189, 214; militia, 174, 178, 179; East Jersey, 170, 171, 174, 175, 180; West Jersey, 174; loyalists, 174, 178; neutrals, 174, 178; Council of Safety, 177; Whigs, 178; war damage, 180–81; war taxes, 181
New Kent County, Va., 47, 49, 52, 56, 60–61, 62, 72, 74
New Lights. *See* New Side-Old Side split
Newport, R.I., 170
New Salem, W.Va., 190–91
New Side-Old Side split, 52, 59, 92–99, 106, 246. *See also* Presbyterians
Newtown, Mass., 16, 19, 27, 34, 36; unhappi-

ness with, 20. *See also* Hartford, Conn.; Thomas Hooker's Company
Newtown, Ohio, 146, 147, 148, 150
New York, 3, 6, 11, 42, 155, 158, 175, 202, 217, 221, 247
New York City, 84, 160, 174, 178, 179, 181, 195, 205
New York Synod, 97, 105
New York Weekly Herald, 231
Noble, Abel, 169
Nobles, Gregory H., 247
Noe, Wilhelm, 196, 204
Nordhoff, Charles, 198
North Carolina, 4, 6, 7, 36, 105
North Dakota, 204, 214
Northern Neck, 67
Northhampton, Mass., 187
Northwest Ordinance, 157
Northwest Territory, 136, 140, 149, 158
Norwalk, Conn., 40
Nova Scotia, 78, 79
Noyes, John Humphrey, 204
Nutfield, N.H., 81

Ocean County, N.J., 171
Ogden Company, 196, 197
Ohio, 137, 156–58, 195, 217, 200, 245
Ohio Country, 11, 135, 140, 143, 149, 156, 157, 189, 190
Ohio River, 135, 140, 146–48, 156, 157
Ojibwa Indians, 157
Oldham, John, 31
Old Lights. *See* New Side-Old Side split
Oliver Lee Bank, 210
Oneida Community of New York (Oneida Perfectionists), 204, 245
Opequon settlement, Va., 101
Oregon, 208, 231
Ortsgemeinen. See Moravians
Oxford, Eng., 169

Padget, John, 125, 127
Padget, Mary, 122
Paget, John, 24
Paine, Thomas, 159, 174
Palmyra, N.Y., 218, 219

San Francisco, Calif., 208
Santa Fe Trail, 221
Saybrook, Conn., 40, 41
Scioto circuit (Ohio), 155
Scotch-Irish Presbyterians, 6, 10, 108, 128,
    192, 245, 246; views of, 75; transatlantic
    migration, 75, 77, 80, 103–5; ethnic identity,
    76, 90–92; internal migration in America,
    77, 99–101, 105–6; and ministerial short-
    age, 83; community formation, 83, 99–101;
    covenanting, 88; communion, 90–92, 95,
    96; catechisms, 91, 96, 142; and role of land,
    100–103; inheritance practices, 103. See also
    Presbyterians
Scotland, 84, 86; wars with England, 87–88;
    Lowland Scots, 88; economy, 102–3; farm-
    ing practices, 102; mobility trends in, 102–3;
    inheritance practices, 103
Seneca, John, 197
Seneca Indian reservation, 196, 197, 198
Seventh-Day Adventist Church, 3
Seventh Day Baptists, 167, 168, 173, 214, 246,
    247; founding of church, 170–71; member-
    ship, 172; congregational life, 172, 181–83;
    statement of faith, 173; in American Revo-
    lution, 174–80; congregational divisions,
    175–80; family rivalries among, 182; 1789
    migration to western Virginia, 182–83,
    189–93
Shakers, 4, 6, 213, 214
Shawnees, 157
Shenandoah Valley, 75, 93, 98, 100–101, 105
Shepard, Thomas, Jr., 29
Shrewsbury, N.J., 167, 169, 171, 174, 175, 177,
    178, 247
Sierra Nevada range, 208, 231
Sing Sing, N.Y., 158, 159
Sioux Indians, 236
Slavery, 135, 136, 138, 146, 181, 207, 245
Smith, Alvin, 228
Smith, Daniel, 125, 126, 127
Smith, Emma Hale, 218
Smith, Hyrum, 215
Smith, James, 139, 141, 150
Smith, Joseph, 200, 216, 221, 222, 224, 233, 243;
    assassination of, 215, 226, 230; early years,

217–18; *Book of Mormon*, 218–20; campaign
    for president, 225; as prophet and leader,
    227–28; theology of, 227–30. *See also*
    Mormons
Smith, Joseph, Sr., 218
Society for the Propagation of the Gospel in
    Foreign Parts, 170
Society of True Inspiration. *See* Inspiration-
    ists
Soelle, George, 123, 128, 129
Solemn League and Covenant, 88
Spangenberg, Augustus, 121, 122
Sparhawk, Nathaniel, 69
Springfield, Mass., 32, 188
Staple Act (1663), 103
Steamships, 206, 210, 232
Stebbin, Edward, 35
Stone, John, 37
Stone, Samuel, 16, 27; differences with
    Thomas Hooker and Hartford congrega-
    tion, 183–87, 193
Stonington, Conn., 41, 170, 176
Stowe, Harriet Beecher, 140
Strang, James, 229
Strange, John, 155
Stratford, Conn., 40
Surry County, Va., 50
A Survey of the Summe of Church-Discipline,
    38, 184
Switzerland, 200

Tabb, Thomas, 72
Taylor, Alan, 247
Tennent, Gilbert, 93, 97
Tennent, William, Jr., 96
Tennent, William, Sr., 96
Tennessee, 156
Texas, 208, 231
Thomas Hooker's Company, 10, 16, 17, 19, 26,
    28, 42, 136, 158, 246; migration to Hartford,
    30–33; demographics of, 32–33
Thompson, William, 101
Thornton, James, 81
Thoughts upon Slavery, 139
Tidewater Virginia, 47, 49, 67, 75
Tinkling Spring meetinghouse, Va., 94, 95, 101